Reading the Qur'an

Dr Alicia Lie

Proverse Hong Kong

2022

Proverse Hong Kong fully supports freedom of artistic expression. The views, statements of fact, interpretations and opinions expressed in "Reading the Qur'an" are those of the writer, Dr Alicia Lie and/or of any other individual writer or writers over whose names various texts appear or who are quoted in this book and not those of Proverse Hong Kong or any of those associated with the editing and publication of this book.

Is Islam necessarily against women's rights? Is Islam at odds with liberal ideals? Dr Alicia Lie argues that neither is true, through a carefully argued textual discussion of the Qur'an.

READING THE QUR'AN aims at rethinking Islam and fighting extremism. Dr Lie argues against literal interpretations of the Qur'an and puts forward a methodology for the interpretation of this key religious text. She argues that the main criterion for being a Muslim should be moral action rather than a confession of faith.

The gist of her argument is that many of the Muslims who follow doctrines derived from the Qur'an and the Hadiths have not given enough consideration to the issues involved in interpreting these texts. She gives textual evidence that Qur'anic passages were not intended to be perfect guidance suitable for all places and all times, and argues for the importance of independent thinking in following Islam.

DR ALICIA LIE was born in Hong Kong, read philosophy, and now teaches subjects investigating the interaction of cultures and communities. She has studied Arabic for many years and considers Egypt her second home. She also plays the oud.

She was first attracted to the Islamic world through the spirituality that effuses from Iranian art-house films. Looking for ways to learn about the religion, she enrolled in Arabic the moment she found that it was available at the University of Hong Kong, where she was a postgraduate student researching Artificial Intelligence and the Philosophy of Mind. Her interest in Islam converges with her interest in the Philosophy of Religion, examining the ultimate pursuit of human salvation, and its social, political, artistic, and literary consequences.

She is drawn to the spirituality of Islam but repulsed by the way women are treated in many Muslim communities. She hopes that this book of hers could bring about some small changes which may in turn bring about more changes, *ad infinitum*.

READING THE QUR'AN

Dr Alicia Lie

Proverse Hong Kong

Reading The Qur'an
by Alicia Lie

First published in Hong Kong by Proverse Hong Kong, 2022.
Copyright © Proverse Hong Kong, 2022.
Paperback: ISBN-13: 978-988-8492-39-8
Ebook: ISBN-13: 978-988-8492-43-5

Distribution (Hong Kong and worldwide)
The Chinese University of Hong Kong Press,
The Chinese University of Hong Kong,
Shatin, New Territories, Hong Kong SAR.
Email: cup@cuhk.edu.hk; Web: https://www.cup.cuhk.edu.hk
Distribution (United Kingdom)
Stephen Inman, Worcester, UK.
Distribution and other enquiries to:
Proverse Hong Kong, P.O. Box 259, Tung Chung Post Office,
Lantau, NT, Hong Kong SAR, China.
Email: proverse@netvigator.com;
Web: www.proversepublishing.com

The right of Alicia Lie to be identified
as the author of this work
has been asserted by her in accordance with
the Copyright, Designs and Patents Act 1988.
Cover design by Artist Hong Kong.
Cover image by Alicia Lie.

All rights reserved. No part of this publication may be reproduced, stored in a retrieval system, or transmitted, in any form or by any means, electronic, mechanical, photocopying, recording or otherwise, without the prior written permission of the publisher or publisher and author. The book is sold subject to the condition that it shall not, by way of trade or otherwise, be lent, re-sold, hired out or otherwise circulated without the author's prior written consent in any form of binding or cover other than that in which it is published and without a similar condition including this condition being imposed on the subsequent owner or purchaser. Please contact Proverse Hong Kong (acting as agent for the author) in writing, to request any and all permissions (including but not restricted to republishing, inclusion in anthologies, translation, reading, performance and use as set pieces in examinations and festivals).

British Library Cataloguing in Publication Data
A catalogue record is available
from the British Library

Contents

1 **Introduction**   **1**
   1.1 A Journey in Time 1
   1.2 Rethinking Islam 2
   1.3 What the Present Book is about 3
   1.4 Why I am Writing this Book 4
   1.5 Who am I to Write this Book? 5
   1.6 Existing Literature 6
   1.7 Synopsis 9
   1.8 Editorial Notes 10
   1.9 Acknowledgements 12

2 **Reformation**   **13**
   2.1 Introduction 13
       2.1.1 Schools of Islam 16
   2.2 Arguments for Change 17
       2.2.1 Logical Gaps 17
       2.2.2 Nation and Period 19
            2.2.2.1 National Prophet 19
            2.2.2.2 Applicability of Punishment .. 20
            2.2.2.3 National Context 24
            2.2.2.4 Period 29
            2.2.2.5 National Scope 31
   2.3 Revising Islam 32
       2.3.1 Internal and External Struggles 33
       2.3.2 A Liberal Religion 34
       2.3.3 Neutrality 40

3 Read! The First Call of Allah — 43
3.1 Reading — 44
3.1.1 Intermediation and Interpretation — 44
3.1.2 Authority — 46
3.2 Methodology of Reading — 47
3.2.1 Uncertainty — 48
3.2.2 Non-literality — 50
3.2.2.1 Textual Difficulties — 51
3.2.2.2 Local Description — 55
3.2.2.3 Spiritual Description — 57
3.2.3 Contextuality — 61
3.2.4 Individuality — 63
3.2.5 Rationality — 66
3.3 The Importance of Interpretation — 67
3.3.1 Coherence — 67
3.3.2 Allegory — 72
3.3.2.1 Time — 72
3.3.2.2 Judgment Day — 75
3.3.2.3 Heaven — 78
3.3.2.4 Hell — 82
3.3.2.5 Discussion — 86
3.3.3 Poetics — 88
3.4 Reading the Qur'an — 91

4 Re-reading Islam — 95
4.1 What is Islam? — 95
4.1.1 Islam and *islam* — 95
4.1.2 The Moral Construal of Faith — 99
4.1.2.1 Textual Evidence — 101
4.1.2.2 Moral Teachings — 104
4.1.2.3 Punishment for Plotting against Allah — 108
4.1.2.4 Frequent Mention of Deeds — 108
4.1.2.5 Relevant Concepts — 115
4.1.2.6 Judgment Day — 127
4.1.2.7 Concluding Remarks — 134
4.2 Teachings of Islam — 136
4.2.1 Intention — 137
4.2.2 The Five Pillars — 138
4.2.3 Faith and Charity — 139
4.2.4 Dedication — 146
4.3 Actions of Muslims — 147

CONTENTS

	4.3.1	Environment	148
	4.3.2	Food and Beverage	149
	4.3.3	Usury	152
	4.3.4	Music	153
	4.3.5	Homosexuality	156
4.4	Attitudes of Faith	157
	4.4.1	Fate	157
		4.4.1.1 Problem of Evil	159
		4.4.1.2 Provision	160
		4.4.1.3 Test	164
	4.4.2	Tolerance and Ease	171
4.5	Status of Non-Muslims	178
	4.5.1	Will	179
		4.5.1.1 Ego	190
	4.5.2	Punishment	192
		4.5.2.1 Fairness	194
		4.5.2.2 National Limitation	197
		4.5.2.3 Lack of Messengers	197
		4.5.2.4 Divine Punishment	220
		4.5.2.5 Conclusion	221
	4.5.3	Violence	221
	4.5.4	Association	228
		4.5.4.1 Belonging to a non-Muslim State	230
	4.5.5	Polytheists	230
	4.5.6	People of the Book	241
	4.5.7	Learning from Non-Muslims	247
4.6	Conclusion	248

5 Re-reading Women — 251

5.1	Context and Background	252
	5.1.1	Scope	255
	5.1.2	Society	256
	5.1.3	Choice	263
	5.1.4	Equal Footing	276
5.2	The Rights of Women	280
	5.2.1	Segregation and Tests	280
	5.2.2	Fornication	288
	5.2.3	Inheritance and Testimony	290
	5.2.4	Marriage	292
	5.2.5	Polygamy	295
		5.2.5.1 Muhammad's Household	296
		5.2.5.2 Pairing	298

- 5.2.6 The Veil 298
  - 5.2.6.1 Muhammad's Household 299
  - 5.2.6.2 General Instructions 304
  - 5.2.6.3 The Practice Today 306
  - 5.2.6.4 Metaphysical Meanings of Covering 307
  - 5.2.6.5 Conclusion 310

6 Reform   311
- 6.1 Refuting Salafism 312
  - 6.1.1 The Incoherence of Salafism 312
  - 6.1.2 Rational Disputation 318
- 6.2 Reshaping Abrogation 327
  - 6.2.1 Origin of Abrogation 327
  - 6.2.2 The Seal of Prophets 328
  - 6.2.3 Nation and Prophet 330
  - 6.2.4 Allah and King 333
  - 6.2.5 Islam as a Compromise 336
  - 6.2.6 Abrogation by Exaltation 344
  - 6.2.7 Deviation 351
  - 6.2.8 Ending Note 352
- 6.3 Re-examination 354
  - 6.3.1 Postponement................ 354
    - 6.3.1.1 Judgment is for Allah 355
    - 6.3.1.2 Reminder Only 356
    - 6.3.1.3 Against Postponement 358
    - 6.3.1.4 Conclusion 359
  - 6.3.2 Shari'a 360
    - 6.3.2.1 Original Sense 360
    - 6.3.2.2 Modern Usage 362
  - 6.3.3 Islam is Law? 362
    - 6.3.3.1 Reductio ad Absurdum 367
- 6.4 Reaction 367
  - 6.4.1 Regression 368
  - 6.4.2 The New Orientalism 371
  - 6.4.3 Economic v.s. Civil Liberalisation 372
  - 6.4.4 Non-liberal Use of Liberalism 373
    - 6.4.4.1 Gender Equality 373
    - 6.4.4.2 Freedom of Expression 374
- 6.5 Redressing the New Orientalism 374
  - 6.5.1 Islam and Governance 375
  - 6.5.2 Liberalism 376

CONTENTS

	6.5.3	Equality 377
	6.5.4	Reform with Respect to Women 378
6.6	Conclusion 379

7 Reason   **381**
- 7.1 The Realm of Religion 381
  - 7.1.1 The Allegory of Satan 382
  - 7.1.2 Worldly Guidance 383
  - 7.1.3 Spiritual Guidance 384
    - 7.1.3.1 Peace 385
    - 7.1.3.2 Forgiveness 388
    - 7.1.3.3 Remembrance 390
    - 7.1.3.4 Light 396
    - 7.1.3.5 Concluding Remarks 399
- 7.2 Philosophical Religion 399
  - 7.2.1 Religion and Reason 400
  - 7.2.2 Clarification of Terms 404
  - 7.2.3 Jihād 405
- 7.3 The Rebirth of Religion 405
  - 7.3.1 The Fall 405
  - 7.3.2 Prophets and Priests 406
  - 7.3.3 Oneness 409
  - 7.3.4 Directness 412
  - 7.3.5 Summatheism 416

Glossary   **421**

… Reading the Qur'an

Chapter 1

Introduction

1.1 A Journey in Time

Imagine that we live in Baghdad in the eighth century. It was the cultural capital of the world. It was the Golden Age of Islam. Muslims were versed in science, medicine, mathematics, and cultures from the Pacific to the Atlantic.

Muslims were not "returning to the roots" of Islam, they were exploring every field of knowledge, new and old, east and west. Islamic philosophy was thriving.

In the introduction to books there was always a dedication to Allah but after the introduction all kinds of novel ideas were discussed. There was no religious self-censorship, and people even talked about having been inspired by Muhammad, the messenger of God. [1] In this age such a writer would probably get a death threat.

The past is not all roses. But unfortunately we are worse in some aspects despite the advantage of the intervening years.

Let us look at what is happening now.

The opposite.

Now is not a golden age of Islam, now is a rotten one.

What are Muslims doing? Busy fighting each other, busy returning others to the roots of Islam, busy marrying, busy martyring.

Muslim countries are, at worst, in a state of war and chaos, and at best, in stagnation.

Physical attacks aimed at silencing intellectuals and artists are common and a constant threat. This is extremely damaging to the intellectual landscape.

1.2 Rethinking Islam

The aim of the present book is to reposition Islam and to fight extremism.

The radicalisation of Muslim youth is probably due to socio-economic problems, [19] but it is hoped that the present book can help prevent radicalisation in circumstances which lead one to blame Westernisation and change for the problems in society. These are not the things to blame when trying to improve society, nor are they incompatible with Islam, as radical Muslims believe.

On the other hand, people pushing for change are not calling for wholesale Westernisation. They are only demanding things like freedom and equality between the sexes. There should be a middle ground.

What should we do? I think we cannot deny that Islam has a role to play in this, even if the recent wave of Islamic conservatism is itself one of the results of widespread social problems. It should be admitted that Islam is potent and Muslims are more likely to listen to something propagated in the name of Islam than not.

In view of this, I contend that one needs to rethink the role of Islam in individual lives, in societies, in politics, and in the intellectual world. Is Islam all-encompassing, unchangeable, and ideal in its historical form, for all Muslims, regardless of the time, place, and situation they are in?

I argue that this is not the case. I contend that life according to Islam needs not be rigid and unchangeable. On the contrary, it can be fluid and flexible. We cannot follow the same set of rigid rules in various ages spanning a

Chapter 1 Introduction

thousand years. The context of the original messages has changed radically, and so should their interpretation and implementation in daily life.

I shall talk about different aspects in detail in the following chapters. I argue that Islam can be compatible with liberalism.

1.3 What the Present Book is about

The word "Islam" in the present book refers to common notions and common practice as observed today in different sects of Islam, and the content of the Qur'an and Hadiths[1].

There are descriptive and normative senses to this. The descriptive sense is what people who regard themselves and are regarded as Muslims believe and do. Of course this differs across different localities, times, and groups of such people. The normative sense is what Islamic scholars—Muslim or non-Muslim—or leaders of Muslim communities say Islam is. The two senses are not always distinct or clearly defined but I shall make this distinction clear if that is needed.

In the present book I will discuss Islam in the descriptive sense and the normative sense, and also argue for my version of Islam. This last of course also belongs to the normative sense.

The gist of my argument is that many Muslims follow doctrines derived from the Qur'an and the Hadiths, but they have not given enough consideration to the issues in relation to interpreting these texts, so that their conclusions are flawed. I give a demonstration of the methodology of interpretation I argue for, using the Qur'an as an example.

What "Islam" is can be a complicated matter, but a historical study of the notion is not the focus of the present

---

[1] Hadiths are records of what the prophet Muhammad's said and did.

book. Massad tries to tackle this question in the introduction of *Islam in Liberalism* [30]. He emphasises that, for the West, "Islam" has been the "other" but it has also become an integral part of the identity of the West and hence of the conception of liberalism, because it is the "other" which is always referred to as a contrasting case. For the purposes of the present book the perception of Islam in the West is not so important since I am not primarily discussing how Islam should be perceived, but instead I am trying to convince people who identify themselves as Muslims how Islam should be practised, and also presenting to non-Muslims a comprehensive overview of the Qur'an under my interpretation.

The word "liberalism" in the present book refers to the separation between religion and state, individual freedom as long as it does not infringe upon the freedom of others, equality of the sexes, etc., starting with J. S. Mill's harm principle.[2] In other words, I adopt a loose, inclusive version of liberalism, but not a strictly defined set of doctrines according to particular philosophers.

The justification is that the social tension widely seen is not between clearly defined liberal philosophies and Islam, but liberalism broadly construed, in a non-technical sense.

In the present book I will focus on discussing interpretations of the Qur'an. This approach may be seen as problematic in the sense that Islam is not about the Qur'an alone. But what I am trying to do is to show the neglected possibilities in interpreting the Qur'an, the most important text of Islam. In demonstrating these possibilities I hope to argue for a new way of thinking about Islam.

1.4 Why I am Writing this Book

I studied philosophy during my undergraduate and graduate years. I started learning Arabic at the beginning of my doctoral studies because I was interested in the Middle East and Islam, after watching countless Iranian films. It

---

[2]See Section 2.3.2 for more details.

Chapter 1 Introduction

was not related to my research, which was in Artificial Intelligence. I continued my study of Arabic for many years, going to Egypt in the scorching summer to take courses even after becoming a full-time lecturer.

When I read the Qur'an and other Islamic texts, I kept feeling that there are possibilities of interpretation that have been neglected. Some of the parallel issues in Christianity have been thoroughly discussed in the West in the philosophy of religion but seldom have the same approaches been applied to Islam, despite the similarities between these two Abrahamic religions. Therefore I am writing this book to point out these possibilities and hopefully lay out useful points of view, especially for Muslim readers, in order to repay the hospitality I experienced in the Middle East.

1.5 Who am I to Write this Book?

Is the author a Muslim? The reader may be wondering at this point. I said the Islamic creed in Jerusalem so one may say I am a Muslim. But I do not accept and am a most vocal critic of many practices of Muslim communities. If Gandhi really did say that he was a Hindu, a Muslim, a Christian, a Buddhist, and a Jew, then in that sense I am also a Muslim. But for people with a strict view of Islam, I do not qualify.

When reading this book, Muslims or even non-Muslims might feel strange that someone who is not a Muslim should say to Muslims that Islam needs a reformation. But it does not matter who says something if it is true. Read the content as it is and see if it is reasonable, without thinking about who wrote it.

When I use phrases such as "we need to reform," the pronoun "we" is used rhetorically, meaning that people need to reform, or that Muslims need to reform. One can also say that I am using the pronoun "we" to refer to everyone who accepts that there is no god but Allah and that Muhammad is his messenger. I accept this, and Muslims accept this, so the use of "we" is warranted. I hope that in this way both Muslim and non-Muslim would feel comfortable. Otherwise if I use "you" frequently Muslims might feel that I am telling them what to do while identifying as a non-Muslim, or if I use "we" without qualification then non-Muslims might feel that the present book is not intended to be read by them. I feel that this is the best solution and I hope that both Muslims and non-Muslims would find it worthwhile to start with just the creed of Islam, that there is no god but Allah and Muhammad is the messenger of Allah, and review each article of faith. More about this in Section 2.2.1.

1.6 Existing Literature

Let me discuss important existing literature with similar aims and compare the key ideas of the present book in relation to them.

There are books on liberal interpretations of the Islam, for example Hamid Haidar's *Liberalism and Islam: Practical Reconciliation between the Liberal State and Shiite Muslims* [20], Katerina Dalacoura's *Islam, Liberalism and Human Rights* [15], Nader Hashemi's *Islam, Secularism, and Liberal Democracy* [22], Andrew March's *Islam and Liberal Citizenship: The Search for an Overlapping Consensus* [29], and Roxanne Euben's *Enemy in the Mirror: Islamic Fundamentalism and the Limits of Modern Rationalism: A Work of Comparative Political Theory* [17]. But they are not concerned with detailed textual analysis and interpretation of Islamic texts as my book proposes to do.

Haidar's *Liberalism and Islam: Practical Reconciliation between the Liberal State and Shiite Muslims* [20] explores the tension between Shi'ite Islam and Mill's deeply secular liberalism and John Rawls' mildly secular liberalism. Haidar chose Shi'ism because he sees more potential for Shi'ism to be compatible with liberalism. Mill's "traditional comprehensive liberalism" is characterised as the view that "suggests not only that all individuals should

Chapter 1 Introduction

adopt and follow the liberal way of life, but also that the state should promote it using its coercive apparatus. Autonomy, self-determination, privacy, liberty, and the like are universal values; not only can the state impose them on citizens, but the legitimacy of government is also based upon pursuing them." [20, p.9] On the other hand, Rawls' "contemporary political liberalism" is characterised as silent and non-interfering with ideas about the good life. [20, p.10]

In contrast to Haidar's view, I argue that Islam, no matter whether Shi'ite or Sunni, is compatible with liberalism.[3] The reason is that from my point of view "traditional comprehensive liberalism" is not the form of liberalism under debate, and liberals today do not necessarily push for it, while the form of liberalism really at stake is "contemporary political liberalism," as this is the form of liberalism that liberals see as indispensable. Wahhabism for example would be against it and people see this as particularly problematic. So this is the point of contention.

I argue that Islam is compatible with liberalism by means of my interpretation of the Qur'an, demonstrating that with a simple paradigm shift, Islam and liberalism can co-exist without any problem.

Hourani's *Arabic Thought in the Liberal Age, 1798–1939* [24] traces reformist thoughts to medieval thinkers such as al-Farabi who argued that prophecy is a state of powerful imagination compatible with philosophical ideals, and Ibn Sina who went further and asserted that prophecy is the highest state of the intellect. Practical considerations forced Ibn Taymiyya to adopt strict analogy and human welfare as principles of legal interpretation. In the sixteenth century, al-Wahhab put forward a "purified" form of Islam, preaching strict adherence to what Muhammad and his companions did. It was a political as well as a religious movement, since the Ottoman Empire clearly was

---

[3] With the words "Islam" and "liberalism" as defined above in Section 1.3. My use of "liberalism" is closer to Rawls' "contemporary political liberalism" than Mill's "traditional comprehensive liberalism."

endorsing a different form of Islam. Hourani describes the political changes in Arab regions in light of their socio-economic transformations and interactions with Europe. He records Tahtawi's interesting idea, put forward in [7], that the principles of Islamic law and the European concept of natural law are similar.

Hourani's book is good for understanding the reception of European ideas in the Arab world from the time of the Napoleonic occupation of Egypt until the time of the second world war. It is a historical investigation of the entry of European political thought into the Arab world. In contrast, the present book looks at the tensions and resolutions between tenets in liberalism and Islam.

Kurzman's *Liberal Islam: A Source Book* [27] provides a good source of information on liberal Muslim thinkers, but is descriptive, and does not argue for a liberal view of Islam as I do.

I do not agree with Asad's over-problematisation of secularism in his *Formations of the Secular: Christianity, Islam, Modernity* [9]. Western states and media may well be hypocritical, and government always involves coercion, but liberalism and secularism bring real benefit and improvement to human rights, especially women's rights. The hypocrisy of the West does not justify Wahhabism nor discredit social reform in the Islamic world. To dismiss liberalism and secularism as just another way to organise society, and to relativise ideas of a good society, is to be blind to the violation of the right to pursue individual happiness and to ignore the repression and abuse of women in many areas of the world.

On the other hand, I agree with Asad's argument that Shari'a is not static.

Similar to Asad's problematisation of secularism, Binder's *Islamic Liberalism: a Critique of Development Ideologies* [13] questions the idea of development and progress. However, its focus is on government, not on Muslims as individuals, while the present book is concerned with the latter. I want to show the compatibility of Islam and liberalism for a Muslim. As for how a liberal government arises in a Muslim-majority country, that is not the main issue in the present book.

As for feminist versions of Islam, there are also precedents, but my book starts with discussions of liberal interpretations of Islam in general, and reaches a feminist interpretation as a result. Among those related to what I talk about in Chapter 5 "Re-reading Women" are Amina Wadud's *Qur'an and Woman* [40] and Aysha Hidayatullah's *Feminist Edges of the Qur'an* [23].

Philosophical Islam has been discussed in Carlos Fraenkel's *Philosophical Religions from Plato to Spinoza* [18] but Fraenkel worked from Muslim philosophers of the past, whereas I propose to expound my own version of philosophical Islam. My version of philosophical Islam will become clear from the arguments and interpretations regarding Islamic texts presented in the initial chapters of my work.

After a brief survey of available literature, let me give a synopsis of the present book.

1.7 Synopsis

In this book, I shall first deal with passages in the Qur'an, then we shall go deeper and talk about Islam and reason. In this way I can present my arguments in a way that is more convincing and easy to follow.

I shall argue in Chapter 2 that Islam needs reformation, that we urgently need to fight against regressive trends. After that, I set out my principles in re-reading the Qur'an in Chapter 3. I shall review passages in the Qur'an that have to do with the main tenets of Islam in Chapter 4 and reach liberal interpretations according to the principles given.

After that, in Chapter 5, I shall review passages in the Qur'an that have to do with women, giving interpretations and unearthing passages compatible with feminism and gender equality.

These arguments culminate in discussion of liberal reform in Chapter 6. In the end we shall talk about the tradition of philosophical religion and the future of Islam in Chapter 7.

1.8 Editorial Notes

Before I put forward my arguments, however, we need to talk about editorial matters. Why do we talk about such a boring topic instead of important issues? Because we will be discussing interpretations of the Qur'an, and fine points of translation and editing are going to make a difference.

In quoting the Qur'an, the number before the colon refers to the chapter (the term *Sura* which comes from Arabic is also used) while the number after the colon refers to the verse.

I am not exclusively using a particular translation of the Qur'an as I could not find a translation that I always agree with, but I follow al-Mehri's translation of the Qur'an [6] for phrases about which I have no particular preference. As I will be discussing fine points in interpretation, I do not strive to make my translation idiomatic, but rather follow Arabic constructions as far as possible. Sometimes the style seems strange and the wordings unclear because otherwise a great deal of interpretation would be incorporated into the translation. I try my best to give a clear translation but I do not want to impose my reading onto the text which is frequently ambiguous.

Muslims believe that the angel Gabriel started appearing to Muhammad in 610 CE. Passages of the Qur'an were recited by Muhammad throughout later stages of his life, and were often said to his audience in reply to issues Muhammad and his community were dealing with. His followers memorised these passages and they were compiled, one to two decades after Muhammad died, into the standard collection we see now. Without bearing this in mind, we would think that the Qur'an contains mostly general statements, while in fact they were usually advice for a particular situation. There is frequently ambiguity in the

Chapter 1 Introduction

text whose meaning was presumably clear in the context but is not always clear to us now. When rendering in English, if we try to remove the ambiguity in the text, we would not be conveying the meaning accurately. Therefore I try to adhere to the original as much as possible and give the explanation and interpretation after the quotation.

That being said, the reader need not take my translation on faith, and may use other editions, for the arguments I make concerning interpretation give more freedom than any translation does.

I shall occasionally discuss Hadiths, and I shall use Sahih al-Bukhari's text [3] as my primary source, as it is arguably the most trusted and the most influential collection. Some claim that the edition used has undergone Wahhabi modifications. But that is the one Arabic-English version that is in print. Therefore in terms of accessibility it has an advantage. I would not like to use a version that is difficult for the reader to find and refer to, since I hope that laymen as well as academics will read the present book. It is a book aimed at changing society, hopefully not just a book that is *welcomed* by academic reviews but only a dozen people read it. More importantly, I would like to show that my approach works with a text even if it is deliberately edited to promote conservative interpretations. Reading with a keen sense of the historical context enables us to steer clear of incoherently literalist readings. Considering these two points I have chosen this collection. In quoting it, I shall follow the numbering used in the version published by Kitab Bhavan [3]. The number before the colon refers to the number of the book we are quoting, while the number after the colon refers to the number of the Hadith; if there is just one number after the comma, I am referring to the number of the book.

In quoting the Christian Bible, I will give the name of the book, then the chapter, and the verse after the colon.

I shall use the male pronoun for an unspecified individual, as a courteous gesture from a female author. I hope male writers will reciprocate. This is because I think that using "their" or "his or her" is long-winded and awkward.

1.9 Acknowledgements

At the very end of this introduction, the author wishes to thank Dr. Lee Tien Ming. His course "Philosophy of Religion" at the Chinese University of Hong Kong and his books inspired many of the ideas in the present work. She is grateful for her institution, the School of Professional Education and Executive Development, the Hong Kong Polytechnic University, for granting her teaching relief for doing research. She also wishes to thank her editor Dr. Gillian Bickley for her meticulous care in editing the manuscript.

Let us begin.

Chapter 2

Reformation

2.1 Introduction

I contend that Islam needs reformation, that we urgently need to fight against regressive trends. Muslims' views of Islam and the ways it exists in the fabric of society need to be put under scrutiny, and we need to reform Islam in order to refute the views of extremist sects and solve the problems Islam faces or causes in the modern world.

Contrary to popular opinion, modernisation of Islam is not a lost cause, even though, at this particular juncture, many Muslims and non-Muslims seem to think that it is, or think either that modernisation equals strict Westernisation or that it involves giving up Islam.

Some argue that Islam is inherently political since Muhammad was a leader of a community, and that the Hadiths' detailed description of Muhammad's actions and recommendations makes secular life impossible.

I beg to differ. There is a way to adhere to Islam and modernise at the same time. Muhammad was a leader of a community, and there are detailed descriptions of how he lived and regulated the lives of his companions, but it does not mean that modern Muslims have to live exactly in the way his community lived. Muslims can simply learn from his example and adapt lessons from his wisdom to the modern world.

Christianity has a great deal of content that is difficult to reconcile with science and secular society. And yet Christian countries have modernised and secularised. Islam is an Abrahamic religion sharing many beliefs with Christianity. Those beliefs can seem barbaric and unchangeable, but we should be confident that Islamic countries can do the same.

In view of recent events, one may be sceptical, but in the long term we should be optimistic. The West also fought many sectarian wars before succeeding in secularisation and making possible the co-existence of different Christian sects and also other religions.

How to move Islam in the same direction? As an individual it is hard to do anything to change the course of history. But one tries one's best. As an intellectual the most one can do is probably to try to change the currents of thought, being unable to change social, economic, political conditions, etc. And this is my humble attempt, hoping for the best.

As I said at the beginning of the introduction, physical attacks aimed at intellectual ideas are common and a constant threat. Is this a result, a cause, or a symptom of the malaise Islam is suffering from? I do not have an answer, but I do think that the ideological war is important, and the one intellectuals are capable of—and therefore responsible for—fighting. So here I am, in the battle field, fighting against Islamic dogmatism, fighting for Islamic reformation.

Islam needs a reformation, and not a Salafist one. Salafism is a self-defeating cause which cannot survive unless it is hypocritical. And it is doomed to fail if one is sincere because it is totally impractical. I shall talk about this in detail. Please refer to Section 6.1.1 for a discussion of Salafism.

How, then, may Islam be reformed? How may Muslims' ideas be changed? The way is to re-examine mainstream doctrinal views in Islam. We need to question them and be open to other possibilities. It is hard to change one's habits

Chapter 2 Reformation

and beliefs, but we need systematically to ditch those that are unreasonable and unearth those that are reasonable. Otherwise our minds are polluted by a confusing structure of hi-jacked beliefs, serving the interests of people craving for power and influence rather than improving our ethical, communal, and spiritual lives.

We are going to do this together in the present book. As a reader, you are participating in this intellectual exploration.

One may find it heretical to reform Islam, but anyone with clear eyes, Muslim or non-Muslim, can see that the state it is in is terrible. Some may say only Muslims are terrible, Islam cannot be. But that is only a different way to put it. And it is not heresy to reform Islam. The actual state of Islam in this world is in urgent need of improvement. By improvement I do not mean the accumulation of material wealth but attaining a productive and advanced society.

I could be courteous and say that the present book aims to reform Muslims, not Islam. If one prefers to put it this way. But it seems that it is the first thing we need to reform, that one should accept that Islam can and should be reformed. Islam is not perfect.

The bottom line here (Muslims should feel reassured) is, as the creed proclaims, that there is no god but Allah and that Muhammad is his messenger. I do not question that in the present book.

But it does not mean that I accept all Islamic texts unconditionally, not even the Qur'an, because there is a possibility that mistakes crept in in the course of the compilation of Islamic texts. The Qur'an was not written down in one copy in Muhammad's lifetime. People memorised it in their minds. Only later on did they start to write down the Qur'an. Muslims are not divine, and they make mistakes. So there could well be bias and mistakes in the Qur'an because of the compilers. This should not be hard to accept.

2.1.1 Schools of Islam

In order to chart the field and make my position clearer with respect to schools of Islam, I am going to give below a brief description and analysis of different views of Islam in relation to the interpretation of texts and recommended practices.

I will separate followers of Islam into roughly the following categories as to their adherence to the faith, namely literalist, moderate, Qur'anist, reformist, and mystic.

The literalist sees that the Qur'an and the Hadiths have to be followed in the closest way possible.

The moderate sees that the Qur'an and the Hadiths can be followed with allowance for the modern world which is very different from the world of early Muslims.

The Qur'anist sees that the Qur'an only is to be followed, while the Hadiths are not reliable and were for a different time.

The reformist sees that the Qur'an and the Hadiths provide good lessons and examples, but great care should be put into reading and interpreting them, and following them literally is not feasible nor commendable in our time. Most aspects of life have progressed, and it would be a mistake and against Islam's real aim to stick to the way Muhammad's community lived, for example in inheritance. There were nearly no viable means for a woman to live independently in the 7th century on the Arabian Peninsula, and male members of the family were expected to provide for and take care of them, and so women received a smaller part of the inheritance. But the situation is different now, so that it would be less loyal to Islam's aim to keep these laws than to change them.

The mystic sees that Qur'anic passages and the Hadiths have to be interpreted as allegories. The mystic can be very reformist, or not, depending on his orientation.

Others may categorise Muslims into textualist, semi-textualist, and contextualist in interpreting Islamic texts. The textualist would correspond roughly with the literalist, and the semi-textualist would correspond roughly with

Chapter 2 Reformation

the moderate, while the contextualist would correspond roughly with the reformist. Though of course contextualism itself does not imply reformism. It allows reformism but does not imply it. I would say the push for reformism comes from perceived issues in the Muslim world, not from contextual reading.

Kurzman [27, p. 8] contrasts *taqlīd* and *ijtihād*. This pair of concepts summarises the tension between tradition and individual reasoning. People following the path of *taqlīd* are more literalist, while people following the path of *ijtihād* are more reformist.

On the other hand, in the history of Islam, we can see what Kurzman [27, p. 5–6] calls *customary Islam* which refers to the multifarious practices of different groups and regions in the Islamic world. *Customary Islam* follows a tradition but is not literalist at all, because all sorts of traditions with no historical or textual basis have arisen throughout the history of Islam. *Customary Islam* can be mystical but is seldom reformist because *customary Islam* is adapted to the world of the practitioner but came into being before the modern period. So it is not adapted to it. We can also see what Kurzman calls *revivalist Islam*, which sees the practices in *customary Islam* as wrong because they did not exist in early Islam, and seeks to change the way Islam is practised because Islam is seen to be in decay. *Revivalist Islam* can be literalist or reformist but the one people are most familiar with, Wahhabism, is literalist. And finally there is *liberal Islam*, which sees that Islam is compatible with Western ideals of liberalism. This roughly corresponds to the position of the reformist.

Now let me put forward my reformist arguments.

2.2 Arguments for Change

2.2.1 Logical Gaps

People tend to question a co-religionist's faith when his view or practice is different from one's own. A follower of a religion may wonder, "does this person really believe in x when believing in x requires that one have such and such a view and behave in such and such a way, and this person does not?"

Indeed I think the most important lesson in religion is the logical gaps between accepting the existence of a deity, and accepting the doctrines of a religion which worships that deity. The deity could be malevolent, or the doctrines could have been wrongly transmitted, or are for the interests of the priests of that religion rather than in the service of that deity.

As it is said in verse 17:85 in the Qur'an, "the soul is Allah's affair, and mankind have only been given a little knowledge." Analogously, in 33:63, it is said that knowledge "of the hour [of judgment] is with Allah." We have to admit that we are not sure about the spiritual world and we need to examine religious doctrines with caution before accepting them, if we do. Religious knowledge is shaky but logic is demonstrable. We need always to use our reasoning and be aware of the logical gaps between evidence that souls exist, and that non-Muslims would go to hell after death.

Another such gap is that between the claim that Allah exists, and the strength of individual passages in the Qur'an. I shall explore the logical gaps between accepting the existence of Allah and accepting any particular form of Islam.

In view of this, I use the word "we" frequently, referring to everyone who accepts that there is no god but Allah and that Muhammad is his messenger, even just temporarily for the sake of argument.

Let us explore this vast interpretative space together and we shall see that liberalism and feminism are compatible with Islam and do not undermine one's piety. What they undermine is tribal rule and clerical power.

Chapter 2 Reformation

2.2.2 Nation and Period

From numerous passages in the Qur'an we see statements to the effect that prophets are for particular nations, not all mankind.

2.2.2.1 National Prophet

In verse 10:47 of the Qur'an it is said that each nation has its prophet, and that judgment is between this prophet and his people. Similarly, in verse 13:7, it is said that for "every race there is a guide." In verse 35:24 it is said that there is "no nation but that a bearer of warning has passed inside it." In verse 35:42 it is said that people "swore that if a bearer of warning came to them, they would be more guided than other nations but when a bearer of warning came to them, it increased nothing but their aversion." In verses 36:3–6 it is said that Muhammad "is one of the messengers, that this is a revelation of Allah for him to warn a people whose fathers were not warned so that they are heedless." In verse 22:67, it is said that for "every nation Allah has appointed rites which they perform." From these passages we can see that prophets are supposed to be sent to each nation to guide them, and each nation should follow its special messenger.

Even the language of the message should match the nation. In verse 14:4, it is said that Allah "did not send any messenger except one who speaks the tongue of his people, so that he can make things clear for them." In verses 41:43–44 it is said to Muhammad that nothing "is said to you except what was already said to the messengers before you" and that "if we made a non-Arabic Qur'an," they would have asked why are its signs not explained, an Arab messenger giving a non-Arabic revelation. Muhammad is told to say "it is for those who believe a guidance and a cure," and then it is said that for those "who do not believe, there is deafness in their ears and blindness upon them." In verse 44:58 it is said, "we have made it easy in your tongue so that they may take heed." Similarly in

19:97 it is said, "we have only made [the Qur'an] easy in your tongue so that you may give with it good tidings to the righteous and warn with it a hostile people."

The revelation is expressly referred to as being one that is in Arabic in 12:2, 13:37, 16:103, 20:113 26:195, 39:28 41:3, 42:7, 43:3, and 46:12. Among these verses, in 16:103 it is said that people say, "it is only a human being who teaches the prophet" and it is said that the tongue they refer to "is foreign, and this Qur'an is in a clear Arabic tongue."

So we can see very clearly that Muhammad's message is for the Arabic-speaking people he was sent to, and the instructions he gave are meant for this people.

2.2.2.2 Applicability of Punishment

In addition to this, in verse 17:15, it is said that Allah "does not punish until he has sent a prophet." Then in 26:208–209 it is said that Allah "did not destroy any town except one with bearers of warning as a reminder, and that he was never unjust." This is repeated in 28:58, saying that Allah "does not destroy a town without sending a messenger," and that "their people are wrong-doers." In verses 28:46–47 it is said that if Allah does not send a prophet before punishing them with a disaster, then people would question and blame Allah. In verses 37:167–170 it is said that the infidels "used to say that if we have a reminder like the former peoples, then we would have been the servants of Allah that are made sincere. But they disbelieved, so they will know." And in 37:176–177 it is said "when Allah's punishment descends into their territory, then the morning of the warned ones would be terrible." Then in 38:3–4 it is said that Allah "has destroyed many generations before, and they wondered that a bearer of warning came to them, and the infidels said that this is a magician and a liar." In verses 43:74–78 it is said that the criminals "are abiding eternally in the punishment of hell" and "we had already brought you the truth, but most of you hate it." In verses 67:6–9 it is said, "for those who disbelieved

Chapter 2 Reformation

in their lord is the punishment of hell, and wretched is the destination. When they are thrown into it, they hear from it an inhaling while it boils up. It almost bursts with rage. Every time a group is thrown into it, its keepers ask them, 'did there not come to you a bearer of warning?' They will say, 'yes, a bearer of warning came to us, but we denied and said, "Allah has not sent down anything. You are not but in great error." ' " In verses 98:1–4 it is said, "those who disbelieved among the people of the book and the polytheists were not to be abandoned until clear evidence came to them, a messenger from Allah, reciting purified scriptures, within which are correct writings. Nor did those who were given the book become divided until after there had come to them clear evidence." Then in 98:6 it is said, "indeed, they who disbelieved among the people of the book and the polytheists will be in the fire of hell, abiding in it eternally. Those are the worst of creatures." From these passages we can see that for nations to which Allah has not sent a prophet, the severe punishment destined for non-believers and polytheists etc. does not apply.

In verse 30:9 people are told to travel and "look at what happened at the end to people to whom prophets came," and that Allah "did not wrong them." In verse 30:47 it is said that Allah "sent prophets to their people with clear proofs, and Allah took revenge on the criminals." In verses 40:21–22 people were told to travel and "look at the end of those who were before them," that they were "greater than them in strength" but "Allah seized them for their sins" and this is because "their messengers had been coming to them with clear proofs but they disbelieved, so Allah seized them." In verses 43:6–8 it is said that Allah sent many prophets "among the former peoples, and there did not come to them a prophet except that they ridiculed him, so we destroyed greater power than them, and the example of the former peoples has occurred." In verses 43:23–25 it is said that every time Allah sent a bearer of warning to a city, the rich disbelieved, so he "took revenge on them." In verses 44:10–14 it is said that one day "the sky will bring clear smoke, enveloping the people. This is a painful punishment" and "a clear messenger came to them, then they turned away from him and said, a taught lunatic." In verses 50:36–37 it is said, "how many a generation before [the righteous] did we destroy, who were greater than them in power and explored throughout the lands. Is there any place of escape? Indeed in that is a reminder for whoever has a heart or who listens while he is witnessing." From this passage we can see that the message of Muhammad is aimed at an audience who could witness the delivery of the message. It was not the original intention that the Qur'an should be used as strict guidance for every nation on earth. In verses 64:5–6 it is said, "has there not come to you the news of those who disbelieved before? So they tasted the bad consequence of their affair, and there is a painful punishment for them. That is because their messengers used to come to them with clear evidences, but they said, 'do human beings guide us?' So they disbelieved and turned away, and Allah did not need them, and Allah is free of need and praiseworthy." In verses 65:8–11 it is said, "how many a city rebelled against the command of its lord and his messengers, so we took it to severe account and punished it with a terrible punishment. So it tasted the bad consequence of its affair, and the outcome of its affair was loss. Allah has prepared for them a severe punishment, so fear Allah, O you of understanding who have believed. Allah has sent down to you a message, a messenger reciting to you the clear signs of Allah in order that he may bring out those who believe and do righteous deeds from darkness into the light, and whoever believes in Allah and does righteousness, he will admit him into gardens beneath which rivers flow, abiding in them forever. Allah has perfected for him a provision." In verses 73:15–16 it is said, "indeed, we have sent you a messenger as a witness to you just as we sent to Pharaoh a messenger. But Pharaoh disobeyed the messenger, so we seized him with a ruinous seizure." From these verses we can see that the people punished had direct contact with the prophet.

In verse 23:44, while telling stories about Noah and

Chapter 2 Reformation

Moses, it is said, "we sent our messengers successively, and every time a messenger came to a nation, they denied him, so we made them follow each other" in the path of destruction. We see such examples again in 25:35–40, 26:10–190, 27:45–58, 29:14–40, 37:73–148, 38:12–14, 51:24–46, 53:50–56, 54:9–42, 69:4–10, 79:15–26, 85:17–20, 89:6–13, 91:11–15 etc. Messengers, warnings, denial, and then destruction. In verses 43:46–56 the story of Moses and the punishment of the Egyptians is briefly narrated, followed by verses 43:57–66 in which Jesus is introduced, and it is stated that "the denominations from among them differed, so woe to those who did wrong, for [they shall receive] the punishment of a painful day. What are they waiting for, except the hour to come to them suddenly and they do not feel?" In verses 46:21–25 it is said that the brother of 'Aad "warned his people in al-Ahqaf, and bearers of warning had passed on before him and after him," saying "do not worship except Allah, indeed I fear for you the punishment of a grave day" but they ignored him, so a wind came, in which there was "a painful punishment, destroying everything by command of its lord." In verses 50:12–14 it is said, "the people of Noah denied before them, and the companions of the well and Thamud and 'Aad and Pharaoh and the brothers of Lot, and the companions of the wood and the people of Tubba' all denied the messengers, so my threat was justly fulfilled." In verse 71:1 it is said that Allah sent Noah to his people, telling him to "warn your people before there comes to them a painful punishment," then in 71:25 it is said, "because of their sins they were drowned and put into the fire, and they did not find helpers for themselves besides Allah." Here we can see that the prophets came to a community which denied them, and then they were punished. People are not punished for not following a prophet of a distant group. All these are records of prophets being sent and people who do not follow them being punished afterwards.

In verse 51:60 it is said, "woe to those who disbelieved for the day which they are promised." People may conclude from this that all infidels would be going to hell.

But if we read the whole passage, we would see that in 51:52 it is said, "there did not come to those before them any messenger except that they said, 'a magician or a madman.' " So it is referring to peoples to which messengers came, and not to all non-Muslims.

Combined with the above statements, we may conclude that such stories of non-believers being punished are only applicable to groups of people who have direct contact with a messenger, for example Moses's tribe and Pharaoh's people. If no one came to them, they would not be punished. And no one who was not in contact with messengers was punished in the stories told in the Qur'an.

One might say, but the Qur'an is available throughout the world, so people could be punished even if they are not Arabs. However, in 32:3, it is said to Muhammad that this is "the truth from Allah for you to warn a people to which no bearer of warning has come before you so that they may be guided." Muhammad's audience had contact with Jews and Christians so this verse means that a prophet has to come to a nation specifically to warn the people. Indirect contact with the revelations is not sufficient. Therefore we can see that the Qur'an was intended for Muhammad's audience, for his time and region. Other peoples have their own prophets to follow.

2.2.2.3 National Context

Let us examine the verses which reveal the national context of Islam.

In verse 16:11-14, it says that Allah "causes to grow the crops, the olives, the date-palms, the grapes and all kinds of fruits, and that he has subjected the sea for you to eat fresh food from it." In verses 36:33-35 it is said that we "placed gardens of palm trees and grapevines on earth, and made springs to burst forth in them, that they may eat from its fruit." In verses 55:10-13 it is said that Allah "laid out the earth for the creatures. There is fruit and palm tress with sheaths in it, and grain with husks and scented plants, so which of the favours of your lord do you deny?"

Chapter 2 Reformation

In verses 87:1-5 Muhammad is told to "exalt the name of your lord, the highest, who created and proportioned, and who destined, and guided, and who brings out the pasture, and makes it black stubble." In verses 80:24-32 it is said, "let mankind consider his nourishment. How we poured down water in torrents, then We broke open the earth, splitting it, and caused grain to grow in it, and grapes and green fodder, and olive and palm trees, and gardens of dense shrubbery, and fruit and grass, as enjoyment for you and your grazing livestock." In verse 22:36 it is said that Allah has made the camels and cattle "among the symbols of Allah, there is good for you in them." In verse 25:49 it is said that Allah "gives drink to those he created, many livestock and men." In verses 36:71-73 it is said that Allah created livestock, tamed them for men, and they ride them and eat them, and they receive "benefits and drinks" from these animals. Livestock is mentioned as Allah's provision in numerous verses, including verses 6:142, 10:24, 16:5, 16:66, 20:54, 23:21, 26:133, 32:27, 39:6, 40:79-80, 47:12, etc.

These verses show us the lifestyle of the people, and the flora and fauna of the region the Qur'an was intended for. We see desert and oasis. We see date-palms and olive trees. We see pasture and livestock. These verses are adapted for this area at a particular period. People living in other climates or other ages would not find these verses pertinent to their way of life. It does not do to admit the specificity in descriptions involving plants and animals, while asserting that the social and legal commands found in it are universal in time and space.

The level of how specifically Arabian the Qur'an is can be seen in the description of judgment day in 81:1-4. It is said to occur "when the sun is wrapped up, and when the stars fall, dispersing, and when the mountains are removed, and when full-term she-camels are neglected." In other parts of the world, there would not be any she-camels, and people are not concerned about them anyway. So how telling is the sign that she-camels are neglected? From this verse we can see that the Qur'an is not intended except for

Arabians.

In verses 30:48–51 it is said that it is Allah "who causes the rain to fall upon whom he wills of his servants, and they rejoice, and that before it fell, they were in despair." It is also said that if Allah "sent a wind and they saw their crops turn yellow, they would remain infidels after it." In verse 41:39 it is said that among "his signs is that you see the earth stilled, but when we send water down upon it, it quivers and grows. Indeed he who has made it become alive is the giver of life to the dead. Indeed he is able to do everything." In verse 43:11 it is said that Allah is the one "who sends down rain from the sky with measure, so we revive with it a dead land." In verses 50:9–11 it is said that Allah "sent down blessed rain from the sky and with it made gardens and grain of harvest grow, and tall palm trees with fruit arranged in layers as provision for the slaves, and we gave with it life to a dead land. The resurrection is like this." From such passages we can see the importance of rain and the dryness of the region, and the specific environment in which palm trees grow. For people from wet or snowy areas, it is not very impressive, convincing, or relevant.

Water features prominently in Allah's provision. In verses 26:131–134 people are told to fear Allah who "provided you with grazing livestock and children, and gardens and springs." In verses 36:33–35 it is said that Allah brought the earth from death to life and "placed therein gardens of palm trees and grapevines and caused to burst forth therefrom some springs so that they may eat of his fruit."

Water and drinks feature prominently in Allah's promise. In verse 15:45 it is said, "indeed, the righteous will be within gardens and springs." In verses 44:51–52 this appears again, "indeed, the righteous will be in a secure place within gardens and springs." There is another variation in 77:41 in which it is said, "indeed, the righteous will be among shades and springs, and fruits from whatever they desire. 'Eat and drink in satisfaction for what you have done.'" The righteous will be rewarded with

Chapter 2 Reformation

food and drinks for their righteous deeds. In verses 55:50 and 55:66 it is said that there are springs in paradise. In verses 76:5–6 it is said, "the righteous will drink from a cup whose mixture is of Kafur, a spring of which the servants of Allah will drink. They will make it gush forth in force." Even the names of springs that believers will drink from are specifically stated in 76:18 and 83:28. In verses 83:22–28 it is said, "indeed, the righteous will be blissful, on adorned couches, observing. You will recognise in their faces the radiance of pleasure. They will be given to drink sealed wine. Its seal is musk. So let the competitors compete for this. And its mixture is of Tasneem, a spring from which those near [to Allah] drink." In verse 88:12 it is said that there is "a flowing spring" in heaven. From verses like this we can see the concern for water sources and drinks.

In addition to the above, heaven is also nearly always said to have rivers which flow beneath it, as in 2:25, 2:266, 3:15, 3:136, 3:195, 3:198, 4:13, 4:57, 4:122, 5:12, 5:85, 5:119, 6:6,7:43, 9:72, 9:89, 9:100, 19:9, 13:35, 14:23, 16:31, 18:31, 20:76, 22:14, 22:2325:10, 29:58, 39:20, 43:51, 47:12, 48:5, 48:17, 57:12, 58:22, 61:12, 64:9, 65:11, 66:8, 85:11, 98:8, etc. This again shows the obsession with water among Muhammad's audience.

Conversely, in hell, hotness and dryness is emphasised. In verses 78:21–24 it is said, "hell is lying in wait for the transgressors, as a place of return, in which they will remain for ages. They will not taste in it coolness or drink except scalding water and purulence."

In verses 23:19–20 it is said that Allah "brought forth gardens of palm trees and grapevines in which there are many fruits from which you [may] eat," and then it is said that he also "brought forth a tree in Mount Sinai which produces oil and food for those who eat." In verses 95:1–5 it is said, "by the fig and the olive, and by Mount Sinai, and by this secure city, we have certainly created man in the best of stature." "This secure city" refers to Mecca. In verse 27:91 Muhammad is told to say that he is "commanded to worship the lord of this city, the one who made it sacred, and to him all things belong." Even though it says that Allah is the lord of everything, the reference here is very specific. It says that Allah is the lord of Mecca. In verse 6:92 it is said that the Qur'an "is a book we have sent down, blessed and confirming what was before it, so that you may warn the mother of cities and those around it," and in 42:7 it is said that in this way "we have revealed to you an Arabic Qur'an in order for you to warn the mother of cities and those around it and warn of the day of assembly, about which there is no doubt. A group will be in heaven and a group in the fire." Here "the mother of cities" means Mecca. In verses 90:1–2 it is said, "I swear by this city, and you are free in this city." "This city" also means Mecca.

The verses above specifically show the people Muhammad was talking to and the geographical location in which he spread his message and led his community. Mount Sinai and Mecca have been referred to. If we are committed to reading Islamic texts literally, then only nations which fit these descriptions need to and may follow Islam. People in Indonesia for example perhaps should rather follow a god who talks about durian and coconut, and mentions Jakarta and Bali.

The tribe of Quraysh has also been referred to. In verses 106:1–4 it is said, "for the accustomed security of the Quraysh, their familiarity with the caravan of winter and summer, let them worship the lord of this house, who has fed them against hunger and made them safe from fear." In verses 111:1–5 even a specific person is discussed. It says, "may the hands of Abu Lahab be ruined, and he be ruined. His wealth will not avail him or that which he gained. He will burn in a fire of blazing flame, and [so will] his wife, the carrier of firewood. Around her neck is a rope of fibre." These references to specific people show the topicality of the Qur'an. Therefore we cannot read its verses as automatically universal. The assumption should, on the contrary, be that they are specific until convincingly shown otherwise.

People may counter with verse 34:28 in which it is said that Muhammad is "sent to all mankind as a bringer of

Chapter 2 Reformation

good tidings and a bearer of warning." But this should be interpreted as rhetorical because it is a natural way to talk to a group without stating explicitly the limiting conditions. Thus it is much weaker than all the passages above taken together.

Combining these ideas, we can see that Islam can be reformed without any problems, since the Qur'an was meant for the Arabic-speaking people which Muhammad was addressing. In this different time and age, especially for Muslims of different races, the messages in the Qur'an need not be adhered to word-by-word. It is impossible anyway, since the objects mentioned or recommended may not exist in one's environment.

In addition to that, the permission for change is written in the text of the Qur'an itself. Let us look at the following verse.

2.2.2.4 Period

In verses 13:38–39 in the Qur'an, it is said that messengers "have been sent before, and that there is a book for every period of time." It is also said that Allah "eliminates what he wills and confirms what he wills," and that the "mother of the book is with him." In verses 43:3–4 it is said that Allah "made it an Arabic Qur'an so that you may understand, and indeed it is, in the mother of the book with us, exalted and wise." In a similar vein, in 31:27 it is said that if "trees were pen and the sea was ink and seven more seas were added to it, the words of Allah would still not be exhausted." From this verse we can see that the Qur'an is just a small part of Allah's words. Is it not conceivable that it is for a particular audience at a particular stage of development? In verse 40:78 it is said that there are "prophets who have not been mentioned in the Qur'an."

Unlike in history when followers of Jesus abandoned Judaism and founded Christianity, when Muhammad declared the name of his faith as Islam and not Judaism or Christianity, he did not say that Jews and Christians were wrong and they need to become Muslims. Islam means submission and Muhammad claimed only that some of the beliefs of Jews and Christians are wrong. So he is not necessarily advocating that Islam replace Judaism and Christianity. It is plausible to construe his position as saying that Islam includes Judaism and Christianity. For more about this please read Section 4.5.6.

The Islamic position on Judaism and Christianity is controversial. Some argue that, according to Islam, Jews and Christians are going to heaven while some argue that they are not. However, if we accept that new, more suitable messages have been sent through Muhammad because the earlier ones were not suitable for Arabs, then it means that we may look for what is no longer suitable for people different from Arabs in the Arabian Peninsula in the seventh century, and change these ideas because we have reached the expiry date for these ideas and they are no longer suitable for us. We should adopt rules and aspirations that fit with the ultimate goals and fundamental ideas of Islam, not a literal adherence to texts and directions given for another age and place. Islam can be changed and it should not be equated with a rigid set of rules.

To be fair, the period of time referred to in verses 13:38–39 is not specified. So how long is a period of time meant when we say there is a book for for every period of time? Could we say it is the lifetime of Muhammad? This seems too short. The form of social organisation present in Muhammad's time persisted for some time after his death. Could we say it is the period in which human beings exist? This does not seem reasonable, since the different prophets and revelations mentioned in the Qur'an did not come very far apart.

We can only make a reasonable guess, as it is not made explicit in the text. However we may disagree about the number of years to which that period should extend to, it is undeniable that the twenty-first century should not be regarded as the same period of time in which Muhammad lived and in which the same book should be the guiding document for people who submit, i.e. *muslims*.[1]

2.2.2.5 National Scope

As for the nation or people for whom Muhammad is intended as a prophet, it should be reasonable to limit it to Arabs in the Arabian Peninsula. This does not mean that others cannot follow his message, but it means that even Allah did not intend this message to cover other people. So that if other people voluntarily adopt it, they should definitely be allowed to adapt it to their reality. For example, the rituals, diet, or dress recommended for Arabs living in the Arabian Peninsula may be unsuitable for people living in other kinds of terrain or climate. It may be reasonable to fast between sunrise and sunset in the Arabian Peninsula. What about in the Arctic circle? The hours would be impossible for fasting since the time between sunrise and sunset can be months. In addition to this, the regularity of the day and the night, and the sun and the moon have been emphasised in verses 2:164, 3:190, 6:96, 7:54, 10:6, 13:2, 14:33, 16:12, 17:12, 21:33, 23:80, 28:71–73, 31:29, 35:13, 36:37–40, 39:5, 40:61, 41:37, 45:3–5, 73:20 etc. and such regularity is cited as evidence for Allah's work and decree, but this is not convincing at all to people living in areas of high latitude where the length of daytime varies a great deal.

In verses 73:1–7 Muhammad is told to pray at night and "we will cast upon you a heavy word. Indeed, the hours of the night are more effective for concurrence and more suitable for words," meaning that it is more effective to receive Allah's message at night. Similarly in 76:25–26 Muhammad is told to "mention the name of your lord morning and evening, and during the night prostrate to him and exalt him a long night." But we can see that this is not applicable everywhere, it just happens to be so in the desert. In other parts of the world, maybe it is better to do it at sunrise, or sunset, or any other time of the day.

---

[1] For more discussions on Muslims and muslims, Islam and islam, please refer to Section 4.1.1.

It could be too cold at night. Therefore we can see that what is said in the Qur'an is very specific, it was a message tailored for Muhammad to transmit to his fellow Arabs and not intended for general application without modification.

From these points one can see clearly and indisputably that the instructions were given for Arabs living in the Arabian Peninsula. They were not intended for every group of human beings living on earth.

From the arguments above we can see that the conditions as to nation and time period each permit us to reform Islam because the rules for living were given in a very particular context.

But then we may be asking ourselves, where is the new guide for my nation and age? Remember that Allah gave us rationality to guide ourselves, even if a new guide in the form of a human being is not found. We can reform without a new prophet, because clearly this is a different age from the time the Qur'an was revealed. Its term has been fulfilled, and we can modify its tenets and laws so that it can adapt to and survive in this modern, globalised, yet fragmented world.

This is what we should do for Islam. A reformation. Islam will have a new position in the lives of Muslims.

2.3 Revising Islam

How can we achieve this?

In the present work, I would like to propose a revised reading of Islamic texts, in particular the Qur'an—a way of reading that existed in some forms in the history of the Islamic world, but unfortunately is nearly lost today.

The present book aims to serve two purposes, the first is to provide a liberal interpretation of Islam, and the second is to provide a feminist interpretation of Islam. They are in fact one interconnected project.

Muslim secularists may implicitly hold such interpretations, but find it difficult to articulate the principles and the reasoning process for bridging Islam, liberalism,

Chapter 2 Reformation

and feminism. This is especially true in recent decades in which proponents of fundamentalism and conservatism have been vocal and influential, and secularists are frequently marginalised or accused of losing authenticity and co-operating with the "enemies," whoever they are.

In writing the present book, it is hoped that secularists will no longer be accused of giving up Islam without being able to give a powerful defence of themselves. And I hope that secularists will become the mainstream of Islam in all aspects, i.e. in number, in influence, in what others think about Islam, etc.

2.3.1 Internal and External Struggles

I would like to embark with Muslims and non-Muslims on a re-reading of Islamic texts and rethink some of the important ideas in Islam.

I hope to promote liberal interpretations of Islamic texts among Muslims through careful textual analysis and argumentation. I would also like to review the historical development of Islam, and show that it can be brought in line with modern standards of human rights, gender equality, and liberal ideals of free human development, among other issues. I would like to win over the dominion of discourse from conservatives and extremists.

This is the *internal* side of the struggle, that among Muslims. On the *external* side, I would like to change external views about Islam, emphasising the liberal ideas that are seldom seen in popular portrayals. I would like to provide alternative views of Islam for people wanting to learn more about this religion, rather than simply receiving propaganda materials from conservative sources which either draw them towards regressive versions of Islam or repel them and leave them with the impression that Islam never left, and never can leave, the Middle Ages.

Hopefully the present book would promote understanding and dialogue between the two sides, because the discrepancy of liberal Muslims' idea of Islam and conservative non-Muslims' entrenched idea of of what Islam must be has been making communication difficult.

In a word, the aim of both the internal and the external side of the struggle is to work towards mutual understanding. This is the struggle. This is *jihād*.

Non-Muslims may question the value of re-reading Islamic texts in order to promote liberalism and the place of women within Islam.

The short answer is that people do not give up a religion easily. If we can provide a compelling re-reading of Islamic texts and revise the accepted tenets, then social change is more easily engendered than if we try to persuade people to leave the faith.

Secondly, if we can show that Islam can be brought in line with modern standards of human rights, gender equality, and liberal ideals of free human development, etc., then Muslims would be able to accept such ideals painlessly. I do not propose to cast aside Islamic views as outmoded and irrelevant. On the contrary, I would like to enlist the Islamic traditionalists to embrace an authentic tradition that did exist in Islam but which has been purposely neglected in recent years due to unfortunate socio-political circumstances and currents of thought. I would like to retake the right of interpretation.

These are the reasons why I do not think that Islam's views on individual rights and women's position should simply be condemned and abandoned, as some suggest. I will attempt to unearth possibilities of interpretations which were prevalent in earlier periods of Islam and also to contribute my own suggestions.

2.3.2 A Liberal Religion

What exactly do I mean by the word "liberal" in this book?

There are many different schools in liberalism. But since we concentrate on one aspect, that is, religion, the choice of which brand of liberalism to adopt is not that complicated.

I use the word "liberal" in the sense of respecting individual choice, not overriding it with religious doctrines by

Chapter 2 Reformation

coercion. A Muslim or non-Muslim is free in their actions, and the only thing governing him is secular law.

As a reference one can look at J. S. Mill's formulation of the basic principle of liberalism, which came to be known as the harm principle,

> That the only purpose for which power can be rightfully exercised over any member of a civilised community, against his will, is to prevent harm to others. His own good, either physical or moral, is not a sufficient warrant. [32, p. 14]

When applied to the religious realm, it means that religious teachings and rulings cannot be forced onto individuals, regardless of whether they are followers of that faith or not. For liberals, the only kind of law enforcement allowed is to prevent physical harm to others. Words cannot cause physical harm to others. They may cause anger, resentment, displeasure, affront, etc. but these are not physical harm. So law enforcement should not be used to prevent speech considered offensive by adherents to any particular religion.

Of course if we read the laws of liberal democracies, the actual situation is not so simple. There are libel laws, privacy laws, etc. but they are not guided by religious teachings and people of any religion—or with no religion—are treated in the same way. This is something that we have to look at when we think about the domain of religion.

This idea cannot be found in the Qur'an, but it also disregards Christian texts and traditions, and for that matter, all other religious teachings. Non-Muslims can live with it happily, and why is it a problem for Muslims? I contend that it is because of an unnecessarily political interpretation of Islam, which has largely sprung up as a reaction to colonial rule and the decline of Muslim-majority areas such as the Eastern coast of the Mediterranean Sea. We shall deal with this in Section 6.5.

I shall also try to discuss and emphasise the ideas in Islam that promote or are consistent with individual freedom, gender equality, tolerance of and coexistence with other faiths, etc. These ideas have been frequently ignored in mainstream discussions inside Islam because of patriarchal traditions.

However, even if there are some liberal ideas in Islam, can we claim that Islam is a liberal religion?

It is something which Muslims decide for themselves. The content of a religion is determined by its believers. The majority of followers can determine what the religion is perceived to be in the world.

A religion is not a purely external reality existing on its own, which cannot be changed by its followers. If the followers change, the religion changes. If you choose that Islam is a liberal religion, it can become one. Of course it is not totally unrelated to its textual and practised content. But there are already liberal aspects and tendencies in it. The issue is what followers choose from the ideas and traditions in a religion and how they practise that religion in everyday life. Do they avoid liberal ideas, remove them, do nothing particular about them, or try to actively promote them and emphasise them? That is what determines whether Islam is a liberal religion or not.

The present book sets out to do exactly this—promote the liberal ideas in Islam. Therefore let me make it clear from the outset, that the present book is not just an "external" "objective" description of Islam, but actually it takes part in its development and is normative in the sense of trying to promote a certain way of reading Islamic texts, i.e. in a broadly liberal way.

Be careful though. In the present book, liberalism is the basis, but we should not tolerate intolerant religions and I do not agree that liberalism means "respecting" religions in the sense of not criticising them. If religions violate liberal principles, for example gender equality, we should criticise them vocally, and they should definitely not be part of the legal system. This is because if we police our speech out of "respect for religion" then eventually no liberal society would be left because religions are free to promote non-liberal ideas and enforce non-liberal laws,

Chapter 2 Reformation

while liberals are tongue-tied and cannot criticise nor campaign against non-liberal religious practices.

This is a dangerous development that we should do our best to prevent. People are confused about liberalism, thinking that criticising cultures, traditions and religions originating from less developed places is a form of bigotry and racism, not realising that the criticism is directed toward violation of modern principles such as equality, which we all benefit from. Without adopting these principles, girls would still suffer genital mutilation and be married off at nine years old in Egypt, for example. It is bigotry and racism of a much grander proportion implicitly to assume that such practices should not be criticised, in order to preserve the good will of the traditionalists from these cultures, at the price of and ignoring the immense suffering on the part of girls and women who did not choose these traditions and practices for themselves. These confused liberals become accomplices of the perpetrators of these terrible practices.

Equality is not saying that savages are as good as civilised people. On the contrary, allowing them to become members of modern society is a manifestation of the principle of equality. To deny that savages can become civilised and to claim that it is their culture to mutilate girls is in fact demeaning them, not respecting them. I am not saying that equality means that we need to do everything in the same way, eradicating all the differences in cultures, but the principles of maximum freedom and gender equality etc. should be upheld.

Saying that anything goes in religion is not what we mean by "liberal" in the present book. People have freedom of worship but we should not allow evil cults which tell people to kill randomly, right? So by the same token, if there is anything wrong with any religion, however large and mainstream it is, we should criticise it so that people are not harmed. The harm principle says that power can be rightfully exercised when we need to prevent harm to others. So of course criticism is allowed, since even government intervention is allowed. To be sure we need to delineate very carefully where to start preventing people from harming others. But we do not need to stand with our hands tied until actual harm is done. The case is similar to that of gun laws. People can argue for gun control, because people can easily use guns to harm others. So in the case of religion, people should respond and prevent people from harming others by means of wrong information and slippery reasoning. Criticism of religion is not a violation of liberal principles. It is even necessary for their preservation in some cases.

It is my aim in the present book to defend liberal values, try to reform Islam, and persuade Muslims of the compatibility of Islam and liberal principles. I support an Islam which conforms to liberal principles, not liberals acquiescing to whatever Muslims do, out of political correctness, timidity, laziness, etc. We have to admit that there are terrible forms of Islam, that even though they are terrible, they have the right to claim that they are also Islam on the grounds of the books they use, the culture they adhere to, the terminology they adopt, etc. And what we must do is to eradicate such terrible forms, not by means of violence, but by means of the weapons of argument and reason.

Political correctness has its benefits in deterring people from hasty generalisation and from perpetuating prejudices and stereotypes which will frequently become normative and reluctantly conformed to in a community. It is something that I as a woman have encountered repeatedly during my course of education, in which I have been told women aren't good at mathematics, logic, philosophy, postgraduate studies, etc. and the implication is that *I should avoid these*. That is a lamentable state of affairs and luckily I have never been deterred by such talk. Political correctness would prevent people from saying these things. That is a good thing.

However, political correctness also prevents people from speaking the truth, the inconvenient truths, about groups of people. But groups do have common properties, and if discussion is prevented, human progress would be stalled or even reversed. For if we are not allowed to speak

Chapter 2 Reformation

against the oppression of women in a culture, how can we change it? If it cannot be changed, how can women be liberated? We have to review the content and interpretations of Islamic texts and root out any problems that can be found. Otherwise injustice and oppression will be done in God's name. We should not pretend that there are no problems in Muslim communities and countries. There are structural and developmental problems that could have a link with Islam.

I contend that the issues of liberalism and women are the most urgent and problematic ones facing Muslims. That is the reason why I shall address them in great detail in Chapters 4 and 5.

Liberalism requires vigilance. It is not something that will thrive without active support from liberals. We need to fight non-liberals in order to preserve liberalism. Liberal societies can easily deteriorate into non-liberal ones if liberals—too accustomed to them—think that it is human nature to preserve liberal societies. Arguably it is not, since the power of propaganda is immense and the vulnerability and susceptibility of human beings to conform to the strong and the mainstream is seen throughout history. So we have to arm ourselves with strong will and critical thinking in order to uphold liberal principles and defend liberal ideals.

It is a complicated matter to be critical of religions and still keep an eye on the positive sides. It is easier just to take one side and be done with it, i.e. either follow a religion blindly, ignoring its critics, or ditch a religion completely and say that it is the opium of the people and has only harmful effects. But we need to challenge ourselves, not be blinded by emotion and habit, and try to look at Islam in a critical way without necessarily giving it up, and without being malicious or spiteful. And it is my hope that I do not offend Muslims by what I say in the present book but invite them to think about and reflect on Islam together.

This is the aim of the present book. I aim at salvaging Islam from blind conservatism as much as at salvaging liberalism from self-defeating leftists, who think that liberalism entails defending all cultures and their practices, even oppressive ones. It is a difficult project but we shall try our best together. I hope we all emerge better after this arduous but colourful journey.

2.3.3 Neutrality

One may question the neutrality of the present book and say that this is not a serious academic work that has no assumption. Indeed I have assumptions. Let me make it clear here. In the present book I assume that Allah exists and that Muhammad is his messenger. I do not argue against that. Non-Muslims would ask why I assume that. Not necessarily because I accept that, but because I think that it is important to point out the subtle shades of faith one can adopt under these assumptions. Atheist arguments are relatively common in publication, and I do not want to repeat them here. On the contrary, rigorous but theist re-examination of religions is harder to find, and especially hard to find in Islam.

That is the reason why I would like to concentrate on this area. I would like to point out the rich possibilities within Islam, and how many different combinations of stances regarding different issues are possible from reading the Qur'an.

I do not aim to persuade Muslims to leave this faith, which plenty of books try to do, but to change the way it is practised, on both the individual and the collective level. I think this is a more needed book than another one arguing for atheism.

Furthermore, if by "a serious academic work" one means something that is archaic and empty, promoting no position or view, then this is not a serious academic work. But it is a serious work, arguing for a way of interpreting Islamic texts that is intentionally neglected and suppressed in this age. We need to bring this back to the forefront.

It is a tragedy of this age that conservative interpretations occupy doctrinal discussions. One can see scan-

Chapter 2 Reformation

dalous viewpoints of crazy clerics ridiculed by the whole world from time to time. Many people start to assume that people born into Muslim families only have a choice between being culturally Muslims (i.e. practically atheist, only participating in the ceremonies and festivities) and being Salafist. I aim to highlight other possibilities and argue that these positions are more reasonable from the standpoint of the texts and from the standpoint of a human being.

In the West, criticism of Christianity is no problem because it was the dominant faith. It was seen as an intellectual's duty to make the church tolerant, or even to fight it. On the other hand, Islam is seen as the minority, and open criticism is seen as hostile and intolerant. However, it is precisely not treating Muslims as fellow humans to think that criticism of Islam should be avoided.

I am not from the West, perhaps that is why I see a dangerous tendency of Westerners to be either mindlessly complacent or mindlessly negative about Islam and Muslims. I contend that openness and honesty is urgently needed. Otherwise Huntington's dim vision [25] of the inevitable hostility between the West and Islam would indeed obtain.

To prevent this from happening, let me present my principles for reading the Qur'an.

Chapter 3

Read! The First Call of Allah

When Gabriel first talked to Muhammad, he ordered him to read, though the prophet-to-be was said to be illiterate. According to al-Bukhari's Hadiths [3, 1:3], Gabriel caught and pressed him three times to urge him to read, and then passed to him the first revealed verse of the Qur'an, 96:1-5. It says, "Recite (or read) in the name of your lord who created, created man from a clinging substance. Recite, and your lord is the most generous—who taught by the pen, taught man that which he knew not." Here we see the power of words and reading, and the positive perception of knowledge.

We can see from the very beginning the importance of the word and reading for Muslims.[1] What is regrettable is that many Muslims only care about Islamic knowledge, but not knowledge in general.

---

[1] A parallel could be seen in the Bible. In John 1:1 it says "In the beginning was the Word, and the Word was with God, and the Word was God."

3.1 Reading

Following Gabriel's call, let us discuss *reading*. This is not as simple or as straightforward as it looks. Reading involves understanding, organising, interpreting, not to mention one's bias and selective mentality. So let us look at issues one should be aware of when reading religious texts, in particular the Qur'an.

3.1.1 Intermediation and Interpretation

Muslims love to read or rather recite the Qur'an. Unfortunately, the Qur'an is not always very explicit about actual acts, so that there is much room for mullahs', imams', sheikhs', kings', and others' intervention, false representation, and theft in the name of religion.

We have to remember that mainstream teachings become mainstream not necessarily because they are the best, but because they are popular or because the people with influence or power prefer them. So it is very dangerous to accept religious teachings without placing them under the microscope of one's intellect.

We should not accept religious teachings simply because everyone we know—or our teacher, or whomever we respect—tells us that these doctrines constitute the one true version of our religion. They may be sincere but they can at the same time be fooled. If one does not check one's beliefs skeptically before adopting them, in all probability one becomes unwittingly a servant of others' interests, thinking that one is serving God, or whatever name we use for the deity one is following.

Even assuming that God exists and that the prophets are real and carried messages from God, each link in the chain of transmission of religious texts throughout the long history after the age of the prophets could go wrong, not to mention the possibility of misinterpretation internalised in the tradition, however authoritative it appears to be.

Consequently, to avoid being misled, we should read the Qur'an and other Islamic texts carefully, on which much

Chapter 3 Read! The First Call of Allah

of the concrete content of Islam is built. We should review these texts and then think about what their messages are, and what conclusions regarding guidance of actions are to be drawn. And we need to think about the doctrinal implications if some parts of it are fake or distorted. In this way we can have an authentic version of Islam, not just one that has been handed down to us.

In the end, one has to take responsibility for one's religious life. If one chooses a terrible sect, one might think that one can simply say, "it is just the fault of the leaders of the sect, and I myself am not responsible." But the truth is, we could have picked a better sect. Therefore we are responsible. We should not let others intercede between us and our God, since it does not absolve us from blame if the interceders use the powers unjustly. And the reasonable line to take is to read and decide for oneself as much as possible.

In the case of Islam, the Qur'an is considered the most important text to read and base one's beliefs on. Apart from that there are the Hadiths. Given that there are such complicated texts in the study of Islam, interpretation is an important issue.

Historically, authenticity and truthfulness have easily been side-stepped when people bring in their own biases and agenda when trying to build up a body of rules from different collections of Hadiths. Patriachal and despotic tendencies in history crept into Shari'a, bits and pieces of cultural vestiges displacing the reformist aims of early Islam.

A case in point is the leader of the community. It should be someone with the wisdom and integrity deserving of the position. But this was clearly not the case after Muhammad and the first Caliphs. Muslims accepted them because they did not have a choice, but many of them started to think that this is what good Muslims should do.

The daunting size and scope of the Hadiths contribute to these issues no doubt. First of all, people do not want to read them all. Secondly, people can choose what they like from them. They can also choose what they like for incorporation into Shari'a, the laws governing the lives of Muslims.

Therefore it is a Muslim's duty to read the Qur'an and the Hadiths and think of a reasonable view of Islam. I shall reflect on this topic at length in Section 3.3. We cannot leave the work of interpretation to others totally. It is dangerous and certainly taken advantage of by powermongers and politicians.

This leads to the issue of authority.

3.1.2 Authority

But are not people who study these texts all their lives experts and authorities on these matters, therefore we should rely on them, rather than on our own judgment?

In science, this is certainly a reasonable attitude, since it takes long years of study to understand the research done to resolve scientific disputes. But for other subjects, the reliability of experts is not as good. In the matter of religion, when we are doubtful about whether an action is permissible in the eyes of Allah, going to a scholar of Islamic texts may not give us a very reliable answer. These scholars have radically different opinions, unlike in science, where there is a high level of consensus.

History shows us the danger in delegating religious beliefs to others, in whichever religion. In the Middle Ages, Christian churches were oppressive and impeded scientific progress.

To be fair, people tend to cling to their old beliefs and old ways of doing things, ignoring new situations or new evidence. This exists in any organisation. However, the problem is more severe in religion because even simple issues like how to hold a fork could get entangled with the issues of whether one respects the deity or not, whether one is pious or not, and whether one is going to hell or not. Therefore critical thinking is crucial and unreflecting reliance on religious authority is perilous.

Apart from that, in recent years, mosques and *madrasas* are frequently centres of regressive and even ex-

tremist thoughts. These do not make good authority.
Because of the above considerations, one should rely on oneself in matters of religious stance.

One may argue that interpretations given by traditional authorities and the circumstances of the revelations they present should be relied upon to make our interpretations. Regarding this point I would argue that this is not necessary. The Qur'an itself provides many hints as to how it should be read. Records about the context of the revelations are less reliable than the Qur'an itself, and traditional authorities may just be perpetuating traditional prejudices. We can and even should read the Qur'an by itself first. If one has to review and discuss all the major commentaries in history one would never reach a conclusion. It complicates the issue and tends to cause people to give up on the matter and delegate the responsibility to theologians.

Tackling the Qur'an itself directly is a better approach.

3.2 Methodology of Reading

If we do not delegate the interpretation of religious texts to others, what should we do? We are very busy with life and supporting ourselves and our families.

One does not need to become a religious student fulltime to take matters into his own hands. One only needs to invest some time in reading and thinking, as Gabriel told Muhammad, "Read!"

One should read the Qur'an and, if one has time, the Hadiths, and read the arguments in them carefully. Then one would be able to reach his own conclusions without spending a lifetime studying in a seminary.

So the question is: how should we read them?

Let me set out some principles in interpreting Islamic texts and give justifications for them.

The methodology I argue for in reading Islamic texts consists of five principles, namely uncertainty, non-literality, contextuality, individuality, and rationality.

3.2.1 Uncertainty

There are many uncertainties surrounding the exact meaning of many passages in the Qur'an and the Hadiths and we are not really sure what they mean. We cannot impose punishment if we are not sure which actions are wrong according to Islamic texts. Therefore we should adopt the principles of liberalism because we should leave judgment to Allah.

Allah's covenant was laid down a long time ago. We are not sure how to apply his laws in contemporary life, which is vastly different from Muhammad's time when the Qur'an was revealed. If life were the same then application of the Qur'an and the Hadiths as guides for everyday life would be easier. But the world has changed, and it is impossible to turn back.

So the safe way is to give people maximum freedom and let them live their lives the best way they can and let Allah judge them in the last judgment. If applying Allah's laws is so simple, we do not need the last judgment, we could just have a village tribunal. But it does not seem to be the picture laid out in the Qur'an. In verses 23:102-103, it is said that those "whose scales are heavy with good deeds, they are the ones who are successful, but those whose scales are light, they are the ones who have lost their souls and in hell." We do not need scales if we only look at who believe and who do not believe. We need to look at how people behaved during their lives. Similarly, in 34:26 it is said that Allah will "gather us together, then he judges between us in truth, and he is the all-knowing judge." We do not need Allah to judge if it is a simple yes-no question of believing or not.

There are some laws given explicitly in the Qur'an, but the circumstances we face are very different. It would be presumptuous to assume we know how to modify those laws for implementation today. For laws given without qualification may be only a shorthand since the qualification was not needed at the time it was given. Therefore it is dangerous to apply these laws *verbatim* even though

Chapter 3 Read! The First Call of Allah

they may look universal and absolute.

It does not make sense, either, to assume that since we do not know how to modify these laws, we should stick to them ignoring the change in circumstances, or artificially make life the same as then so that we can apply those rulings. We need to be realistic. However enthusiastic you are about Islamic law, if you were put back into such an anachronistic environment as the Taliban tried to enforce, you would definitely choose to escape if possible. Therefore it is in line with Islamic texts that everyone is given maximum freedom to practice Islam as he sees fit.

Some might say this seems a serious distortion of Islam. That is because vocal self-appointed spokesmen[2] of Islam have been very conservative. But this does not have to be the case. Christianity has very liberal sects and people do not find it so strange. One may reply, "but the New Testament has liberal passages.[3] In Matthew 5:44 one is told to love one's enemies."

Actually we can also find liberal passages in the Qur'an and the Hadiths. And in terms of illiberal passages, both the Qur'an and the New Testament have many. For example, we may look at Matthew 19:3–12 in the New Testament. In this passage some Pharisees asked Jesus about divorce and Jesus answered that husband and wife are one flesh and that a man who divorces his wife, except for sexual immorality, and marries another woman, commits adultery. If a Christian reads this passage literally he cannot even divorce unless his wife first commits adultery. Therefore Catholics do not permit divorce. But we have the Protestants who do allow divorce. People could claim that Protestants were not Christians when the Protestant movement first began, but no one could claim that Protestants are not Christians now.

In this example one can see that if we establish liberal

---

[2] There is no need to say "spokespersons" because there are practically no women among them.

[3] Just understand "liberal" in the sense of not having many restrictions when there is adult mutual consent, in order not to get into a lengthy discussion of its definition.

communities of Muslims, they can become the mainstream and no one will be able to contest that they are Muslims, after, say, a century. As with the majority of changes, it is only hard to accept in the beginning.

We should remember that judgment lies with Allah (Qur'an 6:57, 6:62, 12:40, 12:67, 28:70, 28:88, 40:12, 42:8–10), that all matters are returned to him (2:210, 3:109, 8:44, 35:4, 57:5) and the outcome of matters is his (22:41, 31:22). Therefore we should postpone our own judgment and leave it to Allah. We should be aware that we cannot be certain about our interpretation. This is connected to discussions in Section 4.1.2 and Section 6.3.1.

In view of this uncertainty, the best strategy is to let people decide for themselves. Uncertainty points towards advocation of civil and liberal government, so that people have the freedom to practise the form of Islam they choose, and leave judgment to Allah. From this discussion we can see that religiosity actually does not necessarily call for religious rule but could advocate, rather paradoxically, civil rule.

3.2.2 Non-literality

Religious texts are frequently allegorical, because the subjects discussed are frequently something the audience have not experienced, for example the afterlife, and similes and allegories have to be employed to make the content easier to understand. But it would be a disaster to read the allegories literally.

One also has to keep in mind that maybe some of the context is lost to us so that we do not know the whole picture. It does not mean that we never know what the texts mean, but it does mean that we have to be very careful and always keep in mind that our interpretation is tentative and may be wrong. And we must not cause any harm by interpreting the religious texts wrongly and enforcing that interpretation. For example, some of the passages in the Qur'an are given in the context of war. Verses given during a war are probably not applicable to life in peace. There is a huge change in circumstances between then and now, so we cannot take such passages literally in contemporary life.

3.2.2.1 Textual Difficulties

Another rationale for non-literality is the textual problems literal interpretation creates.

For example, let us look at the issue of time. In verse 50:38 it is said that Allah "created the heavens and the earth and what is between them in six days, and nothing touched us of fatigue." This is also mentioned in 7:54, 10:3, 11:7, 25:59, 32:4, and 57:4. With the advancement of science and what we know about the beginning of the universe, this account is extremely problematic. But if we just view it as a simplified rhetorical account for the level of Muhammad's pre-modern audience, then it would not harm the credibility of Allah.

In connection with this we can examine verses in which time periods in the afterlife are mentioned. In verses 20:102–104 it is said that the criminals would be "gathered in the day of judgment and that they will say that they have only spent ten days or even one day," presumably between their death and the day of judgment. In verses 23:112–114 it is said that on judgment day Allah will "ask people how many years did they remain on earth after death, and they would say we remained one day or less, but in fact it was a long time." Similarly, in 46:35 Muhammad is told to be patient and it is said that on judgment day it will be "as though they had not remained except an hour of a day." In verse 70:4 it is said, "the angels and the spirit will ascend to him during a day the extent of which is fifty thousand years."

In these passages we can see that time periods in the spiritual world have a different sense from what they have in our earthly existence. Therefore we should not take the words "six days" too literally. We should remember that in 54:17, 54:22, 54:32, 54:40 it is emphasised that Allah "has certainly made the Qur'an easy for remembrance."

These passages should be viewed as metaphors only.

On the other hand, if we insist on reading every word literally, then discoveries in science which contradict the content of Islamic texts would create crises in Islam. We should choose the wiser approach to religion, and give up insisting that Islamic texts should be read literally and adhered to strictly.

Descriptions of the creation of men pose problems if we read them literally. In different verses human beings are said to be created from different materials, including clay (Qur'an 15:26), a clot of blood (96:2), etc. If we interpret such passages literally, then there is a contradiction, for it does not seem to be the case that human beings are a mix of all these materials. I shall discuss this in detail in Section 3.3.1.

In verse 40:64 it is said that Allah "formed you and so perfected your forms and provided you with good things." In verse 64:3 it is said that Allah "created the heavens and earth in truth and formed you and so perfected your forms, and to him is the destination." We know that human beings' forms are not perfect. Our eyes have blind spots. Our bodies are inferior in many aspects to other animals. One might say, "but perhaps it is for the best." But we do not have perfect forms. If we use the word "perfect" in this way, then I can say someone has a perfect intellect, even though he is stupid, but his stupidity gives him a happy life. This is not a sensible usage of the word, and it causes misunderstanding. We can only understand this verse as not saying it seriously or literally, like the words and phrases we use for social purposes. When I say your children are beautiful and cute, I do not necessarily think so, but it is good manners to say it.

A similar example can be found in 67:3–4 in which it is said that Allah is the one who "created seven heavens in layers. You do not see in the creation of the most merciful any flaw. So repeat the sight, do you see any breaks? Then repeat the sight twice again. Your vision will return to you humbled while it is fatigued." The world is not perfect. There are natural disasters. We should read

Chapter 3 Read! The First Call of Allah

such passages as effective communication to eighth-century tribes and not read them too literally. It would not have been practical to explain natural science to them from first principles. If we continue to read 67:5 this position is even stronger. It says, "and we have certainly beautified the nearest heaven with stars and have made them missiles for the devils and have prepared for them the punishment of the blaze." Whether it is referring to stars or meteoroids, it does not make sense given what we know in astronomy. Such passages should be read as metaphors. And if we read some passages as metaphors, we are allowed to read any passage in Islamic texts as metaphor. In view of all these textual difficulties, literalism is defeated,.

Another example is found in 67:19 which says, "do they not see the birds above them with wings spreading and folding? None holds them except the most merciful. Indeed he is seeing everything." We have a much better explanation for flying now. Do we say that Allah holds planes too? The verb would be empty of meaning if we use it for everything whose mechanics we have already explained. It is supposed to be a physical force in this context, as the passage is not talking about things like "holding the family together." Therefore with the advance of science, the only way to maintain the credibility of Islamic texts containing such problematic passages is to take the position that Islamic texts are not perfect and are only meant for Muhammad's audience, so that we are allowed to change and discard its commands if they are unfit for our age. This is not an insult to the exaltedness of Allah, rather it is the only way to preserve it. For of course it is not stupidity to talk at the level of one's audience, and it is, on the contrary, wisdom.

If we read 79:27–33 we can see that the Qur'an was intended as simple guidance for a simple people. It says, "are you a more difficult creation or is the heaven? Allah constructed it. He raised its ceiling and proportioned it. And he darkened its night and extracted its brightness. And after that he spread the earth. He extracted from it its water and its pasture, and he set the mountains firmly, as provision for you and your grazing livestock." From this example we can see that we should not read the Qur'an literally and follow the content strictly, for it does not fit with advanced understanding of science and does not fit with modern society. And it is not consistent to concede scientific inaccuracies while insisting that the legal injunctions are perfect and timeless.

From these examples we can see that we should not read the Qur'an rigidly. We need not take each word and each sentence of the Qur'an literally without flexibility, and we need to take account of the context, the audience, the tone, and the occasion for which a passage is meant. Appropriate non-literal interpretation is essential, and the Qur'an should not be read like a computer programme.

After this discussion we can see that reading the text of the Qur'an itself carefully and critically tells us that we need to read Islamic texts non-literally. Those who would have us believe that reading them literally is more pious than reading them non-literally are frequently using these texts for their own benefit or personal gain. Telling us to read Islamic texts literally, when the old practices—for example male dominance—portrayed in these texts, fits their interests, is the best and most effortless way to preserve their prestige and power. We can see their hypocrisy and farcicality if we look for inconsistencies in their adherence to literality. They do not practise literal interpretation if it hinders their convenience or power. No Muslim leaders give up cars in favour of camels, even though camels have been mentioned frequently in the Qur'an (e.g. 11:64, 17:59, 91:13) while cars have not been mentioned. In verse 22:27 Muhammad is told to proclaim to the people the pilgrimage, and it is said that they will come to him on foot and on every lean camel and from every distant pass. If we read this literally, then people need to go on pilgrimage on foot or at most on a lean camel. Do Muslim leaders follow this? No, I have a hard time finding any one that does. They only practise literal interpretation if it is helpful to their agenda.

However, in general, what about people who travel by

Chapter 3 Read! The First Call of Allah

planes and cars? They are not really doing the pilgrimage, if we read the text strictly and literally. But surely it is reasonable that people coming from afar use modern modes of transport?

In verses 43:12–13 in the Qur'an it is said that Allah is the one "who created all the species and made for you ships and animals on which you ride, so that you may settle on their backs and then remember the favour of your lord." At the time of revelation, this was appropriate for Muhammad's audience, but perhaps not in other places, and if we stick to strict literal interpretation, then this passage is very irrelevant today, for the dominant modes of transportation are no longer ships and animals in most places on earth.

From these examples we see the necessity to be flexible and use our own rationality. It does not do to follow the text blindly.

3.2.2.2 Local Description

Another set of examples which is usually ignored is passages such as 16:11–14 in the Qur'an. These verses say that Allah causes to grow the crops, the olives, the date-palms, the grapes and all kinds of fruits, and that he has subjected the sea for you to eat fresh food from it. In verses 23:19–20 it is said that Allah "brought forth gardens of palm trees and grapevines in which there are many fruits from which you eat." And then it is said that he also "brought forth a tree in Mount Sinai which produces oil and food for those who eat." In verse 25:49 it is said that Allah "gives drink to those he created, many livestock and men." In verse 22:36 it is said that Allah has "made the camels and cattle among the symbols of Allah, that there is good for you in them," and then one is told to "mention the name of Allah upon them when they are lined up for sacrifice, and when they are lifeless on their sides, then one can eat from them and feed the needy and the beggar." At the end of the verse it is said that Allah has "subjected them to you in this way so that you may be grateful."

One can see clearly these types of food and animals are only available in certain areas. Surely these are not found in Alaska. If we read the Qur'an literally, then only areas in which people feed from these kinds of food are supposed to be governed by the rules of Islam. Because only these types of food have been said to be the work of Allah in these passages.

One may say, but elsewhere Allah is said to be the creator of everything. But such general statements sometimes conflict with each other and it is reasonable to give more weight to more specific statements and concentrate on the explicitly mentioned kinds of vegetation. We can safely conclude that areas where these kinds of food are found are more likely to be the contexts for which Allah's orders are intended, than other areas. Therefore it is reasonable to suppose that Islam's rules are intended for these areas. However, people do not read such passages so strictly and literally. They think that such passages are only for illustrative purposes, showing the power of Allah. But when they see rules they read it literally, and do not take them as illustrations for a moderate form of life.

In verse 27:91 Muhammad is told to say that he is "commanded to worship the lord of this city, the one who made it sacred, and to him all things belong." Even though it says that Allah is the lord of everything, the reference here is very specific. It says that Allah is the lord of Mecca. In verse 6:92 it is said that the Qur'an "is a book we have sent down, blessed and confirming what was before it, so that you may warn the mother of cities and those around it," and in 42:7 it is said that, in this way "we have revealed to you an Arabic Qur'an in order for you to warn the mother of cities and those around it and warn of the day of assembly, about which there is no doubt. A group will be in heaven and a group in the fire." Here "the mother of cities" means Mecca. For people of other places, this is slightly alienating. This should tell us that, while other people may become Muslims, the Qur'an was not intended for the various contexts that Muslims all over the world now encounter. If it were, it would have been hard for

Chapter 3 Read! The First Call of Allah

Muhammad's audience to comprehend. It is not advisable to follow the Qur'an literally when the context is different. We need to read for its spirit rather than its literal meaning.

Another passage that urges for non-literality is to be found in Sura 26 of the Qur'an. In verses 26:192–195 it is said that the Qur'an is "the revelation of the lord of the two worlds, brought by the trustworthy spirit, so that Muhammad can be one of the bearers of warning, in a clear Arabic language." Then in 26:198–200 it is said that even if Allah "revealed it to some of the foreigners, they would not have been believers, in this way he inserted this disbelief into the hearts of the criminals." If we read this passage literally, then all non-Arabs have been determined beforehand not to believe in Allah and receive punishment. This is just not acceptable. Maybe acceptable to some Arabs with a taste for Schadenfreude. But not others.

3.2.2.3 Spiritual Description

In verse 47:15 it is said that "the parable of paradise, which the righteous are promised, in which there are rivers of unpolluted water and rivers of milk the taste of which never changes and rivers of wine delicious to those who drink and rivers of purified honey, in which there will be for them from all the fruits and forgiveness from their lord" is not like "one who abides eternally in the fire and given to drink scalding water, then it severs their intestines?" It explicitly says that this is a parable or example only. It is hard to convey what the afterlife is like exactly, so the Qur'an gives simple descriptions in which paradise is full of things that Muhammad's audience desired and hell is horrifying. We should not take these passages literally.

In verses 20:102–104 it is said that the criminals would be "gathered in the day of judgment and that they will say that they have only spent ten days or even one day," presumably between their death and the day of judgment. In verses 23:112–114 it is said that on judgment day Allah will "ask people how many years did they remain on earth after death, and they would say we remained one day or less, but in fact it was a long time." Similarly, in 46:35 Muhammad is told to be patient and it is said that on judgment day it will be "as though they had not remained except an hour of a day." In verse 70:4 it is said, "the angels and the spirit will ascend to him during a day the extent of which is fifty thousand years." Frankly I do not understand how the extent of a day can be fifty thousand years. The measure of time probably differs totally in the afterlife. Therefore we should not pretend that we understand such passages.

From these examples we can see that people have a very different perception after death, so that any description of the spiritual world can only be allegorical and approximate. We need constantly to remind ourselves of this when reading the Qur'an. Otherwise we distort the meaning it is meant to convey.

In verse 18:31 it is said that people in heaven are "adorned with golden bracelets and wear clothes made of green silk and heavy brocade." While this is a sumptuous sight, it is not necessarily one of comfort and beauty. It probably was attractive to Muhammad's audience, but not to people with different tastes. It is reasonable to conjecture that this description is only an allegorical one, the aim of which is to convey the desirability of heaven. Such a description is not attractive to most people of this age. People do not read this description literally. So why should we read other passages literally?

As for punishment, in verses 19:81–86 it is said that the polytheists "would be driven to hell in thirst." Thirst is terrifying, but definitely more so to Muhammad's audience than to people living in other areas. Therefore it is reasonable to conjecture that it is a description that is intended to convey the terror of the polytheists' punishment, but not the actual physical condition. If such rhetorical tools have been used in the Qur'an, then we cannot assume that Islamic texts are always to be read literally. We need to be wary and have to decide for each case whether it is more reasonable to read literally or not. Otherwise we cannot

Chapter 3 Read! The First Call of Allah

get the true intended meaning of Islamic texts.

In verse 27:88 it is said that on judgment day "mountains will pass like clouds, which is the work of Allah, who perfected all things." Let us ask ourselves honestly, is everything perfect? No, there are problems, sickness, defects, etc. Even if their existence has some benefits, the world is definitely not perfect. We can only read this verse loosely. If we read it literally, we cannot accept it, given what we know. One may say, oh it is just your limited perception which does not let you see the perfection of the world. The word "perfect" is used in our sense. If it requires an enhanced perception to see, it is a different sense. We have to say honestly that in the ordinary sense it is simply not true. If it is used in an idiosyncratic way, we need more explanation; if it is read literally in the ordinary sense, it is not true.

In verses 75:7-9 there is an interesting passage about the day of resurrection. It says that it is on the day "when vision is dazzled, and the moon darkens, and the sun and the moon are joined." Perhaps this is referring to the expansion of the sun? But we have no idea what this is really talking about. If part of the text is so obscure, we cannot read other parts and assume that we understand exactly what they mean and how they are to be applied. We should be cautious and allow each person to read and interpret the text for himself.

In verse 72:8 the jinn say, "we have sought to touch heaven but found it filled with powerful guards and burning fires." This is a very mysterious description. If the physical sky is meant, there do not seem to be guards or fire. Therefore this is probably on the spiritual plane. But we must be honest and admit that we do not know exactly what exists in this realm. Therefore we need to read such passages very cautiously, and this caution should be extended to many seemingly straight-forward passages, for a religious text should not be assumed to be literal. Frequently some background or context is left out, and spiritual description cannot be read literally since our language is not adequate for describing these scenes precisely, due to our lack of experience of this realm. We need to be very conscious of our ignorance in this aspect, otherwise we would be too confident and think that these texts can be used against science, whereas history has proved that religious figures always lose in the end. But the way to do justice to these texts is not to take them at face value, but to read them with caution and care.

The best textual support for non-literality is found in 18:65–82 in the Qur'an. In this segment of the text, the story of a wise servant of Allah is told. Moses asked if he could follow this servant and he agreed on the condition that Moses would be patient and never ask him about anything. But then Moses forgot his promise and kept asking questions and making comments. First this servant of Allah tore open a ship, then he killed a boy, and then he restored a wall. None of these actions Moses understood. At the end this servant of Allah explained that he tore open the ship so that the king would not seize it, that the boy he killed would overburden his parents who are believers and he would be replaced with a better son, and lastly that the wall is to cover a treasure intended for two orphan boys whose father was righteous. To be honest I still do not understand these stories very well even after the explanations have been given, but before they were given these stories were clearly incomplete.

The Qur'an is similar to these stories. There are hidden intentions in the message given through Muhammad but the audience at that time was not yet mature enough for that message. The rules given are compromises between the ideal and the societal stage at that time. Therefore when we read the Qur'an we have to be very careful and not just read the literal meaning and try to apply that inflexibly in the modern world which has changed beyond recognition from Muhammad's time. It is true that some elements of human society have not changed, but we need to consider whether each of the claims and injunctions given are still applicable here and now.

In conclusion, if we can say that certain passages are for illustrative purposes only, then why should we read the

Chapter 3 Read! The First Call of Allah

passages about inheritance and testimony so strictly and literally? Double standards have been unconsciously used in reading Islamic texts. It is utterly unconvincing to be inconsistent in applying the principle of non-literality. We cannot just say let's read this non-literally when for example science clearly contradicts a verse. We need to adopt the principle of non-literality on all Islamic texts, including both descriptive or historical texts as well as normative texts.

We have to review and remove double standards in interpretation, otherwise Islam is but a tangled web of inconsistencies and a treasure trove for impostors and charlatans to exploit.

Like uncertainty, non-literality also points towards civil and liberal rule, because the injunctions in the texts cannot be applied directly in everyday life. Since religious authority cannot give us concrete rules in human transactions, we need civil and liberal rules to arbitrate between people. As for private life, it should be left to the individual, because if the texts are not taken literally, they do not really tell us how and what to do with others' "sins." So, broadly speaking, the government should interfere only if people are physically hurt or prevented from exercising their equal freedom.

3.2.3 Contextuality

When we read the Qur'an and the Hadiths, we have to keep in mind the historical context in which such texts came into being. The Qur'an and the Hadiths come from an age of cruel environment and constant warfare. Therefore the people viewed fighting and killing in a much lighter way than today, and these texts talked to its audience within their cultural acclimatisation. But for a modern audience, we need not adopt the same attitude in order to be a pious Muslim. We should read the texts allowing for this difference in context and extract appropriate lessons from the advice and models of action from a different age. It is more reasonable to follow these models with some modification rather than follow them in a rigid *verbatim* way.

Such a difference in context from today can sometimes be seen in the text itself. But frequently it is not set out explicitly. Therefore we have to keep this background in mind when reading. A passage which shows the context of a messenger being opposed directly is 47:32–35 in which it is said, "those who disbelieved and averted from the way of Allah and opposed the messenger after guidance had become clear to them, they will never harm Allah at all, and he will make their deeds worthless. O you who have believed, obey Allah and obey the messenger and do not invalidate your deeds. Indeed, those who disbelieved and averted from the way of Allah and then died while they were disbelievers, Allah will never forgive them. So do not weaken and call for peace while you are superior, and Allah is with you and will not deprive you of your deeds." We can see that the so-called disbelievers had direct contact with the messenger, rejected him, and prevented others from following him. From this passage we can see that the menacing rhetoric in the Qur'an is directed to people threatening the safety of Muhammad and his followers. This is the context of such verses. People were fighting as a result of differences in religious practices. If we consider the historical difference, we can see that we need not and should not adopt the same attitude in this age. It is only while forgetting and ignoring the historical context that people would be able to maintain that we should follow the warlike passages. But in modern civil society, we can co-exist and let each one of us find God in his own way.

In verses 110:1–3 it is said, "when the victory and the conquest of Allah has come, and you see the people entering into the religion of Allah in multitudes, then exalt [him] with praise of your lord and ask forgiveness of him. Indeed, he is ever accepting of repentance." People might read this as promoting religious war. But it was probably referring to specific conquests Muhammad's community made. Therefore we cannot read it as saying that in general Muslims should fight in order to convert people to Islam. Muhammad fought oppression and for the freedom of worship. We should not read this as saying that religious war in general is lauded.

The lack of contextual considerations is probably what led to the widespread malaise of literal ultra-conservatism. I shall give a detailed argument against this in Section 6.1.

3.2.4 Individuality

The third principle I advocate is individuality.

In Abraham's story as recounted in 37:83–110, he sees, in a dream, that he has to sacrifice his son. When he is getting ready to kill his son, God tells him to stop. But how does he know that it is Allah and not the devil who tells him to sacrifice his son? Even after the "happy ending," we can still say that maybe that is the devil's delusion, and after his death Abraham could be burning in hell for succumbing to the devil's temptation. Whatever he did and whatever the result, Abraham used his own judgment, just as we all need to do. In following any religion, in choosing which sect to belong to, in reading which religious text, in picking which rule to follow, and in interpreting any text or rule, we are using our own judgment. Even when a person decides to rely on another's authority, that individual is the one who makes this decision, using his judgment.

Additionally, in Islam, there is no agent between Allah and a Muslim. It is written in the Qur'an that no one can intercede for us. For example, in verse 6:51, it is said that there will be "no protector and no intercessor for them besides Allah." This is repeated in verses 6:70 and 32:4. In verse 36:23 it is said that if Allah "wills me any harm, other gods' intercession does not save me from anything." In verse 39:44 it is said that all intercession belongs to Allah. In verses 2:48, 2:123, 2:254 it is said that on judgment day "intercession from another would not be accepted." In verse 66:10 it is emphasised that even Noah and Lot could not help their wives. Since there is no agent between Allah and a Muslim, everyone should decide how to live his life in general and how to live his religious life in particular. It does not make sense that we can just follow someone and attribute all the blame to him if he led us astray. We chose the person in the first place.

One may object that the verses quoted above are probably criticising polytheism and emphasising that people only need to worship Allah and not any lesser gods. Whatever their reference, they still tell us that no one can take responsibility for our actions except us, so that we need to choose each statement in our belief system carefully. We cannot evade responsibility by saying that we follow Islam and the version taught to us is not our choice. We need to construct our own belief system, even when we have decided to be a Muslim. There are so many different types of Muslim for us to choose to be.

Sometimes it is said that there is no intercession with Allah except for those whom he permits, as in 2:255, 20:109, 21:28, 34:23, 53:26. Similar passages include 19:87, in which it is said that there is "no intercession except with whom Allah has a covenant" and 43:86, in which it is said that there is "no intercession except one who bears witness to truth." But what these passages say does not seem to allow for people to interpret and take responsibility for others, and no intercessor has been named.

In verses 33:67–68 it is said that the infidels will say on judgment day that they only obeyed their masters and big bosses, and they led them astray from the way, and Allah is urged to give them double punishment. But it does not seem to be useful. Similarly in verses 34:31–33 we see the powerful and the oppressed accusing each other, but the oppressed cannot evade the blame for behaving unjustly by saying that they were only following the orders of the powerful. In verses 40:47–50 it is said that in hell, the weak ones will say to the arrogant ones, "we were only your followers, so are you going to relieve us a share of fire?" And it is said that the messengers "came with clear proofs," and "the prayer of the disbelievers is but in vain." From these verses we can see that there is no intercessor taking the responsibility of interpretation. Even the weak cannot blame the powerful, and coercion does not remove

Chapter 3 Read! The First Call of Allah

responsibility.

As there is no interpretative intercessor, no one can claim a special place in excusing another person's behaviour in the face of Allah. If no one can acquit human beings during the final judgment, it seems reasonable to conclude from this that no one has absolute authority over what Islam is. If no one has absolute authority over what Islam is, then each individual has to find out and decide for himself.

The principle of individuality is related to the principles of uncertainty and non-literality. According to the principle of individuality, every Muslim should explore Islam and reach a satisfactory interpretation of the texts and traditions for himself. According to the principle of uncertainty, we cannot be sure that any particular interpretation of the Islamic texts and traditions is the only correct one. According to the principle of non-literality, Islamic texts and traditions should be read as allegories and Muslims should revive the spirit of the records rather than follow the written rules inflexibly, for they were not intended for the time and place we live in.

Because of these principles, individual judgment in religious matters becomes possible and desirable, with the wide possibilities of views and interpretations for different situations and personalities.

The principle of individuality also highlights one's responsibility in choosing one's beliefs and actions even after choosing a religion. This is because a religion can contain vastly different sects, and because the individual is the agent sowing and reaping the result of one's beliefs and actions, in this world or the next.

Once clear about this point, it also encourages one to take the initiative and cleanse one's belief system of the debris of dogma and unjustified articles of faith.

One should read Islamic texts and critically review what to adopt in one's time and place. One should not accept the views of religious scholars or officials blindly.

It is obvious that this principle also points towards civil and liberal rule, for followers of a faith should be given the freedom to decide how to follow that faith, so no coercion based on religion should be imposed upon anyone, because no one can decide for others what to follow and how to follow. Adoption of individual judgment means that forcing others to adopt Islam is not necessarily a good thing, even if some passages in the Qur'an seem to imply that it is. A religion that is not accepted actively, willingly, and critically does credit to no one.

3.2.5 Rationality

Lastly, let me talk about the principle of rationality. As I use the term "rationality" here with reference to interpretation, it means induction, deduction, modification, extrapolation, using analogical reasoning, etc.

In the Qur'an, the phrase أولي الألباب *ūlī al-albāb*, meaning "people of understanding," appears many times, in verses 2:179, 2:197, 2:269, 3:7, 3:190, 5:100, 12:111, 13:19, 14:52, 38:29, 38:43, 39:9, 39:18, 39:21, 40:54, 65:10, etc. The verb عقل *'aqala*, meaning "to reason," is used about 50 times, from 2:44 to 67:10. The word is mostly used to urge people to use their reason. From these turns of phrase we can get a hint that understanding is seen as important and blind following is not encouraged in Islam. We need to reason about interpretations and necessary modifications.

In the history of Islam, there was a group called the Mu'tazilis. The word "Mu'tazili" means "one who withdraws." They were a group that emphasised rationality, analogy, and individual judgment in Islamic law.

They became extinct in the Islamic legal tradition at some point in the history of Islam, but rationality is the only plausible path for Islam in the modern world. For Islamic texts were written in a different age and the structure of society was radically different. How is one going to live one's life in the contemporary world according to a text that does not mention any of the modern daily appliances, means of transportation, tools of communication, etc.? In order to live one's life in a way desirable in or compatible with Islam, one has to re-interpret the texts in the context of this time and age, with respect to the new forms of technology, social organisation, commercial transactions, etc.

How to do it? The only plausible way is by rationality, finding a reasonable interpretation of Islam by means of modification and extrapolation, deciding which are key tenets and which are age-specific and non-essential.

Again, like the other four principles of uncertainty, non-literality, contextuality, and individuality, this principle points towards civil and liberal rule because people should be allowed to employ their own God-given rationality to decide how to follow Islam, and not be forced to accept one form of it. The right of self-determination in religion belongs to the individual, not to the majority of the community. People can be as strict as they like with their life but there is no reason to force it onto others, even if they belong to the same religion.

3.3 The Importance of Interpretation

3.3.1 Coherence

The issue of interpretation is very important in achieving a coherent religious outlook.

Let us look at an example. In verse 4:159 in the Qur'an, it says that all of the people of the book do "believe in Jesus before his death." But in 4:158 it has just been said that

Jesus "has not been killed, but raised by Allah to him." If he is raised and not killed, it is not appropriate to talk about his death.

There are interpretations in which Jesus's death is placed in the future. In such interpretations Jesus ascended, he will come again, and then dies. But they look rather complicated and convoluted. And they come from later traditions that seem designed to explain away the problem with these verses. I remain skeptical.

Therefore if we interpret the Qur'an too literally, it is hard to respond to Christians' questions regarding the seeming discrepancy between 4:158 and 4:159 in the Qur'an. But if we take "death" merely as a shorthand covering death in the narrow sense and other ways of leaving the material world, then it poses no problem.

A strong argument can be made by means of the problem of who is the first Muslim. In verse 6:14 in the Qur'an, it is said that Muhammad has been commanded to be the "first to submit to Allah," and in 6:163 it is said that Muhammad is the "first Muslim" but in other verses, for example 2:132, there are Muslims before Muhammad. A similar situation appears in 26:51 where the magicians who has lost to Moses say "we hope that our lord will forgive us our sins because we were the first of the believers." Reading these verses alongside each other we can see that the appropriate interpretation is not to take the word "first" strictly but simply as referring to the first one submitting to Allah as a result of the messages Muhammad himself brings. Otherwise there would be a contradiction between these verses.

An even stronger example concerns the creation of mankind. In different verses human beings seem to be created from different materials, including clay (15:26), a clot of blood (96:2), etc. If we interpret such passages literally, then there is a contradiction, for it does not seem probable that human beings are a mix of all these materials.

In verses 6:2, 7:12, 17:61, 32:7, 38:71, and 38:76 it is said that Allah created human beings from clay. In 37:11 it is said that Allah created man from sticky clay. In 15:26,

Chapter 3 Read! The First Call of Allah

15:28, and 15:33 it is said that human beings are created from dry clay from black mud. In 55:14 it is said that Allah created man from dry clay like pottery.

In verse 3:59 it is said that Allah created Adam from dust. In 30:20 it is said that Allah created you from dust.

In verse 25:54 it is said that Allah is the one who created a human being from water. In 24:45 it is said that Allah created every creature from water.

In verses 16:4, 36:77, and 80:19 it is said that Allah created human beings from a sperm-drop. In 76:2 it is said that Allah created man from a sperm-drop mixture. In 77:20 it is said that Allah "created you from a disdained liquid." In 86:6–7 it is said that man was created from an ejected fluid, coming forth from between the backbone and the ribs.

In verse 96:2 it is said that Allah created man from a clinging clot.

In another group of verses, the account is more complicated. In verses 18:37 and 35:11 it is said that Allah created human beings from dust and then from a sperm-drop. In verses 32:7–8 it is said that Allah began the creation of man from clay, then he made his posterity from an extract from a despised liquid. In verses 75:37–38 it is said that when man was a sperm-drop emitted from semen, then he was a clinging clot, Allah created and proportioned him. In verse 22:5 it is said that Allah created human beings from dust, then from a sperm-drop, then from a clinging clot, and then from a lump of flesh, formed and unformed.

In verses 23:12–14 it is said that men have been "created from an extract of clay, then it is placed in a sperm-drop, then it is made into a clot, then it is turned into a lump, then bones are made from it, then the bones are clothed in flesh, and in the end it is turned into another creation." People might say, look, there is no contradiction, since the use of clay was at the first stage. But the problem remains that we do not know what it corresponds to in the actual development of an embryo. We know the role of semen but we know of nothing that resembles clay in this process.

In verse 40:67 it is said that Allah created human beings from dust, then from a sperm-drop, then from a clinging clot, then he brings you out as a child, for you to reach maturity.

Yet another different account appears in 71:15–17 in which it is said, "do you not see how Allah has created seven heavens in layers and made the moon a light in them and made the sun a lamp? And Allah made you grow from the earth as a growth."

How is it possible to create a person from clay and then from semen? And is a person created from clay, semen, dust, water, or all of them? In its literal sense, these verses are contradictory and incomprehensible. They simply look capricious and confusing. If we were to read these passages literally, then they conflict with each other. But if we read the words of the Qur'an as allegories and similes, then these seeming inconsistencies do not matter. For example, if we read the word "dust" as denoting the tiny size of the basic components human beings are made of, then it makes sense in a poetic way. Or if we read the verses as talking about the mythical beginnings or spiritual qualities of men (clay) versus the coming-into-being of each person (sperm-drop), then the different accounts become much more comprehensible. But this needs our filling-in and interpretation. Perhaps the account given in 71:15–17 is the most sensible in the light of modern science, for if we read it metaphorically, it hints at a kind of autonomous evolution. But we are the ones choosing how to read these passages, because they were given a long time ago for a distant society.

The discussion above shows that our work as readers is not passive. We have to provide appropriate background to the different stories. It is the same with rules given in the Qur'an and Hadiths. We have to read them actively and qualify them with our own intellect, according to the personal and social context in which they were given.

In contrast with this are the passages saying that Satan was created from fire (7:12, 17:61, 38:76), and other passages saying that jinn were created from fire (15:27) or its

Chapter 3 Read! The First Call of Allah

flame (55:15). These passages are not comprehensible on the literal level. They need the same kind of active reading above, so that we can make sense of them and perhaps acquire interesting spiritual insights.

Such textual issues are very puzzling and frequently explanations worsen the matter. But if we view such passages as metaphorical, then there is no problem. It just means that Allah had a hand at the beginning of life. And that could be compatible with modern scientific discoveries. But anything more specific risks scientific refutation. And we cannot ignore scientific refutation. It means a distrust of science as a whole and then it would be self-defeating[4] if we use any technology based on modern science.

On the other hand, some Muslims like to use this passage as evidence for the divine nature of the Qur'an, as it shows advanced scientific understanding. But this is not very impressive since ancient Greeks already had more detailed accounts with regard to human biology. And viewed with the rigour of science, the Qur'anic passages are not correct.

Thus we can see that, in many circumstances, the Qur'an should be read metaphorically. It is not a distortion of the text. On the contrary, it is the only way to read it reasonably.

In summary, we see repeatedly that very different or even opposite conclusions can be drawn from the same passages! Hence one should be able to see the crucial role an interpreter plays. One should not delegate this role to others. The moral responsibility cannot be evaded. If we choose a bad authority and follow blindly, we are the one doing bad things. We cannot blame it on the authority we are following.

The general lesson is to reject the intrinsic superiority of Islamic texts and be sceptical about religious authorities. One has to review critically what religious teachers say

---

[4]To be self-defeating is to do things that do not fit with what you say. For example, to say aloud that you cannot speak.

about the Qur'an and the Hadiths and not accept their views blindly. One should interpret for oneself, with reason and flexibility, according to core doctrines carefully chosen after reflection.

3.3.2 Allegory

When we read religious texts, we have to remember that similes, metaphors, allegories, and other rhetorical techniques are used, especially since we have no direct experience of the afterlife, so that any discussion of it is very approximate, and such rhetorical tools are employed to make it easier for us to understand, but misunderstandings can also occur because of this wide gap of experience. Therefore we have to read flexibly, otherwise absurdities will result.

Let us discuss the topics of time, judgment day, heaven, and hell, to illustrate this point.

3.3.2.1 Time

The first thing I would like to talk about is time.

The story of the cave serves as an important example. Apparently Allah put a group of people into a long sleep and then woke them up. In verses 18:9–12 it is said, "have you thought that the companions of the cave and the inscription were a wonder among our signs? When the youths retreated to the cave, then they said, 'our lord, grant us from yourself mercy and prepare for us right guidance for our condition.' So we cast [sleep] over their ears within the cave for a number of years. Then we awakened them so that we might show which of the two factions was more precise in calculating how long they had remained." In verses 18:19–20 it is said, "we awakened them so that they might question one another. Said a speaker from among them, 'How long have you remained?' They said, 'we have remained a day or part of a day.' They said [to one another], 'your lord is most knowing of how long you remained. So send one of you with this silver coin of yours

Chapter 3 Read! The First Call of Allah

to the city and let him see which is the purest food and bring you provision from it and let him be cautious, and do not make anyone become aware of you. Indeed, if they come to know about you, they will stone you or return you to their religion, and you will never succeed then.' " This story seems to emphasise that it is hard for people to calculate time in unusual circumstances. But it is hard to grasp the phenomenon that a group of people could be put into sleep a number of years together. The sense of the whole story is not clear. It could be just a metaphor. It becomes even more confusing when in 18:22 it is said, "They will say there were three, the fourth of them being their dog, and they will say there were five, the sixth of them being their dog, guessing at the unseen, and they will say there were seven, and the eighth of them was their dog. Say, 'my lord is most knowing of their number. None knows them except a few. So do not argue about them except with an obvious argument and do not inquire about them among them from anyone.' " I think the numbers symbolise very well people's confusion about religious matters. The solution to this problem is not literalism, but caution and postponement. For we cannot make a difficult text artificially simple by reading it word-by-word, that is not doing it justice. On the contrary, it is caution and admitting one's ignorance that would be doing justice to the text.

Now one may object, but in 18:25–26 it is clarified that they were in the cave for 309 years, and Muhammad is told to say, "Allah is most knowing of how long they remained. The unseen of the heavens and the earth belongs to him. How seeing is he and how hearing! They do not have any protector besides him, and he does not share his command with anyone." Does this not tell us that we can follow Allah's words literally?

No, not really, since we still do not know the unseen, and Allah's advice is for the particular situation of Muhammad's followers, therefore we have to reason and learn from what is said in the Qur'an, rather than applying what is written word-for-word.

In verse 22:47 it is said that people urge Muhammad

"to hasten the punishment, and Allah will not fail in his promise, and indeed, a day with your lord is like a thousand years of those which you count." There is a very similar saying in Chinese, that a day has passed in the mountains (among the gods), while it has already been a thousand years in the world. From this passage we can see that the sense of time in the spiritual world is different from that of the physical world in which we dwell. Therefore it is very difficult for us truly to understand what it is like after death. And we have every reason to suppose that descriptions given are only metaphorical, not intended to be literal, since there may be no equivalence to our experience in this world.

In the Qur'an it is emphasised that people's perception about time is different after death. In verse 10:45 it is said that on judgment day Allah will gather the deniers "as if they had stayed [after death] but an hour of the day. They will know each other. Those who denied the meeting with Allah [on judgment day] will have lost and were not guided." In verse 17:52 Muhammad was told to say to people that on judgment day Allah "will call you and you will respond with praise of him and think that you had not remained [after death] except for a little." In verses 20:102–104 it is said that the criminals would be "gathered in the day of judgment and that they will say that they have spent only ten days or even one day," presumably between their death and the day of judgment. Here we can see that the sense of time after death is very different from that in this world. In verses 23:112–114 it is said that on judgment day Allah will "ask people how many years they remained on earth after death, and they would say we remained one day or less, but in fact it was a long time." In verse 30:55 it is said that on judgment day when "the hour appears the criminals will swear they had remained but an hour. They were deluded like this." Similarly, in 46:35 Muhammad is told to be patient and it is said that on judgment day it will be "as though they had not remained except an hour of a day." Finally, in 79:46, it is said, "it will be, on the day they see it, as though they had not remained except

Chapter 3 Read! The First Call of Allah

for an afternoon or a morning." From these passages we can see that in the afterlife people do not perceive things the ways we do in this world. Therefore all descriptions of the afterlife should be read cautiously and we should admit to ourselves our ignorance of what it is really like after we die. Once we admit this ignorance we can see that it is more sensible to read such descriptions allegorically since they have probably been worded in a way that is geared towards Muhammad's audience who had as little idea about the afterlife as we do, but had tastes and social precepts different from us. Therefore we should not read such descriptions literally and rigidly.

3.3.2.2 Judgment Day

Descriptions of judgment day are frequently obscure. Let us read some examples.

In verses 77:7–11 it is said that judgment day comes "when the stars are obliterated, and when heaven is opened, and when the mountains are blown away, and when the messengers' time has come." Let us ask ourselves seriously. What is meant by "stars are obliterated"? How can heaven be opened? How could mountains be blown away?

Similarly, in 78:17–20 it is said, "indeed the day of judgment is an appointed time. The day the horn is blown and you will come forth in multitudes, and heaven is opened and will become gateways, and the mountains are removed and are a mirage." Does it mean that everyone who has ever been alive will come forward at this point? The scale alone is unimaginable. This could well be true but we should not pretend that we really understand such passages.

In verses 77:28–33 it is said that the deniers will be told to "proceed to that which you used to deny. Proceed to a shadow having three columns, no cool shade and availing not against the flame. Indeed, it throws sparks like a fortress, as if they were yellowish camels." In what sense should we interpret this imagery? It is not comprehensible to a human being.

In verses 79:1–14 it is said, "By those who extract with violence, and by those who remove with ease, and by those who glide swimming, and those who race each other in a race, and those who arrange matter, on the day the blast will convulse. The subsequent one will follow. That day hearts will tremble, their eyes humbled. They are saying, 'will we indeed be returned to the former state? Even if we were decayed bones?' They say, 'that, then, is a losing return.' Indeed, it will be just one shout, and suddenly they will be awakened." This passage seems more straightforward, but do we know how people's souls are extracted? What exactly is referred to by "former state"? Does it mean the state of being alive, or even before becoming alive?

In verses 80:33–42 it is said, "when there comes the deafening blast, on the day a man will flee from his brother, and his mother and his father, and his wife and his children. For every man, that day, there will be a matter adequate for him. Faces, that day, will be bright, laughing, rejoicing at good news, and faces, that day, there will be dust upon them. Blackness will cover them. Those are the disbelievers, the wicked ones." What is the deafening blast? What happens afterwards? This passage is very sketchy, and we can get only a vague sense of a significant event. Other than that there is very little information.

Frankly the scenes described in these verses are not of phenomena that we understand. They are too remote from everyday experience. Therefore we need to be very cautious when reading. People tend to add what they like when they read vague descriptions. We need to guard against wishful thinking when we read such descriptions. People who enjoy seeing others punished would see the future of infidels as they identify them. But we should remember that we are not so sure about what would happen then.

Actually it is wise to withhold views about the afterlife, since we do not have concrete evidence about it. The most reasonable approach is to assert as little as possible, as that

Chapter 3 Read! The First Call of Allah

would have the least chance of being falsified by experience or data. This is what the philosophy of science teaches us. [37]

It is worse if the text makes definite statements that do not seem to make sense in the face of science. In verses 81:1–14 it is said, "when the sun is wrapped up, and when the stars fall, dispersing, and when the mountains are removed, and when full-term she-camels are neglected, and when the wild beasts are gathered, and when the seas are filled with flame, and when the souls are paired, and when the girl that was buried alive is asked for what sin she was killed, and when the pages are laid open, and when the sky is stripped away, and when fire is set ablaze, and when paradise is brought near, a soul will know what it has brought." In verses 82:1–5 it is said, "when the sky breaks apart and when the stars fall, scattering, and when the seas are made to gush forth, and when the graves are scattered, a soul will know what it has presented and kept back." In verses 84:1–6 it is said, "when the sky has split asunder, and has responded to its lord and was obligated, and when the earth has been extended, and has cast out that within it and relinquished, and has responded to its lord and was obligated, O mankind, indeed you are labouring toward your lord with exertion and will meet it." These events seem very hard to imagine. For example, how does the sky break apart? And it is questionable whether such events fit with the law of physics. These passages seem even to conflict with each other. One says that seas are made to gush forward, and the other says that seas are filled with flame. Does it mean a volcano erupts under the sea? A conservative might say, "look, this shows our ignorance, we should hold our tongues and listen to the sheikhs." But that does not do, if you use science, especially modern technology, in any way in your life, which any person living in a modern world definitely does. You cannot say that you trust scientists when it comes to electricity, but you trust sheikhs more when it comes to astronomy. They are aspects of the same scientific enterprise with strongly confirmed content, whereas Islamic texts might have been misread and wrongly copied, to say the least, and we cannot go back in time to check that. So they rest on much weaker evidence. Therefore we have to give in when there is a conflict between statements in the texts and science. We have two options, namely

1. Non-literality

   Interpret such passages as metaphors or as how people will perceive the extraordinary and shocking things happening then.

2. Abrogation

   Cancel such passages on the ground that they might be wrongly transmitted.

Either way it means that the Qur'an is not unchangeable. But then we need to hold the same attitude towards passages with social or legal implications. They cannot be refuted as in science, but the change in circumstances and the arguments presented above should convince us that in this case too the Qur'an and of course the Hadiths are not unchangeable and need not be accepted as a complete inviolable whole.

3.3.2.3 Heaven

In verse 18:31 it is said that people "in heaven are adorned with golden bracelets and wear clothes made of green silk and heavy brocade." And in 22:23 it is said that Allah will admit those "who believe and do righteous deeds to gardens beneath which rivers flow." It is also said that they will be "adorned with bracelets of gold and pearl, and their garments will be made of silk." This is repeated in 35:33. In verse 76:21 it is said that people in paradise will wear "green garments of fine silk and brocade. And they will be adorned with bracelets of silver." In verses 44:51–55 it is said that the righteous "will be in a safe place within gardens and springs wearing fine silk and brocade, facing each other like this and we will marry them to fair

Chapter 3 Read! The First Call of Allah

women with large eyes. They will call there for every fruit, in safety." In verses 43:70–73 it is said that in paradise "plates and vessels of gold are circulated among" Muslims, and there is "much fruit for you to eat." In verses 55:46–59 it is said, "there are two gardens for one who feared the place of his lord" "having branches." "There are two springs flowing in them" and "two kinds of every fruit." People are "reclining on couches whose linings are of silk brocade, and the fruit of the two gardens is low." "There are women limiting their glances, untouched by any man or jinn before them," "as if they were rubies and coral." In verses 56:15–26 it is said that those in heaven would be reclining on woven thrones "facing each other, young boys made eternal circulating around them with vessels, and pitchers and a cup from a flowing spring, no headache from them and they will not be intoxicated, and fruit of what they select, and meat of fowl from what they desire, and fair women with large eyes, like well-protected pearls, as a reward for what they have done. They will not hear in it ill speech or commission of sin, only a saying of peace and peace." In verses 56:27–38 it is said that the companions of the right will be "among thornless lote trees, and trees layered" with fruit, and extended shade, and poured water, and abundant fruit, "not limited and not forbidden, and raised beds. Indeed we created women anew, and made them virgins, devoted and of equal age, for the companions of the right." In verses 69:22–24 heaven is described to be "an elevated garden, clusters of fruits to be picked hanging near. 'Eat and drink in satisfaction for what you presented in the gone-by days.' " In verses 88:11–16 it is said that people in heaven "will not hear vain talk. There is a flowing spring in it. There are raised couches in it, and cups put in place, and cushions lined up, and carpets spread."

While such descriptions are luxurious, they might not fit the tastes of our time. One can see that they are attractive to Muhammad's audience, but not to people with different tastes. The emphasis on unlimited food is more enticing to pre-modern people than to us because we do not crave for food so much, now that hunger is not a problem in most areas of the world, while instead obesity poses more health risks. We can also see that these descriptions are more attractive to heterosexual men than women, as the presence of beautiful women is emphasised.

The passage 76:12–21 touches on many aspects of heaven that are not given as completely as in other verses. It is said that the servants of Allah will be rewarded with "paradise and silk, reclining in it on couches. They will not see any sun or cold in it, and shades are close above them, and clusters of fruits are dangling low, and vessels of silver and cups that were crystal-clear are circulated among them, crystals made from silver the measure of which they have determined, and they will be given to drink a cup whose mixture is of ginger, [from] a fountain in it named Salsabeel, and young boys made eternal circulate among them. When you see them, you would think that they are scattered pearls, and when you look, then you see pleasure and great dominion. Green garments of fine silk and brocade are on them, and they are adorned with bracelets of silver, and their lord gives them a purifying drink." From this passage we can see what was considered desirable in ancient times, especially seventh-century Arabia, for example silk, couches, moderate climate, shades, drinks in silver vessels, young boys, pearls, and silver. If another group of people is addressed, fresh sashimi, the finest tea picked in early spring, exquisite china in pale celestial blue, handsome young men, etc. might have been mentioned instead.

As soon as we read these descriptions carefully, we can see that Muhammad's message is tailored to his audience, and we need not fuss over details of his instruction. It is the ideal way of life, being upright, just, brave, etc. that really matters. We have to remember that the Qur'an is designed for Muhammad's people, not all human beings from the past to the future. Therefore we need to read and interpret actively, not blindly following the text.

It is interesting and significant that the word "bracelet" is used five times in the Qur'an, four times describing paradise, and the remaining one is verse 43:53, in which it is

Chapter 3 Read! The First Call of Allah

said that Pharaoh questioned with respect to Moses, "then why have there not been placed upon him bracelets of gold or come with him the angels joined together?" From this we can see that the sumptuous description of paradise is highly influenced by Egyptian standards.

Very frequently when heaven is mentioned, rivers are said to flow beneath it. This is seen in verses 2:25, 2:266, 3:15, 3:136, 3:195, 3:198, 4:13, 4:57, 4:122, 5:12, 5:85, 5:119, 6:6,7:43, 9:72, 9:89, 9:100, 19:9, 13:35, 14:23, 16:31, 18:31, 20:76, 22:14, 22:23, 25:10, 29:58, 39:20, 47:12, 48:5, 48:17, 57:12, 58:22, 61:12, 64:9, 65:11, 66:8, 85:11, and 98:8. This list includes only the verses in which the rivers are said to flow below the gardens. It does not include the verses in which the rivers are in the garden. This emphasis on the availability of water is probably a product of the scarcity of water in the Arabian Peninsula, which creates a kind of anxiety about and longing for water. This expression would definitely have been attractive for Muhammad's audience. The other significant point again has something to do with Egypt. In verse 43:51, the only time in which a river is said to flow under something else than paradise, it is said to flow under Pharaoh. This shows us what ideas the Qur'an is responding and referring to. The Nile River is an enviable asset and the picture of paradise in the Qur'an is modelled after the Nile Valley.

It is reasonable to conjecture that such descriptions are only allegorical, the aim of which is to convey the desirability of heaven. If we read them literally they do not seem very enticing to us in this age. Therefore many people do not read these descriptions literally.

If we are allowed to read some passages metaphorically, then no one can claim that he has the right to dictate to us which passage is to be read literally and which allegorically.

One has to be honest. We do not know for sure what life after death is like, whether it is heaven or hell. But of course people using religion to gather followers of a religion under their command would like us to believe that they do know. We need to use our common sense, and cannot totally rely on others. The clues are given in the texts, we need to think about what they mean ourselves. We cannot afford to be lazy.

3.3.2.4 Hell

Similarly in the case of hell. In the Qur'an and the Hadiths it is occasionally said that non-Muslims will be going to hell to stay there forever after death. But since we are not sure what life after death looks like, we cannot be sure if we should take such passages very literally.

Maybe it just means that people would feel bad and feeling bad would make time pass very slowly so that to the disembodied soul even a short time of mental torture would seem like eternity. For the notion of time after death may not be the same as that before death.

Many religions have some concept of hell and use it to push followers to do good things, not to do bad things, to be pious, etc. From the way the organisation and structure of hell varies according to the cultural background, it is reasonable to think that if there are souls and if different religions did try to portray life after death as realistically as possible in their texts, then it seems that people's concepts shape how they see their surroundings when they die. Maybe it helps to form some kind of non-physical but intersubjective world.

Allah is most compassionate and merciful, so comments about hell are probably just to scare people from doing bad deeds. In verse 74:31 it is said, "mention of hell is but a reminder to humanity." This passage shows this idea most clearly. I think this is how we should read passages such as 78:21–26 in which it is said, "indeed, hell has been lying in wait for the transgressors, a place of return, remaining in it for ages. They will not taste in it any coolness or drink except scalding water and pus, an appropriate recompense."

A hint of this is also found in verse 33:24 in which it is said that Allah "rewards the truthful for their truth and punishes the hypocrites if he wills, or accepts their repentance," and that Allah is forgiving and merciful. In

Chapter 3 Read! The First Call of Allah

juxtaposition with Allah's love of mercy and forgiveness, sending people to hell for not believing in the existence of Allah and abiding by all his rules seems too harsh and cruel. There is a conflict between these two sets of descriptions about Allah. As a Muslim, one has to choose for oneself when there is conflicting content. However strong one's faith is, one cannot endorse what one does not understand, so at most one can say, "I do not know what will really happen" or one can choose to adopt a more reasonable interpretation. It is more reasonable to think that hell is just an idea to scare people into behaving well, or that it is reserved for the truly evil, than saying that Allah is most compassionate and merciful but people who displease him are going to be tortured in hell forever and ever.

In verse 11:107 in the Qur'an, it is said that the wretched ones "are going to abide in hell as long as the heavens and the earth exist, except what Allah wills." So it means that if Allah wills that they do not abide in hell, then they are saved immediately. If Allah is most compassionate and merciful, he will definitely save them, so people will not spend an eternity in hell. This kind of interpretation is reasonable and within the limits of the text. Why do we seldom see such views? I believe it is because of a bad trend in Islam. But hopefully it will pass. Once we adopt this methodology in interpretation the possibilities in reading Islamic texts open up before us. These possibilities have been deliberately obscured by different interest groups, especially militant political ones, and thus are inadvertently overlooked by many Muslims.

In verse 6:36 in the Qur'an, it is said that Allah will "gather the dead and resurrect them, and then they will return to him." From the context it is probable that he means everyone rather than just believers, because in 6:38 it is said that all "animals and birds will be gathered towards Allah." Being gathered could mean they will be judged and punished, but returning to Allah could mean that they are with Allah for good, maybe at the same time as or after punishment. So we could take it to mean everyone and base our position on this verse rather than the others which talk about non-Muslims going to hell forever.

In verse 10:23 it is said that the rebels against Allah will return to him in the end and he will inform them of what they have done. Again there is no mention of hell and we need not assume that they are going to hell. In verse 29:8 something similar is said. It is said that if "parents strive to make you associate others with Allah, do not obey them," and that your "place of return is to Allah and he will tell you what you have done." For comparison, in 10:69–70 it is said that those "who invent a lie against Allah will return to him and receive severe punishment." And there is no talk about hell. By comparing these verses we could conclude that there are different grades of punishment and it is not reasonable to assume that eternal flame in hell is always the case.

In verse 18:87 in the Qur'an it is said that a person "who is unjust will be punished, then he will be returned to Allah, and he will punish him with a terrible punishment." No mention of hell is made here and the unjust person is returned to Allah for punishment. In verse 29:57 it is said that every soul will "taste death. Then to [Allah] you will be returned." We are not really sure about who would be sent to hell and what really happens there.

In verses 19:81–86 it is said that the polytheists would be "driven to hell in thirst." Thirst is something terrible, but more to people in dry areas than to people in lush areas. Therefore this description seems to be one geared towards Muhammad's audience rather than one that is rigidly accurate. Similarly, in 56:41–44 it is said that the companions of the left will be "in scorching fire and scalding water, and a shade of black smoke, not cool and not pleasant." Then in 56:51–55 it is said that the deniers will be "eating from trees of zaqqum, and filling their bellies with it, and drinking on top of it scalding water, and drinking as thirsty camels drink."[5] All these descriptions focus on fire, heat, and thirst, that which scares people in Arabia most. From such examples we can see that the

---

[5]Zaqqum is the tree of hell. It bears a poisonous fruit.

Chapter 3 Read! The First Call of Allah

Qur'an is not meant to be read inflexibly, for it is tailored for Muhammad's people. We have to take account of the context in order to understand the real message that is intended to be conveyed. If we read without taking into account the historical context then we are not reading more accurately, but less.

An example to the same effect is 69:30–32 in which it is said, "Seize him and shackle him. Then burn him in hellfire. Then into a chain whose length is seventy cubits, insert him." The tone is supposed to be scary, but frankly in this age I think we have much more terrible images of torture than a long chain. It does not seem very convincing to a modern mind. But it should have been suitable deterrence against disbelief and immorality. Again this shows that such descriptions should be read as metaphors only. And if we read such descriptions non-literally, we are bound to allow non-literal interpretation of Islamic texts.

In verses 74:27–31 it is said, "what makes you know what is hell? It lets nothing remain and leaves nothing, scorching the skin, over it are nineteen [angels]. And we have not made anyone the keepers of the fire except angels, and we have not made their number except as a trial for those who disbelieve." Frankly this passage is not very informative. There is some imagery of fire, but it is unclear what the significance is of the number nineteen as the number of angels overseeing hell. This shows the allegorical nature of the descriptions of hell, and the lack of context of many Qur'anic passages. Therefore we have to read with every caution and uncertainty.

In verses 87:12–13 it is said that he "who burns in the greatest fire does not die in it and does not live." This description shows the non-literality of the text, since for a person to be neither dying nor living is not comprehensible in ordinary usage. Therefore we can see that the Qur'an should be read with careful interpretation and reflection, rather than mechanically and literally.

Similarly in 88:4–7 it is said that some "will burn in an intensely hot fire. They will be given drink from a boiling spring. For them there will be no food except from a bitter thorny plant, which neither nourishes nor avails against hunger." How can one be burning and still eat? Again, this seems to be allegorical rather than a literal description of what happens after death for some people. They perhaps would be punished but this is not a straightforward picture. It could also be their own perception, tortured by their conscience.

In verses 33:64–65 it is said that Allah "cursed the infidels and prepared for them a blaze, in which they are abiding forever and do not find a protector or a helper." But just before this, in 33:63, it is said that knowledge of the hour [of judgment] is with Allah. And in 17:85 it is said that the soul is "Allah's affair, and mankind has been given only a little knowledge." So we need to guard against taking descriptions of hell and the afterlife too seriously. They are probably not intended to be accurate since it is hard to describe a radically different state of being. This is a source of much confusion in any religion.

3.3.2.5 Discussion

From the examples above we can see that it would be more prudent to emphasise and remember the passages talking about our lack of knowledge rather than those that offer simple descriptions of the afterlife, Allah's plan, etc., i.e. all the grand and mysterious things that are hard to understand in our current state of being. It is better that we live with a sense of spirituality, but base our judgment and moral considerations on the consequences of actions, for example harm and suffering, rather than follow written rules blindly without adequate contextual interpretation.

Due to our lack of knowledge regarding the afterlife, it is more advisable to read descriptions of heaven and hell and conditions for going to hell in a rhetorical and allegorical way. The description of heaven is very simple and repetitive in the Qur'an. It is always said that there are rivers flowing underneath. The lack of a detailed account probably shows that it is very hard for human beings to understand what it is like in the afterlife, so that the de-

Chapter 3 Read! The First Call of Allah

scriptions are intended only to convey a general sense of peacefulness and comfort in the case of heaven and a general sense of pain and horror in the case of hell.

All in all, I think the simpler description of heaven and hell in 76:11, in which it is said that Allah will protect his servants from the evil of the judgment day and "give them radiance and happiness," is more suitable for spiritually advanced people, while the ones with concrete descriptions are more attractive to beginners in spiritual cultivation.

Some people propose that the talk about hell after death was just a way to scare people, as the Islamic texts are not always consistent about it. One may then ask, if the postulation of hell in Islamic texts was just a way to scare people, why was it necessary to scare people into believing in the existence of Allah too, is not just scaring them to do good deeds enough? If Allah exists, why should it matter that people believe in him or not? Most people would not care if everyone in the world does not know about their existence. Is Allah that narcissistic?

I think that it is because postulating a being who would punish them is more powerful than just postulating heaven for good deeds and hell for bad deeds. In verse 39:15 in the Qur'an, Muhammad is told to say that the losers are the "ones who will lose themselves and their families on the day of resurrection," that this is definitely "the clear loss," that there will be "canopies of fire above them and canopies below them," that Allah "makes his servants fear him by this," and then Muhammad is told to "tell his servants to fear Allah." From this example we can see that terrible punishment and an awe-inspiring god have a strong influence on people's minds, and make an indelible impression.

Another reason why belief in Allah was regarded as essential was probably because that was the form of religion that was most easily accepted, given the Jewish and Christian traditions that already existed in the region. In other words, I think that the cause is circumstantial.

I am not disputing Allah's existence but the supposed punishment for not believing in his existence. These are two very different issues. People questioning the latter frequently question the former, but what is important is that people not doubting the former attain a sense of skepticism for the latter. Allah's existence does not entail a severe punishment for not believing in him, unless Islamic texts are read in a certain way. There is a logical gap between the two. Remembering that would be a cure for most religious extremism.

I think we should remember soothing sayings such as "your place of return is to Allah" (5:48, 5:105, 6:60, 6:108, 6:164, 10:4, 10:23, 10:46, 10:70, 11:4, 29:8, 31:15, 31:23, 39:7), "the destination is to Allah" (2:285, 3:28, 5:18, 24:42, 31:14, 35:18, 40:3, 42:15, 50:43, 60:4, 64:3), "you will be returned to Allah" (2:28, 2:245, 2:281, 3:83, 6:36, 10:56, 11:34, 19:40, 21:35, 23:115, 24:64, 28:70, 28:88, 29:17, 29:57, 30:11, 32:11, 36:22, 36:83, 39:44, 40:77, 41:21, 43:85, 45:15), and "we are returning to our lord" (7:125, 26:50, 43:14). Such statements are found throughout the Qur'an. Allah in all probability does not live in hell. Therefore we in all probability are not returning to him in hell.

I shall explicate my reading strategies, known as abrogation by exaltation, and relevant issues in Section 6.2.6.

3.3.3 Poetics

> So I swear by the retreating stars,
> Those that run and disappear
> And by the night as it closes in
> And by the dawn when it breathes
> Indeed, the Qur'an is a word of a noble messenger.[6]

> By the sun and its brightness
> And by the moon when it follows it
> And by the day when it displays it
> And by the night when it covers it
> And by the sky and who constructed it
> And by the earth and who spread it

---
[6]Qur'an 81:15–19.

Chapter 3 Read! The First Call of Allah

And by the soul and who proportioned it
And inspired it its wickedness and its righteousness,
He has succeeded who purifies it,
And he has failed who buries it.[7]

The Qur'an, especially the earlier verses, is very poetic. Verses frequently rhyme and there is a beautiful and powerful rhythm.

The verses 91:1–10 above talk about the idea of a test[8] in a poetic way. It is even more powerful than the later verses (91:11–15) recounting the story of Thamud, and it does not have to give any detail regarding what counts as purifying one's soul and what counts as burying it. It is a spiritual declaration.

Let us look at another example. We mentioned before, that in 96:2 it is said that Allah created man from a clinging clot (علق *'alaq*). If we read the whole passage we can see that it rhymes with the verb خلق *khalaqa* (created) in the previous verse. To continue the discussion above, it shows that the material human beings are said to be created from is perhaps not very important. The rhyme was probably more important than the material named, not because Allah is a bad poet, but because the whole thing is allegorical and not intended to be precise.

Most of the shorter Suras are clearly of this character, for example the verses giving a vision of judgment day. In verses 75:22–25 it is said, "faces, that day, will be radiant, looking at their lord. And faces, that day, will be contorted, expecting that there will be done to them

---

[7] Qur'an 91:1–10.
[8] The idea that life is a test to see what we do with what we have with us. It is a test for us to work out what do we need improve in our soul. Please refer to subsubsection 4.4.1.3.

something backbreaking." The vision is vivid but allegorical, for it seems to be against the precepts of Islam that Allah can be seen. All the verses here rhyme with each other. In verses 99:1–2 "when the earth is shaken with its earthquake, and the earth discharges its burdens," The words "earthquake" and "burdens" rhyme, and the passage is clearly not literal. In verses 100:1–5 it is said, "By the racers, panting, and the producers of sparks, striking, and the chargers at dawn, stirring up thereby dust, arriving thereby in the centre collectively." The scene is probably allegorical, and all the verses rhythmically resemble each other and share a rhyme. In verses 104:5–9 it is said, "and what can make you know what is the crusher? It is the fire of Allah, fueled, which mounts directed at the hearts. Indeed, it will be closed down upon them in extended columns." Again in this passage the vision is obscure but the linguistic element is strong. All the verses have similar rhythms and the final words have a similar structure.

These Suras are poems. Therefore when we read them we should read them like poems and should try to feel the approximate sense rather than the literal meaning of each word.

Let us look at another example. Sura 78 rhymes throughout its forty verses. In verses 78:6–7 it is said, "have we not made the earth a resting place? And the mountains as stakes? And we created you in pairs, and made your sleep as rest, and made the night as clothing, and made the day for livelihood, and constructed above you seven strong [heavens], And made a burning lamp, and sent down, from the rain clouds, pouring water, so that we may bring forth with it grain and vegetation, and gardens of thick foliage." It is clear from the rhythm of the Sura that it should be read poetically rather than literally. Therefore we need not take the declaration that the earth is created as a resting place and that the mountains are created as stakes too seriously. This displays a characteristically anthropocentric attitude of many pre-modern human beings. In contrast, if we read such passages poeti-

Chapter 3 Read! The First Call of Allah

cally, we enjoy the artistic expression in these verses without assuming that the universe exists just for our sake.

However, this way of reading should not be limited to shorter Suras, for we can see that longer Suras that are revealed later also have such passages.

If we read the Qur'an in this way, we would be much less fussy about details of religious adherence, for we can see that morality and spirituality are what matter in the end, not particular rules, which may become obsolete in later times.

3.4 Reading the Qur'an

In the present book, I shall focus on the Qur'an. I shall quote the Hadiths when they are particularly illuminating, but in general I shall leave the Hadiths to another book, which together with this would constitute a comprehensive treatment of Islamic texts.

One might ask, then the present book is only a partial account of Islam, and how are we supposed to believe its views and conclusions? I would argue that even though the Qur'an alone is not always sufficient in determining what Islam is, it lays the foundation and should be given more weight than the Hadiths, which are not as reliable in provenance as the Qur'an. The Qur'an alone tells us a great deal about what our basic attitude in Islam and in reading Islamic texts should be. Because many discussions and arguments need to be made with respect to the Qur'an, I decided to write one book on the Qur'an which could stand alone, and afterwards another one on the Hadiths, building on my arguments in this one.

The issues about reading the Qur'an are comparatively simple, since we do not have as much controversy regarding the authenticity of each passage as is the case for the Hadiths. But the Qur'an has its own status issues.

Most Muslims assume that the Qur'an is perfect. But it is possible to construe it as something secondary. What do I mean? In verse 10:37 of the Qur'an, it is said that the Qur'an is "a confirmation of the revelations before and an explanation of the book." So a reasonable way to conceptualise this situation is that there is a perfect book but it is with Allah and not the particular compilation of the Torah, the Gospels, or the Qur'an. Given the widespread Muslim stance that the Qur'an is perfect and uncreated, it is a bit surprising that this idea is actually written in the Qur'an.

In verses 13:38–39, it is said that messengers "have been sent before, and that there is a book for for every period of time." It is also said that Allah eliminates what he wills and confirms what he wills, and that the mother of the book is with him. In verses 43:3–4 it is said that Allah "made it an Arabic Qur'an so that you may understand, and indeed it is, in the mother of the book with us, exalted and wise." In verse 31:27 it is said that if "trees were pen and the sea was ink and seven more seas were added to it, the words of Allah would still not be exhausted." Clearly the Qur'an does not consist of so many words, so Allah could add many more words.

If one accepts this idea that the perfect book is with Allah and adapted, partial versions have been sent to human beings, then doctrinal problems would be infinitely easier to solve since one could accept that particular passages are mistaken and miscommunicated. And then the problem is solved. Or one could say that this passage is no longer relevant in our time. And so on and so forth. Even though this position sounds rather unorthodox, it is firmly based in the Qur'an itself.

Additionally, in 15:10–13, it is said that messengers have been sent before, that they have always been mocked, and that their way has passed. In general this is interpreted as saying that messengers have been sent to different peoples and their denial of these messengers is typical, just as many Arabs denied the prophethood of Muhammad. But it is possible—and fits with the content of similar passages—to construe these verses as implying that messengers have been sent before to their respective groups of people, and Muhammad is sent to promote a way of life

Chapter 3 Read! The First Call of Allah

suitable for his people, for the time and place in which they lived.

For people who read the Qur'an for the first time, this would probably appear to be an acceptable reading. But for people who read it while being told that it only means that there were precedents to Muhammad, it would feel odd. But what basis do we have to be sure that the "traditional" interpretation is right? Probably nothing more than an instinctive aversion to interpretations that seem "dangerous" and threaten the currently widespread assumption that the Qur'an is intended to be true and applicable literally and forever. This assumption is highly questionable if we look at the history of Abrahamic religions and the context of revelations during Muhammad's lifetime.

If we read verses 13:38–39, in which it is said that messengers have been sent before and that there is a book for every period of time, without trying to explain it away, it gives strong support for the view that Muhammad's message is meant for his time and people and that modern followers of this faith are permitted, and even encouraged, to modify the rules of conduct written in the Qur'an and to review the lessons to be drawn from the models of conduct recorded in the Hadiths.

However, if this is, for the time being, too radical for your taste, we can begin with more orthodox positions and keep to the standard construal of the Qur'an as holy and unchangeable. We have a place to work even under this assumption.

If we keep to the standard construal of the Qur'an as holy and unchangeable, we may highlight one issue: the context in which a verse is revealed.

We need to consider carefully the context in which a verse is revealed because it could change the meaning completely. If we take one verse to be part of a rousing speech in preparation for fighting, then the scope of application of the injunctions in it would be enormously different from part of a declaration of a strict covenant to be observed everyday in every situation.

Reading in this way could yield opposite conclusions from reading the same passage under the assumption that the context of revelations does not matter. From this we can see the vital role of context and interpretation in reading the Qur'an and the Hadiths.

In view of this issue it is as a rule more advisable to read liberally and allegorically to avoid injustice being done in the name of religion. I shall chart the vastness of this hermeneutic space in the following chapters.

Chapter 4

Re-reading Islam

It is the duty of a Muslim to find out the important tenets of Islam and adhere to them in thinking and in action.

However, from observation one can say that for as many Muslims, there are nearly as many Islams.

How are we then to set out and promote our liberal vision of Islam? I will show that this liberal vision is reasonable and fits with a careful reading of and reflection on Islamic texts, even though the conclusions reached below do not seem to be the mainstream in this particular time in Islamic communities.

Let me present my analysis of Islam by means of reading. The important tenets of Islam are in various places in the Qur'an, and they are set out in the initial books of al-Bukhari's Hadiths [3], for example intention, the five pillars, love of Allah and Muhammad, etc.

4.1 What is Islam?

4.1.1 Islam and *islam*

What is Islam?

One may say it should be clear enough, that Islam is based on the Qur'an and the Hadiths. The key tenets of

Islam are widely available in summarised form, containing the five pillars of faith, and other spiritual and social rules.

But the verbal noun إسلام *islam* means submission and the active participle مسلم *muslim* means "one who submits." To what does one submit? To Allah to be sure. But what does it mean to submit to Allah?

One common problem of Islamic commentators is that they emphasise that *islam* means submission but after that forget all about it and talk about Islam the way people usually do, using it to refer to the specific historical religion that arose after Muhammad started spreading his message. In the Qur'an, the word "submission" is used in the general sense and Abraham, Noah, Solomon etc. are among the submitters to Allah. Clearly Jewish law is different from Islamic law, even though they share many similarities. So such submitters, i.e. *muslims*, are not necessarily the *Muslims* we think of today.

In verse 2:131 it is said that Allah said to Abraham, "Submit!" (أسلم *aslim*, the imperative form) And Abraham said "I submitted (أسلمت *aslamtu*, the past tense) to the lord of the two worlds."

In verse 27:31 it is said that Solomon writes to the Queen of Sheba and tells her and her people, in the name of Allah, to come in submission—مسلمين *muslimīn*—which is the plural of one who submits, or submitters. And in 27:42 he said that "we have been given the knowledge before her and we have been submitters (*muslimīn*)."

Another example of this usage is found in 3:19 in the Qur'an in which it is said that the religion which is "close

Chapter 4 Re-reading Islam

to God" is إسلام *islam*, submission, and those "who are given the book do not differ except out of jealousy among them." So one should see that the picture given in the Qur'an is that different groups have been given God's guidance and they have deviated in some ways since. So Muhammad is sent to give a correct version but it is not necessarily the only correct way.

These examples show the central role the verb أسلم *aslama*, to submit, plays in Islam, and the original sense before Muhammad's message was delivered.

In verse 10:47 in the Qur'an these two different senses of the Arabic word إسلام *islam* are shown clearly. This verse says that for each nation there is a messenger, and judgment is between this messenger and his people. If we accept this statement, then it would nullify the universality of Islamic laws, so that perhaps only Arabs or Semites are supposed to be governed by *Islam* as taught by Muhammad. But anyone following the messages of the messenger of his own people would be following *islam* and Allah.

One can see that we now have *islam* and *Islam*, so that *Islam* is the religion we talk about conventionally, but *islam* is the religion or collection of religions that follow God and their followers would not be punished. In verse 14:4 in the Qur'an, it is said that Allah did not send any messenger except one who speaks the tongue of his people, so that he make things clear for them. So Muhammad's message is for the Arabic-speaking people he was sent to.

Therefore any non-Muslims of other nations should not be threatened or scared by all the alarming passages about going to hell for not following the messages transmitted by

Muhammad. For the messages were not intended for every human being.

In view of the above, a Muslim, or more strictly speaking a Muhammadan, reading the Qur'an carefully, would become very easy about non-Muhammadans, because each nation has their own messenger and their own version of *islam*. One should not be offended by the term "Muhammadan" as used here since it does not mean a worshipper of Muhammad. It just means a *muslim* following *islam* in the way taught through Muhammad.

From the above we can see that Qur'an 10:47 is a very important verse in the construal of the status of Islam as taught *through* Muhammad. This allows the position that *islam* can be taught differently to other nations and those versions could be as true as the one Muhammad transmitted. All religious strife can be annihilated if one truly follows this verse.

Another hint can be found in the creed. How does one become a Muslim? By saying the creed, "I bear witness that there is no god but God and that Muhammad is God's messenger." Why is there a specific acknowledgement of Muhammad but no others in the creed while Islam also accepts Jewish and Christian prophets? I think there are two points to note here.

1. Muhammad's status as prophet was contested, that is why it was important to emphasise that he was one, and it was a key difference between Muslims, Jews, and Christians.

2. People were told to bear witness to Muhammad during his lifetime as people could get to know him and observe him for themselves, thus gathering evidence that the Qur'an was not from himself.

After his death, Muslims never reviewed the practice of uniquely bearing witness to Muhammad because it is nearly impossible without someone as authoritative as Muhammad himself, and I doubt if Muslims would accept that, given the importance of Muhammad and his companions' stories in the collective consciousness of Muslims. But I think the use of the verb *to bear witness* suggests a more direct contact with Muhammad than it would be possible for people more than a thousand years after his time. You may say, "but people were told to bear witness to God too, is God not visible?" I would say it is a totally different matter in the case of God since for monotheists God is everywhere and eternal, so there is no problem in bearing witness to him. But there is a problem in bearing witness today to Muhammad who is merely a human being (as is emphasised in verse 18:110 in the Qur'an) who lived more than a thousand years ago.

From the above discussion we can see that Islamic texts were pragmatic and provisional, and were not meant to be followed without modification by later generations.

4.1.2 The Moral Construal of Faith

But perhaps the best way to understand what Islam is, is to ask who is a Muslim, and who is not?

In Islam it is generally agreed that human beings are categorised into Muslims and non-Muslims, while the latter include the people of the book (أهل الكتاب *ahl al-kitāb* which I shall discuss in Section 4.5.6) and infidels (singular form كافر *kāfir*, meaning "one who does not believe"). Most Muslims believe that infidels are going to hell.

Given this scheme, the next question would be, how to determine who is a Muslim and who is an infidel?

According to the principle of إرجاء *irjā'*, i.e. postponement, of المرجئة *al-murji'a*, the postponers, we should postpone—that is to say—leave judgment to Allah. He is the one who knows, and we should not be hasty and label others non-believers.

This view is commonly thought of as heresy in Islam, but is it a reasonable view?

I think it is, because there are many controversies surrounding all aspects of Islam, and it is not prudent to condemn people for not abiding by some of the rules which are given in the Qur'an or extracted from the Hadiths, because those rules may be non-essential to being identified as a Muslim by Allah. So we should be cautious and reserve judgment. Let Allah be the judge. To do otherwise is arrogant and not respecting Allah.

In verses 42:8–10 we can find textual support for this position. Here it is said that if Allah had "willed, he could have made them one nation" and that in "whatever you disagree, its ruling belongs to Allah." Additionally, in 6:57, 12:40, and 12:67 it is said that judgment "is only for Allah." In verses 6:62, 28:70, 28:88, and 40:12 it is said that judgment is his. To postpone judgment and leave it for Allah would point towards secular liberal government, so that people have the freedom to adhere to their own religious views. We should remain doubtful about doctrinal points that are not clear, and leave judgment to Allah. We need not enforce our religious views on others. It would be to distrust Allah's ability if we did so.

If Allah is most gracious and most merciful, he should not be concerned with petty crimes in faith. As a confirmation of this we can see in 4:31 in the Qur'an that it is said that if you avoid great sins your bad actions would be removed and you will enter paradise. It is reasonable to assume that he is only concerned with serious crimes that are terrible regardless of faith.

Let us look at passages pointing towards a moral construal of Islam.

Chapter 4 Re-reading Islam

4.1.2.1 Textual Evidence

In verses 40:7-8 there is a direct piece of evidence supporting a good end for non-believers who do good. Here it is said that those (angels) who carry the throne and those around it praise Allah and believe in him and ask forgiveness for those who believed, saying "O our lord, you encompassed everything in mercy and knowledge, so forgive those who repented and followed your way and protect them from the punishment of hell. O our lord, admit them to gardens of Eden which you promised and whoever was righteous among their fathers, spouses, and offspring. Verily you are strong and wise." The fathers of Muslims may not have known Islam and become Muslims. But they could still be admitted to paradise for their good deeds. Therefore we can see that belief is not essential, but righteousness is essential for a good end.

In verses 81:8-9 it is said that on judgment day the girl that was buried alive would be asked "for what sin she was killed." Among all the things that human do, this is the only human behaviour mentioned in a description of what happens during judgment day. From this passage we can see that Islam was a social and moral project aimed at improving a nation. From this we can also see the wretched state of Arab society at that time, which explains the frequency of threatening people with hellfire. This is a very good example which shows us the importance of social context in reading Islamic texts.

Another passage emphasising the importance of moral behaviour in determining one's position in the eyes of Allah is in 73:20. It is said that Allah "knew that there will be among you those who are ill and others traveling throughout the land seeking the bounty of Allah and others fighting for the cause of Allah. So recite what is easy from it and perform prayer and give alms and loan Allah a good loan, and whatever good you present for yourselves, you find it with Allah. It is better and greater in reward, and seek forgiveness of Allah. Indeed, Allah is forgiving and merciful."

In verses 89:15–26 it is said, "and as for man, when his lord tries him and is generous to him and favours him, he says, 'my lord has honoured me.' But when he tries him and restricts his provision, he says, 'my lord has humiliated me.' No! But you do not honour the orphan, and you do not encourage one another to feed the poor. And you eat up inheritance completely, and you love wealth immensely. No! When the earth has been levelled and crushed, and your lord and the angels have come, rank upon rank, and hell is brought forth on that day. That day man will remember, but what good to him will be the remembrance? He will say, 'Oh, I wish I had presented [some good] for my life.' So on that day, none will punish as he does, and none will bind as he does." Then in contrast, in 89:27–30 it is said, "O reassured soul, return to your lord, well-pleased and pleasing. So enter among my servants, and enter my paradise." From this Sura we can see that reward and punishment is granted in proportion to one's moral performance in life.

In verses 90:4–20 the moral dimension of Islam is shown clearly. It says, "we have certainly created man [to live] in hardship. Does he think that no one will ever overcome him? He says, 'I have spent wealth abundantly.' Does he think that no one has seen him? Have We not made for him two eyes? And a tongue and two lips? And have shown him the two ways? But he has not broken through the difficult pass. And what can make you know that it is the difficult pass? It is the freeing of a slave, or feeding on a day of severe hunger an orphan of near relationship or a needy person in misery, and then being among those who believed and advised one another to patience and advised one another to compassion. Those are the companions of the right. But they who disbelieved in our signs, those are the companions of the left. Over them a fire will close in." This passage promotes the idea that life is a test in which one chooses between the compassionate way and the other way. The ones who choose the compassionate way would be rewarded well while the ones who choose the other way would be punished. But one should not think that it is

Chapter 4 Re-reading Islam

just about becoming a Muslim or not, as the injunctions make it clear that it is about moral actions rather than anything else.

This idea is repeated in verses 91:7–10 in which it is said, "by the soul and he who proportioned it, and inspired it with its wickedness and its righteousness, he has succeeded who purifies it, and he has failed who buries it." The purpose of life is to live a purified life rather than a soiled one in face of the vicissitudes and temptations of life.

In verses 92:4–11 it is said, "indeed, your efforts are diverse. As for he who gives, and fears Allah, and believes in the best, we will ease him toward ease. But as for he who withholds and considers himself free of need, and denies the best, we will ease him toward difficulty. And what will his wealth avail him when he falls?" From this passage we can see that the most important quality of a Muslim is to give to good causes. Then it is said in 92:14–21, "so I have warned you of a fire which is blazing. None will burn in it except the most wretched one, who had denied and turned away. But the righteous one will avoid it, [he] who gives his wealth to purify himself, and not to anyone who has a favour to be rewarded, but only seeking the countenance of his lord, the highest, and he will be pleased." From this we can see that punishment and reward is given according to one's moral life, not the nominal status of being a Muslim or not.

In verses 93:6–11 there is an appeal to Muhammad's poor childhood and a command to treat orphans and others like them well. It says, "did he not find you an orphan and give shelter? And he found you lost and guided [you], and he found you poor and made [you] self-sufficient. So, as for the orphan, do not oppress [him]. And as for the one who asks, do not repel [him]. But as for the favour of your Lord, report [it]." This passage shows the moral nature of Muhammad's message.

In verses 96:9–18 it is said, "have you seen the one who forbids a servant when he prays? Have you seen if he is rightly guided or enjoins righteousness? Have you seen if he denies and turns away, does he not know that Allah sees? No! If he does not desist, We will surely drag him by the forelock, a lying, sinning forelock. [...] We will call the angels of Hell." Again a list of contrasting behaviour is given, and punishment is threatened for bad behaviour.

In verse 98:5 it is said that those who were given the book "were not commanded except to worship Allah, be sincere to him in religion, be upright, and to perform prayer and to give alms, and that is the correct religion."

In verses 107:1–7 it is said, "have you seen the one who denies the judgment? For that is the one who drives away the orphan, and does not encourage the feeding of the poor. So woe to those who pray, who are heedless of their prayer, those who make show, and withhold assistance."

From these passages we should be able to see that Islam is largely about moral guidance, i.e. how to live one's life morally, and reward and punishment is based on this. One might argue, "then it means that we should follow its commands literally and strictly, right?" I argued against this in Section 3.2 and I shall argue against it more comprehensively in Section 6.2.

In other words, we can construe Islam as a body of moral guidance but we need not follow the rules and commands in Islamic texts literally, due to the difference in time and context. We can follow Islam as a moral and social enterprise without living as a seventh-century Arab. Many assume that purity and piety entail following the texts as closely as possible, but if we consider the circumstances thoughtfully we can see that it is a false impression. Allah was giving practical advice suitable for Muhammad's audience. We should learn the lessons, not the letters.

4.1.2.2 Moral Teachings

Another piece of evidence for the moral construal of Islam is the frequency of the phrase سبيل الله *sabīl allāh*, the way of Allah, which appears in the Qur'an more than a hundred times. For example, in verse 2:195, one is told to spend in the way of Allah. The phrase "the way of Allah" points to

Chapter 4 Re-reading Islam

actions rather than just faith. The way is something one needs to walk in, rather than just think about. A similar word is صراط ṣirāṭ, which means a path. It occurs 40 times in the Qur'an, most of the time as the phrase صراط مستقيم ṣirāṭ mustaqīm, i.e. a straight path, and a prominent example is to be found in the opening chapter, 1:6–7, the straight path, the path of the people on whom Allah bestowed favour. From this we can see that, in the context of Islam, it is very important to determine which actions are good and are the ones we should take. If we do not do good things, it could be the case that we do not qualify as Muslims at all, however loudly and frequently we say the creed.

Another point showing the moral nature of faith is the emphasis on thankfulness which is prominent in the Qur'an. In verses 2:152, 2:172, 16:114, 29:17, 31:12, 31:14, and 34:15, people are told to be grateful to Allah. In verses 2:52, 2:56, 2:185, 3:123, 5:6, 5:89, 8:26, 14:37, 16:14, 16:78, 22:36, 28:73, 30:46, 35:12, and 45:12, it is said that Allah does something so that you would be grateful. In verses 3:144 and 3:145 it is said that the grateful ones will be rewarded. In verses 4:147, 14:7, and 39:66, being thankful and worshipping Allah are mentioned together. This emphasis on thankfulness shows that requiring people to believe in or worship Allah is not something for the sake of Allah, but for the sake of the spiritual cultivation of that person. If one is thankful, one tends to do good deeds because he does not feel that the world is treating him badly so that he is justified in doing whatever he wants.

A connected emphasis is the warnings against miserliness, attachment to wealth, and greediness. The injunctions against miserliness are found in 3:180, 4:37, 9:76, 57:24, and 92:8, and people are told to spend in doing good in 2:215, 2:270–273, 3:134, and 9:121. We discussed this in Section 4.2.3.

People are told to see wealth and children as a trial in which their behaviour is shown. In verses 64:15–16 it is said, "your wealth and your children are but a trial, and Allah has with him a great reward. So fear Allah as much as you are able and listen and obey and spend, it is better for you, and those who are saved from the miserliness of their souls, they are the successful ones."

In verses 100:6–11 it is said, "indeed mankind, to his lord, is ungrateful. And indeed, he is to that a witness. And indeed he is, in love of wealth, intense. But does he not know that when the contents of the graves are scattered, and that within the breasts is obtained, indeed, that day their lord is acquainted with them." In verses 102:1 8 it is said, "competition in increase diverts you until you visit the graveyards. [...] If you only knew with knowledge of certainty, you will surely see hellfire. Then you will surely see it with the eye of certainty. Then you will surely be asked that day about pleasure." In verses 104:1–4 it is said, "woe to every scorner and mocker who collects wealth and counts it. He thinks that his wealth will make him immortal. No! He will surely be thrown into [...] the fire of Allah" In these passages we see that love of wealth seems to have pushed people onto the wrong way. Surely this has to do with one's attitude towards justice and charity rather than just entering the Islamic faith or not.

In verses 96:6–8 it is said, "indeed, man transgresses because he sees himself as self-sufficient. Indeed, to your lord is the return." This is a warning to people who think only about wealth, and not about other issues such as social justice and charity. The verb استغنى *istaghanā*, meaning "to consider oneself free of," is an interesting concept in this context. Its use in the Qur'an is accorded a metaphysical dimension. People who consider themselves free of need (of Allah) can be seen as materialists, not spiritual, and not behaving morally because they do not believe in punishment in the afterlife. They live only for the physical life, its pleasure and enjoyments. They would not have scruples in obtaining these at the expense of others. The word is also used in this sense in verses 80:5 and 92:8. However, I do not think that atheists in this age should be seen this way because they refuse to believe due to the logical inconsistencies and scientific inaccuracies in religious texts. But it was probably the case in Muhammad's time.

We should also read verses 103:2–3 in this way. It says, "indeed, mankind is losing, except for those who have believed and done righteous deeds and advised each other to truth and advised each other to patience." The role of belief is to support and guide people towards moral behaviour, and away from a purely materialistic form of life. But the nominal status of being a Muslim or not is not the main point. The main point is the subsequent state of mind and the choices one makes. As we can see in this passage, righteous deeds, truth, and patience are the goals, not belief itself.

Similarly, in the following passage, perhaps one or more specific persons are meant, but the moral lesson against greed is clear. In verses 74:11–19 it is said about a rich man that Allah, "granted to him extensive wealth, and children present [with him], and made [life] easy for him, then he desires that [Allah] add [to that]. No! Indeed he has been obstinate towards our signs, I will cover him with a laborious torment. Indeed, he thought and plotted. May he be destroyed for how he plotted." This person still desires more when he has extensive wealth and everything one needs. This type of greed is something that Islam warns against.

4.1.2.3 Punishment for Plotting against Allah

In the Qur'an, it is sometimes said that the infidels and polytheists plot against Allah or Muslims.

In verse 3:120 it is said of the disbelievers that "if good touches you, it distresses them, and if harm strikes you, they rejoice at it, and if you are patient and fear Allah, their plot will not harm you at all." In verse 8:18 it is said, "Allah is weakening the plot of the disbelievers." In verses 40:23–25 it is said that when Moses "brought them the truth from us, they said, 'kill the sons of those who have believed with him and keep their women alive.' But the plan of the disbelievers is not except in error." In verses 86:15–17 it is said, "indeed, they are planning a plan, and I am planning a plan. So allow time for the disbelievers. Leave them awhile." In verses 105:1–5 Muhammad is told, "have you not considered how your lord dealt with the companions of the elephant? Did he not make their plan into misguidance? And he sent against them birds in flocks, striking them with stones of hard clay, so he made them like eaten straw."

From these verses, talking about the punishment for infidels and polytheists, we can see that they were punished because of their actions against and intention to do harm to Muslims or others, rather than just for disbelief. There was a specific context of clashes and war between believers in an Abrahamic religion and non-believers. But this context no longer obtains in this age, in which after years of sectarian wars people have a sufficient level of political wisdom and religious tolerance for followers of different religions and sects to live together peacefully.

4.1.2.4 Frequent Mention of Deeds

Apart from the mention of plots, the frequent reference to deeds in the Qur'an points even more strongly towards an Islamic conflation of belief and good action.

Let us think about the following question. Are disbelievers going to hell no matter what?

Chapter 4 Re-reading Islam

Of course there are passages that support the view that if one is not a Muslim, then one's good deeds are not counted and one goes to hell. That is why it is a common view. But let us examine one such verse closely and reflect on it. In verse 5:5 in the Qur'an, it is said that whoever "rejects the faith his good deeds are wasted." But the faith could be simple, just the creed that Allah is the only God and Muhammad is his messenger. For people who do not consciously think about it, maybe that is what they accept, even though they do not know much about Islam. So officially they are not Muslims, but are their good deeds wasted?

On the other hand, there are also passages where it is said that Allah will "not allow the reward of any who did well in deeds to be lost (18:30)." Maybe he will receive some punishment for not believing, but it seems unjust that he would not receive any reward for doing good deeds. In verses 22:54–57 one again sees this ambiguity. In this passage it is said that Allah will "judge between people who believe and who disbelieve." The ones who believed and did righteous deeds will go to heaven, and there will be a humiliating punishment for the ones who disbelieved and denied the signs of Allah. What about people who believed but did not do good deeds, and people who did not believe but did good deeds? One cannot get a clear answer from this passage. And looking at Islamic texts in general we do not have a clear answer, some point to one direction, that only faith matters, others point to the other direction, that good deeds are very important.

As a confirmation of the close-knitted conception in Islam of morality and belief, in 28:54 it is said that Muslims are those "who avert evil with good," and believing and being righteous or doing good (عمل الصالحات *'amila al-ṣāliḥāt*) is almost always mentioned together, for example in 2:25 Muhammad is told to "give good tidings to those who believe and do righteous deeds so that there would be for them gardens beneath which rivers flow." In verse 2:62 it is said, "those who believed and those who were Jews or Christians or Sabeans, those who believed in Allah and the last day and did righteousness, there is their reward with their lord, and there is no fear concerning them, and they are not going to grieve." In verse 2:82 it is said, "those who believe and do righteous deeds, those are the residents of paradise. They will abide in it eternally." In verse 2:277 it is said, "those who believe and do righteous deeds and perform prayer and give alms, there is their reward with their lord, and there is no fear concerning them, and they are not going to grieve." In verse 3:57 it is said, "as for those who believed and did righteous deeds," Allah "will reward them fully with their rewards, and Allah does not like the unjust ones." From this verse we can see that punishment is for being unjust, not for disbelief.

Believing and being righteous or doing good are also mentioned together in 4:57, 4:122, 4:173, 5:9, 5:69, 5:93, 7:42, 10:4, 10:9, 11:11, 11:23, 13:29, 14:23, 16:97, 17:9, 18:2, 18:30, 18:88, 18:107, 19:60, 19:96, 20:75, 20:82, 20:112, 21:94, 22:14, 22:23, 22:50, 22:56, 24:55, 25:70, 26:227, 28:67, 28:80, 29:9, 29:58, 30:15, 30:45, 31:8, 32:19, 34:4, 34:37, 35:7, 38:24, 38:28, 40:40, 40:58, 41:8, 42:22, 42:26, 45:32, 45:30, 47:2, 47:12, 48:29, 64:9, 65:11, 84:25, 85:11, 95:6, 98:7, and 103:3. The frequency of believing and being righteous or doing good being mentioned together highlights the inseparability of belief and righteous deeds in Islam. Thus when we look at punishment for disbelievers, it should be seen as an alternative term for unjust people. This was probably true of Muhammad's Arab contemporaries. But it is not necessarily the case in other times and places. We need not apply this conflation in other contexts.

Chapter 4 Re-reading Islam

Now let us look at the use of the word عمل *'amal*, meaning "deed." Let us consider whether non-believers' deeds are lost or not. This word occurs about seventy times in the Qur'an. Of these, there are 18 passages in which the stance is ambivalent or the content irrelevant, 31 passages in which one's deeds are said to determine one's afterlife, and 16 passages in which it is said that for people who do not believe, their deeds are not counted.[1]

However, in the verses in which infidels' deeds are said to be worthless, the word frequently refers to their acts preventing Muslims from practising their faith, and it seems that we should not read it as saying that even their good deeds are lost and worthless in the face of Allah. For example in verse 2:217, it is said that people "will continue to fight you until they make you retract from your religion if they are able. And whoever of you reverts from his religion and dies while he is an infidel, then for those, their deeds have become worthless in this world and the hereafter, and those are the companions of the fire, they will abide in it eternally." In verses 3:21–22 it is said that for "those who disbelieve in the signs of Allah and kill the prophets unjustly and kill people who enjoin justice, give them tidings of a painful punishment. Those are the ones whose deeds have become worthless in this world and the hereafter, and there will not be helpers for them."

In verse 5:5, after talking about what is lawful and what is not regarding food and sex, it is said, "and whoever denies the faith, his deeds have become worthless, and he is among the losers in the hereafter." From the context of this verse we can see that even though it says non-believers'

---

[1] Deeds determining reward is mentioned in verses 2:139, 2:167, 3:195, 5:90, 9:94, 9:102, 9:105, 9:120, 10:61, 11:7, 11:15, 11:46, 11:111, 18:7, 18:30, 18:103, 18:110, 25:70, 27:4, 29:38, 35:10, 40:37, 46:19, 47:4, 47:14, 47:30, 47:35, 49:14, 52:21, 67:2, and 99:6, adding to 31 times in total. Deeds becoming worthless is said in verses 2:217, 3:22, 5:5, 5:53, 9:17, 9:69, 14:18, 18:105, 24:39, 25:23, 33:19, 47:1, 47:8–9, 47:28, 47:32–33, and 49:2, appearing 16 times in total. Ambivalent or irrelevant occurrences can be seen in verses 6:108, 7:147, 8:48, 9:37, 10:41, 10:81, 16:63, 21:82, 23:63, 26:168, 27:24, 28:15, 28:55, 33:71, 35:8, 39:65, 42:15, and 66:11, coming to 18 times in total.

deeds have become worthless, it does not refer to just any deed, but refers to deeds violating the rules.

In verses 5:52–53, it is said that "those in whose hearts there is a disease hastening into them" are in doubt and in fear, "and those who believe say 'are these the ones who swore by Allah their strongest oaths that indeed they were with you?' Their deeds have become worthless, and they have become losers." Here we can see that their deeds have become worthless because they were spreading fear and doubt when Muslims were fighting and struggling, so we can conclude that the deeds here do not refer to any deeds, but deeds harming the Muslim community at that time.

In verse 9:17 it is said, "it was not for the polytheists to maintain the mosques of Allah witnessing against themselves with disbelief. For those, their deeds have become worthless, and in the fire they are abiding eternally." Again here the "deeds" are specific, they are occupying Allah's mosques. We cannot extend this to all deeds of polytheists, and conclude that all of their deeds are worthless and they are going to hell.

In verse 9:69 the disbelievers are warned that they are "like those before you. They were stronger than you in power and more abundant in wealth and children. They enjoyed their portion, and you enjoyed your portion as those before you enjoyed their portion, and you have engaged like that in which they engaged. For those, their deeds have become worthless in this world and the hereafter, and they are the losers." Here even though the disbelievers' deeds are said to be worthless, we should not read it as as general statement, but as one referring to their acts related to the attainment of worldly enjoyment, because the passage is talking about this part of their lives and not every type of their deeds.

In verse 14:18 it is said that for "those who disbelieve in their lord, their deeds are like ashes which the wind blows forcefully on a stormy day. They are unable to hold onto anything from what they earned. That is the extreme error." Here "what they earned" could be inter-

Chapter 4 Re-reading Islam

preted as worldly things rather than good rewards from good deeds, so we cannot conclude that this stipulates that non-believers' good deeds are void. The other verses should be interpreted in similar ways.

From the discussion above, we can see that most of the verses discussing deeds state that people are rewarded according to them. As for verses which seem to say that as long as people do not believe, their deeds are void, we have shown that if they are read with adequate consideration of context, it would be clear that they mean that disbelievers' worldly advantages are of no use in Allah's judgment, that they are doing wrong, or that their bad deeds would cancel their good deeds, but not simply that non-belief means that one's good deeds are completely ignored.

In verses 22:64–65 in the Qur'an it is said that what is "in the heavens and what is on the earth belongs to Allah." And that Allah is the one who is "free of need, and worthy of praise." And then afterwards it is said that Allah is kind and merciful. In verse 14:8 it is also said that even if all the "people on earth disbelieve, Allah is free of need." In verse 35:15 it is said that people are the "ones in need of Allah and Allah is free of need and praiseworthy." In verse 39:10 it is said that for those "who do good in this world [there is] good." Can we conclude from these passages that Allah will not punish people for not believing in him, for this is a sign of need, unkindness, and a lack of mercy? And can we also conclude from this passage that he will definitely reward people for doing good deeds, since this is worthy of praise?

In verse 46:12 it is said that the Qur'an is a book confirming the book of Moses "in an Arabic tongue to warn those who have done wrong and as good tidings to the ones doing good deeds." From this verse we can see that the aim of the Qur'an is to warn of punishment of the evil and to announce rewards for the good. In verses 46:13–14 it continues, "indeed, those who have said, 'our lord is Allah' and then remained firm, there will be no fear concerning them, and they are not going to grieve. Those are the residents of paradise, abiding in it eternally as a reward for what they have done." The mentioning of remaining firm makes it clear that the emphasis on belief should be read as talking about belief in punishment in the afterlife, and the continued adherence to morality that comes as a result. In verse 46:15 it goes on to say, "and we have enjoined upon man good treatment of his parents. His mother carried him with hardship and gave birth to him with hardship, and his weaning is thirty months, until he reaches maturity and reaches forty years. Then he says, 'lord, enable me to be grateful for your favour which you have bestowed upon me and upon my parents, and to do righteousness which pleases you and make righteous for me my offspring. Indeed, I have turned to you, and indeed, I am among the submitters (مسلمين *muslimīn*)." From the prominence of righteousness in talking about faith we can see that it is ultimately about good and evil rather than belief and disbelief.

In verse 28:10 when telling the story of Moses after his mother put him "in the river" so that he would not be killed, it is said that she "almost exposed him had Allah not strengthened her heart so that she would be one of the believers." From this passage it seems that Allah decides whether people remain believers or not. So why does he not strengthen everyone's heart so that they become or remain believers and go to heaven after death? In verse 28:14 we can find some elucidation regarding this question. It is said that Allah "gave Moses judgment and knowledge when he was mature," and that Allah "rewards the ones doing good in this way." In verse 15:12 and 26:200 it is said that Allah inserts "denial into the hearts of the criminals." So maybe in the end it is doing good or not that is the choice? If

Chapter 4 Re-reading Islam

you do good things, Allah makes you a believer. If you do bad things, Allah makes you a non-believer. Then perhaps people have been wrong all along in the classification of Muslims and non-Muslims. It should be that the people doing good things are Muslims, and the people doing bad things are non-Muslims, rather than that people who say they are Muslims are Muslims, and people who say they are not Muslims are non-Muslims. Islam then equals to doing good things rather than primarily the creed.

In verse 42:13 it is said that "what you invite polytheists to do is difficult for them. Allah chooses whom he wills to him." At this point it seems that Allah determines in whatever way he likes who believes. However, if we read on, we see that he "guides who repents to him." Here again we see a moral connection to belief. Repentance is usually connected to regret for bad deeds and a change in one's way for the better. Therefore we can see that action plays a key role in determining who is a "believer" and who is not.

4.1.2.5 Relevant Concepts

In this connection, the use of the word محسن *muḥsin*, meaning "one who does good," in referring to believers and rewards, is significant. This word has been used nearly 40 times in the Qur'an from 2:58 until 77:44. "Allah loves the ones who do good" is repeated in 2:195, 3:134, 3:148, 5:13, and 5:93. "We reward in this way the ones who do good" is reiterated in 6:84, 12:22, 28:14, 37:80, 37:105, 37:110, 37:121, 37:131, and 77:44. In verse 2:58 we are told to recall that it was said to Moses that when people say, "relieve us of our burdens" Allah will forgive their sins and "increase the doers of good" in goodness and reward. In verse 3:134 it is said that there are those "who spend during ease and hardship and the ones who restrain anger and the ones who pardon the people, and Allah loves the ones who do good." A particularly good example is 4:125, in which it is said, "who is better in religion than one who submits himself to Allah while being one who does good and follows the religion of Abraham, uprightly? And Allah took Abraham as an intimate friend." In verse 5:85 it is said, "Allah rewarded them for what they said with gardens beneath which rivers flow, abiding in it eternally, and that is the reward for the ones who do good." In verse 7:56 one is told not to "cause corruption on earth after its reformation, and [to] invoke him in fear and aspiration. Indeed the mercy of Allah is near to the ones who do good."

In verse 55:60 after giving a description of heaven it is said that the reward of good is nothing but good. This again emphasises the importance of doing good rather than just saying that one believes in Allah.

These verses show that doing good is an integral part of belief. If one does not do good, it is questionable whether one is really a believer and should receive heavenly rewards.

The use of the word متق *muttaqin*, meaning "God-fearing" or "righteous," which is used about 50 times throughout the Qur'an from 2:2 until 78:31, is also relevant, for it highlights the connection between belief in Allah and being moral. "The believing ones" and "the righteous ones" are used interchangeably. We have to remember the historical context. At that time life was hard and people were ruthless in the Arabian Peninsula. People would not care about morality if they did not believe in a god who would punish them for evil deeds. This is the reason why people who disbelieve were viewed as punishable, for they usually were also morally bad, so it was convenient to conflate the two. But it does not mean that punishment for disbelief itself is justifiable. We need to separate these concepts when we see clearly that people can be ethical atheists and that there are diverse systems of beliefs in which people are induced to be moral. In Islamic texts terms like "infidels" were more of a shorthand for being morally bad than solely referring to the lack of belief, for in pre-Islamic Arabia society was cruel and dangerous, there was no effective government, and people killed each other easily. It is in this context that punishment is frequently mentioned for the disbelieving. But in fact righteous deeds are what place one in heaven. In verses 44:51–52 it is said, "the righteous ones will be in a safe place in gardens and springs."

This conceptual scheme is explained beautifully in verse 2:177. "Righteousness is not that you turn your faces toward the east or the west, but righteousness is one who believes in Allah and the last day and the angels and the book and the prophets, and gives wealth, in spite of loving it, to relatives and orphans and the needy and the traveler and those who ask, and in freeing slaves." It is one who "performs prayer and gives alms, and ones who fulfill their promise when they promise, and ones who are patient in poverty and hardship and during battle. Those are the ones who have been true, and those are the righteous."

There are still other examples. In verse 31:22 it is said that whoever "submits his face to Allah and is at the same time one doing good, then he has taken hold of the most trustworthy handle." In verse 41:33 it is said that no one is better in speech than one who invites people to Allah and does righteous deeds and says, "indeed I am a Muslim." Even more explicitly, in 41:6–8 it is said, "woe to the polytheists" that is, those "who do not give alms, and do not believe in the hereafter, for indeed there is an uninterrupted reward for those who believe and do righteous deeds." In verse 41:46 there is another piece of indirect evidence. Here it is said, "whoever does righteous deeds, it is for his soul, and whoever does evil deeds, it is against his soul," and Allah "is not unjust to his servants." In verse 45:15 it is said, "whoever did a righteous deed, then it is for his soul, and whoever does evil, then it is against it. Then to your lord you will be returned."

In verses 42:20–22, it is said, "whoever desires the harvest of the hereafter, we increase his harvest, and whoever desires the harvest of this word, we give him of it but there is no share in the hereafter for him. Or do they have other deities who ordained for them a religion to which Allah did not give permission?" After that it says, "indeed there is a painful punishment for the unjust ones. You will see the unjust ones fearing what they earned and [the punishment] will befall them. And those who believed and did righteous deeds will be in grasslands in heaven, having what they will with their lord. This is the great favour." In these verses, being unjust and being punished are linked, while believing, doing good deeds, and getting rewarded are also linked. We can see that punishment for the unbelieving is more about punishing unjust deeds and causing suffering, than for saying that one believes in Allah or not per se.

The discussion so far has dealt with concepts involving believers, being good, and good rewards. Now let us turn to the opposite cluster, concepts involving disbelievers, being bad, and bad rewards.

When we look at how the word ظالم *ẓālim*, meaning

Chapter 4 Re-reading Islam

"unjust" or "wrongdoer," is frequently used together with the word "disbelieve" or "infidel," we see that belief is morally construed; it has to manifest itself in good action, and is not just a declaration. In verse 2:254 it is said that the infidels "are the unjust ones." In verse 2:258 it is said that the one "who disbelieved was overwhelmed, and Allah does not guide the unjust people." In verse 3:86 it is said, "how does Allah guide a people which disbelieved after their belief and witnessed that the messenger is true and clear signs came to them? And Allah does not guide the unjust people." In verse 62:5 it is said, "wretched is the example of the people which denied the signs of Allah, and Allah does not guide the unjust people." In these verses the concepts of disbelief and injustice are linked together.

In verse 9:109 it is said that he "who bases his building on righteousness from Allah and his approval" is better than he "who bases his building on the edge of a bank, so it collapsed with him into the fire of hell," "and Allah does not guide the wrongdoing people." In verse 18:29 it is said that Allah "prepared for the wrongdoers a fire whose walls will surround them." In verses 43:74–76 it is emphasised that the criminals going to hell are not wronged, "but they were the wrongdoers." From these verses we can see that being wrongdoers and going to hell are linked together.

The verb form of the same root, ظلم *zalama*, meaning "to oppress," "to do wrong," "to commit injustice," etc. is also used frequently in the Qur'an. It appears more than 100 times, from 2:54 until 65:1. The following verses talk about people who did wrong. In verse 3:117 it is said, "the example of what they spend in this worldly life is

119

like that of a wind in which there is frost which strikes the harvest of a people who have wronged themselves and destroys it, and Allah has not wronged them, but they wrong themselves." In verse 4:168 it is said, "those who disbelieve and do wrong, Allah will never forgive them, he will not guide them to a path." In verse 39:51 it is said that on judgment day "the evil consequences of their deeds struck them, and of these people, those who did wrong will be afflicted by the evil consequences of their deeds." In verse 42:42 it is said, "the way is only against those who wrong the people and tyrannise on earth unjustly. Those will have a painful punishment." In verses 43:64–65 it is said, "Allah is my lord and your lord, so worship him. This is a straight path, but the denominations from among them differed, so woe to those who did wrong, for [they shall receive] the punishment of a painful day." Here we can see that people who do not act according to the way enjoined by their prophets will be punished, but the criterion is not simply a verbal declaration of faith.

From the verses discussed above we can see how often wrongdoing is condemned in the Qur'an.

Similarly, in verses 45:34–35 it is said that on judgment day "we will forget you as you forgot [the judgment day], and your refuge is the fire, and there are no helpers for you. That is because you ridiculed the signs of Allah, and worldly life deluded you." From this passage we can see that it is not just disbelief that is the issue, but being concerned only with worldly life, which seems to imply harming others in order to obtain goods and pleasure. This is what leads to punishment. And then in verse 46:20 it is said on judgment day those who disbelieved will be exposed to the fire, for "you exhausted your pleasures during your worldly life and enjoyed them, so today you will be awarded the punishment of humiliation because you were arrogant on earth unjustly and because you were defiantly disobedient." From this verse we can see that the problem is not just disbelief, but living only for worldly pleasures, and probably having done bad things to obtain them.

Chapter 4 Re-reading Islam

Another word that occurs frequently is مجرم *mujrim*, meaning "criminal," the active participle of أجرم *ajrama*, "to commit crime." This is also linked to disbelief and there are many negative passages about criminals and their punishment. This can be contrasted with the use of the word محسن *muḥsin* in referring to believers and rewards above. I shall give below examples of verses talking about criminals and examples of verses talking about their punishment.

In verses 6:54–55 it is said that Allah "decreed upon himself mercy, whoever among you does wrong in ignorance and repents after that and reforms, then [Allah] is indeed forgiving and merciful." In verse 6:147 Muhammad is told to say that Allah's "punishment cannot be repelled from the criminal people." This is repeated in 12:110. In verse 7:40 it is said that those "who denied our verses and were arrogant towards them, the gates of heaven are not open for them, nor are they entering paradise until a camel enters into the eye of a needle, and we reward the criminals in this way." In verse 8:8 it is said that Allah "should establish the truth and abolish falsehood, even if the criminals disliked it." In verse 7:133 it is said that Allah "sent upon them the flood and locusts and lice and frogs and blood as distinct signs" but Pharaoh's people "were arrogant and were a criminal people." In verse 9:66 it is said that if "we pardon one faction of you, we are punishing another faction because they were criminals." In verse 11:52 people are told to "ask your lord for forgiveness and then repent to him, and not to "turn away as criminals." In verse 11:116 it is said that those "who did injustice pursued what [provided luxury], and they were criminals." The verses above talk about criminals negatively.

In verses 14:48–49 it is said that on judgment day "you see the criminals bound together in shackles." In verse 18:49 it is said that when the record is placed then you see the criminals fearing what is in it," and that Allah does not wrong anyone. In verse 18:53 it is said that the criminals will "see the fire and be certain that they are falling into it." In verse 19:86 it is said that Allah will "drive the criminals to hell in thirst." In verse 20:74 it is said that whoever "comes to his lord as a criminal, then indeed for him is hell. He will neither die therein nor live." In verse 20:102 it is said that on judgment day "the horn is blown and we gather the criminals on that day blue" from terror. In verse 25:22 it is added that they "see the angels. There will not be good tidings on that day for the criminals, and [the angels] will say, 'Prevented and inaccessible.'" In verse 30:12 it is said that on judgment day when "the hour is established the criminals will be in despair." In verse 32:22 it is said that Allah "is taking revenge on the criminals." In verse 43:74 it is said that the criminals "will be in the punishment of hell, abiding eternally." In verses 45:31–34 it is said that the signs were recited to the infidels but they "were arrogant and were a criminal people" and "the bad deeds that they did will appear to them, and they will be surrounded by what they ridiculed," and that their "refuge is the fire." In verses 54:47–48 it is said that the criminals "are dragged into the fire" on judgment day. In verses 55:41–43 it is said that the criminals "will be known by their marks" and that this is "hell, which the criminals deny." In verse 70:11 it is said that on judgment day "the criminal will wish that he could be ransomed from the punishment of that day by his children."

Above are the verses talking about criminals' punishment in hell, while the following verses talk about criminal people being destroyed on earth.

In verse 10:13 it is said, "we had already destroyed generations before you [referring to the people to whom Muhammad was reciting this] when they committed injustice, and their messengers came to them with clear proofs, but they were not to believe. We recompense the criminal people in this way." In verse 27:69 people are told to "travel in the land and see what was the end of the criminals." In verse 44:37 it is said that Allah destroyed the people of Tubba' and those before them for "indeed they were criminals." In verses 46:21–25 it is said that a wind destroyed everything of the people of 'Aad, and that of them "nothing is seen except their dwellings. We recompense the criminal people in this way." In verses 51:31–34 it is said that messengers told Abraham that they "were sent to a people of criminals in order to send upon them stones of clay, marked in the presence of your lord for the transgressors." In verses 77:16–18 it is said, "did we not destroy the former [disbelievers]? Then we will make the later ones follow them. We deal with the criminals in this way."

If we read these verses carefully we should be able to see that non-believers are punished because they commit crimes, not because they do not believe.

A similar word is مسرف *musrif*, meaning "transgressor" or "one who commits excess," the active participle of أسرف *asrafa*, "to commit excess." In verse 5:32 it is said that Allah "decreed upon the children of Israel that whoever kills a soul, unless [avenging a murder] or for corruption on earth, it is as if he had killed all mankind, and who saves one, it is as if he had saved all mankind. And our messengers had certainly come to them with clear proofs. Then indeed many of them, after that, were transgressors on earth." In verses 6:141 and 7:31 it is said that Allah "does not like those who commit excess." In verses 10:83 and 44:31 it is said that Pharaoh was a transgressor, and in 21:9 it is said that Allah "destroyed the transgressors." In verses 26:150–152 we are told to fear Allah and obey Muhammad, and "do not obey the order of the transgressors, who cause corruption in the land and do not amend." In verse 40:28 it is said that Allah "does not guide one who is a transgressor and a liar." In verse 40:43 it is said that our place of return "is to Allah, and indeed, the transgressors will be companions of the fire." In verses 51:31–34 it is said that messengers told Abraham that they "were sent to a people of criminals in order to send upon them stones of clay, marked in the presence of your lord for the transgressors."

From these passages we can see that being a Muslim and getting good rewards in the afterlife are closely linked to doing good deeds, and not believing is linked to injustice and being punished. But we need to be aware that probably it is the case that doing good deeds leads to good rewards, and doing bad deeds leads to bad rewards, rather than the case that belief leads to good rewards, and disbelief leads to bad rewards. A mere verbal affirmation that there is no god but God and Muhammad is his prophet is not a ticket to heaven.

In verses 36:54 and 37:39 it is said that you will "not be recompensed except for what you have done." Although such verses are frequently preceded by verses about punishment for people who do not believe, we can see that in Islam what people do is probably more important than saying that one believes or not.

In verse 38:49 it is said that there is a "good place of return for the righteous," while in 38:55, the active par-

Chapter 4 Re-reading Islam

ticiple طاغي *ṭāghī* of the verb طغى *ṭaghā*, meaning "to transgress" or "to oppress," is used for denoting infidels and it is said "indeed, for the transgressors is an evil place of return, hell, in which they will burn, and wretched is the resting place." From this we can see that the line between the believers and the non-believers is not so much what they say, but how good they are morally. This is also seen in 79:35–41, in which it is said that on judgment day "for him who transgressed and preferred the life of the world, then indeed hellfire will be the refuge. And as for him who feared the standing of his lord and prevented the soul from vain desires, then indeed paradise will be the refuge." This passage clearly shows the moral construal of faith, and that reward is given in proportion to moral behaviour.

In verses 89:6–14 it is said, "have you not considered how your lord dealt with 'Aad, with Iram, who had lofty pillars, the likes of which had never been created in the land? And with Thamud, who carved out the rocks in the valley? And with Pharaoh, owner of the stakes? Who oppressed (طغى *ṭaghā*) within the lands, and increased therein the corruption. So your lord poured upon them a scourge of punishment. Indeed, your lord is in observation." This passage makes clear that punishment is for oppression and corruption, not allegiance to Allah or the lack thereof per se. From this we can see the moral nature of Islam.

Many passages refer to the arrogance of disbelievers. The most famous of them is perhaps 2:34 in which it is said, "when we said to the angels, 'prostrate before Adam,' they prostrated, except for Satan.[2] He refused and was arrogant and became one of the disbelievers." In verse 4:172 it is said that whoever disdains the worship of Allah "and is arrogant, he will gather them to himself all together. And as for those who believed and did righteous deeds, he will give them fully their rewards and grant them extra from his bounty, and as for those who disdained and were arrogant, he will punish them with a painful punishment, and they will not find for themselves besides Allah any protector or helper." In verse 7:36 it is said, "the ones who deny our verses and are arrogant toward them, those are the companions of the fire. They will abide therein eternally." In verses 7:75–76 it is written "said the chiefs who were arrogant among his people to those who were oppressed, to those who believed among them, 'do you know that Salih is sent from his lord?' They said, 'indeed we are believers in what he was sent with.' Said those who were arrogant, 'indeed we, in that which you have believed, are disbelievers.' " In verses 75:30–34 it is said, "to your lord, that day, will be the procession. And the disbeliever did not believe, and he did not pray. But he denied and turned away. And then he went to his people, swaggering. Woe to you, and woe!" From these passages we can see the frequent link between disbelief and pride, and I think it is reasonable to assume that punishment is for pride rather than disbelief. Most importantly, there is an emphasised message against pride and enlarged egos.

Related to this, in 4:36 people are commanded to "worship Allah and associate nothing with him, and to parents do good, and to relatives, orphans, the needy, the near neighbour, the neighbour farther away, the companion at your side, the traveler, and your slaves. Indeed, Allah does not like those who are self-deluding and boastful." The last sentence is repeated in verses 31:18 and 57:23.

---

[2] For more discussion on Satan, see Section 7.1.1.

Chapter 4 Re-reading Islam

4.1.2.6 Judgment Day

In this part I shall talk about issues connected to judgment, namely, bearing witness, weighing of deed, records of what one has done, and their connection to the moral construal of faith. This part gives further evidence that Islam was a spiritual, moral and social campaign, aiming at an improvement of the lives seventh-century Arabs were living.

Let us first look at passages in which people are said to bear witness against themselves.

The concept of bearing witness is very important in Islam. The creed is literally a testimony bearing witness that there is no god but God and that Muhammad is God's messenger. On judgment day, people also bear witness, but this time it is against themselves. If we reflect upon this, we should be able to see that it also points towards a moral construal of faith. For people bear witness not just to whether they believed or not, but, more importantly, to how they lived out their lives, what they have done with it. If it is just a simple yes-or-no matter of having been a Muslim by confession or not, then one does not need to bear witness against oneself.

In verse 6:130 it is said, " 'O assembly of jinn and mankind, did there not come to you messengers from among you, relating to you my verses and warning you of the meeting of [the judgment day]?' They will say, 'we bear witness against ourselves,' and worldly life had deluded them, and they will bear witness against themselves that they were disbelievers." Even though some of the passages which talk about this emphasise that people bear witness against themselves that they were disbelievers, if we take into consideration the arguments for moral construal above, that disbelief is a shorthand for immorality, then these passages actually make much more sense and become more coherent. They tell a cautionary tale of people disregarding spiritual cultivation and justice, regretting it when faced with judgment in the afterlife and reviewing what they have done.

Directly in support of my proposal of the moral construal of belief are passages in which people's actions are mentioned as justification for punishment. In verses 24:23–24 it is said, "indeed, those who accuse chaste, unaware, and believing women are cursed in this world and the hereafter, and there is a great punishment for them on a day when their tongues, their hands, and their feet will bear witness against them as to what they have done." In verse 36:65 it is said that on judgment day "we will seal over their mouths, and their hands will speak to us, and their feet will testify about what they used to earn." In verses 41:19–22 it is said that on judgment day "the enemies of Allah will be gathered to the fire while they are assembled in rows, until, when they reach it, their hearing and their eyes and their skins will testify against them about what they have done. And they will say to their skins, 'why have you testified against us?' They will say, 'we were made to speak by Allah, who has made everything speak, and he created you the first time, and to him you are returned. And you were not covering yourselves, lest your hearing or your sight or your skins testify against you, but you assumed that Allah does not know much of what you do.' " In verses 99:6–8 it is said that on judgment day "the people will depart in scattered groups to be shown their deeds. So whoever does an atom's weight of good will see it, And whoever does an atom's weight of evil will see it."

Also in support of my proposal are passages in which persecution of Muslims is mentioned as justification for punishment. In verse 7:37 it is said, "and who is more unjust than one who invents a lie about Allah or denies his verses? Those will receive what is destined for them, until, when our messengers come to them to take them in death, they will say, 'where are those you used to invoke besides Allah?' They will say, 'They have departed from us,' and will bear witness against themselves that they were disbelievers." In verse 85:7 it is said, "they are witnesses to what they were doing against the believers."

In addition to bearing witness, weighing (presumably one's good and bad deeds) is frequently mentioned in connection to judgment day and resurrection. It is said to happen at that time. If one's reward is simply determined by whether one believes in Allah or not, then there is no need to weigh what one has done. The occurrence of weighing shows that each of one's deeds counts, and one's overall morality determines one's reward. Let us look at these passages. In verse 21:47 it is said, "and we place the scales of justice for the day of resurrection, so no soul will be treated unjustly at all, and if there is the weight of a mustard seed, we will bring it forth. We are sufficient as accountant." In verses 7:8–9 it is said, "the weighing that day will be the truth. So those whose scales are heavy, those are the ones who succeed, and those whose scales are light, those are the ones who lost their souls for [wrongfully denying] our signs." In verses 23:101–103 there is a very similar passage. It says, "so when the horn is blown, then no relationship would be between them on that day and they are not asking about each other, then those whose scales are heavy, those are the ones who succeed, and those whose scales are light, those are the ones who lost their souls, abiding eternally in hell." In verses 101:6–11 it is said that on judgment day "as for one whose scales are heavy, he will be in a pleasant life. But as for one whose scales are light, his refuge will be an abyss. And what can make you know what that is? It is a fire, intensely hot."

From such passages we can see that reward and punishment are based on a comparison of one's good deeds with one's bad deeds. It is not about being a nominal Muslim or not.

Allah is also said to be the one who sent down the balance. So people's deeds would be weighed and rewarded according to their record of good and bad deeds. In verse 42:17 it is said, "It is Allah who has sent down the book in truth, and the balance, and what will make you perceive? Perhaps the hour is near." In verses 55:7–9 it is said, "and he raised heaven and imposed the balance, so that you do not transgress with the balance. And establish weight in justice and do not make deficient the balance." In verse 57:25 it is said, "we have already sent our messengers with clear evidences and sent down with them the book and the balance in order that the people may stand with justice." In verses 101:1–9 it is said that during the calamity (probably the judgment day) "as for one whose scales are heavy, he would have a pleasant life, and as for one whose scales are light, his refuge would be an abyss."

In verses 50:16–22 in the Qur'an, it is said, "we have already created man and know what his soul whispers to him, and we are closer to him than the jugular vein. As the two [recording angels] observe, seated on the right and on the left, man does not utter any word without having a ready observer, and the intoxication of death will bring the truth. That is what you were trying to avoid. And the horn will be blown. That is the day of the threat. And every soul will come, with it someone driving [him there] and a witness. You were certainly heedless of this, and we have removed from you your cover, so your sight today is sharp." From this passage we can see the importance of morality in Islam. If people are just rewarded and punished according to their belief and disbelief, then there is no need for a witness to observe everything one does. It is the inter-connection between faith and morality in Islam which leads to an emphasis on punishment for disbelievers. But disbelief itself is not the target.

The emphasis on a record being presented on judgment day also tells us that what a person has done is very important, that the link between a believer and receiving rewards is really the conflation of believing and doing good deeds, for if only declaration of faith and prayers are important, then there is no need to keep a record of everything a person has done in life. This conflation is probably a result of Allah and Muhammad trying to promote moral behaviours among his people rather than a factual declaration of these two being the same thing, or always occurring together.

Many verses talk about a record being presented on judgment day. For example in verse 17:71 it is said that on judgment day "we will call forth every people with its record. Then whoever is given his record in his right hand, those will read their records, and they will not be wronged even to a thread."³ In verse 18:49 it is said that the book of deeds "leaves nothing small or great uncounted, and they will find what they did present, and your lord does not wrong anyone." In verse 39:69 it is said that on judgment day "the earth will shine with the light of its lord, and the record will be placed, and the prophets and the witnesses will be brought, and it will be judged between them in truth, and they will not be wronged." In verses 54:52–55 it is said, "everything they did is in the written records, and every small and big thing is written down. Indeed the righteous will be in gardens and rivers in a seat of honour near a powerful king." In verses 58:6–7 it is said that on judgment day "Allah will resurrect them all and inform them of what they did. Allah recorded it, while they forgot it, and Allah is a witness over everything." In verses 82:10–12 it is said, "indeed, over you are keepers, noble and recording. They know whatever you do. Indeed, the righteous will be blissful, and indeed, the wicked will be in hellfire. They will burn in it on the day of judgment, and never therefrom will they be absent." These verses all emphasise that one's actions are recorded clearly for the sake of judgment.

In verses 84:6–15 it is said, "O mankind, indeed you are labouring toward your lord with exertion and will meet him. Then as for him who is given his record in his right hand, he will be judged with an easy account, and return to his people in happiness. And as for him who is given his record behind his back, he will cry out for destruction, and burn in a blaze. Indeed, he had been among his people in happiness. Indeed, he had thought he would never return [to Allah]. But yes! Indeed, his lord constantly saw him." From this passage we can see that disbelief is seen as a cause of immoral behaviour. This is why there are so many threats of hell. It is to scare people in order to make them behave morally.

In verses 69:18–32 it is said that on judgment day "you

---

³The verse shifts between a group of people and an individual. But the general sense should be clear.

will be exhibited, no secret will be hidden. So as for him who is given his record in his right hand, he will say, 'here, read my record! Indeed, I was certain that I would be meeting my account,' " and he will go to heaven. "And as for him who is given his record in his left hand, he will say, 'oh, I wish I had not been given my record and had not known what my account is. I wish my death had been the end. My wealth has not availed me. Gone from me is my authority,' " and he goes to hell. In verses 69:33–34 there is a further explanation of the sentence. It is said, "indeed, he did not believe in Allah, the most great, and he did not encourage the feeding of the poor." In verses 83:1–16 it is said, "woe to those who give less, who, when they take a measure from people, take in full. But if they give by measure or by weight to them, they cause loss. Do they not think that they will be resurrected for a tremendous day, a day when mankind will stand before the lord of the worlds?" And then it says, "woe, that day, to the deniers, who deny the day of judgment. And none deny it except every sinful transgressor," and they will burn in hell. Here we can see the significance of all of one's deeds rather than just belief or disbelief. Belief is used as shorthand for being concerned with the spiritual and the hereafter, and thus being moral. Belief itself is not the criterion of judgment.

There is a similar passage in 75:13–15 in which it is said, "man will be informed that day of what he sent forth and [what he] kept back. Rather, man will be a witness against himself, even if he presents his excuses." It means that man will be informed of what he did and did not do. Similarly, in verse 82:5 it is said that on judgment day "a soul will know what it has sent forth and [what it has] kept back." In verses 81:10–14 it is said that on judgment day "the pages are laid open" and "a soul will know what it has brought [to the world]." In verse 78:40 it is said, "indeed, we have warned you of a near punishment on the day when a man will observe what his hands have put forth and the disbeliever will say, 'oh, I wish that I were dust!' " Again these passages show the importance of what one has done in one's life, rather than just being a Muslim or not as a

Chapter 4 Re-reading Islam

matter of formality. This is another confirmation of the moral construal of belief in Islam. The emphasis on belief is just a short-hand for moral behaviour.

In verse 67:11 it is said that on judgment day the disbelievers "will admit their sin, so away with the companions of the blaze." The word "sin" here would not be limited to their disbelief. I think the reasonable interpretation is that since they do not believe in the hereafter, they did not hesitate in committing injustices in order to benefit themselves, and they were punished for their moral deficiency. But in another context people would not need faith as much as Muhammad's audience did to be moral. Therefore we need not take threats of punishment to non-Muslims literally.

In verse 74:39–47 it is said that the companions of the right will be "in gardens, questioning each other about the criminals (and asking them) 'what led you into hell?' They will say, 'we were not among the praying ones, and we did not feed the poor, and we used to talk vainly with the vain-talkers, and we used to deny the day of judgment until the certainty came to us.' " From this passage we can see a list of punishable traits, and though prayer and belief in the judgment day can be taken to be religious requirements rather than moral ones, one can conjecture that the real motives for mandating these two items are spiritual cultivation and the promotion of just actions respectively. Thus one can see that with a change of mindset Islam does not need to be a religion advocating hell for disbelievers, but simply a movement promoting moral actions, social justice, and spiritual cultivation at a specific point in history, doing good in a way that would be effective at the time.

After all, in verse 95:8 it is said, "is not Allah the most just of judges?" How could it be just to base reward and punishment on pledging allegiance to Allah or not, rather than on one's moral behaviour?

4.1.2.7 Concluding Remarks

From these passages we can see that there are strong reasons to believe that the criterion for being a Muslim is being a good person, that the two are closely linked in the original version of Islam. If one is not good, then he cannot truly be a Muslim. Taken in this sense, punishment would be for doing bad things, but there is no point punishing people for whether they claim to be a Muslim or not.

We see more support of this view in verses 31:2–3, in which it is said that these are the "verses of the wise book, as guidance and mercy for the ones who do good." We can see the firm link between morality and faith in Islam. However, potentially this link could be used for justifying any action in the name of Allah. Therefore it is very important to reflect critically on what counts as good in Islam.

Of course this is a very tough question, since for example in 28:16 it is said that, after killing someone, Moses asked for forgiveness, and Allah forgave him, for he is forgiving and merciful. But if one is so easily forgiven, is killing someone not a very serious crime or sin? Then how do we measure what is good and what is bad? We shall will talk about the issue of choice in following rules in Islam in Section 5.1.3.

Abraham's story is also difficult to understand. In verses 37:83–110 he nearly killed his son in response to a vision in his dream. Are we to interpret this as an act of obedience, cruelty, or delusion? We need to think carefully. There are no simple rules to follow, and even if there are, we need to judge if the circumstances fit the conditions of those rules.

Faith is based on acts but that does not imply that rules do not change. A prophet improves on what is happening, he does not work in a vacuum. He cannot go too far. Thus we should not apply a set of revelations from another age without adapting it. Thus the reasonable and the brave thing is probably to face this uncertainty and do the best to one's ability. Reading the Qur'an literally is not really using one's ability in the best way, as we touch

Chapter 4 Re-reading Islam

on in Section 3.2, Section 3.3, and Section 6.1.

Moral judgment is definitely difficult. Maybe that is the reason why people like a system in which belief suffices, and reading the Qur'an literally provides a feeling of security. Passages such as 12:24, 15:40, 19:51, 37:40, 37:74, 37:128, 37:160, 37:169, and 38:83 which include the word مخلص *mukhlaṣ* tend to support this view. The reason is that this word, as a passive participle for "being sincere," means someone who is divinely made sincere, and thus by derivation, one who is divinely chosen. One can argue that if everything happens by Allah's will then this derivation does not work since one can also be divinely made evil, and that person does not seem to be "chosen." Still it is a common way to read this word. If one is divinely made sincere and a Muslim, then demarcation of Muslims by good deeds does not seem necessary. Since Allah determined the list, one does not need to identify its members by some criteria.

However, I argue that this is not the case because Allah can choose Muslims on the basis of their behaviour. The passages linking good behaviour and belief testify to this stance. Therefore even if believing or not is divinely chosen, it could be based on one's prior qualities and behaviour.

Now we should be able to see that even though literalism seems to provide a relief from the complication and nuances of moral judgment, in the end that is an illusion, since it is just putting the bet in a wholesale way, adhering to a system of rules rigidly, rather that choosing case by case what to do and what to advocate.

After the discussion in this section, we should be able

to see the inseparability of belief and righteous deeds in the conception of Islam. When the Qur'an talks about punishment for disbelievers, it should be read as referring to unjust people, especially people persecuting Muslims. I think it was probably the case that in the Arabian Peninsula at the time of Muhammad's campaign non-Muslims had a lower level of morality. But it is not necessarily the case in other times and places. We need to read Islamic texts with this in mind but need not apply this conflation in other contexts.

One is free to take his own position regarding the issue of demarcation as long as it is according to reason and no violence is involved, or not, since perhaps Allah determined it already.[4] Nevertheless, we should ask ourselves whether it is my ego that is speaking when I think or accuse someone of being an infidel or polytheist, whether it is because it feels good to think that I am on the right path but others are not. But are we really sure? Are we sure that, for example, doing five prayers a day and giving the designated amount to charity and thinking ill of non-Muslims, in total, is better than someone doing good deeds alone?

4.2 Teachings of Islam

If you find the ideas propagated above rather adventurous, we can continue with more commonly accepted ideas first. Let us look at the main teachings of Islam.

---

[4]From my point of view the discussion about chosen-ness is just for the sake of argument, since the textual support is not strong to begin with. It is more reasonable to stick to the view that belief is chosen by oneself and the criteria differentiating Muslims and non-Muslims are doing good deeds and not doing bad deeds. If we accept that belief is determined by Allah, we shall run into problems which will be discussed in Section 4.5.1.

4.2.1 Intention

In the very first item al-Bukhari put in the first book of his collection of Hadiths [3, 1:1], Muhammad stresses that the intention of an act matters most. What people intend in an act is what their reward would be based on.

This is in line with the Qur'an, which in 20:15 says, "each soul is rewarded for what it strives for," and in 53:39 declares, "there is nothing for man except that for which he strives, and that his effort is going to be seen. Then he will be recompensed for it with the fullest recompense." According to this principle of reward, if you intend to help people, then you would be rewarded accordingly. But if you intend to get people's praise, then that is all you get.

Similarly, if one intends to do good and for that reason neglects prayer times, he should still be rewarded for doing good. This is something that many adherents of religions forget. They measure piety just by looking at the explicitly coded rules. Life cannot be explicitly coded easily. That is the cause of many issues in religions. People want a simple guide, but in the process get stuck to a set of rules without considering individual situations. In sticking to the rules this way the rules become twisted and this goes against the *intention* of law-setters. Such adherents are not using their God-given intellect properly.

An example that demonstrates this point can be found from 22:36–37 in the Qu'ran, in which it is said that Allah has "appointed the camels and cattle as among the symbols of Allah," and Muslims are told to "mention the name of Allah upon them when they are sacrificed." But it is said, "their meat will not reach Allah, nor will their blood, but what reaches him is our piety." And the goal of all of this is for Muslims to glorify Allah for his guidance. From this passage we can see that the sacrifice itself is only a symbol of one's piety. And it is highly conceivable that in different situations another symbol can be used. It is the duty of a religious person to figure out the changeable, symbolic part versus the essential, important part. The example here illustrates this point. Piety is the important part. The sacrifice used is only one of the symbols. Other rituals can be viewed similarly.

Looking for the intention should also be a guiding principle in reading Islamic texts themselves because a long time has passed after Muhammad's revelations, and the world is profoundly different from his time. Therefore when we read Islamic texts we need to look for the intended message in the historical context, and apply appropriate modifications in view of the changes in the fabric of society, gender roles, economic activities, etc. Otherwise the only conclusion we can get is an anachronistic call to return, in every aspect of life, to Muhammad's time.

We should bear this in mind when reading Islamic texts, for it means that, for example, if modesty is intended, the actual mode of dress does not matter as much. It could be that more conspicuous kinds of dress actually flaunt one's piety and attract attention rather than embody modesty. Then the corresponding reward would be one for exhibition, not modesty.

People care about external things because they can be seen. In contrast, intention is not as easily seen. It is usually visible only to oneself and God. Therefore it needs to be emphasised in order not to be neglected. Intention is paramount in Islam. It is something we need to keep in mind in reading the Qur'an and the Hadiths, because it lets us and requires us to use our own judgment in interpreting texts with a context profoundly different from the world we live in now.

4.2.2 The Five Pillars

What are the main requirements of Islam? Definitely they are the five pillars mentioned in the Hadiths, namely the creed, daily prayers, almsgiving, pilgrimage to Mecca, and fasting during Ramadan. [3, 2:7] The most important ones are prayers and almsgiving, as one can see in verse 27:3 of the Qur'an when a summary is given of what a believer is, it is said that they are whose who pray, give alms, and believe in the hereafter with certainty; and pilgrimage is not compulsory, as it is not always mentioned in such lists, for example [3, 2:44].

Among these pillars, is there anything having to do with the veil or other "protection" for women? No, nothing in particular about women is mentioned. But when one looks at instructions for female Muslims, and the understandably negative reaction from the non-Muslim world, one might think that those things instead are the pillars of Islam.

Viewed together with other passages (such as those in [3, 6]) we may understand that women follow Islam in the same way that men do. As long as they accomplish these five tasks, they are good Muslims. The veil is not one of these tasks.

To focus on other issues but not on these five pillars is a sign of the decay of Islam and its being eaten away by jealousy and inferiority complexes etc. arising from economic underdevelopment and threatened patriarchal institutions, to name a few of the prominent issues in Muslim-majority societies.

4.2.3 Faith and Charity

It should now be clear that Islam is mainly about the five pillars, which can be summarised as *faith* (the creed, daily prayers, pilgrimage to Mecca, and fasting during Ramadan) and *charity* (almsgiving). Islam should be about these and not other external actions, societal affiliations, or kinds of dress. It should be about improving one's spiritual level (faith) and helping the people in need (charity).

One issue related to charity is the injunction against miserliness (3:180, 4:37, 9:76, 57:24, 92:8) and the frequency of characterising Allah as the provider (for example in 2:212, 3:37, 10:31, 22:58, 35:3). In verse 3:180 it is said that "those who withhold what Allah has given them of his bounty" should "not think that it is better for them. Rather, it is bad for them. Their necks will be encircled by what they withheld on the day of resurrection." In verses 9:76–77 it is said that when Allah gave people who made a covenant with him gifts from his bounty, "they were stingy with it and turned away [from people] indifferently. So he penalised them with hypocrisy in their hearts until the day when they meet him, because they failed Allah in what they promised him and because they lied."

One is also told to spend out of what Allah provides (2:3, 2:254, 2:267, 4:39, 8:3, 13:22, 14:31, 22:35, 28:54, 32:16, 34:39, 35:29, 36:47, 42:38, 63:10, 65:7). In verses 64:15–16 it is said, "your wealth and your children are but a trial, and Allah has with him a great reward. So fear Allah as much as you are able and listen and obey and spend, it is better for you, and those who are saved from the miserliness of their souls, they are the successful ones." Since God tells us to spend and says how good it is, why worry about money at all? Spend anything you have!

As a result of this, Muslims tend not to save money for the future, thinking that miserliness and the propensity to save are bad qualities. Actually, as one can see from verse 9:79, what verses 8:76–77 are trying to say is that miserliness is bad if money is withheld from charity. It is said in 9:79 that people ridicule "those who criticise the contributors among the believers concerning [their] donations and the ones who find nothing except their effort." It warns that "Allah will ridicule them, and there is a painful punishment for them." It does not mean that a person can spend everything without a plan for the future and think that he can just depend on Allah who will take care of him. This is irresponsibility rather than faith. If you feel doubtful about this issue, look at verses 17:26–27, where it is said that one should not spend wastefully and that the wasteful ones are "brothers of the devils." In verse 25:67 it is said that the servants of Allah are "those that spend not excessively and not stingily but between that, moderately."

The true aim of advising against miserliness is to encourage people to spend in the way of Allah and spend in charity. People are told to spend in the way of Allah in verses 2:195, 2:261–262, 2:274, 8:60, 47:38, and 57:10. It is also said in 8:36 that people who disbelieve "spend their wealth to avert from the way of Allah." In verse 9:34 it is said, "those who hoard gold and silver and spend it not in the way of Allah, give them tidings of a painful punishment."

With Muhammad's frequent military campaigns (which started because Muslims were persecuted) "spending in the way of Allah" frequently referred to fighting for the freedom of Islamic worship, but in this age it should be limited to charity because a great variety of military campaigns invoke Allah's name unjustifiably. People are told to spend in doing good in 2:215, 2:270–273, 3:134, and 9:121. We should remember this when trying to understand what is meant by "spending in the way of Allah."

In verses 47:36–38 it is said "worldly life is only amusement and diversion, and if you believe and fear Allah, he will give you your rewards and not ask you for your properties. If he should ask you for them and press you, you would withhold, and he would expose your hatred. Here you are—those invited to spend in the way of Allah—but among you are those who withhold, and whoever withholds only withholds from himself, and Allah is free of need, while you are the needy ones." Once we read the whole passage, we see that people are told to spend and not to withhold **with reference to the specific goals of helping the cause of Islam and helping the needy**. People are not told to spend aimlessly.

Another passage shows us this point clearly. In verse 57:7 people are told to "believe in Allah and his messenger and spend from that of which he has made you trustees. For those who have believed among you and spent, there will be a great reward." It seems that it is just about spending and perhaps not tied to material possessions, as a general piece of advice. But we have to read on to see the whole story. In verses 57:10–11 it is said, "why do you not spend in the cause of Allah while to Allah belongs the heritage of the heavens and the earth? Not equal among you are those who spent before the conquest and fought. Those are greater in degree than they who spent afterwards and fought. But to all Allah has promised the best, and

Allah is informed of what you do. Who is it that would loan Allah a good loan so he will multiply it for him? And there is a noble reward for him." Its reference is specific, alluding to Muhammad's military campaigns. Therefore we should not think that such verses apply generally.

The metaphor of a loan to Allah which appears above is interesting. It is mentioned in 2:545, 5:12, 57:11, 57:18, 64:17, and 73:20. In verse 57:18 it is said, "Indeed, the charitable men and the charitable women and [those who] have loaned Allah a good loan, it will be multiplied for them, and there is a noble reward for them." And in 73:20 it is said that Allah "knew that there will be among you those who are ill and others traveling throughout the land seeking the bounty of Allah and others fighting for the cause of Allah. So recite what is easy from it and perform prayer and give alms and loan Allah a good loan, and whatever good you present for yourselves, you find it with Allah. It is better and greater in reward, and seek forgiveness of Allah. Indeed, Allah is forgiving and merciful." From such passages we can see that human beings are trustees of Allah's provision, but they can loan it to Allah. This hints at the temporal nature of the world, and the concept of the world as a test, which I shall expand on in subsubsection 4.4.1.3.

In verses 9:53–55 Muhammad is told to say, "spend willingly or unwillingly, never will it be accepted from you [as good deeds]. Indeed, you have been a defiantly disobedient people. And what prevents their spending from being accepted from them but that they have disbelieved in Allah and in his messenger and that they do not come to prayer except while they are lazy and that they do not spend except while they are unwilling. So let not their wealth or their children impress you." From this example we can see that it is not any kind of spending that would please Allah. If it is not spent right, it is not viewed favourably. Only specific types of spending are actively encouraged in the Qur'an. Belief is mentioned here but please refer to the discussion in Section 4.1.2 regarding the moral construal of faith. Another verse which shows that

Chapter 4 Re-reading Islam

only certain kinds of spending is encouraged is 63:7, in which it is said that the hypocrites say, "do not spend on those who are with the messenger of Allah until they disband." Here we can see that the cost of war was a constant subject in discussion. This is the context of telling people to spend.

To add to this discussion, we can also see from the Qur'an that people who do not have excess to spend for good causes should not feel uneasy. The thought also counts. In verses 9:91–92 it is said "there is not upon the weak or upon the ill or upon those who do not find anything to spend any discomfort if they are sincere to Allah and his messenger. There is not upon the doers of good any way [for blame], and Allah is forgiving and merciful, and not upon those who, when they came to you that you might give them mounts, you said, 'I can find nothing for you to ride upon.' They turned back while their eyes overflowed with tears of sorrow that they could not find something to spend."

Furthermore, we should remember that the order to spend from what Allah provides had frequently a specific reference. For example in verse 8:3 it is said that the believers are the ones who perform prayer, and spend from what we have provided them. But people frequently forget the context. The first verses of Sura 8 are actually talking about the bounties of war. In verse 8:1 Muhammad is told "they ask you about the bounties. Say, 'The bounties are for Allah and the messenger.' So fear Allah and amend that which is between you and obey Allah and his messenger, if you should be believers." One can sense that people had disputes about the division of war spoils, and these verses are to talk about this problem. Therefore we should not think that it is telling people always to spend without worrying. It is just encouraging people to spend the gains in proper ways. This specific reference is also assumed in verses 9:98–99 where it is said, "among the bedouins are some who take what they spend as a loss and await your turn of misfortune. A turn of evil is upon them. Allah is hearing and knowing. And among the bedouins are some who believe in Allah and the last day and take what they spend as a means of nearness to Allah and of [receiving] the prayers of the messenger."

In verses 65:2–3, it is said that for everyone who "fears Allah, he makes for him a way out, and provides for him from where he does not expect, and whoever relies upon Allah, then [Allah] is sufficient for him. Indeed, Allah accomplishes his order. Allah has already set a quota for everything." It seems that we do not need to think about anything as long as we fear Allah. However, if we read the accompanying verses we can see that the Sura is talking about divorce, which in Muhammad's time involved a deal of monetary problems, as it sometimes still does today. Therefore it is reasonable to infer that the revelation is mostly trying to ease people's concern, rather than encouraging financial foolhardiness in general. It would be a grave mistake to read it broadly and think that one has earned the right to spend recklessly since one has pledged allegiance to Allah and he will provide for one.

One of the best explanations of this topic is to be found in Sura 59 which was revealed when Muhammad and his followers prevailed in war and it talks about the distribution of spoils. Some of the gains will go to people who were driven from their homes in Mecca. Then, in verse 59:9 it is said that there is a share for those who were settled in Medina and adopted the faith before the Muslims who were driven away from Mecca came, and "they love those who emigrated to them and find not any want in their breasts of what the emigrants were given but prefer them over themselves, even though they were poor, and whoever is protected from the miserliness of their souls, they are the successful ones." If a person can be poor and yet provide for others before himself, we can be quite sure that he is magnanimous, and such a person can face the hardships of life without bitterness. It is a very precious virtue. But it is a totally different story from spending lavishly and throwing grand parties.

Another one is in 76:8 in which it is said that the servants of Allah "give food, in spite of love for it, to the needy, the orphan, and the captive." This is the spirit of telling people to spend. Not for luxury, but for charity. We should understand verse 64:16 similarly. It says, "so fear Allah as much as you are able and listen and obey and spend. It is better for your souls, and whoever is protected from the miserliness of their souls, they are successful." It does not describe how to spend, and we should adopt the explication of verse 59:9 for this command too.

Reading and combining the teachings of these passages one should see that a Muslim is supposed to spend on charity and not be stingy about it, but one should not be wasteful. Allah will not take care of you if you starve because you have been wasteful. One is only supposed to spend the excess of one's income (2:219), and not for the sake of being seen by people (2:264–265, 4:38), for it is better to conceal it (2:271).

One of the neglected teachings of Islam is that the world is a "trial" which one has to work through ethically and sensibly (c.f. verse 8:28 in the Qur'an and the discussions in Section 4.4.1). Muhammad was a trader working for Khadija. They were prosperous, and one can be sure it was not by spending all the money earned. Muhammad was famous for being honest and upright, not spending all the money in his hands. So as soon as we reflect, we find that one has to save and plan for oneself. We should not act as if Allah will take care of us, the way children are taken care of. This is not non-miserliness, just childishness.

In verse 94 it is said to Muhammad, "did we not expand for you your breast? And we removed from you your burden which had weighed upon your back, and raised high for you your repute. For indeed, with hardship is ease. Indeed, with hardship is ease. So when you have finished [your duties], then labour hard, and to your lord direct your longing." Even Muhammad needs to work hard and finish his duties. Despite all the warnings against being overly concerned with riches, one does have to work hard and be responsible for oneself. Allah does not just give provisions and sustain people without conditions.

Weber's *The Protestant Ethic and the Spirit of Capital-*

ism [42] lauds the Protestant Puritanical spirit in promoting saving and investment and speculates that this leads to prosperity in Protestant countries. Weber may not be right, but many Muslims seem to derive from the abhorrence of miserliness expressed in the Qur'an and the commendable cultural emphasis on hospitality a tendency towards recklessness in financial planning.

4.2.4 Dedication

To realise the teachings of Islam in faith and charity requires a great deal of dedication in terms of one's own action and improvement. However, one very important problem comes from human beings: the love of poking into the affairs of others. True, Islam has societal visions and Muslims should aspire to the strength of faith of some of Muhammad's companions, but one's first priority is one's own piety, not others' behaviour. Human beings like to meddle in the affairs of others while neglecting their own moral and spiritual cultivation. So Islam in many communities has become an excuse for that, and not much else. This is a tendency that one has to guard against carefully and vigilantly. People seem to mistake being a nosy neighbour checking on others' Shari'a-approved behaviour for being a pious Muslim.

In verse 7:54 in the Qur'an, Muslims are told to call their lord privately. It means that one should not practice religion as a show. It is between oneself and Allah, not between others' views and Allah. One should spend one's energy on improving oneself, not policing others with regard to their religious practice. That is their own business. For example, we may look at the five prayers. Even though communal prayer is good, it is not mandatory. And one should not judge others by whether they go to the mosque frequently or not. Maybe they are very pious and pray a great deal at home. No one else knows.

In verse 7:205 Muslims are told to remember Allah inwardly, humbly, and without loudness in words. Administrators of mosques with loudspeakers blasting their call to prayer day and night seem not to have read this verse. Muslims care about building large mosques with high minarets. But do we care as much about building our inner faith and humility?

One should remember and constantly remind oneself of such issues because it is human nature to find fault with others and to find ways to feel superior. Muslims frequently satisfy this urge by checking others' piety. This is not good for religious practice and especially not good for society. People are too busy nominally satisfying Islam's rules so that they have no time or energy for improving either their minds or their societies.

For example, during Ramadan, people are angry if they see someone else eating. But even the most fastidious adherent of Islamic law admits that there are exceptions to the fasting requirements during Ramadan, such as menstruation, sickness, travelling, etc. But people do not care about these details, they are just angry because they hate to see people eat when they cannot.

If we compare this to most Buddhist traditions we see the difference. Among most lay people vegetarianism is not seen as a duty but as something good to do. So people are reasonable about it and they might do it themselves but do not use their energy to monitor if others do it or not.

If one has the time and energy to poke into others' affairs, why not do some volunteering? It requires more determination and work than criticising one's neighbour, but it would be much more commendable in the eyes of a benevolent deity.

4.3 Actions of Muslims

For a critical reflection on what qualifies as good in Islam, please refer to Section 4.1.2 and Section 5.1.3. In this part we shall look at concrete issues.

4.3.1 Environment

In general it seems that there is a lack of concern among Muslims for the environment, perhaps out of the belief that Allah is the provider and he controls everything so there is no need to worry about the environment. Allah is said to be the best of the providers in verses 22:58, 23:72, 34:39, and 62:11 but we should see that Allah does not interfere with every issue. In verse 36:47 it is said that when people are told to "spend from that which Allah has provided for you," disbelievers asked the believers, "should we feed one whom, if Allah wills, he would have fed?" If Allah is supposed to interfere with every issue, then he is very unjust not to save everyone from crimes or help everyone in need. But the world does not seem to work this way. We are given the freedom to act and show our inner selves. We can see this in verse 67:2 in which it is said that Allah "created death and life to test you" to find out which of you is "best in action." Therefore we need to take care of the environment in which we live, instead of behaving recklessly and assuming that Allah will maintain it well for us.

In verse 67:15 it is said that Allah "made the earth subservient (or tame) for you, so walk in its paths and eat of his provision, and to him is the resurrection." Some people may read this and say, "the earth is just for our use, we do not need to be so careful about it." But the word ذلول *dhalūl*, meaning "subservient" or "tame," is worth some reflection. For in using this word a conceptual parallel is established between the earth and domestic animals, especially if we read 36:71–72 in which it is said, "do you not see that we created for them from what our hands have made, grazing animals, so that they are owners of them? And we have tamed them for them, so they ride on them, and they eat from them." Now how would we treat domestic animals? We take good care of them, otherwise we would not benefit from them. Are we doing the same about the environment? It seems that we are not.

In verse 57:7 people are told to "believe in Allah and his messenger and spend out of that of which he has made you trustees. For those who have believed among you and spent, there will be a great reward." The word "trustees" is important. We are supposed to be caretakers of what Allah has given us, not take whatever we can from the environment without thinking about the future.

4.3.2 Food and Beverage

One issue that frequently causes a problem between Muslims and non-Muslims is that of Halal food and the banning of alcohol.

In verses 5:90–91 in the Qur'an it is said, "intoxicants, gambling, altars, and divining arrows are but dirt from the work of Satan, so avoid them so that you will succeed. Satan wants to institute animosity and hatred through intoxicants and gambling and to turn you away from the remembrance of Allah and prayer."

For most Muslims, this passage shows that alcohol is to be avoided because it existed and the word "intoxicant" refers to it, so the alcohol ban is vehemently enforced in many Muslim countries. In contrast, since items such as cigarettes and soft drinks had not appeared yet in Muhammad's time, so of course they have not been expressly banned, or spoken of negatively, in the Qur'an or the Hadiths. Consequently, it is not as clear whether they need to be avoided. But these are materials that many people are intoxicated with. They consume a great deal of them to feel light and good, with no willpower to stop themselves.

To see that the banning of alcohol is only a means,

while the avoidance of intoxication is the main aim, we should read 37:43–47, in which it is said that in paradise, "on thrones facing each other, a cup (of wine) from a spring would be passed among them, white and delicious to the drinkers, without bad effects and they are not going to be intoxicated." Similarly, in 47:15 it is said that "the parable of paradise, which the righteous are promised, in which there are rivers of unpolluted water and rivers of milk, the taste of which never changes, and rivers of wine delicious to those who drink and rivers of purified honey, in which there will be for them all the fruits, and forgiveness from their lord" is not like "one who abides eternally in the fire and given to drink scalding water, then it severs their intestines?" Again in the description of heaven in 56:15–24 an idealised version of wine is presented as an attraction. It is said that those in heaven would be reclining on woven thrones "facing each other, young boys made eternal circulating around them with vessels, and pitchers and a cup from a flowing spring, no headache from them and they will not be intoxicated, and fruit of what they select, and meat of fowl from what they desire, and fair women with large eyes, like well-protected pearls, as a reward for what they have done."

Since wine is said to be available in heaven, we can see that there is nothing fundamentally abhorrent about alcohol, just that intoxication causes problems for the individual and society. And it is difficult to ask people to drink without getting drunk. That is the reason the consumption of alcohol is banned in Islam.

So if we are to be consistent, we should ban such things as cigarettes and soft drinks along with alcohol. But they are not banned, because they did not exist and so were not mentioned in the Qur'an and the Hadiths, and also because people are hypocritical and they obey Allah only in an inflexible and lazy way. They are too lazy to think about why Islamic texts tell us to avoid certain things and whether the reason applies to other things as well. This is probably the reason why the obesity rate is high in many Muslim countries, because they pay too much attention

Chapter 4 Re-reading Islam

to alcohol but forget about staying alert and not getting addicted to sugar. They think they are better because they do not eat pork or drink wine, but they eat compulsively as if in compensation for all the enjoyments that are banned by Islam.

In verse 7:31 in the Qur'an Muslims are told to "eat and drink but not excessively" and that Allah "does not like those who commit excess." This is a verse that Muslims should pay more attention to, rather than obsessing about pork and alcohol. This is something that is not as straightforward to implement but governs the consumption of food and beverage overall. This injunction should not be neglected just because it is not rigidly set down and it is hard to judge people by it. We should observe this rule carefully for our own benefit. See the irony that such verses are emphasised neither in Muslim circles nor in non-Muslim circles when discussing Islam. If we are serious and not hypocritical about adhering to what we are told to do according to Islamic text we should calculate our calorie intake as carefully as avoiding pork and alcohol.

Similarly in Ramadan people sleep in the day and eat a great deal at night, thinking that they have achieved what Allah asked. Again this is hypocrisy. Fasting is not supposed to be like this. One is supposed neither to just sleep through the day nor overeat during the night. And the ridiculous thing is they condemn anyone eating during the day in their country or within their sight, while they themselves only fulfil this requirement hypocritically, following the letter but not the spirit.

Of course not only Muslims suffer from this hypocritical attitude, the elevators in some buildings in Israel stop on each and every floor during Sabbath, so that observant Jews do not have to operate these machines directly, thus not breaking the rules of Sabbath and yet do not have to climb the stairs, thus achieving both convenience and lawfulness. Smart? Or ridiculous?

Each follower of each religion should reflect on this. It is hard to be aware of the problems caused by double standards in religious observance. It is devastating to the image of a religion especially if it affects non-believers.

4.3.3 Usury

Another controversial issue is usury, the issue of lending and interest.

In verse 30:39 in the Qur'an, it is said that whatever "you gave for the sake of interest, in order for it to increase in the wealth of people, will not increase on the side of Allah. But what you gave in charity desiring the face of Allah, those are the ones who multiply." From this passage we can see that using money to get interest is not viewed as favourably as charity. But we need to be reasonable here. Lending for interest is not a good thing when it exacerbates the lives of poor people, but it can be a form of investment in which people borrow to do business and make a profit, and the lender benefits from this profit too. There is nothing wrong with that. In the modern financial system, it is comparatively convenient to get interest in some form, but hard to invest without bearing a semblance to lending. The important thing is just to ascertain as far as possible that the deposit is not leeching off the effort of others. But capital in itself is an important element in the modern business world. It is not realistic to avoid interest altogether.

Islamic finance tries to deal with this, modifying some of the transactions to avoid charging interest. But I doubt if this is necessary at all since textually in the Qur'an it is just saying that taking interest is worse than giving to charity. But there are so many things done on a day-to-day basis that are worse than charity. Very very few people are living their lives solely doing charity. So we need not be so severe against receiving interest. It caused more misery in the past because of the consequences of not being able to repay debts with interest. But now we can declare bankruptcy if necessary and we will not be sold into slavery. If we make sure that we are not causing suffering such as by charging exorbitant interest, then it should not be a problem.

Chapter 4 Re-reading Islam

In the Middle Ages, Christians did not think it right to charge interest, due to passages such as Luke 6:34–35 in which one is told to lend without expecting to get anything back. If one should not expect to be repaid, interest is probably out of the question. But lending without expecting to be repaid or without interest is something that very few people would do. It is not in one's self-interest to do so. So people in need may not even be able to get a loan at all. Arguably this is worse than getting a loan with interest. At least you postpone the crisis.

As for Jews, it is said in Exodus, "If thou lend money to any of My people, even to the poor with thee, thou shalt not be to him as a creditor; neither shall ye lay upon him interest." [35, Exodus 22:24] Based on such verses they reason that they could lend to non-Jews with interest.

In the contemporary world, most Christians and Jews do not bother with these rules. One could see those verses as historical or ideal, so that the verses were addressing the terrible forms of lending seen in the ages in which they were written. It is the same with Islam. The key issue is to be just and not to oppress people. But it is not realistic to ban interest across the board.

4.3.4 Music

The uneasiness with music shows another kind of malaise among conservative Muslims.

Is music unlawful, and the term *Islamic music* an oxymoron? Let us start with the way the Qur'an is experienced. It can be experienced by reading, silently or loudly, as calligraphy, and most importantly, as pitched recitation. In verses 73:2–4 people are told to "arise [to pray] at night, except for a little, half of it, or subtract from it a little, or add to it, and recite the Qur'an with measured recitation."

Pitched recitation as regularly practised in mosques *is* music, though vocal, not instrumental.

In some conservative circles, secular songs are prohibited. But Qur'anic recitation is in fact a type of singing, by any standard. Unaccompanied singing is also singing, consider the *a cappella* tradition in Western music.

For Muslims, reciting the Qur'an aloud is something very different from (secular) music. But for non-Muslims, it is situated firmly in the Abrahamic tradition of liturgy-chanting that evolved into church music in Christianity and very musical varieties of prayer service in some Jewish sects.

Because of some Hadiths such as [3, 15:70] and [3, 15:72] mentioning the devil's *mizmara* (a double-reed wind instrument, or any musical instrument in general), instrumental music is particularly suspect in Islam. In verse 31:6 of the Qur'an it is said that for the people who "buy the amusement of speech to mislead others from the way of Allah without knowledge and who ridicule it, there is a humiliating punishment." Some commentators take this to refer to music and argue from this that music is unlawful. Others argue from the example of 17:55 in the Qur'an in which it is said that Allah gave David the psalms, that one can see that music is permitted as David's psalms are clearly sung.

Christians also had some problems with music. We can take the book of psalms as evidence that music is approved by God and Ecclesiastes 7:5 which says that "it is better to heed the rebuke of a wise person than to listen to the song of fools" as evidence that music is not approved. We can argue either way but now we have a vast repertoire of Catholic and Protestant church music with all sorts of instrumental accompaniments.

We can also look at the case of poetry. At the end of Sura 26 of the Qur'an, i.e. 26:224–227, some negative things are said about poets. It is said that only deviators follow poets, that they roam in every valley, that they say what they do not do, except those who believe and do righteous deeds and remember Allah a great deal, and defend themselves after they were wronged. Muslims do not have as many problems with poetry as they do with music but this passage can be seen as a fairly negative comment on poetry. Of course we should remember the context, that there were probably poets mocking Muhammad, and that

Chapter 4 Re-reading Islam

this passage only condemns some, but not all, poets.

Incidentally it has been emphasised that Muhammad is not a poet. In verses 69:40-41 it is said that the Qur'an "is the word of a noble messenger. And it is not the word of a poet, little do you believe." But that does not imply that there is anything inherently bad about poetry, just that Muhammad is not the one who composed the message he was reciting, and the people who did not believe him said that he was a poet (21:5, 37:36, 52:30) who wrote the verses of the Qur'an.

The case of music is similar to the case of poetry. Something negative was associated with music, but we should not read these negative comments as saying that music is unlawful. It is just that some music should be avoided.

For example in 8:34-35 it is said, "why should Allah not punish [those who disbelieved] while they obstruct from al-Masjid al-Haram and they were not its [true] guardians? No one but the ones who fear Allah are its [true] guardians, but most of them do not know. And their prayer at the house was not except whistling and hand-clapping. So taste the punishment for what you used to disbelieve." People might use this verse against any association of music with Islam or its rituals, but perhaps what people were doing was very unbecoming? From this brief description we have no idea what the disbelievers were actually doing and we are not sure what kind of activity is condemned in this passage. One might say, "then we should be on the safe side so as not to err. Therefore we should not do anything remotely similar to whistling and clapping, hence any music and rhythm should be banned in mosques."

Now for the sake of argument, let me agree with this position. I would argue that in this case we should not do any pitched recitation of the Qur'an, for it does remotely resemble "whistling," since it is in a sense music. It shares the same melodic system as Middle Eastern musical traditions.

What would be the reaction of an imagined conservative opponent? The most extreme conservatives do say that pitched recitation of the Qur'an should be avoided, but most conservatives do not. Most conservatives *love* it, listening to it day and night. For conservatives who do not condemn pitched recitation of the Qur'an, it is hard to justify banning music based on some vague passages *and* making an exception of pitched recitation, at the same time.

How should we decide on this issue? As the principle of Islamic law is to work with explicit prohibition, and there is no explicit prohibition of music across the board, therefore the legal position that all music is prohibited is not strong.

Again, if we adopt the principle of uncertainty as explained in Section 3.2.1, then we need not formally prohibit music. Everyone should decide for himself on a case-by-case basis, whether a certain piece of music incites immoral behaviour, and therefore should not be listened to.

4.3.5 Homosexuality

In verses 7:80–84 in the Qur'an the story of Lot and his people is told. It is said that Lot said to his people, "you approach men with desire, instead of women, rather, you are a transgressing people."

Should homosexuals be punished on the basis of this passage? Note that in the stories it was Allah who punished Lot's people, not human beings who punished them. Therefore it is not the duty of Muslims to punish homosexuals. This is the minimum that we could agree about the text.

Now I would like to argue further. Again, we need to read with consideration of the age and context. Perhaps homosexuality threatened tribal existence. Therefore it was vehemently condemned. But I do not see why we have to worry about it in this age. Yes, in the developed world the birth rate is dropping. But can it be remedied by punishing people who have anal sex? I doubt it. Or can it be remedied by forcing homosexuals to marry a person of the opposite sex and have children? I do not think so. For the sake of fairness we need to force everybody to have children, heterosexuals and homosexuals alike. And heterosexuals are not raising the birth rate either.

Anyway there could be an historical context that we are not aware of, which leads to such condemnation of homosexuality. According to the principle of uncertainty as explained in Section 3.2.1, we are not really sure of the Qur'anic stance on homosexuality now, and therefore we should consider its legal status as a civil matter, not a religious one.

4.4 Attitudes of Faith

4.4.1 Fate

Let us think about one issue that surely has troubled many a soul. The problem of fate and freedom. Under this topic we shall touch on the problem of evil, Allah as a provider, and life as a test.

The Qur'an is full of passages that assert Allah's ultimate power and control of the world. Everything happens according to his will.

Even though this seems to be a compliment to Allah and a glorification of his elevated status, it has sometimes become an excuse for Muslims to be lazy and irresponsible. Many Muslims seem to think that since Allah ultimately controls everything, then if I am lazy, it is Allah's will. If I spend all my money, it is Allah's will. If I fail to keep promises, it is Allah's will. And so on and so forth. Nothing is my fault.

Societies are doomed to fail if people attribute failure to someone else without making an effort. If I fail, it is Allah's will. If I am poor, it is Allah's will. If I go back on my word, it is Allah's will. What about the other possibilities? If I succeed, it is also Allah's will. If I am rich, it is also Allah's will. If I keep promises, it is also Allah's will. However it turns out, it is Allah's will.

Indeed in many stories in the Qur'an it seems that the fate of people is predetermined, for example in verse 11:81

when the angels are telling Lot what to do, they tell him to travel during the night with his family and not to let any of his family members look back, except his wife, for what will strike the evil ones will strike her as well. In verses 15:59 and 27:57 it has been repeated that it has been decreed that Lot's wife is "among those who remain behind." In verses 29:32–33 it is said twice that she is of those who remain behind.

Do these descriptions mean that Allah wills that Lot's wife disobeys or that Allah already knows that she will disobey? Either way it seems futile to try to change the course of events.

But this is a Qur'anic story, so the degree of Allah's intervention may be different. Who can be sure if our everyday events are run under the same system? Such Qur'anic stories do not imply that our everyday events involve Allah's intervention to the same degree. Therefore there is not enough evidence that all events are determined or predictable to this degree.

There is a similar case in 33:36–38. If we only read on the level of words, it says that it is "not for a believing man or a believing women to have the choice about their affair when Allah and his messenger have decided it." But from the passage that comes after this declaration it is clear that this seemingly absolute rule is referring to the marriage between Muhammad and his adopted son's ex-wife. It is only talking in strong terms about this controversial marriage in order to stop any strife that might develop from it. We should not read from this that Allah and Muhammad decide everything for people to follow passively.

In verse 17:13 in the Qur'an it is said that Allah has "fastened everyone's fate upon his neck, and a record will be produced on the day of resurrection." In verse 28:68, it is also said that Allah "creates what he wills and chooses, the choice was not for them." But from reading the Qur'an carefully we should be aware that the seemingly universal quantification here should not be read as such, because it is aimed at the audience Muhammad was talking to, and in other passages of the Qur'an we can see that its message and injunctions are not intended for every human being in the universe. For discussions on the domain of applicability of the Qur'an, see Section 2.2.2 and Section 6.2. If everything is determined by Allah, retribution does not seem just at all. Therefore we are not sure whether everyone's fate really is fastened upon his neck beforehand.

In verse 28:70 it is said that the decision (maybe wide-ranging, or maybe referring to the one on judgment day only) belongs to Allah. In verse 30:5 it is said that Allah "helps whom he wills." In verse 29:21 it is said that Allah "punishes whom he wills and is merciful to whom he wills." This can be interpreted to mean that Allah is capricious and does whatever he decides to do, or that Allah rewards and punishes according to what a person has done in his life out of his own volition. This is corroborated in 29:23 in which it is said that those "who disbelieve in the signs of Allah and his meeting will not have his mercy, and there is a painful punishment for them." Thus we can see that fatalism is not the only possible interpretation.

What we should take away from this uncertainty is that one should not just adopt a passive attitude and let things happen by themselves. If one is not sure of determinism, one might as well live as if the world is not governed by it, for if everything is determined, this attitude does no harm, but if at least something is not determined, it makes all the difference.

4.4.1.1 Problem of Evil

In verses 113:1–5 one is told to say, "I seek refuge in the lord of daybreak, from the evil of that which he created, and from the evil of darkness when it spreads, and from the evil of the blowers in knots, and from the evil of an envier when he envies." Even without this passage, if everything is created by Allah, then crimes, pain, and evil are also surely his work. Can we reconcile this with his power and mercy? Does it mean that human beings are not responsible for crimes and evil?

Theological problems like this show us that we should

not rely on religious texts too much. They say one thing in a passage and then say something contradicting it in another one. The cause is that they are frequently trying to convey ideas removed from everyday experience, and so the actual meaning is not always clear and unequivocal. We should rely more on reason and rational discussion. It is dangerous to govern by religious texts.

4.4.1.2 Provision

The word "provision" is mentioned frequently in the Qur'an. The noun رزق *rizq* itself is used more than fifty times.

In verse 29:62 it is said that Allah "extends and restricts provision for whom he wills of his servants" and that he knows everything. That Allah extends and restricts provision for whom he wills is repeated in 2:245, 13:26, 17:30, 28:82, 30:37, 34:36, 34:39, 39:52, 42:12, and 42:27.

Allah is also frequently characterised as the one who provides (رزق *razaqa*), as in 2:3, 2:57, 2:172, 2:212, 2:254, 3:27, 3:37, 4:39, 5:88, 6:140, 6:142, 6:151, 7:160, 8:3, 8:26, 10:31, 10:93, 11:88, 13:22, 14:31, 16:56, 16:72, 16:114, 17:31, 17:70, 20:81, 20:132, 22:28, 22:34, 22:35, 24:38, 27:64, 28:54, 29:60, 30:28, 30:40, 32:16, 34:24, 35:3, 35:29, 36:47, 40:64, 42:19, 42:38, 45:16, 63:10, and 65:3. People are told to spend from what he provides to them.

In verses 22:58, 23:72, 34:39, and 62:11 it is said that Allah is the best of the providers (خير الرازقين *khair al-rāziqīn*).

In verses 65:2–3, it is said that for everyone who "fears

Chapter 4 Re-reading Islam

Allah, he makes for him a way out, and provides for him from where he does not expect, and whoever relies upon Allah, then he is sufficient for him. Indeed, Allah accomplishes his order. Allah has already set for everything an extent." It seems that we do not need to think about anything as long as we fear Allah.

With so many passages talking about Allah as a provider, we seem compelled to accept our lot and do nothing. All in all, these passages on provision seem to promote fatalistic non-action. And since we are told to spend from what he provides for us, we do not need to worry about saving for the future at all. If I am poor, it is his will because he restricts my provision. However, I can also say the opposite, that if I strive and succeed, it is again his will to extend my provision. Furthermore, it is said only that Allah is the best of the providers, it is not stated that Allah is the only provider. It is a fallacy to reason from the former to the latter. Thus people can also be providers and provide for themselves through their own effort.

As for the verses 65:2–3 cited above, I have taken them out of context as an example of the importance of holistic interpretation. The Sura is talking about divorce, which in Muhammad's time involved many worries about what the women would live on, so the revelation is trying to ease people's concern. It would be a mistake to read this broadly and think that one has earned the right to spend recklessly since one has pledged allegiance to Allah and he will provide for me.

It should be clear with reflection that his provision is second-order. One has to do something to trigger the provision. From all that we can observe, it does not come without doing anything. And textually we can find a reference to this reasoning. In verse 36:47 it is said that when people are told to "spend from that which Allah has provided for you," disbelievers asked the believers, "should we feed one whom if Allah wills, he would have fed?" From this conversation we can see that if we assume Allah would do and determine everything, then the inevitable conclusion is that he is evil in causing suffering and not making good things always happen. It makes much more sense to assume that he does not interfere and that we are the ones to work out everything ourselves with our intellect and abilities.

However, people may produce verse 39:49 and say, "look! here it is said that when harm touches a person, he called us, and when we bestowed a favour on him, he said that he was given it on the basis of knowledge, while in fact it is a trial but most of them do not know. So Allah wants us to believe that everything is done by him and our knowledge is useless." In verses 41:49–50 it is also said that man "is not weary of prayer for the good and if evil touches him, he loses hope and despairs, and if we make him taste mercy from us after harm has touched him, he would definitely say this is due to me and I do not think the hour is going to stand, and if I were returned to my lord, indeed there will be for me the best with him. But we will definitely tell those who disbelieved about what they did we will make them taste an enormous punishment." From such verses it seems that attributing anything to oneself is wrong and would bring divine punishment.

But we do not have to read these verses in this way. We should not extend a negative comment on thanklessness into a full-fledged call for irresponsibility and passivity, or use it as an excuse for laziness. Maybe knowledge itself is the favour, and Allah granted him the chance to attain knowledge and thus he solved his problem. It is probably the case that we still have to do our best, do everything in our capacity, to save ourselves. Perhaps Allah has a hand in it, but we do not know for sure, and it is stupidity to sit there and wait for Allah's favour. Even if he interferes and helps, he probably helps people who have striven and exerted themselves with endurance and perseverance.

In verse 42:20, it is said that who "desires the harvest of the hereafter, we increase his harvest, and who desires the harvest of this world, we give him of it but there is no share in the hereafter for him." But it does not mean that as long as we desire the harvest of the hereafter, we do not need to work, for here the word used is "increase,"

Chapter 4 Re-reading Islam

so if you do not have any harvest to begin with, how can it be increased? Therefore when we read this we need to be careful and not assume that once we are believers, we do not need to work hard for our own sake, and God will take care of everything. This attitude is very harmful for the development of the community, for no one is dedicated to his work, and trade and services would be very inefficient. We should remember that even miracles occur only when the people involved have done all they could, for example Hagar ran around searching for water, when she and her son Ishmael were nearly dying of thirst. Even divine intervention needs mortal exertion, let alone in a normal situation.

In verse 36:82 it is said that if Allah wills anything, he only needs to say "be!" and it is. In verse 40:68 it is also said that when he decrees a matter, he only needs to say "be!" and it is. Do these verses mean that everything in the world happens by his will? Strictly speaking it does not imply that, because when he does not have any will regarding something, then probably that thing develops by itself, without his will and intervention. It only implies that he has the power to effect any change but it does not mean that he uses it. Therefore we should not think that Allah will be active in the affairs of this world. We should rely on ourselves. It is stupid and a waste of time to say that something happened because Allah wanted to punish someone. We have no way to know that. The reasonable way to live is to assume no divine intervention and work as best we can. Maybe a person whom someone thinks of as an infidel actually was the best person in the eyes of Allah. To look at others and judge if they are going to hell or not is a petty thing to do. If Allah wanted someone punished, he would do it. If not, shouldn't we mind our own business?

Rationally speaking, even if Allah wills everything that happens, no one can know Allah's will except by what has already occurred. Therefore, it is better that one leaves such talk to the afterlife. It is not fruitful at all to attribute any event to Allah's will, especially when it is not finalised yet. It takes away one's own will power. It may be good for one's feelings after something has happened, especially something tragic. But it diminishes one's initiative before the result is determined. It often becomes a shallow show of piety and an excuse for not trying hard, because one can always say it is Allah's will, even for cases in which, if we look at it in a secular way, we would surely say the person is to blame. Saying it is Allah's will is easy on oneself and one can at the same time appear pious. What a good bargain.

In philosophy, there is a great deal of doubt about the existence of free will, but people seldom adopt this attitude in talking about moral responsibility. It is interesting to contrast how Allah's will is implicitly used by some Muslims to evade human responsibility.

4.4.1.3 Test

In this regard, many Muslims ignore the fact that the Qur'an is full of passages saying that what happens in this world is a test. The verb بلا *balā*, meaning "to test," occurs about twenty times in the Qur'an, and each time it is about Allah testing people.

In verse 2:155 it is said that we will "test you with something from fear and hunger and lack of wealth and souls and fruits." In verse 5:48 it is said that if Allah "had willed, he would have made you one nation, but in order to test you in what he has given you" he had not, "so compete in doing good." In verse 5:94 it is said that Allah will "test you with something of what you hunt with your hands and spears so that he may know who fears him with the unseen." In verse 7:168 it is said that Allah "divided them into nations on earth. There were among them the righteous ones, and others," and he "tested them with good things and bad things so perhaps they would return." In verse 16:92 one is told not to be like the female "who untwisted her yarn into untwisted strands after it was strong, taking your oaths as deception between you because one community is more plentiful than another one. Allah is only testing you with it." In verse 18:7 it is said that Allah has "made what is on earth adornment for it so that we may test them" as to which of them is "best in action." In verse 67:2 something similar is said. It is said that he "who created death and life to test you" as to which of you is "best in action and he is the strong, the forgiving." In verse 21:35 it is said that Allah "tests you with evil and good as a trial and to us you will be returned." In verse 47:31 it is said that Allah will "test you until he knows the striving ones among you and the patient ones," and he will "test your affairs." In verse 68:17 it is said that Allah tried the former peoples "as he tried the companions of the garden, when they swore that they would cut its fruit in the morning."

Other forms of the root are also used in emphasising that Allah tests people. In verse 3:186 and 8:17 the form IV verb أبلى *ablā*, meaning "to test," is used. In verse 3:186 it is said, "you will surely be tested in your possessions and in yourselves." In verses 3:152, 3:154, 4:6, 33:11, 76:2, 89:15–16 the form VIII verb ابتلى *ibtalā*, meaning "to test" or "to try," is used in saying that Allah tests people. In verse 76:2 it is said, "indeed, we created man from a sperm-drop mixture that we may try him."

From all these verses above we can see that what we do with what we have with us is a test for us to work out the next stage. It is not just a result to be accepted and be done with. This is not just for the sake of Allah. It is also for us to know our souls, our will, and our inner strengh. What we need to do is to work hard (and this is truly *jihād* as one has to fight against one's strong tendency to be lazy), and not passively accept everything as determined by God. We should put the responsibility on ourselves, rather than Allah.

In verse 30:37, it is again said that Allah "extends and restricts provision for whom he wills." But the interesting point comes next, in 30:38, when the verse goes on to command people to "give relatives their rights, and the needy and the people on the road," and to say that this is "best for those who desire the face of Allah, and these are the successful ones." From this passage we can see that the talk about Allah's control of provision is meant to emphasise that giving to relatives and people in need probably would not harm one's material life and is definitely good for one's moral account. It is not saying that everything is Allah's doing. If so, Allah could directly will people to be charitable, and there is no need to convince them.

Another passage in the Qur'an points in the same direction. In verse 13:11, it is said that Allah "does not change the condition of a people until they change what is in themselves." According to this passage, human beings are the ones who should take the initiative. As the proverb says, "God helps those who help themselves." When you really make the effort, God helps you. But if you do not, things will not happen by themselves. This drive to work for what one hopes for is something that many Muslims lack. They just sit there and call upon Allah. Some may think that prayer is enough, but if we were to use the same zeal for work, probably more would be achieved, for action is as much a manifestation of will as prayer, or more.

To purify and strengthen one's will is important, but after that, or at the same time, one can work and put the

Chapter 4 Re-reading Islam

will into actual action, and change the world for the better. This is a point of tension between esoteric and exoteric teaching, for sometimes it seems that esoteric teaching tells you that the material world is not important, what matters is the inner world. But the inner world and the material world interact and influence each other. If you have good will in your inner world, you can do good things with it, for example help reduce suffering in the material world. On the other hand, if there are bad things in the material world, maybe they would prompt your will to change the world for the better, and you would actually *do* something to change the situation.

From these discussions we should see that cultivating the inner world is not necessarily in conflict with becoming involved in the material world. On the contrary, it is the manifestation and test of one's inner world and strength of will. If you have a pure mind and a strong will, you will act and change the world for the better, and maybe Allah would help you in the process. This is the scenario described by verse 13:11 of the Qur'an, saying that Allah does not change the condition of a people until they change what is in themselves. But if you have a confused mind and a weak will, and you do nothing, probably Allah would not do anything to help you. And if you have a pure mind but do nothing, Allah probably would not help you either. If you have a confused mind but you are active, maybe you will have some effect in the world, but it could be worse than if you did not try to do anything.

Therefore we can see that it is important to work on one's inner world and will power and also make changes in the material world. The world is a test and Allah helps those who change themselves and take the initiative.

People are frequently told to strive in the Qur'an. For example, in 49:15 it is said, "the believers are only the ones who have believed in Allah and his messenger and then doubt not but strive with their properties and theirselves in the way of Allah. Those are the truthful ones." If what people do is not important, then people do not need to strive. They can just sit there and wait for miracles to happen.

Some passages in the Qur'an such as 4:79 seem to point to another system of attribution. It says that good things "come to you from Allah, but bad things come from yourself." On a first look, there is no problem in such passages. But if we reflect on this issue, doubts arise. For example, this does not sit well with babies suffering painful illnesses, unless the parents are the ones punished, or this is bad karma from past lives. A more reasonable interpretation is that this passage is specific to the context of battles which the surrounding passages refer to. It means to say that if one behaves like a coward then bad things would happen to him and if one fights bravely then he either enters heaven or receives worldly rewards. Therefore such passages should not be generalised.

The above example highlights the importance of context and reference; without deliberating over these one would reach hasty, problematic, and even dangerous interpretations.

Just a cursory view of philosophical discussions on free will and determinism enables one to see that determinism makes ethical judgment questionable. In contemporary Western philosophical discussions, determinism comes from classical physics. In Islam, some passages seem to assert determinism by Allah. Whatever the brand of determinism, the same questions regarding ethical responsibility arise. If one is determined by external force to do something, it seems unjust to lay the praise or blame on the forced party.

In verses 11:47–48 in the Qur'an it is said that some "nations receive blessings from Allah, while some nations are granted enjoyment and then painful punishment." This is given as news of the unseen. Indeed it is mysterious, for how does Allah determine which nations to give blessings to and which nations to give punishment to? Is it out of the prior desires of the nations or out of the whims of Allah?

In verses 26:192–195 it is said that the Qur'an is the "revelation of the lord of the two worlds, brought by the

Chapter 4 Re-reading Islam

trustworthy spirit, so that Muhammad can be one of the bearers of warning, in a clear Arabic language." Then in 26:198–200 it is said that even if Allah "revealed it to some of the foreigners, they would not have been believers, in this way he inserted this disbelief into the hearts of the criminals." So Allah had decided beforehand that non-Arabs would not believe? And on judgment day they are going to be punished for this disbelief which Allah inserted into their hearts? What is the point and where is justice and fairness?

Is it fair that Allah simply decides to bless some people and punish some people? Where is justice, which I believe is universally understood as people doing good deeds receiving rewards and people doing bad deeds receiving punishment? If we put the decision of doing good and bad on Allah, then it does not seem fair to punish anyone because of their actions, since their actions are not what they choose to do.

In verse 18:101 it is said that the infidels' "eyes were covered from" the remembrance of Allah. It is not said that the cover is placed by Allah, but in 50:22–25 it is said that on judgment day the infidels would be told, "you were certainly heedless of this, and we have removed from you your cover, so your sight today is sharp" and "every obstinate infidel, preventer of good, aggressor, doubter" would be thrown into hell. So Allah is capable of removing this cover. Then why does he not remove it earlier? Because we need to be tested. Fair enough. It is alright to be tested. But is it necessary to send the people who have failed the test to hell? It seems too harsh. How can this fit with the claim that Allah is compassionate and merciful?

Especially problematic is the way some Muslims seem to enjoy seeing others punished, citing it as the will of Allah. But if people are punished without doing bad things out of their own volition, how can we be sure that we will not be the next to suffer from this whim for no bad intentions or evil deeds of our own? Do we really feel secure by becoming a Muslim and thus obtaining the favour of Allah? But maybe the next minute he will decide that we are going to do bad deeds and then he will punish us for it. Do you think this would be just?

We should remember this when we say everything is Allah's will. If we also give ethical praise and blame to human beings, then there may be inconsistencies. The reason is that if everything is Allah's will, then every ethical praise and blame should also be given to Allah, not to the puppets, i.e. we human beings, that he controls.

If we go on, this section could turn into never-ending arcane discussions about free will and divine predestination. But what has been said should have given us a taste of the potential problems of attributing everything to Allah's will and attributing ethical praise and blame to others. Before we leave this topic let me briefly state my recommendations:

1. We should take care of and be responsible for our own affairs in this world. We should pray only when we have done everything possible. We should not easily think that praying is everything possible.

2. We should not think of others' fate as favour or punishment. This is because the reward system in the Qur'an is by Allah's will alone and there is no satisfactory rationalisation. Whatever happens is Allah's will, and whatever does not happen Allah wills it not to happen. Therefore the relationship between human choice or agency and subsequent events is not established. It does not fit with reasonable standards of justice.

One may try to make a defence and say that whatever Allah says must be right, but the truth is that you do not understand it either, and on close examination, one inevitably finds it unreasonable. In this difficult situation one had better stay silent about Allah's punishment and rewards, as Wittgenstein recommends,

> Whereof one cannot speak, thereof one must be silent. [43, §7]

4.4.2 Tolerance and Ease

In verse 22:78 in the Qur'an, one is told to "strive for Allah with the striving due to him." It is said that he has chosen you and that he has not placed upon you any difficulty in the religion. One is told to perform prayer, give alms, and hold fast to Allah. In this passage we can see that the key points of Islam are just praying and alms-giving. It is stressed that Allah does not make it difficult for a Muslim to follow Islam. In verse 23:62 it is said that Allah "does not charge any soul except within its capacity." We should remember that any overly strict and unrealistic rules are against the conception of Islam. Such rules are probably established for the benefits of the priests or the powerful.

In verse 35:32 it is said that Allah "made those he chose from his servants inherit the book, and among them is one who wrongs himself, one who is moderate, and one who is foremost in good deeds by the permission of Allah." From this passage we can see that the admired qualities in Islam are to care about others more than oneself, to be moderate, and to be eager in doing good. All of this points towards an easy-going personality that is moderate, not one who is harsh and difficult.

Similarly, in many Hadiths we can see that Islam is a religion that stresses non-extremity and ease for its adherents. These include [3, 2:38] and [3, 2:41], the latter recording Muhammad's distaste for a woman who prays excessively. Moderation is an extremely important virtue in Islam. This can actually explain many passages in which the practices of the day were approved or only small improvement was suggested—regarding the rights of women for example, not because they were what Allah likes, but because drastic change was not practical.

In the Hadiths [3, 3:83 and 3:84], when people came to Muhammad asking about anything in the ceremonies of the pilgrimage that they did in the wrong order, Muhammad told them to do it and that there is no harm in it. We could see from such passages it is a good thing to follow the rituals, but if we commit any mistake, there is no need to worry. In verse 22:32 in the Qur'an, it is said that whoever "honours the symbols of Allah is from the piety of hearts." The rites are just symbols, but the important thing is the piety of hearts that is shown through such rites.

In verses 23:51–54 in the Qur'an it is said that your nation is "one nation and Allah is the lord of this nation, but people divided it into sects. So leave them in their confusion for a time." In this passage we can see that factional disputes are man-made and should not touch the core of Islam. Details of rituals and antiquated rules of social interaction become points of contention and division but if we look at the non-attachment Muhammad shows in answering questions about ceremonies of the pilgrimage, it should be clear to us that people are caught up in unimportant things but forget about the truly important ones such as faith and charity.

In a Hadith, Allah is recorded to have said that people with just the weight of a mustard seed of faith would be taken out of hell. [3, 2:21] A seed of faith is probably not a requirement that is difficult to fulfil, anyone who believes in a higher deity should be able to qualify. Similarly, in 27:89–90 in the Qur'an it is said that people are rewarded on judgment day according to what they do; if they do good things, their reward would be good, and vice versa. In verse 28:84 it is said that who "comes with a good deed will have something better than it, and who comes with a bad deed would be repaid likewise." In verse 30:44 it is said that whoever "acts righteously, they are preparing for themselves." Allah is recorded in a Hadith to have said that people with just the weight of a barley grain, a wheat grain, or an atom of good would be taken out of hell. [3, 2:42]

Similarly, in 9:120, 11:115, 12:56, 12:90 etc. in the Qur'an it is said that Allah does not let the reward of the ones doing good go to waste. If people doing good suffer forever in hell for their disbelief, surely their reward has gone to waste. So we can be confident that these people are not going to be in hell forever, if at all.

From these passages we can see that it is possible to

Chapter 4 Re-reading Islam

construe Islam as a religion in which good people will go to heaven and bad people will go to hell, and not one in which Muslims will go to heaven and non-Muslims will go to hell. We discussed this in detail in Section 4.1.2.

However, verse 33:19 seems to say something different. It says that when fear "came to the hypocrites, you saw them looking at you, their eyes turning like one dying, but when fear went away, they smote you with sharp tongues, these did not believe so Allah made their deeds worthless." But here it is their terrible and harmful behaviour that discounts their good actions, not belief or disbelief per se. It is not appropriate to interpret this as saying that people who do not believe automatically get their good actions wiped from the record.

In verse 4:31 in the Qur'an it is said that if you "avoid great sins your bad actions would be removed and you will enter paradise." And in 11:114 after telling people to "pray at the two ends of the day and at the approach of the night" it says that good acts remove bad ones. If good acts can remove bad acts, promised punishment might not obtain if good acts have been done. So perhaps for at least some of the people who are said to be going to hell, their good acts have removed their bad acts and they are not going to hell.

In verses 53:31–32 it is said, "to Allah belongs whatever is in the heavens and whatever is on earth so that he may recompense those who do evil with what they have done and recompense those who do good with the best. Those who avoid the major sins and immoralities except small ones, indeed your lord is vast in forgiveness. He was most knowing of you when he produced you from the earth and when you were fetuses in the wombs of your mothers." In verse 42:37 it is said, "those who avoid the major sins and immoralities, and when they are angry, they forgive," they will not be blamed. From these passages we can see that Allah is in a very high position and he is forgiving. Therefore he does not care about small faults. He only rewards people according to their significant deeds.

Such verses could be reasonably interpreted to mean

that if someone avoids great sins or does good acts then he should have no problem entering heaven. One should remember this especially regarding fellow Muslims. If according to the Qur'an they are going to heaven, who are we to despise them for not fasting, for drinking alcohol, etc.?

Reviewing Qur'anic passages and Hadiths similar to the ones above should remind us that Allah is merciful and not petty about small details connected with a particular age and a particular form of society.

In verse 27:40 in the Qur'an it is said that Solomon said, "Whoever is grateful, he is grateful for his soul (or himself). Whoever is ungrateful, then Allah is self-sufficient and generous." In verse 31:12 Luqman also received this piece of wisdom. In verse 27:92 it is said that whoever "accepts guidance he accepts for his soul." In verse 29:6 it is said that who "strives (جاهد *jāhada*, the verb for *jihād*), only strives for his soul, for Allah is free from need of the worlds." In verse 45:15 it is said that who "did a righteous deed, then it is for his soul, and who does evil, then it is against it. Then to your lord you will be returned." This line of thinking should be more important and generally applicable than the verses urging for war and violence and threatening with hell and punishment. Because they were given in the context of ongoing war and persecution under the need to unify and strengthen a small group of Muslims facing severe challenges. When reading the Qur'an, we are the ones deciding how to read it and what to learn from it, using our God-given faculty of reasoning and capacity for compassion.

Chapter 4 Re-reading Islam

On the other hand, in verses 11:15–16 in the Qur'an, it is said that a person "who desires the life of the world will have nothing but fire in the hereafter." This seems to mean that Muslims should not care about this world at all, and should only be concerned about religious deeds and the afterlife. But this interpretation ignores the emphasis of Islam on charity (c.f. Section 4.2.3) and how to behave in everyday life. So the reasonable interpretation is that it refers to people who desire the life of this world *to the detriment of piety and justice*. Those people will be punished by hellfire. This is the reading that makes sense, in view of the overall message of Islam. But one can see how such seeming nonchalance about this world in occasional passages has been used as an excuse not to work for advancement of society and used for violent propaganda and brainwashing people to be terrorists.

In verse 18:87 in the Qur'an it is said that a person "who is unjust will be punished, then he will be returned to Allah, and he will punish him with a terrible punishment." No mention of hell is made here and the unjust person is returned to Allah for punishment. In verse 29:57 it is said that every soul "taste death. Then to [Allah] you will be returned." From such passages we should be able to see that we cannot be sure that bad people are always sent to hellfire, it is just a turn of phrase used in the Qur'an. Perhaps it is not something that is really practised. We should not be too confident about the claim that non-Muslims would be sent to hell. Spiritual descriptions cannot be taken literally, as I argued in subsubsection 3.2.2.3.

In verse 13:27 in the Qur'an, it is said that Allah "leads astray whom he wills and guides to himself those who turn back to him." From this verse we can see that if people turn back to Allah, then they will be guided, so even if people do not follow Allah and are wrong in our opinion, maybe in future they will turn back and be guided to Allah. So if we say or do anything bad to them it would only decrease their chances of becoming a Muslim, right? What we should do is be a good, hard-working, and knowledgeable person, then people will think that Islam is good. If one were none of that, then he would be a person who turns people away from Islam, because they see that Islam does not make people good, or even that it makes people lazy and ignorant.

There are truly such tendencies in some Muslim communities. Some Muslims think that they do not need to do anything and Allah will determine and do everything for them, so they become lazy. Some Muslims think that they only need to know Islam and any other knowledge and skills are not important, and the education of women is neglected or even prohibited. And the result is that the education levels of such Muslims are low in comparison with other communities.

Muslims should remember that Allah cannot be harmed by people (Qur'an 9:39). In verse 14:8 it is also said that even "if all the people on earth disbelieve, Allah is free of need." In verse 35:15 it is said that people are the "ones in need of Allah and Allah is free of need and praiseworthy." In verses 22:64–65 in the Qur'an it is said that what is in the heavens and what is on the earth belongs to Allah, that Allah is the one who is free of need, and worthy of praise, and then afterwards it is said that Allah is kind and merciful. The pronouncement that Allah is free of need is repeated frequently in other verses too, for example in 2:263, 2:267, 3:97, 4:131, 6:133, 10:68, 27:40, 29:6, 31:12, 31:26, 39:7, 47:38, 57:24, 60:6, and 64:6. Therefore we should be able to see that any interference in other people's lives to please God is probably selfish in intention rather than to "protect" or enrich Allah, which is neither necessary nor possible. To be a good Muslim, one should concentrate on doing what is required of oneself. Let others worry about their own business. One should help others but should not force them to conform to our ideas of what Muslims should or should not do. The world would be much more peaceful and people would make much more progress if people would become strict about themselves instead of others.

Reading Islamic texts and reflecting on the nature of re-

Chapter 4 Re-reading Islam

ligions and institutions, one would probably conclude that what is important is faith and charity. To be concerned with historical details is in the interest of religious professionals, not in the interest of believers. For example, the more people worry about the lawfulness of their food, the more people would be employed to cater to this issue.

In general, the fussier people are about details in religious practice, the more people would be employed in this field and the more power they would get. If people worry about spiritual cultivation rather than small details, then more spiritual teachers would be supported rather than literalist scholars.

Which state of affairs is more desirable?

To worry about small details in religious practice rather than actually helping people is an unwise way to act in religion, because we do not have complete contextual details of the revelations, and we could easily be getting things wrong, obeying the form rather than the intention. In verse 17:85 in the Qur'an, it is said that the soul is Allah's affair, and mankind has only been given a little knowledge. We should do things about which we have more knowledge, such as ethical and altruistic acts in everyday life. These can be the same acts that are morally desirable for non-Muslims, but such acts are surely good in the eyes of Allah. This is a safer route than fastidious adherence to rules gleaned from the Islamic texts.

We should choose our own beliefs one by one. We should not accept everything people say Islam contains because we see some great things in Islam. People smuggle things that are good for their power or interests into Islam.

For example in 56:77–79 it is said, "indeed it is a noble Qur'an, in a well-guarded book, none except the purified touch it." Some Muslims would read this literally and narrowly and say that non-Muslims should not touch a copy of the Qur'an, and it is sacrilegious to do so. This is a bad interpretation. We should see that it is said in a symbolic sense, and could even be taken to mean that only the purified reach the level of teaching given in the Qur'an.

It is a classic example of bad religious interpretation. It is narrow and self-important, thinking that people not in one's religion are inferior and even dirty. It is opposite to the best teachings of Islam.

I hope this section has convinced you that tolerance and ease are what Islam really intends to promote, and that we should actively choose, follow, and disseminate such teachings.

4.5 Status of Non-Muslims

In the preceding sections we dealt with a Muslim's personal behaviour. Now let us move on to Islam's recommended treatment of non-believers.

I advocate the principle of postponement,[5] but when discussing issues about what the Qur'an and the Hadiths say about how Muslims should behave towards non-believers, we need to remember the discussion in Section 4.1.2 as to how to determine whether one is a Muslim or not and consider ideas other than conventional views. For we need to contemplate and review the concept of infidels first, before we can adequately discuss what to do with them.

The categorisation in Muhammad's time was simple, because it was a period of war, and non-Muslims did not let Muslims practise their faith. For example, in 22:71–72, it is said that the ones "who worship someone other than Allah, they nearly attack those who recite Allah's verses." It was either friend or foe.

But in modern pluralistic societies, the categorisation is not so simple. To make a reasonable judgment, should it be based on having said that creed or not, or all of one's actions in life should be weighed and considered? People are not supposed to attack followers of another faith just for the reason that their conception of religion is different.

In this plethora of faiths, people born to Muslim parents may not do the five prayers, and they still consider

---

[5]It will be discussed in detail in Section 6.3.1.

Chapter 4 Re-reading Islam

themselves Muslims. And this is not a wrong categorisation. A religion admits of a spectrum of practitioners. And people who do not consider themselves Muslims may be considered by Allah to be Muslims because they are very charitable. Who knows for sure? So no one, however devout he considers himself to be, should presume himself to be authoritative enough to judge who is a Muslim or not. Maybe in the end you are the hypocrite, you are the infidel.

We should adopt a moral construal of Islam argued for in Section 4.1.2 rather than a simple confessional or demographic view.

4.5.1 Will

There is another serious problem apart from demarcation.

In Section 4.4.1, I talked about the issue of fate. Allah is supposed to determine everything. In verse 25:2, it is said that Allah has "created each thing and determined how it is." If it means that every action of a human being has been determined beforehand, then we do not make our own decisions.

Now let us apply this attribution. If someone becomes a Muslim, then it is Allah's will. This is mentioned explicitly in the Qur'an. For one example out of many similar passages we may look at verse 2:213. It says that Allah "guides who he wills." And if someone refuses to become a Muslim or even hates and defames Islam unjustly, it is also Allah's will. Since this action has been determined by Allah, can we blame this person? Allah made him so. Is it his fault?

Another clear example can be found in 10:99-100. Here it is said that if "Allah had willed, everyone on earth would have believed and anyone believing is by the permission of him." And then it is said that there is no need to force people to believe in Allah. So people's belief of Islam or lack thereof is determined by Allah.

In verses 16:106-109 it is said that disbelievers "who prefer the life of this world are the ones over whose hearts, hearing, and sight Allah has set a seal (طبع *ṭabaʿa*)." And then it is said that they are the "losers in the hereafter." This word is used in the same sense in 4:155, 7:100–101, 9:87, 9:93, 10:74, 30:59, 40:35, 47:16, and 63:3. There is a particularly strong contrast in 47:16–17 in which it is said that there are people who listen to Muhammad until they depart from him, and they say to those who were given knowledge, "What did he say just now?" It is then said, "those are the ones over whose hearts Allah set a seal and who have followed their desires. And those who are guided, he increases them in guidance and gives them their righteousness." Why does Allah not increase his guidance for people who gave up their faith? Why does he set a seal over their hearts?

Allah is also said to set a seal (this time using another word ختم *khatama*) on people's hearing and hearts in 2:7, 6:46, 42:24, and 45:23. Of these, in 2:7 and 45:23 it is then said that there is a veil (غشاوة *ghishāwa*) over their vision. In verses 47:22–23 one reads, "So would you perhaps, if you turned away, cause corruption on earth and sever your kinship? Those are the ones who Allah cursed, so he deafened them and blinded their vision." This passage seems to say that some people are cursed by Allah, so they turn away from him and cause corruption on earth. If that is the case, why does Allah choose this fate for them?

If such passages are true, then it seems that Allah is the one who has decided whether a person disbelieves or not. Then why should these people be punished for disbelief if they did not choose to disbelieve? Furthermore, the punishment would come from the one who made them dis-

Chapter 4 Re-reading Islam

believe. This whole system is cruel and ridiculous. People are made to behave badly and then to suffer for behaving badly. This is like an elaborate and mischievous game set up by a tyrannical and evil king.

In verses 43:36–37 it is said that he "who is blinded from the remembrance of the most merciful, we appoint for him a devil, then he is to him a companion." It is very hard to understand why for people who are blinded from the remembrance of Allah, help is not given, but rather a companion who would lead them further astray. It makes one question Allah's mercifulness.

In verse 6:39 it is said that Allah "wills who is to go astray and who is to go on the straight path." In verse 35:8 it is said that Allah "wills whom to go astray and wills whom to guide." Similarly, in 39:23 it is said that this book is the "guidance of Allah by which he guides whom he will and there is no guide for whom Allah leads astray." Why is not everyone willed by Allah to go on the straight path? Is it because Allah also makes crooked paths to divert the traffic? Is it because he does not like everyone to be good and to believe in him?

In verse 18:17, it is said that whoever "Allah guides then he is the guided one, and whoever he leads astray then he has no protector or guide." In verses 39:36 and 40:33 it is said that whoever "Allah misleads, there is no guide for him," and in 39:37 it is said that whoever "Allah guides, there is no misleader for him." In verses 40:69–74 it is said that those who "dispute the signs of Allah" will "be dragged in boiling water," and that Allah "leads the disbelievers astray in this way." In verse 42:46 it is said that whoever "Allah leads astray, there is no way for him."

The causative verb أضل *aḍall*, meaning "to mislead" or "to let go astray," appears in the Qur'an 64 times and frequently it is Allah who misleads people. In verses 14:4, 16:93, 35:8, and 74:31 it is said, "Allah leads astray whom he wills and guides whom he wills." We may try to interpret this very non-literally and say that such verses refer to people who have chosen of their own will to be guided or to go astray, and they get their rewards accordingly, or we may prefer a verse like 13:27 which says, "indeed, Allah leads astray whom he wills and guides to himself whoever turns back," and maintain that Allah misleads and tests people, but they choose to believe or not. However, this would conflict with the view that Allah's will determines everything, and some Muslims might see this as an undesirable limitation of Allah.

In verse 18:28, people are told "not to obey the one whose heart Allah has made heedless about remembering Allah." If it is Allah who made a person's heart heedless, how can he be worthy of blame? It is Allah's decision, not his.

In verse 18:29, it is said that he "wills whoever to believe and whoever to disbelieve." Is Allah playing a game with human beings? Assigning a good role to some, and a bad role to some? But then why are they punished for being assigned to be bad?

In verse 49:7 it is said that Allah "has endeared to you the faith and has made it pleasing in your hearts and has made hateful to you disbelief, defiance, and disobedience. Those are the guided ones." Does it mean that Allah decides who is a believer? Why does Allah not endear Islam to disbelievers too?

In verse 58:11 it is said, "O you who have believed, when you are told, 'space yourselves' in assemblies, then make space. Allah makes space for you. And when you are told, 'arise,' then arise. Allah will raise those who have believed among you and those who were given knowledge, by degrees, and Allah is informed of what you do." If knowledge is given by Allah, and people who are given knowledge will be raised by Allah, what is the point of raising some people and not others? They were chosen by Allah anyway.

In various verses in the Qur'an, Allah says that he worsens people's shortcomings or bad deeds and will give them a severe punishment. For example, in 2:10 it says that there is an "illness in their hearts so Allah increased their illness and there will be a painful punishment for them." If Allah is all-powerful and most merciful, why would he do that instead of decreasing their illness so that they do not go astray and do not get punished? It seems as if Allah enjoys torturing people for its own sake.

Another example is 6:25, in which it is said that among the polytheists there are "people who listen to Muhammad but Allah placed coverings (أكنّة *akinna*) on their hearts and deafness in their ears so that they will not understand." Why does Allah not let them listen and understand and believe and go to heaven? Is it because heaven would be too crowded?

Yet another example is in 36:1–11, in which it is said that Muhammad is sent to "warn a people whose fathers have not been warned, that the word already came true on most of them so they do not believe," that we "put iron collars on the necks up to their chins, so their heads are raised up," that we "put before them a barrier and behind them a barrier, so we covered them and they do not see," that it is the "same whether you warned them or not, they will not believe," that you "can only warn one who follows the reminder and fears Allah in the unseen." So can people choose to believe or not? Why does Allah prevent people from believing rather than help them believe?

In verse 18:57, it is said that no one is more unjust than one "who has been reminded of the signs of Allah but turns away from them and forgets what his hands have put forth." It is then said that Allah has placed over their hearts coverings (أَكِنَّة *akinna*) and in their ears deafness, so that they do not understand. And then it is said that even "if you call them towards guidance, they will never be guided." Why does Allah prevent people from understanding his signs even if they initially rejected these signs? Does this not conflict with the claim that Allah is all merciful and compassionate?

In verses 27:4–5 it is said that Allah "made the deeds of those who do not believe in the hereafter look pleasing to them so that they wander blindly," and that in the hereafter "they will have the worst punishment and they are the greatest losers." Why does Allah not make the deeds of those who do not believe in the hereafter look displeasing to them, so that they would repent? Is it because Allah loves to punish so he does not want them to repent?

Again in 6:35, Allah says that if he "willed then he would have gathered them on the guided way." In verse 32:13, it is even said that if Allah had "willed then he could have given each soul its guidance, but his word is true and he will fill hell with jinn and people together." Why does Allah abandon them and not guide them? Why does Allah aim to fill hell with people? O Allah, are you not all-merciful?

And then in 6:107 it is said that if Allah "had willed, the polytheists would not have associated others with Allah." What does Allah want really? He wants people to worship other deities, and then punish them? So what he wants is to punish people? Is he too bored?

In verse 6:110 it is said that Allah "turns away the hearts and the eyes of the polytheists and leaves them wandering blindly in their transgression, because they had not believed the first time." Why does Allah refuse to give them a second chance? Why does he prevent them from believing? Because he likes to punish people so does not like them to repent because then he has to forgive them?

In verses 17:45–47 it is said that when you recite the Qur'an, "a concealed partition would be placed between you and the non-believers." And then it is said that cov-

Chapter 4 Re-reading Islam

erings (أكنة *akinna*) have been "placed over their hearts and deafness in their ears, so that they do not understand." And when you just mention Allah in the Qur'an, they "turn their back in aversion." This is a terrible passage if read literally, and for us the only reasonable way to read it is to assume that it is to protect believers from unjust arguments by non-believers. But this still casts doubt on the fairness of punishing non-believers if they have been prevented by Allah from understanding the Qur'an. One could argue that Allah knows that they will not believe anyway, but Allah is not the one causing them to disbelieve. However, this conflicts with the claim that everything is by the will of Allah, on the one hand, and even if we were to give up this claim, if Allah really knows it beforehand, then it seems that the non-believers were not free to choose anyway. It has been determined by an unbreakable chain of causation and Allah by his infinite intellect predicts that they will not believe. If they were not free to choose in this world view, then again we need to ask ourselves, would it be fair to punish them?

In verses 6:112 and 25:31 it is even said that for each prophet Allah makes an enemy. So why does Allah makes them enemies of prophets and then punish them? Is Allah a recalcitrant and violent child controlling and watching with enjoyment the misery in the world, and then punishing the unfortunately and unwillingly wrong side?

A whole group of people could be predetermined by Allah to be disbelievers. In verses 26:192–195 it is said that the Qur'an is the "revelation of the lord of the two worlds, brought by the trustworthy spirit, so that Muhammad can be one of the bearers of warning, in a clear Arabic language." Then in 26:198–200 it is said that even if Allah "revealed it to some of the foreigners, they would not have been believers, in this way he inserted this disbelief into the hearts of the criminals." Even if the "foreigners" mentioned only referred to a small group of people and not all non-Arabs that exist, it is still terrible that some people are designated to be non-believers and receive terrible punishment.

In verses 28:41–42 when telling the story of Moses and Pharaoh, it is said that Allah made the "Pharaoh and his soldiers leaders inviting people to the fire, and on the day of resurrection they will not be helped," and that Allah "made a curse follow them, and on the day of resurrection they will be of the despised." Were Pharaoh and his people disbelieving Allah out of their own volition? Probably not. So why should they be punished? It is not just.

In verse 25:20 it is said that Allah has made "some people as trials for others." In verse 6:123 it is said that Allah has "placed within every city its greatest criminals to plot in it, but they did not plot except against themselves, and they do not feel it." It seems that some people have been designated to play villains. I think it is alright to give roles to people, but it is not alright to give roles and then punish them for playing that role. But in conjunction with other passages this seems to be how it works. This is unjust and unfair.

Are such verses not problematic?

Some say such evils come from the devil. But the devil is also made by Allah, and any tricks that the devil performs Allah can neutralise, just like when Moses threw his staff and it swallowed all the magician's tricks, as narrated in 7:116 in the Qur'an.

In various passages, Satan is said to mislead people with Allah's approval. In verses 34:20–21, it is said that the infidels followed Satan, that he "had no authority over them except for us to know who believes in the hereafter and who is in doubt," and that Allah is "guardian over all things." So Satan is an agent of Allah to tempt people into disbelief. They would follow Satan and disbelieve if they are in doubt. Why does Allah play such games with people? Why does he not lead the ones in doubt towards the right way? Is this what a benevolent deity is supposed to do?

Then in 19:83 it is said that Allah "sent devils to the non-believers to incite them." Why does he not try to lead the non-believers to his way, but do the opposite, and drive them away? Is Allah so hard-hearted that if any

Chapter 4 Re-reading Islam

person does not believe in him, then he is doomed to severe punishment in the afterlife and there is practically no way to turn back and earn Allah's grace? Or perhaps it is more reasonable to read this in the context of the particular war Muhammad was fighting and that this passage aimed only at putting the hearts of his followers at ease? Either way, we cannot read Allah's promised punishment literally if we read with reason and the assumption that Allah is merciful.

In verses 82:6–9 it is said, "O mankind, what has deceived you concerning your lord, the generous, who created you, proportioned you, then balanced you, assembled you in any form he willed? Nay! But you deny the judgment." If Allah determined one's form exactly, then one's belief or disbelief may also be pre-determined. In that case judgment, reward, and punishment seem pointless. Everything would be Allah's game only.

Because of Allah's abilities, people who do not believe are so by Allah's permission and according to his will. It is not fair to blame them if they are not the ones who made the decision to believe or not. Therefore it is extremely unjust to put non-believers into hell if Allah is in control. Allah made them non-believers and then put them into hell.

In verses 76:27–28 it is said, "Indeed, these [disbelievers] love the immediate and leave behind them a grave day. We have created them and strengthened their forms, and when we will, we can change their likenesses with alteration." So Allah can change them. Why does he not do so? Then these people would be saved, and would not have to suffer punishment on judgment day.

In verse 7:179 in the Qur'an it is even said that Allah "created many jinn and men for hell." It is said that they have "hearts with which they do not understand, they have eyes with which they do not see, and they have ears with which they do not hear." It is said that they are "like livestock, no, even more astray." Why would Allah create them so that they will go to hell and suffer? Is Allah some kind of a psychopath?

In verse 27:87 it is said that one day "the trumpet

will be blown and whoever is in the heavens and in the earth would be terrified except whom Allah wills." So is it the case that whether people are good or not does not matter? Or that whether they are believers or not does not matter? Or that since all these are determined by Allah, in summary, it is Allah who wills who is going to be terrified and punished or not. Subsequently in 27:89 it is said that whoever "comes with the good, then on judgment day it would be better and they will be safe from the terror of that day." This seems more reasonable, but still according to the text it could be that ultimately only Allah's will matters, since being good or not presumably is his decision.

As Moses says to Allah in verse 7:155 in the Qur'an, "if you had willed, you could have destroyed them before, and me. Would you destroy them for what the foolish among them have done? This is your trial by which you send astray whom you will and guide whom you will. You are our protector, so forgive us and have mercy upon us, and you are the best of forgivers." This is Moses's appeal to Allah. And in 61:5, it is said that when Moses's people "deviated, Allah caused their hearts to deviate, and Allah does not guide the defiantly disobedient people."

One can see here that the responsibility rests really with Allah. He leads people astray so of course he should forgive them. It does not make sense that he misleads whom he wills and guides whom he wills and then punishes the ones who are misled. It is capricious and irresponsible.

With all these verses talking about Allah's will determining whether people believe or not, it is not acceptable to any thinking mind that he will punish people who do not believe because he has determined that they do not believe.

Let us use 30:58-59 as an example to illustrate this issue. Here it is said that if you "bring the infidels a sign, then they will definitely say that you are but falsifiers," and that in this way "Allah seals the hearts of those who do not know." Why does Allah not open their hearts to Islam rather than seal them? Basically we have two choices here,

Chapter 4 Re-reading Islam

1. Allah determines everything, and people can be satisfied with Allah's all-powerfulness. But moral responsibility including the responsibility of belief or disbelief does not lie with the individual.

2. The individual determines whether he believes or not, and moral responsibility rests with oneself. But Allah does not determine everything, and people may feel uncomfortable with Allah's lack of all-powerfulness.

However we look at it, Allah's universal will does not fit with individual moral responsibility. The only way this can make sense is if everyone is a part of Allah and a person's will is Allah's will regarding himself. Allah himself does not have any will about what people should do.

In verse 31:28 it is said that your "creation and your resurrection will not be but as one soul." The division into different souls and persons is obvious in this world, but our perception could be radically different as spiritual beings. I shall elaborate on this idea in Section 7.3.

In a contrary note, in 16:35 it is speculated that polytheists would use Allah's will as an excuse. It is said that they say that if Allah had willed, they would not have worshipped anything other than him. Here Allah's will is seen as an excuse rather than a genuine determinant of everything and every event, the view implied by other passages above.

So who is the one making decisions? Allah or the individual? In my opinion, the only reasonable way to interpret such verses would be to proceed by something similar to one of the following approaches,

1. Read all this non-literally, as a sort of rhetorical device practical in Muhammad's age to exalt Allah's power in order to scare people into behaving morally and controlling themselves. Arabia at that time was in chaos and needed unity and stability urgently.

2. Interpret Allah's will as corresponding to a person's prior moral standing. If he is a righteous person,

then Allah would will him to be a believer and receive rewards.

3. Posit God's benevolence as a *first principle* and disregard verses that assert divine predestination and punishment at the same time. More about this in Section 6.2.

Otherwise Allah seems to be capricious and cruel.

4.5.1.1 Ego

Besides, Muslims should ask themselves, why would Allah will you to believe but others not to? Are we sure that this is what is happening? Do you think you deserve Allah's guidance while others do not? Perhaps this is just your ego? This is not God but your ego pretending to be God.

We need to rethink our faith. We need to remove the egotistical God from it. Allah should be better than this. Even dictators are better than this, because they torture to keep their places. But Allah does not need such petty acts to keep his place. He does it for fun. He does it because he enjoys making crooked paths and punishing people for following them by throwing them into eternal flame.

Is this the kind of deity we believe in? It reflects upon ourselves. In the worldview that Allah decides everything, no one except Allah needs to take responsibility. However, as soon as you would like to blame someone for not believing in Allah, you give that person moral agency and you implicitly deny that Allah determined his lack of belief. It is then reasonable to believe that you grant that people in general have moral agency, including yourself. In that case you would have to take moral responsibility for your beliefs. In that case, if you believe in a god who is not merciful, it seems to show your insecurity, lack of self-confidence, and your need to take refuge in a god who says that you are right and others are wrong and will go to hell.

Even though there is textual support that Allah creates people who he wills not to believe and then throws

Chapter 4 Re-reading Islam

them into hell to suffer, we can reason and choose more reasonable verses. Verses point toward different directions anyway. So when we choose which ones to emphasise, we are choosing the belief system we prefer to adopt, the kind of life we prefer to live, and the kind of person we want to be.

In the end, we should pay more attention to verses such as 6:21, 6:93, 6:144, 7:37, 10:17, 11:18, 18:15, 29:68, 61:7 in the Qur'an, which ask "who is more unjust than he who invents a lie against Allah?" This rhetorical question has been repeated so many times and yet people seldom pay serious attention to it. If people uphold this point firmly, then it means that people need to be absolutely truthful and take great care about what they say regarding Allah, and not use him for their own benefit. But we see Islamic texts interpreted to suit people's needs and to justify the status quo very frequently.

Also in verses 10:69–70 it is said that those who invent a lie against Allah will return to him and receive severe punishment. Clerics interpreting Islamic texts to their advantage or to their own agenda fall into this group. Are they not worse than infidels? Infidels may go to hell themselves, but people who invent lies about Allah mislead others and could cause those who listen to and follow their advice to go to hell.

In verse 10:59, it is said that Allah "sent his bounty but people made some of it lawful and some of it unlawful." So we should be skeptical about religious laws, because they could be the invention of human beings rather than the order of God.

We need to compare verses against each other, for example we should hold phrases such as "exalted is Allah above what they describe" in 37:159 and 37:180 against passages describing a petty, egoist God. It is probably for the sake of scaring people into good behaviour, given the historical context and the level of the audience Muhammad was preaching to. We need to read between the lines, rather than repeating the texts like a parrot without critical thinking and textual juxtaposition.

We have to be wary of religious lies. We have to be skeptical about anything which is said to be Allah's orders. Because they may be just man-made lies after all. They have to be proven to be Allah's order first, if they are to be taken as such.

If there is any uncertainty, we should examine whether a rule is reasonable and ethical in itself. It is much safer and does not expose us to the danger of fake commands of Allah. We should follow the Mu'tazilis (Section 3.2.5) in this regard.

4.5.2 Punishment

In a Hadith, Muhammad is recorded as saying that there are legal things and illegal things, and one should avoid the dubious things in between. [3, 2:49] This seems to encourage an extremist interpretation asking people to renounce everything except if explicitly stated to be legal in Islam.

However, at the end of the Hadith Muhammad said that there is one piece of flesh that if it is good then the whole body is good, and if it is bad then the whole body is bad, and it is the heart. Hence what is to be avoided are things that corrupt the heart. To interpret this as mingling between the sexes, forms of dress, erotic literature, etc. is to be narrow-minded. The main point should be about being conscientious and charitable.

In verse 8:24 in the Qur'an it says, "know that Allah comes between a man and his heart and that to him you will be gathered." I think this is a beautiful verse which deserves much attention. It highlights the importance of the heart and one's mental world rather than rigid rules which could and do become obsolete with time and changes in society. To be a good person is more complicated than following old rules rigidly. All we can do is to have basic ethical principles and to choose between possible actions on a case-by-case basis. To be a good person is to find that fine line in one's heart. And Allah comes between a man and his heart. Allah will judge according to that fine line. Not the length of one's beard or skirt.

Chapter 4 Re-reading Islam

This view of religion puts emphasis on individual conscience rather than on external authority. This way of thinking is not good for the interests of the clerical class but it is good for Islam.

If we take the heart to be the primary centre, we cannot really adopt an extremist position because good intention and compassion would matter most. It is more reasonable to interpret what corrupts the heart as giving no charity, animal cruelty, tyrannical parenting, etc.

However, what should we make of texts like the Hadith in which it is narrated that Muhammad sent a letter to the Governor of Bahrain and he sent it to Khosrow, who tore it to pieces? One of the transmitters tentatively suggested that Muhammad called to Allah to tear them to pieces and disperse them. [3, 3:64] Let us assume this is what happened. What does it mean? Does it mean that people should pray that bad things happen to people who slight them, that we should take up arms against such people, that we should not slight prophets, or all of the above? One should think about this wisely. Violent people choose violent conclusions.

Another important example is the Hadith in which Muhammad is said to have said that الأمة (al-umma, the Muslim nation) will continue to be based on Allah's teachings and that they will not be harmed by any one going on a different path. [3, 3:71] We can take this to mean that anyone harming Muslim communities is to be punished. But we have to be careful what the term means. Can any country with a Muslim majority really claim that she is based on Allah's teachings? I doubt that. So we should not use such Hadiths and, in general, religion in the political arena to incite "religious wars" or anything similar. People reading casually may let politicians use such Hadiths, but not someone reading critically. It is too dangerous and misleading.

I argue that we should not read these as permitting human inflicted punishment on non-Muslims. The reasons are

1. Fairness

2. National limitation

3. Lack of messengers

4. Divine punishment

4.5.2.1 Fairness

It is emphasised frequently that Allah does not wrong people. The following passages are examples of this. From these passages we can draw the conclusion that Allah does not punish people just for disbelief, for example putting them into hell even if they did much good.

Let me put this in a standard form of argument,

1. If Allah punishes people just for disbelief, for example putting them into hell even if they did much good, then Allah wrongs people.

2. Allah does not wrong people.

∴ Therefore, Allah does not punish people just for disbelief, for example putting them into hell even if they did much good.

This argument fits the form called *modus tollens*. In this form, the premises make the conclusion undeniable.

In verses 50:16–22 in the Qur'an, it is said, "we have already created man and know what his soul whispers to him, and we are closer to him than the jugular vein. As the two [recording angels] observe, seated on the right and

Chapter 4 Re-reading Islam

on the left, man does not utter any word without having a ready observer, and the intoxication of death will bring the truth. That is what you were trying to avoid. And the horn will be blown. That is the day of the threat. And every soul will come, with it someone driving [him there] and a witness. You were certainly heedless of this, and we have removed from you your cover, so your sight today is sharp." If people are just rewarded and punished according to their belief and disbelief, then there is no need for a witness to observe everything one does. This is also a piece of evidence for the moral construal of belief we discussed in Section 4.1.2.

Additionally, there are passages explicitly saying that people will not be wronged on judgment day. In verse 2:281 people are told to "fear a day in which you are returned to Allah. Then every soul will be compensated for what it earned, and they will not be wronged." In verse 3:25 it is said that on judgment day "each soul will be compensated what it earned, and they will not be wronged." This is repeated in 3:161. In verse 10:54 it is said that the people who did wrong would "be judged in justice, and they will not be wronged." In verse 16:111 it is said that on judgment day "every soul disputes for itself, and every soul will be fully compensated for what it did, and they will not be wronged." In verse 17:71 it is said that on judgment day "we will call forth every people with its record. Then whoever is given his record in his right hand, those will read their records, and they will not be wronged even to a thread."[6] In verse 18:49 it is said that the book of deeds "leaves nothing small or great except what it has enumerated, and they will find what they did present, and your lord does not wrong anyone." In verse 21:47 it is said, "we place the scales of justice for the day of resurrection, so no soul will be wronged at all, and if there is the weight of a mustard seed, we will bring it forth. And we are sufficient as accountants." In verse 36:54 it is said that on judgment

---

[6]The verse shifts between a group of people and an individual. But the general sense should be clear.

day "no soul will be wronged at all, and you will not be recompensed except for what you have done." In verse 39:69 it is said that on judgment day "the earth will shine with the light of its lord, and the record will be placed, and the prophets and the witnesses will be brought, and it will be judged between them in truth, and they will not be wronged."

The following are examples about people not being wronged but are not explicitly about the judgment day. In verse 45:22 it is said that Allah "created the heavens and earth in truth and in order that every soul may be recompensed for what it earned, and that they are not wronged." In verse 2:272 it is said that whatever "you spend of good it will be fully repaid to you, and you will not be wronged." In verse 4:40 it is said that Allah "does not wrong even to the weight of an atom, and if it is a good deed, he multiplies it and gives from himself a great reward." In verse 4:49 it is said that "Allah purifies whom he wills, and they are not wronged even to a thread." In verse 4:77 it is said, "you will not be wronged even to a thread." In verse 6:160 it is said that whoever "came with a good deed will have ten times the like thereof, and who came with an evil deed will not be recompensed except the like thereof, and they will not be wronged." In verse 8:60 it is said that what "you spend of a thing in the way of Allah will be repaid to you, and you will not be wronged." In verse 10:44 it is said that Allah "does not wrong the people at all." In verse 23:62 it is said, "we charge no soul except its capacity, and with us is a record which speaks with truth, and they will not be wronged." In verse 46:19 it is said that there are "degrees for all for what they have done, so that he may fully compensate them for their deeds, and they will not be wronged."

On the other hand, there are verses in which there is a condition of belief when talking about not being wronged. In verse 4:124 it is said that whoever "does righteous deeds, being male or female, while believing, then those will enter paradise and will not be wronged, even to the speck on a date seed." In verse 19:60 it is said that those who repent,

Chapter 4 Re-reading Islam

believe, and do righteousness "will enter paradise and will not be wronged at all." Even though there is a condition of belief here, this is not always stated, and logically it does not say that those not believing will be wronged, or that their good deeds do not count. All it says is that those who believe will not be wronged. We should look at other passages without the condition of belief for the fate of non-believers, not imposing the implication of the necessity of belief for being treated justly simply because there is the condition of belief in some passages. The condition here means that this passage concerns believers, but it does not mean that non-believers' good deeds do not count and that they would be punished whatever the circumstances.

4.5.2.2 National Limitation

For a more detailed discussion of this point see Section 2.2.2.

In verse 10:47 of the Qur'an it is said that each nation has its prophet, and that judgment is between this prophet and his people.

The Qur'an is an Arabic message for Arabs. We can see that in 14:4, in which it is said that Allah "did not send any messenger except one who speaks the tongue of his people, so that he makes things clear for them."

The Qur'an is a message for its times. We can see that in 13:38–39 where it is said that messengers "have been sent before, and that there is a book for every period of time."

Therefore the punishment for disbelievers at most applies to Muhammad's Arab audience, but not others.

4.5.2.3 Lack of Messengers

In verses 50:24–26 it is said that on judgment day Allah will say, "throw into hell every obstinate disbeliever, preventer of good, aggressor, doubter, who made another deity alongside Allah. Then throw him into the severe punishment." From this passage people may conclude that every disbeliever is going to hell. But I contend that the word "obstinate" is crucial here. It hints at the proximity of prophets. If you do not have close contact with the message and the prophet, how can you qualify to be an *obstinate* disbeliever? You can only be a disbeliever without such emphasis. There are many passages mentioning the existence of a prophet in one's people as a precondition for punishment for disbelief. The quantity of such passages supports my interpretation of 50:24–26 above. Many of the following passages have been quoted in Section 2.2.2 in order to clarify to whom Muhammad's message applies but here we discuss them in the context of punishment for non-Muslims.

The following passages show that Allah punishes only when he has already sent a prophet. In verse 17:15, it is said that Allah "does not punish until he has sent a prophet." In verses 26:208–209 it is said that Allah "did not destroy any town except one with bearers of warning as a reminder," and that he was "never unjust." This is repeated in 28:58, saying that Allah "does not destroy a town without sending a messenger," and that "their people are wrong-doers." In verses 28:46–47 it is said that Moses is sent as a bearer of warning, and if Allah does not send a prophet before punishing them with a disaster, then people will question and blame Allah. In verses 37:167–170 it is said that the infidels "used to say that if we have a reminder like the former peoples, then we would have been the servants of Allah that are made sincere, and that they disbelieved, so they will know." And in 37:176–177 it is said "when Allah's punishment descends into their territory, then the morning of the warned ones would be terrible." Then in 38:3–4 it is said that Allah "has destroyed many generations before, and they are astonished that a bearer of warning came to them, and the infidels said that this is a magician and a liar." In verses 43:74–78 it is said that the criminals "are abiding eternally in the punishment of hell" and "we had already brought you the truth, but most of you hate it." In verses 67:6–9 it is said, "for those who disbelieved in their lord is the punishment

Chapter 4 Re-reading Islam

of hell, and wretched is the destination. When they are thrown into it, they hear from it an inhaling while it boils up. It almost bursts with rage. Every time a group is thrown into it, its keepers ask them, 'did there not come to you a bearer of warning?' They will say, 'yes, a bearer of warning came to us, but we disbelieved and said, "Allah has not sent down anything. You are not but in great error." ' "

The following are examples of Allah's messengers and the punishment of their people. In verses 23:23–54 the stories of Noah, Moses, and Jesus are told, and it is said that Allah sent his "messengers successively, and every time a messenger came to a nation, they denied him, so we made them follow each other in the path of destruction (23:44)." Similar enumerations of prophets and destruction are made in 25:35–40, 26:10–190, 27:45–58, 29:14–40, 37:73–148, 38:12–14, 50:12–14, 51:24–46, 53:50–56, 54:9–42, 69:4–10, 79:15–26, 85:17–20, etc. where the stories of Noah, Moses, Abraham, Thamud, Lot, etc. are told or hinted at. In verses 43:46–56 the story of Moses and the punishment of the Egyptians is briefly narrated, followed by 43:57–66 in which Jesus is introduced, and it is stated that "the denominations from among them differed, so woe to those who did wrong, for [they shall receive] the punishment of a painful day. What are they waiting for, except the hour to come to them suddenly when they do not feel?" In verses 46:21–25 it is said that the brother of 'Aad "warned his people in al-Ahqaf, and bearers of warning had passed on before him and after him," saying "do not worship except Allah, indeed I fear for you the punishment of a grave day" but they ignored him, so a wind came, in which there was "a painful punishment, destroying everything by command of its lord." In verses 50:12–14 it is said, "the people of Noah denied before them, and the companions of the well and Thamud and 'Aad and Pharaoh and the brothers of Lot, and the companions of the wood and the people of Tubba' all denied the messengers, so my threat was justly fulfilled." In verse 71:1 it is said that Allah sent Noah to his people, telling him to "warn your people before there comes to them a painful punishment," then in 71:25 it is said, "because of their sins they were drowned and put into the fire, and they did not find helpers for themselves besides Allah." All these are records of prophets being sent and people who did not follow them being punished afterwards. In the Qur'an, there are lists of prophets and the destruction of their people after ignoring the messages they brought, and prophets without bringing destruction, but never destruction without a prophet. We see from such stories that non-believers being punished is only applicable to groups of people who have received a messenger.

In verse 51:60 it is said, "woe to those who disbelieved for [they shall receive punishment on] the day which they are promised." People may conclude from this that all infidels would be going to hell. But if we read the whole passage, we would see that in 51:52 it is said, "there did not come to those before them any messenger except that they said, 'a magician or a madman.'" So it is referring to peoples to which messengers came, not all non-Muslims.

From the following passages we can see that the people punished had direct contact with the prophet. In verse 30:9 people are told to "travel and look at what happened at the end to people to whom prophets came," and that Allah "did not wrong them." In verse 30:47 it is said that Allah "sent prophets to their people with clear proofs, and Allah took revenge on the criminals." In verses 40:21–22 people were told to travel and "look at the end of those who were before them," that they were "greater than them in strength" but "Allah seized them for their sins" and this is because "their messengers came to them with clear proofs but they disbelieved, so Allah seized them." In verse 39:25 it is said that those "before them denied, so punishment came to them." In verses 43:6–8 it is said that Allah sent many prophets "among the former peoples, and there did not come to them a prophet except that they ridicule him, so we destroyed greater power than them, and the example of the former peoples has occurred." In verses 39:57–60 it is said that a soul would say, "if only Allah guided me, I would have been among the righteous," that Allah's verses

Chapter 4 Re-reading Islam

"did come to you but you denied them and were arrogant," and that there is "residence in hell for the arrogant." In verse 39:71 it is said that when the infidels reach the gates of hell, its keepers would ask "did messengers from among you not come to you, reciting to you Allah's verses and warning you of the meeting of your day?" They will say, "yes but the word of punishment came true on the infidels." In verses 43:23–25 it is said that every time Allah sent a bearer of warning to a city, the rich disbelieved, so he "took revenge on them." In verses 44:10–14 it is said that one day "the sky will bring clear smoke, enveloping the people. This is a painful punishment" and "a clear messenger came to them, then they turned away from him and said, a taught lunatic." In verses 50:36–37 it is said, "how many a generation before [the righteous] did we destroy, who were greater than them in power and explored throughout the lands. Is there any place of escape? Indeed in that is a reminder for whoever has a heart or who listens while he is witnessing." In verses 64:5–6 it is said, "Has there not come to you the news of those who disbelieved before? So they tasted the bad consequence of their affair, and there is a painful punishment for them. That is because their messengers used to come to them with clear evidence, but they said, 'do human beings guide us?' So they disbelieved and turned away, and Allah did not need them, and Allah is free of need and praiseworthy." In verses 65:8–11 it is said, "how many a city rebelled against the command of its lord and his messengers, so we took it to severe account and punished it with a terrible punishment. So it tasted the bad consequence of its affair, and the outcome of its affair was loss. Allah has prepared for them a severe punishment, so fear Allah, O you of understanding who have believed. Allah has sent down to you a message, a messenger reciting to you the clear signs of Allah in order that he may bring out those who believe and do righteous deeds from darkness into the light, and whoever believes in Allah and does righteousness, he will admit him into gardens beneath which rivers flow, abiding in it forever. Allah has perfected for him a provision."

In verses 73:15–16 it is said, "indeed, we have sent you a messenger as a witness to you just as we sent to Pharaoh a messenger. But Pharaoh disobeyed the messenger, so we seized him with a ruinous seizure." From these passages we can see that a messenger is always sent to warn a people before they are punished.

Another passage which shows the context of a messenger being opposed directly is 47:32–35 in which it is said, "those who disbelieved and averted from the way of Allah and opposed the messenger after guidance had become clear to them, they will never harm Allah at all, and he will make their deeds worthless. O you who have believed, obey Allah and obey the messenger and do not invalidate your deeds. Indeed, those who disbelieved and averted from the way of Allah and then died while they were disbelievers, Allah will never forgive them. So do not weaken and call for peace while you are superior, and Allah is with you and will not deprive you of your deeds." Here we can see that the menacing rhetoric in the Qur'an is directed to people threatening the safety of Muhammad and his followers, for the text clearly has a background of fighting going on. We should never adopt this attitude in a peaceful environment.

The frequent use of words of the root ر - ذ - ن *n–dh–r* is very telling. The root is closely linked to the concept of warning. The verb أنذر *andhara*, meaning "to warn," is used more than forty times in the Qur'an, from 2:6 to 92:14, and it always has to do with prophecy and punishment. In verse 6:19 Muhammad is told to say that the "Qur'an was revealed to me so that I can warn you with it and whom it reaches." In verse 6:51 Muhammad is told

Chapter 4 Re-reading Islam

to warn by the Qur'an "those who fear that they will be gathered before their lord," "so that they might become righteous." In verse 6:130 it is said that on judgment day people will be asked "did there not come to you messengers from among you, telling you my verses and warning you of the meeting of this day of yours?" and they will say, "we bear witness against ourselves," and it is then said, "worldly life deluded them, and they will bear witness against themselves that they were infidels." In verse 7:2 Muhammad is told that the Qur'an is "a book revealed to you, so let there not be in your breast distress from it, that you may warn with it and as a reminder to the believers." In verse 7:63 Noah said, "do you wonder that there came to you a reminder from your lord through a man from among you, in order that he may warn you and that you may fear Allah so you might receive mercy." In verse 7:69 Hud said basically the same thing, "do you wonder that there has come to you a reminder from your lord through a man from among you, in order that he may warn you? And remember when he made you successors after the people of Noah and increased you in stature extensively. So remember the bounties of Allah in order that you may succeed."

Another important word from the same root is نذير *nadhīr*, meaning "a person who warns." I use the translation "bearer of warning." It is used nearly sixty times in the Qur'an from 2:119 until 74:36. Of these, 7:184, 11:25, 15:89, 22:49, 26:115, 29:50, 38:70, 46:9, 51:50–51, 67:26, and 71:2 emphasise that a clear bearer of warning is sent. Let us look at some examples in detail. In verse 2:119

Muhammad is told, "we have sent you with the truth as a bringer of good tidings and a bearer of warning, and you will not be asked about the companions of hellfire." In verse 5:19 it is said, "O people of the scripture, our messenger has come to you clarifying to you after a period of messengers, lest you say, 'no bringer of good tidings nor a bearer of warning has come to us.' A bringer of good tidings and a bearer of warning has already come to you. And Allah is capable of everything." In verses 11:25–26 it is said that Allah has sent Noah to his people to say, "Indeed, I am a clear bearer of warning to you not to worship except Allah. Indeed I fear for you the punishment of a painful day." In verse 25:1 it is said, "blessed is he who sent down the criterion [distinguishing between right and wrong] upon his servant so that he may be a bearer of warning to the worlds." If one is not informed of the criterion of judgment, it does not make sense to punish with it. In verse 46:21 it is said that the brother of 'Aad "warned his people in al-Ahqaf, and bearers of warning had passed on before him and after him," saying "do not worship except Allah, indeed I fear for you the punishment of a grave day." From these passages we can see that a bearer of warning is needed before punishment can be fairly brought to people, so if no prophet comes to one's nation, it would not be punished.

The appearance of the words منذر *mundhir*, meaning "a person who warns" (translated as "bearer of warning") in 2:213, 4:165, 6:48, 13:7, 18:56, 26:194, 26:208, 27:92, 37:72, 38:4, 44:3, 46:29, 50:2, 79:45, and منذر *mundhar*, meaning "the warned," in 10:73, 26:173, 27:58, 37:73, 37:177, is also significant. We can see that prophets also come as bearers of warning, and their peoples are the warned. This shows that the Islamic view of monotheism is that if a prophet comes to a people, they are warned, and if they do not reform, then they are punished. It is not in line with the original intention of the texts that people are using them to justify oppression of other people, forcing them to follow Islam. Only Muhammad's people is eligible for Allah's punishment. Other people would only be punished if they have their own bearers of warning.

From these verses we can see that a prophet has to come to a people to warn them and then and only then will there be punishment for not heeding the warnings.

From the evidence given above we can see that if we do not have a messenger warning us, then there would not be divine punishment. Examples are given below for the co-occurrence of the designated conditions.

Case 1. Prophet sent and ignored, therefore destruction, e.g. Lot.

Case 2. Prophet sent and not ignored, therefore no destruction, e.g. David.

Case 3. Prophet not sent, no destruction, e.g. Arabs before Muhammad.

Case 4. Prophet not sent, destruction. No example in the Qur'an.

We can see that an ignored prophet is a necessary condition for divine punishment.

Now let us examine other relevant points. Besides the frequent occurrence of words related to warning which supports the thesis that a prophet needs to come and warn his people, many other words in the Qur'an, if we reflect upon it, convey the idea that one needs to receive the message in a direct way, in order to reject it and be punished. Other non-believers are not the target of threats of punishment.

First of all, let us look at the use of the verb كفر *kafara*, meaning "to deny" or "to disbelieve," which is a very prominent word in the Qur'an and in Islam. Especially in the context of radical Muslims' promotion of تكفير *takfīr*, a word from the same root, the practice of excommunicating other Muslims based on the claims that they are not pious enough, they do not adhere to the right set of doctrines, etc. What is the original sense of this verb?

The word كفر *kafara* originally means to cover. Then it came to mean covering the truth and thus denial and disbelief of Allah. This act is frequently associated with punishment. We can see this in 2:39, 2:90, 2:121, 2:126, 2:161, 2:257, 3:4, 3:10, 3:12, 3:56, 3:106, 3:116, 3:151, 4:56, 4:84, 5:10, 5:73, 5:78, 5:86, 5:115, 6:30, 6:70, 8:35–36, 8:52, 8:59, 9:3, 9:26, 9:90, 10:4, 10:70, 11:17, 13:31–32, 14:7, 14:18, 18:106, 21:39, 22:19, 22:57, 22:72, 29:23, 29:52, 33:25, 35:7, 38:27, 39:63, 39:72, 40:22, 41:27, 41:50, 45:11, 46:20, 46:34, 47:1, 48:25, 51:60, 54:14, 57:19, 64:10, 67:6, 98:6 etc. In all these verses it is said that the ones who disbelieve will be punished. For example, in 2:126 Abraham said, "my lord, make this a secure city and provide its people with fruits, whoever of them believes in Allah and the last day," and Allah said, "and whoever disbelieves, I will grant him enjoyment for a little while, then I will force him to the punishment of the fire, and wretched is the destination."

But we need to read carefully. Let us look at more verses. In verse 2:39 it is said that those "who disbelieve and deny our signs, those will be companions of the fire. They will abide in it eternally." In verse 2:90 it is said, "how wretched is that for which they sold themselves, to disbelieve in what Allah has revealed through outrage that Allah would send down his favour upon whom he wills from among his servants. So they returned with wrath

Chapter 4 Re-reading Islam

upon wrath, and for the disbelievers is a humiliating punishment." In verse 2:121 it is said that those "to whom we have given the book recite it with its true recital. They believe in it. And whoever disbelieves in it, then those are the losers." In verse 64:10 it is said, "the ones who disbelieved and denied our signs, those are the companions of the fire, abiding in it eternally, and wretched is the destination." From these verses we can see that you are given the message by a messenger and then if you reject this message you would be punished. If you are not given this, punishment is not applicable to you. Even though this is not said explicitly in verse 2:126 cited above, the presence of Abraham fulfilled this condition.

Because of this, when we read verses such as 66:9 in which Muhammad is told to "strive against the disbelievers (كافر *kāfir*, one who refuses) and the hypocrites and be stern upon them, and their abode is hell, and wretched is the destination," we should remember that one cannot be a *kāfir* and be punished unless a prophet came and warned one's people.

The use of the word كذّب *kadhdhaba*, meaning "to deny," is also illuminating. To deny (كذّب *kadhdhaba*) the signs of Allah is frequently associated with punishment and losing. We can see this in 2:39, 3:11, 5:10, 5:86, 6:49, 6:148, 7:36, 7:92, 7:96, 7:147, 7:182, 8:54, 10:45, 10:73, 10:95, 16:113, 20:48, 22:42–44, 22:57, 23:48, 25:11, 25:19, 25:36, 25:37, 26:139, 26:189, 30:16, 32:20, 34:42, 38:12–14, 39:25, 50:12–14, 52:14, 54:18, 54:42, 57:19, 62:5, 64:10, 67:18, 83:10–11, 84:22–24, 91:14, 92:15–16, 96:13–18, etc. In all these verses it is said that people who deny the signs of Allah will be punished or will lose. For example, in 2:39 it is said, "those who disbelieve and deny our signs, those will be companions of the fire. They will abide eternally in it." In verses 3:10–11 it is said that those who disbelieve are following the habit of the people of Pharaoh and those before them. "They denied our signs, so Allah seized them for their sins, and Allah is severe in penalty." In verses 5:10 and 5:86 it is said, "those who disbelieve and deny our signs, those are the companions of hellfire." In verse 6:49 it is said that for "those who deny our signs, the punishment will touch them because they used to disobey defiantly." In verse 6:57 Muhammad is told to say, "indeed, I am on clear evidence from my lord, and you denied it. I do not have that for which you are impatient. The decision is only for Allah. He tells the truth, and he is the best of deciders." From these verses we can see that the message was brought to people by the prophet but they denied it, and they were threatened with punishment and hellfire. But we cannot say that this automatically applies to people who do not have a prophet. In verses 52:11–12 we find a particularly explicit specimen. It says, "woe to the deniers" on judgment day "who are playing in vain discourse." This shows that people who deny Islam and Muhammad after contact would be punished on judgment day, and they were playing in vain discourse, probably slandering Muhammad. But it is not appropriate to think that this is automatically applicable to all non-believers.

The following passage demonstrates the moral construal of following Islam clearly. In verses 68:7–13 it is said that Allah "is most knowing of who has gone astray from his way, and he is most knowing of the guided. So do not obey the deniers. They wish that you would soften, so they would soften. And do not obey every worthless habitual swearer, scorner, going about with malicious gossip, preventer of good, transgressing and sinful, cruel, in addition to being useless." All the descriptions point towards evil-doing, which is seen as a result of a world view with no afterlife. But non-belief itself does not deserve to be punished. It is the associated lack of morals that would be

Chapter 4 Re-reading Islam

judged and punished.

Another example is the word to reject (جحد *jaḥada*). It appears in 6:33, 7:51, 11:59–60, 16:71, 27:13–14, 29:49, 31:32, 40:63, 41:15, 41:28, 46:26, etc. Each time it refers either to the rejection of Allah's signs or his favour. For example, in 6:33 Muhammad is told, "we know that you are saddened by what they say, and indeed, they do not say that you are lying, but the wrongdoers reject the signs of Allah." In verse 7:51 it is said that on judgment day "we forget them in the same way as they forgot the meeting of this day of theirs and rejected our signs." In verses 11:59–60 it is said that 'Aad "rejected the signs of their lord and disobeyed his messengers and followed the order of every obstinate tyrant and they were followed in this world with a curse and on the day of resurrection." In verses 27:13–14 it is said that Pharaoh and his people rejected "our manifest signs," "while their souls were convinced, out of injustice and haughtiness. So see what the end of the corrupters was." In verse 29:47 it is said "we have sent down to you the Qur'an in this way, and those to whom we gave the book believe in it, and among these are those who believe in it. And none reject our verses except the disbelievers."

Having gone through the long lists of verses above having to do with refusing to believe, you might be thinking that all non-Muslims are destined for punishment in hell. But if we think about it we should be able to see that these verbs, to disbelieve and to deny, imply contact with the message. If you have never heard about something, you cannot deny it. In verse 46:7 it is said that when Allah's "signs are recited to them as clear evidences, those who disbelieve (كفروا *kafarū*) say about the truth when it came to them, that this is magic." From this example we can see that normally you need to have the message from the prophet in order to disbelieve, deny, or reject it. And when we look carefully at the verses that talk about rejection, we realise that one has to have news of Allah's signs and his favours in order to reject them. This is a logical precondition. The only question is how direct it has to be. If it does not have to be direct, then anyone who has heard of the content of Islam would fulfil this precondition. But if one has to be told by a prophet in person, then that is another story. And modern Muslims seem to have forgotten this. But it is clear in the text that Muhammad's message catered to his contemporaries, and it was a version that was suitable for the knowledge, social condition, and understanding of his audience.

Along with the context above, it is reasonable to read these verbs as presupposing a prophet having come to one's nation. Otherwise you cannot deny the prophet directly. In verse 3:101 people are asked "how could you disbelieve (تكفرون present second-person plural of *kafara*) while the signs of Allah are recited to you and his messenger is among you?" In verse 45:31 it is said that for those who disbelieved (كفروا past third-person plural of *kafara*), "were not our signs recited to you but you were arrogant and a people of criminals?" We should pay attention to the fact that the passive verb to be recited (تلى *tuliya*) is used frequently in the Qur'an in 4:127, 5:1, 8:2, 8:31, 10:15, 17:107, 19:58, 19:73, 22:30, 22:72, 23:66, 23:105, 28:53, 29:51, 31:7, 33:34, 34:43, 45:8, 45:25, 45:31, 46:7, 68:15, and 83:13. It

Chapter 4 Re-reading Islam

is said that the signs of Allah, the favours of Allah, the book, etc. are *recited* to people. These verses show the original sense of denying and disbelieving the prophet in person, with the Qur'an recited to you.

Another interesting word to pay attention to is the word معرض *mu'riḍ*, a person who refuses, it is used in 2:83, 3:23, 6:4, 8:23, 9:76, 12:105, 15:81, 21:1, 21:24, 21:32, 21:42, 23:3, 24:48, 26:5, 36:46, 38:68, 46:3, and 74:49. In verse 2:83 it is said that the children of Israel were told, "do not worship except Allah, and to parents do good and to relatives, orphans, and the needy. And speak to people good things and perform prayer and give alms" but "then you turned away, except a few of you, and you refused." From this example we can see that it is to people who actively turn away from God's message, after having received it from a prophet, that threats of punishment are directed. This word is sometimes used together with the verb to turn away (تولّى *tawallā*). The verb appears quite frequently and occurs nearly eighty times in the Qur'an, from 2:64 to 96:13. In verses 2:204–205 it is said that there are "people whose speech pleases you in worldly life, and who ask Allah to witness what is in their heart, while they are the fiercest of the opponents. And when they turn away (تولّى *tawallā*), they strive throughout the land to cause corruption in it and destroy crops and animals, and Allah does not like corruption." This passage describes people who, having known about Allah, turn away from him and spread corruption. This is a paradigmatic example of people who turn away from Allah. Therefore we can see that the use of both the words معرض *mu'riḍ* (people who refuse) and تولّى *tawallā* (to turn away) conveys the notion that people unjustly rejected Allah's message. And the precondition to doing that is to have the message first, which need to be brought by one's national prophet, as we learn from the verses discussed above.

A less frequent word is مبطل *mubṭil*, meaning "falsifier," which is an active participle of the verb أبطل *abṭala*, to nullify. It is used in 7:173, 29:48, 40:78, and 45:27 to refer to people who do not believe. In verse 29:48 it is said that Muhammad did not recite before the Qur'an any scripture, and he did not inscribe one with his right hand, "otherwise the falsifiers would definitely have doubted." In order to falsify, you have to know of the message, and then cast doubt on it, so if you do not receive a messenger, you do not have an authentic version to falsify.

A similar word is خرّاص *kharrāṣ* meaning "liar" or "slanderer." In verses 51:8–11 it is said, "you have different views. He who is deluded, is deluded away from [the Qur'an]. The liars are destroyed, who are in a flood, heedless." People who would like the scope of Allah's punishment to be wide would say that the word "liars" here refers to all disbelievers. But I would argue that it only refers to people spreading lies about Muhammad around the time of revelation. This is what it is referring to. It is clear that people who were deluded away from the Qur'an had to have heard of it from Muhammad or at most people who relayed his message, and have thought or heard negative views about it, and "liars" would only apply to a small group of people who were spreading lies about Muhammad and posing a danger to him or making his life difficult. It is

Chapter 4 Re-reading Islam

anachronistic to think that this applies in general to people who are not Muslims.

We should read these words of rejection in conjunction with verses (2:67, 2:231, 5:57–58, 18:56, 10:106, 21:36, 25:41, 31:6, 45:9, 45:35) talking about how people view Muhammad's message with ridicule (هزو huzuw) and verses (4:140, 6:5, 6:10, 11:8, 13:32, 15:11, 16:34, 21:41, 26:6, 30:10, 36:30, 39:48, 40:83, 43:7, 45:33, 46:26) about how people mock (استهزأ istahza'a) Muhammad and the other prophets. From these verses, together with what we know about people's hostile reaction to Muhammad, we can see that the verses threatening punishment for infidels should be viewed in the context of a doubted prophet struggling to have his message accepted by people surrounding him, who were mocking and attacking him, placing him in physical danger. Otherwise it does not make sense to punish people just for disbelief, for it conflicts with the exalted status of Allah, which is asserted in 2:255, 4:34, 6:100, 7:190, 10:18, 16:1, 16:3, 17:43, 20:114, 22:62, 23:92, 23:116, 27:63, 28:68, 30:40, 31:30, 34:23, 39:67, 40:12, 42:4, 42:51, 72:3, 79:24, 87:1, and 92:20.

Another set of words which points to a narrow applicability of Allah's punishment is the verb فسق fasaqa, to defiantly disobey, its noun فسق fisq, defiant disobedience, and its active participle, فاسق fāsiq, one who defiantly disobeys.

The verb فسق fasaqa, to defiantly disobey, occurs in 2:58–59, 6:49, 7:163–165, 10:33, 17:16, 18:50, 29:34, 32:20, and 46:20. For example, in 2:58–59 it is said that those who did wrong changed Allah's words into something "different from that which was said to them, so we sent down upon those who did wrong punishment from the sky because they were defiantly disobeying.." In verse 6:49 it is said that for "those who deny our signs, the punishment will touch them for their defiant disobedience." In verse 17:16 it is said, "if we want to destroy a city, we command its affluent [to obey Allah] but they defiantly disobey, so the word is justified, and we destroy it with destruction."

Its noun فسق *fisq*, defiant disobedience, occurs in verses 5:3, 6:121, and 6:145. In verse 5:3 people are told what type of meat is prohibited, and that one should not "seek decision through divining arrows. That is grave disobedience." In verse 6:121 people are told not to "eat of that upon which the name of Allah has not been mentioned, for indeed, it is grave disobedience. And indeed the devils inspire their allies to dispute with you. And if you were to obey them, indeed, you would be polytheists." In these verses a clear order is given, and then it is pronounced that it would be grave disobedience to do so. From this we can see the context and precondition for disobedience. Not every one can disobey. You cannot if you are not ordered to do something.

Its active participle, فاسق *fāsiq*, one who defiantly disobeys, is the one that appears most frequently in this set of words. It occurs nearly forty times from 2:26 until 63:6. For example, in 2:99 it is said, "we have certainly revealed to you clear signs, and no one denies them except the defiantly disobedient." In verses 3:81–82 it is said that Allah "took the covenant of the prophets" which says, that with

Chapter 4 Re-reading Islam

"what I give you of the book and wisdom, and then a messenger comes to you confirming what is with you, you would definitely believe him and support him," and that people endorsed it, "so those who turned away after that, they were the ones who defiantly disobey." In verse 3:110 it is said, "you were the best nation produced for mankind. You enjoin what is right and forbid what is wrong and believe in Allah. And if the people of the book believed, it would have been better for them. Among them are believers, but most of them are the ones who defiantly disobey." In verse 5:47 it is said, "let the people of the gospel judge by what Allah has revealed in it, and who does not judge by what Allah has revealed, then those are the ones who defiantly disobey." In verse 5:49 Muhammad is told to judge between the Jews and the Christians "by what Allah has revealed and do not follow their desires and beware of them, lest they tempt you away from some of what Allah has revealed to you. So if they turn away, then know that Allah only intends to afflict them with some of their sins. And indeed, many among the people are defiantly disobedient." From these verses we can see that you need to be given clear signs or to have agreed to a covenant to be able to defiantly disobey. This is how this word is used in the Qur'an and this is what is supposed to be punishable, if there is no prior order or agreement there is nothing to be disobedient to. Otherwise God is just someone merciless and maleficent, instead of merciful and magnificent.

The use of words from the root ف - س - ق *f-s-q*, like the other words discussed before, shows that one has to receive the message and then actively refuse to follow it in order to be among the punished ones. If no messenger comes to your people, how can you be defiantly disobedient? There is nothing you can be disobedient to, since there are no orders.

Someone who hopes to preserve a harsher theology may perhaps retort, using rhetorical interpretation as I do, "but can't we interpret this as rhetorical, emphasising the obstinacy and despicability of the infidels?" However, I argue this is not reasonable, since Allah is supposed to be merciful and wise, it is not fitting that people are accused to be defiantly disobedient, unreformable, etc., if they have *not* received clear warning and instructions. And in Muhammad's time and before, it means no less than getting a prophet among your people speaking in your language. The texts saying this explicitly are given above. Now one may ask, "what about afterwards? We have printing, broadcasting, the internet, etc. I do not need a messenger for my nation specifically, in order to know about God's message clearly." But you are not supposed to be concerned with afterwards, if you are a literalist, because you aim to adhere to whatever is said in the Islamic texts, ignoring the difference between then and now. On the other hand, if you are not a literalist, you do not need to care about threats to non-Muslims, unless you are of the "bad" type of Abrahamic monotheists, who enjoy condemning people to earthly destruction and infernal punishment even when your theology does not compel you to. Now you are either a literalist, or not, so whatever the case, people who do not have a messenger coming to them directly should not be punished by destruction or hellfire.

In verse 48:13 it is said that whoever "did not believe in Allah and his messenger, then indeed we have prepared for the disbelievers a blaze." This seems to say that all non-believers will be punished by hellfire. But if we look at the previous verses of which it is a continuation, we can see that is it referring to Muhammad's contemporaries. In verses 48:10–13 Muhammad is told, "those who pledge allegiance to you, they are actually pledging allegiance to Allah. The hand of Allah is over their hands, so who breaks his oath breaks it against himself, and who fulfils that which he has promised Allah, he will give him a great reward. Those of the bedouins who remained behind will say to you, 'our properties and our families occupied us, so ask forgiveness for us.' They say with their tongues what is not in their hearts. Say, 'then who would be able to prevent Allah from anything if he intended for you harm or intended for you benefit? Rather, Allah is cognisant of what you do. But you thought that the messenger and the believers would never return to their families, and that was made pleasing in your hearts, snd you assumed an assumption of evil and became a ruined people.' " And then in 48:15–16 it repeatedly speaks about people who remained behind that they would be told to fight. Once we take these verses into account, we see that more than disbelief is at stake. People were involved in personal enmity and physical conflict. The group against Muhammad and his followers posed a danger for them. It was not just a matter of spiritual attitude. Therefore verse 48:13 should not be read as a general statement applying to all non-believers, but only the people Muhammad and his followers were dealing with. And even that could be rhetorical and allegorical.[7]

From such examples we can see that the Qur'an frequently talks about specific events and groups, but many Muslims commit the mistake of reading words only, and forgetting to think about the context and circumstances which a verse was addressing. We need to be very careful in reading. Otherwise we are not doing justice to Islam.

Now let us look at other passages that show the necessity of a direct message as a precondition for punishment. In verse 41:41 it is said that those "who disbelieve in the reminder when it came to them and indeed it is a mighty book." This verse shows that when Allah talks about punishment, the assumption is that the message has come to them via a messenger and they refuse to believe. Another passage gives context to the threats to non-believers. In

---

[7]Please refer to my discussion in Section 3.3.2.

verses 45:6–9 it is said, "woe to every sinful liar who hears the signs of Allah recited to him, then persists arrogantly as if he did not hear them. So give him tidings of a painful punishment. And when he knows anything of our signs, he ridicules them. There is a humiliating punishment for those people."

In verses 40:7–8 it is said that those who carry the throne and those around it praise Allah and believe in him and ask forgiveness for those who believed, saying "O our lord, you encompassed everything in mercy and knowledge, so forgive those who repented and followed your way and protect them from the punishment of hell. O our lord, and admit them to gardens of Eden which you promised and whoever was righteous among their fathers, spouses, and offspring. Verily you are strong and wise." The fathers of Muslims may not have known Islam and become Muslims. But they could still be admitted to paradise for their good deeds. Therefore we can see that non-believers are not necessarily sent to hell.

From the above verses and the words used in them we can see the implicit message that if no one came to a people, they would not be punished. And no one who was not in contact with messengers got punished in the stories of the Qur'an.

Of course in the course of history cities and towns have been destroyed but probably not as a punishment from Allah for not adhering to his way, since they have not been discussed in the Qur'an. Therefore we can see that Islam asserts that punishment is given only after a group of people have received a prophet among them.

In verse 6:47 we find another passage for fruitful discussion. It says that if the punishment of Allah comes, "only evil people will be destroyed." In different religions there is some concept of divine retribution. This has led to some random declarations by followers of different religions that such and such events are a punishment of God or a result of karma. But people apparently with no particular fault die in large numbers in terrible accidents or disasters. In such cases, unless we subscribe to the view that they must

Chapter 4 Re-reading Islam

have done something wrong that we do not know about, or that they have done something wrong in their past lives, we cannot fit such disasters with the idea that all destruction is a form of divine retribution. To expend on this point, let us read verse 42:30, in which it is said that whatever "disaster strikes you, it is what your hands have earned, and he pardons a great deal." First of all, the "whatever disaster strikes you" here could well be rhetorical and not intended to be universal. Secondly, if it were intended to be a universal statement, then have babies suffering from an earthquake earned this suffering by their own hands? It then seems that innocent people suffer for what others have brought upon them, so that the phrase "your hands" here does not refer precisely. The whole community could suffer as a result of the bad actions of some of its people, and it does not have to be disbelief or impiety. If this is the case we have to think about whether this fits with Allah's mercifulness. If not, perhaps we should reject the universal reading. Anyway, when we see a disaster and want to attribute it to people's apostasy, we should be aware that we are not sure which hands earned it. We should not be rash in talking about divine punishment. It could well be our wishful thinking.

The passage 57:22–24 should be reviewed similarly. It says, "no disaster strikes upon the earth or among yourselves except that it is [written] in a register before we bring it into being—indeed that is easy for Allah—in order that you do not despair over what has escaped you and not exult over what he has given you, and Allah does not like any self-deluded and boastful persons who are stingy and enjoin upon people miserliness. And whoever turns away, then indeed Allah is the free of need, the praiseworthy." When we read this passage, we should see that the seemingly universal statement "no disaster..." is rhetoric, not really universal, and we should see that the message emphasised here is that people should not be self-deluded and boastful. It should not be read literally word-by-word.

In verse 64:11 it is said, "no disaster strikes except by permission of Allah." This simple statement conjures up the controversy about the problem of evil. If this statement is literal, is everyone who is struck by a disaster punished by Allah? Or is the disaster good for them, maybe for their spiritual growth? But surely Allah can devise some less painful way for people to learn their lesson? It is perhaps easier to read this statement loosely, meaning that some disasters are the work of Allah, with a specific aim and directed for good, but others are perhaps just random processes of life. It would be very hard to think of a way to explain every disaster in terms of Allah's punishment or some similar goal.

I think there are two possible interpretations of such verses,

1. Not all disasters are the punishment of Allah.

2. All disasters are the punishment of Allah, but innocent people are hurt as collateral damage, and such sentences only apply to some specific context which was clear among Muhammad's audience.

Either way, we cannot assume that victims of disasters deserve it.

4.5.2.4 Divine Punishment

All the above punishments come in the form of disasters, from which we can see that Allah will punish whom he wills. It is not human beings' job to punish people for him. What human beings are morally permitted to do is to defend themselves and retaliate if treated unjustly. It is not permissible to fight or kill others just because those people do not believe.

What about passages in the Qur'an which urge people to fight?

In verse 2:190 in the Qur'an one is told to "fight in the way of Allah against people who *fight* against you." Be careful, it does not say people who *criticise* you or Islam. In verse 2:191 it says that persecution is "worse than killing," but remember what kind of harassment and torture Muhammad and his followers were suffering. Do not think of secular rule and non-Muslim societies' practices as tantamount to religious persecution. These are totally different situations. To non-Muslims, such thoughts are terrible and incomprehensible. Co-existence would become impossible, whether in Muslim-majority countries or in Muslim-minority countries. In the long term, such extreme interpretations would be very bad for Muslims living in Muslim-minority countries.

Extremist preachers make violent interpretations of such passages and people accept them easily, because these interpretations and subsequent extrapolations seem to receive the legitimacy of being God's words. One has to be vigilant that such interpretations do not become common, otherwise Muslims will think it is the norm and many people will accept the norm without reflection.

In verse 27:40 it is said that Solomon said, "Whoever is grateful, he is grateful for his soul. Whoever is ungrateful, then Allah is self-sufficient and generous." We should choose to follow what this verse says, rather than what the violent ones call for, because the context in which they were given is not the one we are in today.

4.5.2.5 Conclusion

From the discussions above we can see that it is not for human beings to inflict punishment on non-Muslims, and it is doubtful if non-Muslims would be punished by hellfire in the afterlife, a commonly held notion among Muslims.

In the following sections I shall examine the quintessential non-Muslims, namely the infidels, and the polytheists.

4.5.3 Violence

In most discourses in Islam, it either quotes the violent passages and tells you to fight certain targets the speaker would like you to attack, or does not tell you about aggressive passages in the Qur'an at all. It is no doubt difficult to read such things coherently without either becoming rather violent or turning into a skeptic of Islam. But one has to be honest and truly know one's religion. It does not do to be ignorant about this. At least we have to know that such passages exist and think about an appropriate attitude to adopt, for example one that limits this to historical contexts in the past, one that annuls such passages in a reformist spirit, one that distrusts such passages and the associated mentality, etc. Otherwise we would become a potential target for radicalisation and brainwashing.

Let us examine related passages and reflect on this issue.

In verse 9:29 in the Qur'an, people are told to fight infidels.

Muslims, look! You have permission to fight.

Non-Muslims, look! These people are irrevocably violent, intolerant, and incapable of co-existence.

But wait, the verse continues to say, fight—until they pay the جزية *jizya*, that is, the tax imposed on non-Muslims. So what can we get from this? We need to remember the following points.

1. This was the period when the Muslims were fighting the Meccans, so it is not necessarily applicable in general.

2. Even if it is generally applicable, you only fight until you collect the tax. If the tax is paid, there is no need to fight non-Muslims.

So one should see that, given the unclear domain of application and the clause about taxes, it is hard to find

Chapter 4 Re-reading Islam

cases where violence against non-Muslims is clearly lawful. Do not be incited towards violence simply by the word "infidel," which is a problematic word anyway because the final judgment is with Allah. It would be presumptuous for Muslims to categorise others as believers or not, worse to think that those non-believers are going to be in eternal fire, and worst to feel that one has the right to punish them.

Let us examine another example. In verse 47:4 in the Qur'an it is said, "when you meet those who disbelieve, strike their necks until you have weakened them, then secure their bonds, and either give favour afterwards or ransom until the war puts down its burdens. That is it. And if Allah willed, he could have taken vengeance upon them, but rather to test some of you by means of others, and those who are killed in the way of Allah, their deeds will not be wasted." Now people may say, "see! We have permission to strike disbelievers." But we need to remember the context of Muhammad's struggle. He was violently prevented from practising his faith. This does not happen in civil society. Therefore Muslims cannot use this as a precedent to wage war or fight non-believers. We should not blindly apply texts meant for one situation to other scenarios. To think about this for a moment would make it clear that it does not make sense at all to interpret this passage as generally applicable, for in that case Muslims would be fighting on every front and I do not believe it is practical for them to do so.

One may reply, "but we need not be practical, Allah already made the provisions and it is an honour to die in his way."

However, the verse says "either give favour afterwards or ransom until the war puts down its burdens." It makes it clear that it is talking about war, it would be totally wrong to think that it applies in general. It may sound trivial once I point this out, but people do not read texts word-by-word and then think and rethink about what they mean. So it is important to see the word "war" in the text and not follow what it says in peace. We also have to remember that such texts necessarily speak very strongly because it takes superlatives to prepare people for armed struggle and to encourage people to fight bravely in ruthless battle. Therefore speech before war needs to be read rhetorically and not literally. That is the responsible and reasonable way to read Islamic texts.

In verses 47:20–21, it is said that the believers asked, "why has a Sura not been sent down? But when a precise Sura is revealed and fighting is mentioned in it, you see those in whose hearts there is sickness looking at you with a look of one fainting from death, and obedience and good words are more appropriate for them. So when the matter was determined, then if they had been true to Allah, it would have been better for them." Again people may say, "look! Allah urges us to fight!" But this passage *was for the particular occasion on which it was revealed.* We cannot read it as a general order. The appropriate way to read this is to interpret these passages holistically, looking at the whole historical situation and all the personages involved. We cannot assume that this urges us to fight when we read it. Most orders need to be read as specific. Only commands like giving alms would apply in general, and even then, you cannot give if you cannot feed yourself. So when we read texts we need to think about the scope of application. This is our responsibility and it is not "changing its meaning." On the contrary, to read without consideration of the scope of application is "changing its meaning."

In verses 22:71–72 in the Qur'an, it is said that the ones "who worship someone other than Allah, they nearly attack those who recite Allah's verses." In this state of antagonism, it was comparatively reasonable that menacing and violent language is used against non-Muslims. But it is not applicable in other circumstances.

In verses 45:6–9 it is said, "woe to every sinful liar who hears the signs of Allah recited to him, then persists arrogantly as if he did not hear them. So give him tidings of a painful punishment. And when he knows anything of our signs, he ridicules them. There is a humiliating pun-

Chapter 4 Re-reading Islam

ishment for those people." From this passage we should be able to see that it is in the context of violent competition between different groups that threats of painful punishment to non-Muslims were given. We should not think that this is applicable to every non-Muslim, including people who have no contact with Muhammad's message, and groups that are not attacking Muslims physically.

In verse 31:23 one is told "not to be sad over people's disbelief," and it is said that their "place of return is to Allah and he will tell them what they did." This verse tells us the generally applicable rule. We need not bother about people who do not believe. Allah will take care of that. This is something that does not depend on the historical context of revelation, unlike the statements that conflict with this stance.

In verse 10:23 it is said that the rebels against Allah "will return to him in the end and he will inform them of what they have done." In verse 29:9 something similar is said. It is said that if parents "strive to make you associate others with Allah, do not obey them," and that your "place of return is to Allah and he will tell you what you have done." No mention of hell is made here and the unjust person is returned to Allah for punishment. Since he will be returned to Allah for punishment, there is no need for Muslims to try to do that. We should leave judgment for Allah. This is the reasonable stance taken by المرجئة *al-murji'a*, literally the postponers.[8]

Since the descriptions vary when punishment is discussed, we should be aware of the uncertainty surrounding

---

[8] For related discussions see Section 4.5.2 and Section 6.3.1.

this issue. Therefore, we should not be too confident about the claim that non-Muslims would be sent to hell, and of course we should not think that we have the right to punish these "hell-bound" people. In verse 5:32 it is said that Allah "decreed upon the children of Israel that whoever kills a soul, unless [avenging a murder] or for corruption on earth, it is as if he had killed all mankind, and who saves one, it is as if he had saved all mankind. And our messengers had certainly come to them with clear proofs. Then indeed many of them, after that, were transgressors on earth."

In general, Islamic texts talk about peace a great deal but they also talk about fighting a great deal. What about Hadiths that seem to encourage fighting non-believers, such as the Hadith in which Muhammad said that he has been ordered to fight against the people until they bear witness that there is no god but Allah and that Muhammad is his messenger, perform prayers, and give alms? [3, 2:24] We have to remember that Muhammad was living in an age in which his freedom to believe and preach was threatened, and the requirement was more political allegiance then religious belief, as becoming a Muslim by compulsion or only in outward behaviour is not truly embracing Islam. [3, 2:26]

Similarly, for verse 9:5 in the Qur'an in which Muslims are told to kill polytheists, one should not read it without qualification. It was in the context of survival for Muhammad and his followers. It should not be interpreted as universal. In fact, we could see Muhammad was told to adopt different attitudes under different circumstances. It is not even practical for a Muslim to think that one should always fight non-Muslims, for then we cannot rest until the earth is free of non-Muslims, if that ever happens.

When viewed in their historical context, such passages should not be interpreted to incite general fighting against non-Muslims. Interpreting them to mean fighting against all non-Muslims is just a trick of war-mongers. Harming and killing non-believers is definitely not the best way to spread Islam.

Chapter 4 Re-reading Islam

And verse 4:94 in the Qur'an should be viewed carefully. It says that when you fight in the way of Allah, which presumably refers to Muhammad's military campaigns, you should investigate and not easily place people in the category of infidels. It seems to imply that if someone is not a Muslim, then you may take his life and belongings. However, remember that this is said in the context of battles which Muhammad and his followers were fighting for survival and the freedom to practice Islam. It is wrong to apply this in any other context.

In verse 19:83 it is said that Allah sent devils to the non-believers to incite them. Why does he not try to lead the non-believers to his way, but do the opposite, and incite them to war? Perhaps it is more reasonable to read this in the context of the particular war Muhammad was fighting and that this passage only aimed at putting the hearts of his followers at ease. Again this shows that we must read with reservation, and never assume that passages are meant to be universal and eternal.

We need to ask ourselves if we believe that Allah should incite war and suffering. If not, we should treat such passages skeptically. We should not adopt the attitude that Islamic texts should be accepted completely and literally, and applied universally in time and space.

If you agree with this, you have to establish a firm state of mind about non-harming. Otherwise violent-minded clerics might still be able to move you because of the circumstance and atmosphere of early Islam. Of course it is also a peculiar orientation of our times that tends to think that early Islam is equivalent to a simple, abiding, and thus better Islam. But in fact each of those qualities is independent, needs to be established separately, and they are not necessarily the same thing.

Early Islam was perhaps not simple in the sense of non-corrupt and just. Society was full of chaos and problems.

Abiding by the rules of Islam in the days when those rules were given may be good, but it may be bad in our times.

After considering the issue of violence against non-

Muslims, let us discuss the issue of association with them.

4.5.4 Association

Should Muslims associate with non-Muslims? Let us look at relevant passages in the Qur'an and the Hadiths.

In verse 3:118 in the Qur'an it is said, "O you who have believed, do not take as intimates those other than yourselves." But as the ensuing verses show, Muslims were fighting against non-Muslims, so in a state of war it is reasonable not to take people from the other side as associates. It should not be generalised.

Similarly in 58:14–15 it is said, "did you not see those who take as allies a people with whom Allah was angry? They are not of you and not of them, and they swear to falsehood while they know. Allah has prepared for them a severe punishment. Indeed, what they were doing was evil." This seems to say that under no circumstances should Muslims associate with non-Muslims. But if we read on, we see that 58:16 says, "they took their oaths as a cover, so they averted from the way of Allah, and there is a humiliating punishment for them." The "way of Allah" as used here probably refers to supporting Muhammad's campaigns. Therefore it is very likely that there were military risks at stake, and the passage does not talk about just any association between Muslims and non-Muslims. We should not apply this passage generally.

In verse 60:1 it is said, "O you who have believed, do not take my enemies and your enemies as allies." People might interpret it as saying that non-Muslims are Allah's enemies. But the truth is it refers to people who have "driven out the Prophet and yourselves because you believe in Allah." Therefore Allah's enemies should only include people who actively persecute Muslims. Non-Muslims should not automatically be put into this group. In verses 60:7–9 this is made clear, "perhaps Allah will put, between you and those to whom you have been enemies among them, affection, and Allah is competent, and Allah is forgiving and merciful. Allah does not forbid you

Chapter 4 Re-reading Islam

from those who do not fight you because of religion and do not expel you from your homes [and Allah does not forbid you] from being righteous toward them and acting justly toward them. Indeed, Allah loves those who act justly. Allah only forbids you from those who fight you because of religion and expel you from your homes and aid in your expulsion, to make allies of them, and whoever makes allies of them, then those are the wrongdoers." Here we can see that only people who fight Muslims because they believe in Islam are forbidden as allies.

In the same vein, we have to treat the phrase "a people with whom Allah has become angry" very carefully. In verse 60:13 it is said, "O you who have believed, do not make allies of a people with whom Allah has become angry. They have despaired of the hereafter just as the disbelievers have despaired of the inhabitants of the graves." The descriptions following the phrase do not act as definitions. We should not put everyone who does not believe in the afterlife into the group with which Allah is angry. It is a continuation of the verses above, therefore it is referring to people who fight Muslims because they are Muslims.

In verses 60:10–11 it is said that men should not marry women who are disbelievers. Arrangements regarding dowry are discussed. "O you who have believed, when the believing women come to you as emigrants, examine them. Allah is most knowing as to their faith. And if you know them to be believers, then do not return them to the disbelievers; they are not lawful [wives] for them, nor are they lawful [husbands] for them. But give the disbelievers what they have spent. And there is no blame upon you if you marry them when you have given them their due compensation. And hold not to marriage bonds with disbelieving women, but ask for what you have spent and let them ask for what they have spent. That is the judgment of Allah; He judges between you. And Allah is knowing and wise. And if you have lost any of your wives to the disbelievers and you subsequently obtain [something], then give those whose wives have gone the equivalent of what they had spent. And fear Allah, in whom you are believers." This should be read in connection with the context of war and enmity above. This passage is only talking about male Muslims and female non-Muslims, but in general we need to remember the moral construal of Islam and postponement before we proclaim that someone is not a Muslim and thus an avowed Muslim is prohibited from marrying him or her.

4.5.4.1 Belonging to a non-Muslim State

As for the issue of Muslims belonging to non-Muslim states, it is interesting to note that March discusses this at length in his book *Islam and Liberal Citizenship: The Search for an Overlapping Consensus*. [29] He tries to locate the overlapping consensus among comprehensive doctrines (such as major religions). The idea of overlapping consensus comes from Rawls's work on liberalism. [38] It is argued that despite major differences in the realm of religion and metaphysics, people with different faiths can reach similar political judgements, achieving co-existence in the same state.

4.5.5 Polytheists

In this section, the word "polytheists" corresponds to the word المشركون *al-mushrikūn* in Arabic, literally the ones who associate others with Allah. Polytheists seem to constitute a subset of infidels but since it is repeatedly discussed in Islamic texts, let us further examine this issue separately.

Chapter 4 Re-reading Islam

In verses 2:48, 4:48, 4:116 etc. in the Qur'an, it is said that Allah does not forgive people who worship other gods along with Him. This is a huge issue in Islam, some of the worst sectarian clashes stem from this matter.

First we must reflect on what is really meant by worshipping other gods when we use this phrase in the context of Islam. In the Qur'an, the verb أَشْرَكَ *ashraka* is used in discussing such acts. It is a form IV verb derived from the root ش - ر - ك *sh–r–k* which means to share, so strictly speaking أَشْرَكَ *ashraka* means *to make someone an associate or a partner of God*, not just any acts of devotion to beings other than Allah. Therefore, not just any respect paid to higher beings can be categorised as polytheism, even though this is the view adopted by many Muslims. And this contributes to a great deal of paranoia and farcical declarations by clerics.

In short, one has to put those beings on the same footing as Allah to qualify as having committed polytheism.

Let us illustrate this issue with the following discussion. In Islam, as in Judaism and Christianity, there are angels. If we pay them high standards of regard and respect, it should not constitute polytheism. High standards of regard and respect can range from thinking about them, repeating their names, writing their names, making mementos, celebrating their festivals, visiting their holy sites, burning candles or incense for them, following specific traditions related to them, performing special rituals devoted to them, etc.

In verse 2:158 in the Qur'an it is said that الصفا والمروة

231

(al-Safā and al-Marwa) are "among the symbols of Allah" and that there is "no blame upon pilgrims for walking between them." It is then said that whoever "volunteers good then Allah is appreciative and knowing."

In verse 22:32 it is said that whoever "honours the symbols of Allah is from the piety of hearts." And in 22:34 it is said that for each nation "we have made rites for them to mention the name of Allah over cattle." In some societies they do not have access to cattle. Then surely some other rites can be performed.

In the end, which are acts honouring the symbols of Allah and which are acts of polytheistic rituals? It is not easy to tell. In verse 2:158 one rite is explicitly set out. What about other rites that are not mentioned? Should they be assumed by default to be lawful or unlawful? Performing one of these acts could be the difference between a monotheist and a polytheist, and yet we do not have a clear rule for distinguishing between them. We only have sporadic cases from which we cannot derive a general rule.

In view of this confusion, where should one draw the line between monotheists and polytheists? Remember, those on one side of one line go to heaven, and those on the other side go to hell. Is it reasonable to decide where to send people after death according to this criterion? Is it not more reasonable to decide where to send people according to whether they killed anyone unjustly or not?

In verse 23:44, while telling stories about Noah and Moses, it is said that we "sent our messengers successively, and every time a messenger came to a nation, they denied him, so we made them follow each other in the path of destruction." And no one who was not in contact with messengers got punished in the stories of the Qur'an. This is corroborated in 25:35–40, 26:10–190, 27:45–58, 29:14–40, 37:73–148, 38:12–14, 50:12–14, 51:24–46, 53:50–56, 54:9–42, 69:4–10, 79:15–26, 85:17–20, etc. where there are lists of prophets and the destruction of their people after ignoring the messages they brought, and prophets without bringing destruction, but never destruction without a prophet. In verses 43:46–56 the story of Moses and the punishment

Chapter 4 Re-reading Islam

of the Egyptians is briefly narrated, followed by 43:57–66 in which Jesus is introduced, and it is stated that "the denominations from among them differed, so woe to those who did wrong, for [they shall receive] the punishment of a painful day. What are they waiting for, except the hour to come to them suddenly and they do not feel?" In verses 46:21–25 it is said that the brother of 'Aad "warned his people in al-Ahqaf, and bearers of warning had passed on before him and after him," saying "do not worship except Allah, indeed I fear for you the punishment of a grave day" but they ignored him, so a wind came, in which there was "a painful punishment, destroying everything by command of its lord." In verses 50:12–14 it is said, "the people of Noah denied before them, and the companions of the well and Thamud and 'Aad and Pharaoh and the brothers of Lot, and the companions of the wood and the people of Tubba' all denied the messengers, so my threat was justly fulfilled." In verse 71:1 it is said that Allah sent Noah to his people, telling him to "warn your people before there comes to them a painful punishment," then in 71:25 it is said, "because of their sins they were drowned and put into the fire, and they did not find helpers for themselves besides Allah." All these are records of prophets being sent and people who do not follow them being punished afterwards.

In verse 17:15, it is said that Allah "does not punish until he has sent a prophet." In verses 26:208–209 it is said "Allah did not destroy any town except one with bearers of warning as a reminder," and that he was never unjust. This is repeated in 28:58, saying that Allah "does not destroy a town without sending a messenger," and that "their people are wrong-doers." In verses 28:46–47 it is said that Moses is sent as a bearer of warning, and if Allah does not send a prophet before punishing them with a disaster, then people would question and blame Allah. In verses 37:167–170 it is said that the infidels "used to say that if we have a reminder like the former peoples, then we would have been the servants of Allah that are made sincere, and that they disbelieved, so they will know." And in 37:176–

177 it is said "when Allah's punishment descends into their territory, then the morning of the warned ones would be terrible." Then in 38:3–4 it is said that Allah "has destroyed many generations before, and they wondered that a bearer of warning came to them, and the infidels said that this is a magician and a liar." In verses 43:74–78 it is said that the criminals "are abiding eternally in the punishment of hell" and "we had already brought you the truth, but most of you hate it." In verses 67:6–9 it is said, "for those who disbelieved in their lord is the punishment of hell, and wretched is the destination. When they are thrown into it, they hear from it an inhaling while it boils up. It almost bursts with rage. Every time a group is thrown into it, its keepers ask them, 'did there not come to you a bearer of warning?' They will say, 'yes, a bearer of warning came to us, but we denied and said, "Allah has not sent down anything. You are not but in great error." ' "

In verse 30:9 people are told to travel and look at what happened at the end to people to whom prophets came, and that Allah "did not wrong them." In verse 30:47 it is said that Allah "sent prophets to their people with clear proofs," and Allah "took revenge on the criminals." In verses 40:21–22 people were told to "travel and look at the end of those who were before them," that they were "greater than them in strength" but "Allah seized them for their sins" and this is because "their messengers used to come to them with clear proofs but they disbelieved, so Allah seized them." In verses 43:6–8 it is said that Allah sent many prophets "among the former peoples, and there did not come to them any prophet whom they did not ridicule, so we destroyed powers mightier than [the Meccans], and the example of the former peoples has occurred." In verses 44:10–14 it is said that one day "the sky will bring clear smoke, enveloping the people. This is a painful punishment" and "a clear messenger came to them, then they turned away from him and said, a lunatic taught [by others]." In verses 50:36–37 it is said, "how many a generation before [the righteous] did we destroy, who were greater than them in power and explored

Chapter 4 Re-reading Islam

throughout the lands. Is there any place of escape? Indeed in that is a reminder for whoever has a heart or who listens while he is witnessing." In verses 64:5-6 it is said, "Has there not come to you the news of those who disbelieved before? So they tasted the bad consequence of their affairs, and there is a painful punishment for them. That is because their messengers used to come to them with clear evidences, but they said, 'do human beings guide us?' So they disbelieved and turned away, and Allah did not need them, and Allah is free of need and praiseworthy." In verses 65:8-11 it is said, "how many a city rebelled against the command of its lord and his messengers, so we took it to severe account and punished it with a terrible punishment. So it tasted the bad consequence of its affair, and the outcome of its affair was loss. Allah has prepared for them a severe punishment, so fear Allah, O you of understanding who have believed. Allah has sent down to you a message, a messenger reciting to you the clear signs of Allah in order that he may bring out those who believe and do righteous deeds from darkness into the light, and whoever believes in Allah and does righteousness, he will admit him into gardens beneath which rivers flow, abiding in them forever. Allah has perfected for him a provision." In verses 73:15-16 it is said, "indeed, we have sent you a messenger as a witness to you just as we sent to Pharaoh a messenger. But Pharaoh disobeyed the messenger, so we seized him with a ruinous seizure."

In view of the above verses stating the coming of prophets, disobedience, then punishment, it is reasonable to conclude that punishment for practicing polytheism (and only the kind of polytheism in which other gods are put on the same footing as Allah) is only for people who had prophets sent to them but ignored their guidance. If guidance has not been sent, how could people learn about the difference between polytheist rituals on the one hand, which they are supposed to avoid, and monotheist rituals, on the other, which they are supposed to perform?

In verse 23:17 in the Qur'an, it is said that Allah "has created above you seven layered heavens," and that he is aware of his creation. In 17:44, it is said that the seven heavens and the earth and everyone in them exalt Him. It is also said that everything "exalts Allah by praising him, but that you do not understand their way of exalting." And then it is said that Allah is "forbearing and forgiving." This passage seems to tell us that there are higher beings in the seven heavens, and that there are different ways to exalt and praise Allah. If that is the case, why cannot paying respect to higher beings be a form of exaltation of Allah? Idolatry is a great taboo in Abrahamic religions, but a ban on it is not essential to Islam. We can see it as a historical relic in which the need to follow previous revelations and to establish concentrated authority led to an emphasised ban of idolatrous practice. But these practices could also be in praise of Allah, as he is the ultimate source of life and the highest being.

In verses 53:26–29 it is said "how many angels there are in the heavens whose intercession will not avail at all except after Allah has permitted to whom he wills and approves. Indeed those who do not believe in the hereafter name the angels by female names, and they have no knowledge in support of this. They follow nothing except assumption, and indeed, assumption does not avail at all against the truth. So turn away from whoever turns his back on our message and desires nothing except worldly life." The existence of angels is acknowledged in Islam. From this passage we can see that the mistake of polytheists, according to Islam, is to believe in the power of the intercession of angels, and the consequent attitude of appeasing them for worldly goals. So the real problem is corruption in life. The most important issue is not difference in theology, but being worldly and not caring about morality and spirituality. We see this made explicit in 53:33–35 in which it says, "have you seen the one who turned away and gave a little and refrained? Does he have knowledge of the unseen, so he sees?" It clearly links Islamic belief to giving to the needy. I contend that to make people do good is the motivation for the seemingly strong condemnation of polytheism. But it was linked to the particular

Chapter 4 Re-reading Islam

types of worship Arabs at the time were practicing. Therefore we should not read such condemnations too strongly and also they do not apply automatically to all varieties of polytheism.

We can find more evidence for this account of the condemnation of polytheism and religious reform in 6:137 in which it is said, "to many of the polytheists their partners have made pleasing the killing of their children in order to ruin them and to confuse them in their religion," and then in 6:140 it is said, "lost are those who killed their children foolishly without knowledge and prohibited what Allah had provided for them, inventing lies about Allah. They have gone astray and were not guided." From such descriptions we can see that polytheist Arabs did not have a moral leader. They performed religious rituals but did not need to act justly to earn the favour of their gods. It is this form of religion that Islam protests strongly against.

Throughout history there have been many different approaches in different cultures and sects in the same religion, not to say in different ones. In the recent conservative wave propagated by Saudi Wahhabis nearly anything other than the daily prayers and pilgrimage to Mecca is regarded as polytheism. For example, visiting the graves of Sufi saints is regarded as a form of polytheism. This may seem to be the "correct" one, but in fact it is just one school among many.

From the discussion above one should be able to see that the injunctions against polytheism and idolatry constitute a delicate and confusing matter and we should not be presumptuous and think that we are the ones to determine who is a polytheist and who is not. Allah alone knows that. We should be cautious and open to different views and interpretations.

By the way, more extreme groups even say that portraits are a form of polytheism. Many Muslims reacted with anger when a cartoonist drew Muhammad. This is just paranoia. Do you think non-Muslims are making portraits of Muhammad in order to worship him? If not, what is the problem? On the other hand, if non-Muslims are making portraits of him to make fun of him, what is the big deal? People make jokes about Jesus all the time. Christians do not react violently. Why should Muslims react so strongly when someone makes fun of Muhammad who is in Islam only a prophet? Should we conclude from Muslims' attitude that Muhammad is a god therefore one cannot make fun of him? Is this not committing a form of polytheism where one makes a god of Muhammad? Is this not committing the sin of idolatry? The irony is that Islam emphasises the mistake of Christians in making a god of Jesus.

From this we can see that Muslims who reacted with violent reactions are either too stupid to understand that one can make portraits without the intention of worshipping them, or are themselves polytheists making a god of Muhammad. May Allah forgive them.

The ban against polytheism should be understood on a higher level. In verse 12:108, Muhammad is told to say, "this is my way. I invite to Allah with insight, I and those who follow me. And exalted is Allah, and I am not of those who associate others with him." It is said in 9:31, 10:18, 16:1, 28:68, 30:40, 39:67, 52:43, and 59:23 that Allah is exalted above what they associate with him. In verses 6:100, 21:22, 23:91, 37:159, 37:180, and 43:82 it is said that Allah is exalted above what they describe.

It is even granted that the worshiped entities exist. In verses 46:5–6 it is said that on judgment day "when the people are gathered," the ones people invoked besides Allah "will be enemies to them." This verse shows that those entities exist and will be judged on judgment day.

From such verses we should be able to see that the real reason against polytheism is not that it would incur Allah's wrath, but that it is a lower form of theology. All these verses emphasise that Allah is higher than how people describe him or think about him.[9] In primitive forms of worship people tend to impose their way of being, their likes and dislikes, their ideas, etc. onto the god they are

---

[9] I shall expand on this in Section 7.3.4.

Chapter 4 Re-reading Islam

worshipping, so that the worshipped would be very similar to the worshipper. In contrast, to be able to postulate an abstract, exalted being is a sophisticated development of religion. It presupposes more theological reflection and a more comprehensive conception of religion. Monotheism rises above a great deal of pagan nonsense and chaotic practices.

However, one may say, "for all you have said, what about the assertion that there is no god but Allah, which frequently occurs in the Qur'an and is part of the creed?"

Indeed it is emphasised in verses 2:163, 2:255, 3:2, 3:6, 3:18, 3:62, 4:87, 6:102, 6:106, 7:158, 9:31, 9:129, 10:90, 11:14, 13:30, 16:2, 20:8, 20:14, 20:98, 21:25, 23:116, 27:26, 28:70, 28:88, 35:3, 37:35, 38:65, 39:6, 40:3, 40:62, 40:65, 44:8, 47:19, 59:22–23, 64:13, and 73:9 that there is no god but Allah. In addition, in verse 16:51 people are told not to take two gods, and in verses 17:22, 17:39, 18:14–15, 19:81, 28:88, 50:26, and 51:51 people are warned not to make, take, or call another god alongside Allah.

First, how can one argue against the view that any kind of worship other than the daily prayers and pilgrimage as specified in the Qur'an and the Hadiths is not lawful? As I mentioned before, the distinction between permitted forms of worship and polytheism is not as clear as conservatives would like to say that it is. Secondly, even though it says there is only one god, there are still angels. Why cannot gods in other religions be referred to as angels in Islam? Therefore it is still more reasonable to interpret the assertion that there is no god but Allah as saying that there is no other god with the same exalted status as Allah.

In verses 6:19, 9:31, 14:52, 16:22, 18:110, 21:108, 22:34, 29:46, 37:4, 38:65, and 41:6 it is said that Allah is only one god, but this is probably directed against the trinitarian doctrine. The verse 5:73 says this explicitly. It says, "those who say, 'Allah is a third of three' have certainly disbelieved, and there is no god except one god." The concept of the trinity does not make sense, for it would cause logical inconsistency. For example, how can one be the father and the son at the same time? Then would he be his own grandson too? Since as the son he can be a father at the same time then there would be a grandson. This is total chaos. The father-and-son relation can only take place between two individuals. But this could be rather complicated for the level of the audience Muhammad was speaking to and it was a simpler refutation to say that there is only one god.

Interestingly in verses 7:59, 7:65, 7:73, 7:85, 11:50, 11:61, 11:84, 23:23, and 23:32 it is said, "there is no god for you except him." There is some nuance to be found in this assertion. This is the case *for them*, for the audience of Muhammad. One could interpret it as meaning that Muhammad, as the national prophet of the Arabs, presented Islam to them as an improvement on their system of beliefs. It is not meant to be imposed upon people of other times.

Monotheism has its benefits as opposed to polytheism. But to fight and kill in order to get rid of polytheism goes totally against the advancement of civilisation. Muhammad and his followers were actively persecuted by polytheist groups. But this is not the context we have in modern society. We now have more violence perpetrated in the name of monotheism than paganism. Therefore to follow the example of Muhammad and his followers and fight polytheists is not at all a suitable thing to do now.

Let us look at a passage which exemplifies believers' misplaced touchiness well. In verse 51:56 it is said, "I did not create jinn and mankind except to worship me." Muslims read this and some of them might think, "look, mankind is created to worship Allah. People who do not, they do not even deserve to exist." But they forget that 51:57–58 goes on to say, "I do not want from them any provision, and I do not want them to feed me. Indeed, it is Allah who is the provider, the firm possessor of strength." The sense of "only" in 51:56 really means *not more*, i.e. nothing else is expected except worship. It does not, as some might think without reading the ensuing verses, mean *the only goal of human existence.*

Lastly, what about the injunction in 9:28 in the Qur'an

saying that the polytheists are unclean and should not be allowed to come near the Masjid al-Haram? Again, we need to remember that this was in the age of Muhammad fighting for the control of the mosque. It should not be applied to all non-Muslims and all mosques.

Muslims should not think that non-Muslims are unclean and that they should not be allowed to enter mosques. It is very narrow-minded. This is very harmful to mutual understanding between different communities and can cause problems for people of different faiths living in close proximity in the globalised world. Even from a selfish point of view, this is not good for the image of Islam and the spread of Islam. For if non-Muslims are not allowed to come near mosques, how can they learn about Islam and experience the atmosphere of Islamic religious practice?

4.5.6 People of the Book

In the Qur'an, the position regarding the *people of the book*, i.e. Jews and Christians, is ambiguous. And this has given an excuse for clashes. Let us review this issue thoroughly.

First of all, in verse 2:62 in the Qur'an it is said that those "who believed and those who were Jews, Christians, or Sabeans, those who believed in Allah and the last day and did righteous deeds, will have their reward with Allah," and that there "will not be any fear concerning them and they will not grieve." From this verse we see that they could receive equal rewards that are as good as those granted to Muslims.

In verse 48:29 it is said, "Muhammad is the messenger of Allah, and those with him are forceful against the disbelievers, merciful among themselves. You see them bowing and prostrating, seeking bounty and pleasure from Allah. Their mark is on their faces from the trace of prostration. That is their similitude in the Torah, and their similitude in the Gospel is like a plant which sends out its offshoots then strengthens them so they grow thick and stand upon their stalks, delighting the sowers, in order that by them Allah may enrage the disbelievers. Allah has promised those, who believe and do righteous deeds among them, forgiveness and a great reward." From this verse we can see that the Torah and the Gospel are cited as corroboration and support for what is being said.

Additionally, in verse 22:40 it is said that were it not that Allah "repudiates the people, some by means of others, then monasteries, churches, synagogues, and mosques, in which the name of Allah is mentioned many times, would have been demolished," and that Allah will surely "support those who support him for Allah is powerful and full of might." From this passage we can see that Jews and Christians are seen as supporters of Allah and that they are viewed favourably.

What about the relationship between Muslims, Jews, and Christians? On the surface, it seems that Allah urges Muslims not to be allies with Jews and Christians (5:51), and that Jews and Christians are going to hell. In verse 5:17 it is said that those who say that God is Jesus, son of Mary, disbelieve (كفر *kafara*). In verse 5:49 it is said that many Jews and Christians are "disobedient to Allah."

In verses 62:6–7 Muhammad is told to say, "you who are Jews, if you claim that you are allies of Allah, excluding the people, then wish for death, if you should be truthful." And it is added, "and they will not ever wish for it because of what their hands presented, and Allah is knowing of the wrongdoers." From this passage it seems that Jews are not real believers.

However, one has to read carefully. The Qur'an affirms the Torah (5:44) and the Gospels (5:46), saying that Allah sent them down and there is guidance and light

Chapter 4 Re-reading Islam

in them, and it says that both contain what believers should do (5:66) and the true promise of Allah (9:111). In verse 33:7 it is said that when Allah "took from the prophets their covenant and from Muhammad and from Noah and Abraham and Moses and Jesus the son of Mary, he took a solemn covenant." We also have to remember that Muhammad and his followers were fighting with different groups so taking allies was a risky issue, but we need not apply the injunction not to be allies with Jews and Christians in our own case. And the passage 62:6–7 need not apply to every Jew, for revelations frequently had a context and specific reference which are lost to us.

However, the Qur'an does qualify that Jews and Christians distorted some of the revelations. In verse 5:66 it is said that there is "a moderate community among them" and on the other hand there are "evil-doers among them." In verses 2:213, 3:19, 42:14, and 45:17, it has been said that human beings had one religion and people were given the scripture, but then they differed out of rivalry after receiving this knowledge.

As for Christianity, it is said repeatedly (2:116, 4:171, 6:101, 10:68, 17:111, 18:4, 19:35, 19:88, 19:92, 21:26, 23:91, 25:2, 39:4, 72:3 etc.) that God has not taken a son. In verse 72:3 it is said, "exalted is the nobleness of our lord; he has not taken a wife or a son." This is perhaps also directed at Christianity. The case is similar for 112:1–4 in which Muhammad is told to say, "he is Allah, [who is] one. Allah, the eternal. He did not beget and was not born, and there is to him no equivalent."

In verses 43:81–83 Muhammad is told to say, "if the most gracious had a son, then I would be the first of the worshippers. Glory be to the lord of the heavens and the earth, lord of the throne, above what they describe. So leave them to converse and play until they meet their promised day" referring presumably to Christianity. Note that perhaps judgment day is meant here, but we cannot conclude rashly that they are going into hellfire, for here we can only conjecture that maybe they would be punished, but not necessarily severely.

In verses 57:28–29 it is said, "O you who have believed, fear Allah and believe in his messenger. He gives you a double portion of his mercy, makes for you a light to walk by, and forgives you, and Allah is forgiving and merciful. So that the people of the book may know that they are not able to get anything from the bounty of Allah and that the bounty is in the hand of Allah, giving it to whom he wills." This passage seems to say that only Muslims have the favour of Allah while Allah does not give the people of the book anything. But the clause "they are not able to get anything from the bounty of Allah" should not be read universally, for if everything is from Allah and by the permission of Allah, of course the people of the book have received from the bounty of Allah. Therefore the word "bounty" here is bound to have a definite reference. Perhaps a military victory in a specific battle. Otherwise the clause does not make sense. Since the reference of the clause is specific, we cannot deduce from this passage that none of the people of the book will be received favourably by Allah. Therefore this passage does not prescribe a terrible end for all of them. It was only talking about specific groups with whom Muhammad was dealing and not all of the people of the book are evil ones going to hell. The reasonable view is that each would be judged according to his deeds, as argued in Section 4.1.2.

From the verses above we can see that, according to the Qur'an, Judaism and Christianity both have problems. But it does not go so far as to say that Jews and Christians would be punished and are going to hell. So we cannot draw a clear conclusion as to whether they are saved or not according to the Qur'an. We need to wait for judgment day. In fact, even among Muslims we are not sure everyone who says he is a Muslim is going to heaven, and everyone who has not said that he is a Muslim is going to hell. We also need to wait for judgment day. More on this in Section 4.1.2.

In fact, let us imagine if Allah were to send a prophet today. The messages conveyed by this messenger would probably contain much criticism of Muslims, and would

Chapter 4 Re-reading Islam

probably say that many of them are corrupt. Does it mean that no Muslims are going to heaven? It seems unlikely. Analogously, what is meant in the Qur'an is that many Jews and Christians are corrupt and mistaken, but those who really follow the Torah and the Gospels can still be accepted by Allah and go to heaven, as for example 5:69 says there is "no need to fear for them and they will not grieve."

What about the passages warning against taking them as allies such as 5:51 or 32:23–30 in the Qur'an in which it is said that Allah "gave Moses the book and made it a guide for the children of Israel," that they were "patient and certain about Allah's signs," that Allah will "judge between them on the day of resurrection regarding what they differ about," and in the end one is told to "turn away from them"? We should remember that Muhammad was fighting different groups and such passages are about particular warring circumstances and it is not reasonable to apply their content to other time periods or situations.

In verses 11:110 and 41:45 it is said that Allah "gave Moses the Scripture, but that they had disagreements about it. And if not for a word of your lord that came before, it would have been judged between them." From this passage it seems that Allah prevents judgment against them. Therefore we should remember that we are not really sure about the status of the people of the book. To say that they would be punished is not warranted.

In verses 27:76–78 it is said that the Qur'an "narrates to the Children of Israel what they most differ about," that it is "guidance and mercy for the believers," and that he will judge them. Here we can see that the Qur'an is intended as a correction to Judaism, clarifying the issues Jews disagree about. It seems to imply that Jews are among the believers. And since they are in disagreement, probably at least some of them are right, and they have subscribed to the correct form of *islam*, the usage of which is discussed in Section 4.1.1. As a confirmation of that we see in 29:46 that Muhammad is told "not to argue with the people of the book except in a way that is best, except those who

245

are unjust among them," and Muslims are told to say, "we believe in that which was revealed to us and was revealed to you, and our god and your god is one, and we submit (مسلمون *muslimūn*) to him."

In verses 39:27–33 it is said that Allah "presented every example in this Qur'an so that they may remember, an Arabic Qur'an without any deviance so that they may become righteous," that Allah "presents the example of a man owned by quarrelling partners and a man belonging to one man without dispute, that they are not equal," that you will die and they will die, that you will "dispute on the day of resurrection before Allah," that no one is more unjust that one "who lies about Allah and denies the truth when it comes to him," that there is "in hell a residence for the infidels," that the one "who came with the truth and those who believed in it are the righteous ones." Perhaps people may read from this passage that the people of the book are going to hell, for they are the ones disagreeing about the nature of God. But this is not a meaning that is totally obvious. I would argue that reading this passage as saying that among the people in dispute some denied the truth and are going to hell, while some believed the truth and are going to heaven, that reading it this way makes as much sense, or more, than reading it as saying that the people of the book are the ones denying the truth and that they are all going to hell.

If we are not sure that Allah rejects them, who are we to think that they are wrong-doers going to hell?

In verse 5:48 in the Qur'an it is said that Allah "gave Jews, Christians, and Muslims each their own laws and programmes so that they will compete in doing good." From this verse it is clear that Jews and Christians can receive good rewards from Allah.

And in 22:17 it is said that Allah will "judge between those who have believed, those who were Jews, the Sabeans, the Christians, the Magians, and the polytheists." If everyone except Muslims receives the same treatment, then there is no need to "judge between them." It is reasonable to suppose that the details of one's faith and actions will be judged and it is not as simple as saying the creed and going to heaven, and not saying it and going to hell. We shall see it during the judgment. Before that comes, everyone should be wary and use their good sense. As I argued in Section 3.2.1, the reasonable solution is to advocate secular rule and let everyone choose for themselves.

In verse 28:4 it is said that Pharaoh "exalted himself in the land and made its people into sects, oppressing a group, slaughtering their sons and letting live their women," and that he was one of the corrupters. People tend to read it and see only the evil of Pharaoh, but we should also see that the evil lay in separating people into different groups and oppressing them. If we are overly strict about doctrinal issues, saying that people do not belong to our religion if they think differently on some issues, then we get innumerable sects and factions. If we fight other groups of people because they think differently, then we are just like the evil Pharaoh. The irony is how close militant Islamist groups get to this, fighting every group that does not conform to their own idea of being Muslims, whether they are Muslims of a different sect, Jews or Christians, or polytheists and atheists.

4.5.7 Learning from Non-Muslims

In a Hadith, Muhammad is reported to have said that it is possible for people who hear something indirectly to understand better than the people who hear it directly. [3, 3:67] There is a common misunderstanding among some Muslim communities that Muslims must understand Islam better because they spend more time on it and hear religious figures discuss it more than non-Muslims studying it. But exposure is not a guarantee of understanding. Many non-Muslims make the effort to understand this religion while many Muslims only follow what their families do without much knowledge about Islam.

Research, independent thinking, and reflection make for a better guarantee than hearing it directly from esteemed figures. One needs to study the texts and history of Islam in order to find out what it is. This Hadith serves as a reminder of these issues.

4.6 Conclusion

After detailed discussion of actual passages in this chapter, we should be able to see that Islam is concerned with one's own faith and good actions, and tolerance towards others.

The violent and regressive interpretations of Islam commonly seen today are a reflection of the frustration and despair of many Muslims. If the states of mind of Muslims were optimistic and looking forward to the future, they would concentrate on better aspects of Islamic texts. Sadly, rather than looking forward to the future, they only want to return to the past. And the truth is, such groups do not return to the past in terms of piety and spirituality, they return only in terms of the social injustice and oppression present at that time.

But the irony is, if Muslims stick to this delusionally nostalgic Zeitgeist, it would be very hard to get out of the chaos and tragedies that are happening today in so many Muslim-majority countries.

Muslims as a community need to change their mindset first. It is not enough to be a "moderate" Muslim who is non-violent but secretly thinking that every non-Muslim neighbour is going to hell and that Islamic laws are the best laws in the world, timeless and eternal, so that only communities under Islamic laws are moral. That kind of

Chapter 4 Re-reading Islam

Muslim can be turned into a violent extremist quite easily. We need to clear away all these ancient violent political tendencies. We need to condemn these doctrines and reform our ideas about piety.

The experience and insight from re-reading the Qur'an and the Hadiths as we have done in this chapter connect to the later chapters about reform and liberalism. Because once we find out the main tenets and works required of a Muslim, we shall see that they fit with liberal ideals of free development and progress among human beings. This is not the meddling version one sees today among many Muslim communities, which partly springs from a mistaken understanding of the history of Muslim-conquered countries.

The fact is, after Muhammad's death, religious authority and government were mostly separate in countries ruled by Muslims. Judges settled disputes, but there was no comprehensive state power. [21, Chapter 1] It was during the colonial period when Europeans tried to codify their laws that Shari'a law became the model to modify and modernise from. But the rule of Shari'a law was seldom the reality in countries ruled by Muslims. There was never a Vatican in Islam, and Islamic scholars were at most advisers to rulers, never with actual power to enforce their views directly.

From the discussions above I hope that we all see the need to look beyond the versions of Islamic textual interpretation and Islamic history in vogue today, and try to reach for a more informed and critically reviewed outlook for ourselves.

Chapter 5

Re-reading Women

In the Qur'anic narrative of Adam and Eve's expulsion from paradise, Eve is not the one who initiated it. In verses 20:120–122 it is said that Satan whispered to Adam, "O Adam, shall I direct you to the tree of eternity and possession that will not deteriorate?" Then it is said that Adam and his wife "ate of it, and their private parts became apparent to them, and they began to cover themselves with the leaves of paradise, and Adam disobeyed his lord so he erred. Then his lord chose him and turned to him in forgiveness and guided [him]. He said, 'descend from paradise together, some of you being enemies to others, and if there should come to you guidance from me, then whoever follows my guidance will neither go astray nor suffer. And whoever turns away from my remembrance, then indeed he will have a straitened life, and we will gather him on the day of resurrection blind.'" Unlike in the Bible (Genesis 3:1–24), Eve is not to blame for mankind's expulsion from paradise and subsequent suffering.

In the same vein, in the Qur'an Eve is not said to be created from a rib of Adam. Eve is created from the same soul as Adam. In verse 4:1 it is said, "O mankind, fear your lord, who created you from one soul and created from it its mate and dispersed from both of them many men and women, and fear Allah, through whom you ask one another, and [honour] family ties. Indeed Allah is ever watchful over you." In verse 7:189 it is said, "it is he who created you from one soul and created from it its mate that he might dwell in security with her." In verse 39:6 it is said, "he created you from one soul. Then he made from it its mate." In verse 30:21 it is said, "and of his signs is that he created for you from yourselves mates that you may find tranquillity in them, and he placed between you affection and mercy. Indeed in that are signs for a people who give thought." Even though it is possible to interpret what is said here as the same version as in Christianity, namely that Adam is created first, then Eve is made from his rib (Genesis 2:21–22), it is just one possibility. It could be more equal than that and the two are created from the same soul.

Additionally, it is frequently emphasised in the Qur'an that creatures come in pairs. In verse 51:49 it is said, "of all things we created two mates, so that perhaps you will remember."

But then, given that in the Qur'an women are presented more equally in the story of the origin of human beings, and are not blamed for the expulsion from Eden as they are in the Bible, why in our age does Islam seem to be more at odds with women's rights than Christianity?

In this chapter, let us talk about passages in the Qur'an and the Hadiths that illuminate the place of women in Islam.

5.1 Context and Background

Fundamentalist Muslims think that the Qur'an is timeless and unchangeble, and every word should be followed *verbatim*. But it had an audience, and communication cannot take place if a text does not take into account the social conditions, knowledge, and assumptions of its audience. It shows the arrogance of fundamentalist Muslims to think that the Arabs Muhammad was talking to were on the level to receive the highest eternal unchangeable universal

Chapter 5 Re-reading Women

messages humanity can receive.

People might produce verse 10:64 of the Qur'an which says that there is "no change in Allah's words" and verses 17:77, 33:62, 35:43, and 48:23 which say "you will not find in the way of Allah any change." But it is only to assure Muslims of God's ability and the fulfilment of his promise. In Section 6.2.5 I shall show that the surrounding verses make this clear. Thus there is no conflict between these verses and establishing new versions of Allah's covenant. And even if the words themselves do not change, the way they are followed could change, because we can interpret according to the historical context and follow the reason and spirit rather than the literal command.

Look at the world. Even as a Muslim one has to accept that the world has progressed, not just materially, which is undeniable, but in understanding.

Therefore, as modern readers, we need to read old texts with historical awareness and sympathetic understanding. We need to remember that the context has vastly changed. For this reason, the text itself cannot be treated in the same way. We do not need to accept conservative interpretations to be pious, and do not need to condemn Islam to be liberal.

The guidance given in the Qur'an and the Hadiths is not a body of eternal laws. It was a covenant for the society in Muhammad's time. One might argue that it was not given in this light, it was given as if it were eternal. But if one gave laws without the gravity and authority of eternal-sounding statements to the feuding Arabian tribes, one would doubt if such laws would be accepted, let alone binding, at all. It was the kind of teaching that they were ready for, it was the kind of teaching that was an improvement on what they were doing. But we can do better now. We are ready for more advanced teaching than what they were ready for. We can make better improvements than they could make in their form of society.

As we discussed in Section 6.2.5, the Qur'an and the Hadiths were aimed at and adapted to the level and social environment of Muhammad's followers. Many Qur'anic verses hint at this. In verses 54:17, 54:22, 54:32, and 54:40 it is emphasised that Allah "has certainly made the Qur'an easy for remembrance." In verse 23:62 it is said that Allah "does not charge any soul except within its capacity."

In this age where Islam seems to be at odds with modern society and the rights of women in particular, it is the responsibility of Muslims to preserve the wisdom and discard what is outdated in Islam, while it is the responsibility of non-Muslims to celebrate the wisdom and argue against the outdated in Islam. There should be a reformation in Islam, analogous to what happened in Christianity. There are still very conservative sects in Christianity, but in comparison with Islam at this juncture, Christianity has adapted to the modern world to a larger degree. Islam can do the same. It is orientalistic to argue that Islam is "different."[1]

Unfortunately the opposite of this is happening. Somehow the segregation and covering up of women have been tied to piety and there is a vicious circle of competing in this false piety—I wear long sleeves, I am better than you.—I cover my hair, I am better than you.—I cover my face, I am better than you.

People follow such fads easily. They are like the tails of peacocks. They become more and more ridiculous, but people keep going further and further down the slope.

This is not a fault that only Muslims have been guilty of. It is something that has also existed in some historical periods in other societies. For example, in the 14th century to the 19th century in China, there was a race to prevent widows from remarrying, however young they were when they became a widow. The government built monuments for widows who died without remarrying. Families felt immensely honoured when they had the largest number of such monuments in the village. So widows were treated like prisoners and morally condemned if they wanted another marriage. Once this mindset was in place, widows were destined to live alone for decades.

---

[1] See Section 6.4.2 for relevant discussions.

Chapter 5 Re-reading Women

We should be careful so that we are not affected by such societal trends. It is difficult to evaluate the norms taken for granted in a society. But relativism is not the answer. Do you think it is reasonable that widows should be forced to live as widows for the rest of their lives? Do you think it is reasonable that women should be forced to wear clothing totally inappropriate to the weather because it is their responsibility to cover up? Why is it not, on the contrary, the responsibility of men to keep their desires under control when they see a woman's legs or hair?

It is easy to say that we should not criticise or discriminate against another culture. It sounds nice and one feels good. But what if that culture discriminates against women? Are we discriminatory if we try to stop gender discrimination? How can we fight any kind of discrimination if some group jumps out and says it is our inviolable right to stick to our tradition of discriminating against this sub-group?

Letting "respect for culture" or "respect for religion" trump women's rights is the worst confusion in leftist thought. I agree with Nawaz in calling this moral relativism the "regressive left" in his book *Radical: My Journey Out Of Islamist Extremism* [33, Ch. 27].

It is self-defeating because if moral values are only relative,[2] if there is no right or wrong regarding moral values, and people should not try to change or debate others' values, then this school should not say anything either. But they want people to accept their views.

Let us look at different aspects of women's rights in Islam, criticising whatever is not right.

5.1.1 Scope

How to read Islamic texts in general was discussed in Chapter 3. In connection with the rights and position of women in Islam we need to pay special attention to one point,

---

[2]I forego discussion of aesthetic values here, not because I think they are relative, but because this is a separate issue to which I do not want to divert our attention.

that of scope, because it is very important and frequently ignored in reading rules and commands in Islamic texts, and when we examine the rights and position of women in Islam we frequently need to read and interpret rules and commands in relation to women.

We should distinguish between passages with a wide scope of application and passages intended for a specific audience. I explained my methodology of reading in Section 3.2, and the most relevant concept is contextuality.

In verse 49:13, we have a more generally applicable passage. It says, "O mankind, indeed we have created you from male and female and made you peoples and tribes so that you may know one another. Indeed, the most noble of you in the sight of Allah are the most righteous of you. Indeed, Allah is knowing and informed."

Examples of less generally applicable passages are ones that deal with actual legal arrangements, such as inheritance. Such arrangements have to be suitable for society. It does not make sense to justify sticking to ancient rules by citing them as God-given. It is not necessarily true that God gives only eternal rules. As I shall argue in Section 6.2, it was not practical to give provisions for each generation. It would have been too complicated for a community without archives and filing systems. The Qur'an was not even in complete copies in early Islam.

I have more to say about this in Chapter 6 with reference to the question whether Islam is a timeless system of rules.

5.1.2 Society

We also need to think about the social background of Muhammad's audience. His message had to be comprehensible to them, and in order for his project to be accepted the ideas could not be too alien or the requirements too difficult for his followers.

We need to remember the social milieu Muhammad's followers were in. They were killing female babies. In verse 6:137 in the Qur'an, it is said, "to many of the polytheists,

Chapter 5 Re-reading Women

their partners have made pleasing the killing of their children, in order to ruin them and to confuse them in their religion," and then in 6:140 it is said, "those will have lost who killed their children foolishly without knowledge and forbade what Allah had provided for them, inventing lies about Allah. They have gone astray and were not guided." In verses 81:8–9 it is said that on judgment day a girl who was buried alive would be asked "for what sin she was killed." This is the only human behaviour mentioned in a description of what happens during judgment day. From these passages we can see that Islam was a social enterprise aimed at improving a nation, in which the status of women was terrible.

Let us examine verses purportedly showing the inferiority of women with this consideration in mind.

In verses 53:19–23 it is said, "so have you considered al-Lat and al-'Uzza, and Manat, the third, the other one? Is the male for you and the female for him? That then is an unjust division. They are not but names you have named them, you and your forefathers, for which Allah has not sent down authority. Indeed they follow nothing except assumption and what the souls desire, and there has already come to them guidance from their lord." Then in 53:26–29 it is said "how many angels there are in the heavens whose intercession will not avail at all except after Allah has permitted [it] to whom he wills and approves. Indeed those who do not believe in the hereafter name the angels by female names, and they have no knowledge of it. They follow nothing except assumption, and indeed, assumption does not avail against the truth at all. So turn away from whoever turns his back on our message and desires nothing except worldly life."

These verses seem to show that giving the angels female names is a bad practice and the reason is probably that the female sex is inferior.

But we need not accept this reasoning. The passage itself does not even assert the inferiority of women. This is over-interpretation.

Now for the sake of argument, let us temporarily assume that the passage is talking pejoratively about females. Even if the inferiority of women is assumed, it could well just be following the social convention of the Arabs. It does not necessarily mean that Allah holds this view. Even if there were a sense of disapproval about worshipping angels with female names, we need to remember that this message was given to Muhammad and his companions and it fits their Weltanschauung, but we need not think that this is universally and eternally true. It was something assumed without question. Notwithstanding the unacceptability of this view today, it was effective communication and dissuaded many of them from polytheist worship aiming at worldly gains with no consideration of doing good. But it is clear that the inferiority of females was not an essential part of the message. We as readers should be aware of the social context without accepting the prevalent views at that time.

The description of heaven is a telling case in this connection. The presence of beautiful virgins is an important attraction of heaven. This shows the state of society Muhammad's prophecy was working on.

The first point I would like to talk about is the phrase "purified spouses" أزواج مطهّرة *azwāj muṭahhara*. In verse 2:25 in the Qur'an people are told to "give good tidings to those who believe and do righteous deeds, that there are for them gardens beneath which rivers flow. Whenever they are provided with a provision of fruit from it, they will say, 'this is what we were provided with before,' and it is given to them like [fruits on earth]. There are in [paradise] purified spouses for them, and they will abide in

Chapter 5 Re-reading Women

it eternally." In verse 3:15 Muḥammad is told to say, "for those who fear Allah, will be gardens in the presence of their lord, beneath which rivers flow, wherein they abide eternally, and purified spouses and approval from Allah." In verse 4:57 it is said, "but those who believe and do righteous deeds—we will admit them to gardens beneath which rivers flow, wherein they abide forever. For them therein are purified spouses, and we will admit them to deepening shade."

Many Muslims assume that "purified spouses" means virgins but it does not make much sense, because in paradise if one were to live on forever, being a virgin is just one moment at the beginning, does it mean that the wife is not purified afterwards? Indeed in 55:56 and 55:74 it is emphasised that the women have not been touched by man or jinn. But this points towards the allegorical nature of such descriptions rather than affirms its literality, for still it is not very significant whether they have been touched or not, except in the limited perspective of a jealous man from a pre-modern society. If women are independent beings, not just objects, it is totally reasonable that they have been through life and have been sexually active, what is the problem in that? In fact it would make less sense otherwise. Therefore we can see that these descriptions cannot be read literally.

Or is it the case the women become virgins again after each sexual act? Then as a woman I would never want to enter heaven, because it means that every sexual act is as painful as the first one. It sounds like hell to me rather than heaven. This is an example of how totally male-oriented most of the descriptions of heaven are in the Qur'an.

Or if the wives are purified in the sense of Mary, mother of Jesus, then it is doubtful whether people would be as keen to enter paradise. Mary conceived Jesus without sexual acts. This is a celebrated miracle. But are people who aspire to enter heaven keen about experiencing immaculate conception themselves, making sexual intercourse obsolete?

In one of the six major Hadith collections *Jami' At-*

Tirmidhi [8, Vol. 4, Book 12, Hadith 2562], it is said that the "least in position of the people of paradise is the one with eighty thousand servants and seventy-two wives." And in a less prominent Hadith *Sunan Ibn Majah* [28, Vol. 5, Book 37, Hadith 4337], Muhammad has even been recorded as saying that Muslims in heaven would be married to seventy-two wives, "all of whom will have desirable front passages and he will have a male member that never becomes flaccid."

While getting seventy-two wives in heaven seems a promising prospect for heterosexual males, many women do not endorse such accounts of heaven. Such contradictory ideas about Islam seem like a bad thing, but actually it may be good for its transmission and proselytation, since people could choose what to talk about to different audiences, among the contradictory claims, when they are trying to attract people into the faith.

In verses 78:31–34 it is said, "indeed, for the righteous is attainment—gardens and grapevines, and full-breasted [companions] of equal age, and a full cup." Again these verses reflect the desires of Muhammad's audience rather than the nature of heaven. Indeed, it is perhaps the case that in the afterlife one's desires create one's perceived environment, so that what Muhammad is saying is true, but only for his audience who craved this as ultimate happiness.

However, to be rational believers, we should be aware that whatever that has been said about heaven was probably intended as metaphorical, since our state of being would definitely be so different, that it is difficult to make us understand what it is like in heaven. That is probably why descriptions suitable for the level of understanding of the audience at the time have been given.

In fact, it is not enough that we are aware of it. It is necessary for the dignified survival of Islam in the modern world that we proclaim loudly to everyone, both Muslims and non-Muslims, that anything in this line was intended as metaphorical and that it is no long suitable and acceptable in our age in view of the subjugation and objectifica-

Chapter 5 Re-reading Women

tion of women. We have to agree with people finding fault with this that it is terrible, and we should establish the consensus that it is not part of Islam anymore. We should not defend and uphold it in any way out of pride or for the sake of our self-esteem. It makes us feel better in the short term but is disastrous for our religion in the long term.

Let us look at other passages describing heaven. In verses 37:40–49 it is said that there are "women with eyes of modest gaze, as if they were well-protected eggs" for the chosen servants of Allah. In verses 38:49–52 it is said that in heaven there are "women with modest gaze and of equal age" for the righteous ones. In verses 44:51–55 it is said that the righteous "will be in a safe place within gardens and springs wearing fine silk brocade, facing each other like this and we will marry them to fair women with large eyes. They will call for every fruit safely." In verses 52:17–20 it is said that the righteous will be in heaven and will be married to "fair women with large eyes." In verses 55:46–59 it is said that for him who has feared the position of his lord there are two gardens in which "there are women limiting their glances, untouched by any man or jinn before them" "as if they were rubies and coral" and in 55:70–76 that there are "good and beautiful women," "fair ones reserved in pavilions," "untouched before them by man or jinn," "reclining on green cushions and beautiful fine carpets." In verses 56:15–24 it is said that those in heaven would be reclining on woven thrones "facing each other, young boys made eternal circulating around them with vessels, and pitchers and a cup from a flowing spring, no headache from them and they will not be intoxicated, and with any fruit they choose, and meat of fowl from what they desire, and fair women with large eyes, like well-protected pearls, as a reward for what they have done." In verses 56:27–38 it is said that the companions of the right will be "among thornless lote trees, and trees layered" with fruit, and extended shade, and poured water, and abundant fruit, "not limited and not forbidden, and raised beds. Indeed we created women anew, and made them virgins, devoted and of equal age, for the companions of the right."

In verses 78:31–34 it is said, "indeed, the righteous will gain—gardens and grapevines, and full-breasted [companions] of equal age, and a full cup."

Descriptions of heaven in the Qur'an are never complete without beautiful women. From this obsession with women we can see the Qur'an was a message for the level and social environment of Muhammad's people. Indeed it is made easy for them to remember (54:17, 54:22, 54:32, 54:40). His audience were men craving for women, unlike the composition of society today, where women and men both take part in society and people do not care only about marriage and children. Probably it is as verse 25:16 says, that in heaven, "there is for them whatever they wish, abiding eternally," analogous to verse 52:22 in which it is said, "and we will provide them with fruit and meat from whatever they desire." Since they craved women, that was what they would have in heaven.[3] This shows the limitation of Muhammad's audience and therefore the provisional nature of Islamic texts. They contained Allah's message but it was adapted to the level of Muhammad's community. If the message was too intellectual or complicated people would not have been able to follow his teachings and improve upon what they were doing. The Qur'an was the best message possible for Muhammad's community, not for every place and time. We need to accept that and should not feel that this view is an insult to Islam.

From the above discussion we can see that the Qur'an is not universally applicable, and the Hadiths even less so because of their concreteness and rootedness in the social conditions of seventh-century Arabia. They were tailored for Muhammad's community and its level of social development. We need to distill carefully the wisdom in Islamic texts suitable for our time and discard unsuitable content. We cannot simply adopt everything said in these texts. That does not do justice to our divine endowment of a highly sophisticated mind.

---

[3]See Section 3.3.2 for the allegorical nature of descriptions of the afterlife.

Chapter 5 Re-reading Women

5.1.3 Choice

As can be seen from previous discussions, the reader plays a great role in what he takes away from such an extensive body of text as the Qur'an and the Hadiths. In this section we shall look at the issue of choice, that is, which passages to choose to place more weight on when we try to form an overall picture of Islam.

Let us look at a key passage in the Qur'an, namely 6:151–152, in which Allah's commands are listed. It says, in summary,

1. Do not associate anything with Allah.

2. Be good to your parents.

3. Do not kill your children out of poverty.

4. Do not go near immoral behaviours.

5. Do not kill except by [legal] right.

6. Be fair to orphans.

7. Give full measure and weight.

8. Testify justly about relatives.

We can see it does not include anything regarding women as a separate group. From reading Islamic texts holistically one can see that the injunctions about men and women are more of an expedient nature given for the audience to which Muhammad spoke. They were at times explicit and detailed but it does not mean Muslims have to stick to them rigidly without taking into account the changes societies have undergone.

Another list of requirements is given in verses 23:1–5, as follows,

1. Be submissive when you pray.

2. Turn away from ill speech.

3. Practice alms-giving.

4. Guard your private parts except from your wives and slaves.

Some more rules are found in verses 23:57-61,

1. Anxiously fear Allah.

2. Believe in the signs of Allah.

3. Do not associate anything with Allah.

4. Give alms with your heart fearful that you will be returning to Allah.

These rules apply to both men and women except the fourth one in verses 23:1-5 which emphasises the importance of virtuous behaviour in men, unlike what imams frequently do, emphasising the need to limit the freedom of women in order to build a virtuous society. This shows the important role of Muslims as agents actively choosing what to believe in Islam and what to pay attention to in Islamic texts.

In verses 25:63-74 we can find another list, which in summary runs as follows,

1. Walk humbly.

2. Pray prostrating and standing at night.

3. Ask Allah to avert you from the punishment of hell.

4. Spend moderately.

5. Do not invoke Allah with another god.

6. Do not kill any human being except by [legal] right.

7. Do not commit unlawful sexual intercourse.

8. Repent, believe, and do righteous deeds.

9. Do not bear false witness.

10. Pass by foolish talk with dignity.

11. Do not fall deaf and blind when reminded of the signs of Allah.

12. Ask Allah to grant you wives and offspring who will be the joy of your heart and make you a leader for the righteous.

In this list there is one injunction against unlawful sexual intercourse, but it is not limited to women and no particular specification is made as to their freedom of movement or association. The responsibility to avoid unlawful sexual intercourse lies on both sexes. It is the patriarchal mindset of human beings which shifts it all upon women. This again shows the important role of Muslims as agents actively choosing what to believe in Islam and what to pay attention to in Islamic texts.

In verses 28:86–88 there is a short list, which in summary runs as follows,

1. Do not be an assistant to the infidels.

2. Do not be averted from the signs of Allah.

3. Invite people to Allah.

4. Do not associate others with Allah.

5. Do not invoke another god with Allah.

Again, there is nothing said about women's behaviour specifically.

In verses 31:17–19 we see yet another list when Luqman, a wise man in the Qur'an, instructed his son. It is summarised below.

1. Pray.

2. Command what is right.

3. Forbid what is wrong.

4. Be patient about what befalls you.

5. Do not show people contempt.

6. Do not walk about exultantly.

We see here a list for both men and women to act uprightly in life. There is no distinction needed in their rules of action.

In verses 32:15–16 there is also some guidance. It says that, when reminded by Allah's signs,

1. Fall down prostrating.

2. Praise Allah, not being arrogant.

3. Get up from the bed, supplicating Allah in fear and hope.

4. Spend from what Allah provides.

This list specifies the correct attitude for a Muslim. Again it has nothing to do with whether one is female or male.

In verses 42:36–43 there are some directions. According to these verses a Muslim should

1. Believe.

2. Rely on Allah.

3. Avoid major sins and immoralities.

4. Forgive when you are angry.

5. Respond to Allah.

6. Pray.

7. Consult your affairs by consultation.

8. Spend from what Allah provides.

9. Defend yourselves against tyranny.

10. When an evil act is done, return with the same, but those who pardon and seek reconciliation will be rewarded by Allah.

11. Revenge when you are wronged, there is no blame.

12. Avoid wronging people or tyrannising on earth.

13. Be patient and forgiving.

Again, this list gives a number of recommendations, but none distinguishes a man from a woman. The same goes for the instruction below.

In verses 61:10–11, people are told to do the following and they will be saved from a painful punishment.

1. Believe in Allah and his messenger.

2. Strive in the way of Allah with your wealth and yourselves.

Now let us look at commands specifically for women or about relationships between men and women.

Unlawful sexual intercourse or adultery (الزنى *al-zinā*) is mentioned in verses 17:32, 25:68, 60:12, and 24:2–3. I shall discuss the last one in Section 5.2.2.

In verses 17:31–37 people are told to follow the following rules.

1. Do not kill your children for fear of poverty.

2. Avoid situations which might lead to unlawful sexual intercourse.

3. Do not kill any human being except by [legal] right.

4. Do not approach the property of an orphan, except in the way that is best, until he reaches maturity.

5. Fulfil commitments.

6. Give full measure when you measure, and weigh with an even balance.

7. Do not stand by that of which you do not have knowledge.

8. Do not walk upon the earth exultantly.

In this list there is only one rule regarding the relationship between men and women, and that is to warn against unlawful sexual intercourse. It applies to both men and women.

In verses 25:67–68 there is another list of directions.

1. Spend moderately.

2. Do not invoke another deity with Allah.

3. Do not kill any human being except by [legal] right.

4. Do not commit unlawful sexual intercourse.

Again even though there is a rule about sexual intercourse, it applies to both men and women.

In verse 60:12 it is said, "O prophet, when the believing women come to you pledging to you that they will not associate anything with Allah, and they will not steal, and they will not commit unlawful sexual intercourse, and they will not kill their children, and they will not bring forth a slander they have invented between their arms and legs, and they will not disobey you in what is right, then accept their pledge and ask forgiveness for them of Allah. Indeed, Allah is forgiving and merciful." In this list the content is similar to what has been given in general for Muslims.

Chapter 5 Re-reading Women

From this discussion we should be able to see that verses that talk about men and women separately constitute but a small segment of Allah's orders. We should understand the general advice first before considering how gender-specific passages should be interpreted, otherwise our reading would not be accurate.

It cannot be stressed enough that following a religion does not mean that we do not need to make any choices in the matter of doctrine. We choose the sect to follow and which rules to follow. We are the ones who decide whether Islam is a misogynous religion or a progressive one. The texts are open to interpretation.

It depends on the level of the reader to reach an appropriate interpretation because it is an old religion and because religious texts talk about spirituality and the afterlife. In the limited minds of the uneducated, the virgins in the descriptions of heaven are important and taken literally. In the liberal minds of the enlightened, these passages are not important. They are but metaphors to convey the beauty of another experience, another world. As Rabi'a, a famous Sufi mystic says, "O God! if I worship Thee in fear of Hell, burn me in Hell; and if I worship Thee in hope of Paradise, exclude me from Paradise; but if I worship Thee for Thine own sake, withhold noßt Thine everlasting beauty!" [34, p. 82]

If Muslims want to defend women's rights, they could pay more attention to verses such as 6:139 of the Qur'an, in which it is said that Allah will "punish people who said that what is in the wombs of these cattle is only for our males, but if they are born dead, then their spouses can share."

One can say that this verse is only about eating dead animals which is forbidden in Islam. But it is more reasonable to interpret it as also referring to the unfair treatment of women, especially since in the following verse (6:140) infanticide is mentioned, the victims of which were usually female. Therefore we can see that according to the Qur'an unfair treatment of women would be punished by Allah. If we apply this to all areas, there would be gender equality in society.

In verses 16:58–60 in the Qur'an it is said that people grieve when they have a daughter, and that they would choose to bury her. It is then said that those who commit female infanticide "do not believe in the hereafter." This shows the stage of social development Muhammad's community and target audience were in. Members of this community were still burying baby girls alive because of their perceived uselessness for the family. It is easy to imagine that more radical reform would not be possible and they were not ready for messages that push for gender equality. The message Muhammad conveyed was already an improvement on the situation. More reform would have to wait. Unfortunately the age-specific passages which were meant for them have become an impediment to women's liberation in Muslim communities.

In verse 18:46 it is said that wealth and children are "adornments of worldly life but the enduring good deeds are better in the view of Allah for reward and hope." Some people choose to remember the first part of the sentence, and marry many women and have many children, but they forget about the second part of the sentence, which is more important than the first part. They also conveniently forget that in 26:88–89 it is said that on judgment day "neither wealth nor sons would be of any use, but only one who came to Allah with a sound heart." From examples like these we can see the significance of individual choice and interpretation in reading Islamic texts, especially with respect to women. In Muhammad's lifetime, women had low status, and his message could not be too radical in that context. And after Muhammad's lifetime, men were still in power in most places, and they tended to keep their higher status. Most people do not read such passages with enough awareness of the historical context and enough critical thinking. They do not stress the importance of the second part of the sentence, but are still caught in the first part of the sentence and enslave women for the sake of having as many children as possible, forgetting that, without enough education and discipline, such children will only

Chapter 5 Re-reading Women

lead miserable lives in modern society.

For another example, look at slavery. In the Qur'an, numerous verses imply that slavery is permitted (4:3, 4:25, 4:33, 4:36, 23:6, 24:31, 24:58, 30:28, etc.). In verse 24:33, one is told not to force his slave girls into prostitution if they desire chastity. It means that slavery is sanctioned, though forced prostitution is not. In verses 30:27–28 it is implied that Allah is not equal to men just as men are not equal to their slaves and would not fear the slaves in the way they fear their partners. The relationship between a master and his slaves is even used as a metaphor for the one between Allah and his servants. Muhammad is called Allah's slave (عبد 'abd which can also mean servant but probably people liked the sense of being owned by Allah) in 2:23, 17:1, 18:1, 25:1, 53:10, 54:9, 57:9, and 72:19, David is called Allah's slave in 38:17, Ayyub is called Allah's slave in 38:44, Abraham, Issac, and Jacob are called Allah's slaves in 38:45, Jesus is called a slave in 43:59, Noah and Lot are called Allah's slaves in 66:10 and Muslims are called Allah's slaves in 2:90, 2:186, 2:207, 3:15, 3:20, 3:30, 3:182, 5:118, 6:18, 6:61, 6:88, 7:32, 7:128, 8:41, 8:51, 10:107, 12:24, 14:11, 14:31, 15:40, 15:42, 15:49, 16:2, 17:17, 17:30, 17:53, 17:65, 17:96, 18:65, 18:102, 19:2, 19:61, 19:63, 20:77, 21:105, 22:10, 23:109, 25:17, 25:58, 25:63, 26:52, 27:15, 27:19, 27:59, 28:82, 29:56, 29:62, 30:48, 34:13, 34:39, 35:28, 35:31, 35:32, 35:45, 37:40, 37:74, 37:81, 37:111, 37:122, 37:128, 37:132, 37:160, 37:169, 37:171, 38:83, 39:10, 39:16, 39:17, 39:53, 40:15, 40:31, 40:44, 42:19, 42:23, 42:25, 42:27, 42:52, 43:68, 44:18, 50:11, 76:6, and 89:29. The word slave appears 131 times in the Qur'an and most of the time refers to Muslims. What a holy form of social bonding being a slave is indeed! Therefore undoubtably we can see that there was no social stigma against owning slaves as we have today.

In verse 43:32 it is said that Allah "raised some of them above others in degrees so that they may make use of one another for service." People could also argue from this verse that Allah approves of social inequality and slavery, and that he does not think that social mobility is good or necessary.

However, would people argue using all the verses above that we should bring back slavery? Very very few Muslims do. Then why do people insist that the views and rules in the Qur'an and the Hadiths about women should be kept? From these contrasting stances we can see that it is really down to the choice of Muslims. We do not care so much about what is said in the Qur'an. We think that slavery is too repugnant, so we give it up. But backward rules about women are not repugnant enough to Muslims, especially male ones, so these rules are kept.

Allah's words do not settle these issues, people's views do. Why do we not choose to see how repugnant misogyny and inequality are, and get rid of such traditions? Early Muslims tried to improve the status of women within the historical context. Why do Muslims now not do the same thing, but instead choose to keep unequal rules about women which harm society as a whole in the name of Allah?

In verses 31:29 and 35:13 it is said that Allah makes night enter day and day enter night, and has subjected the sun and the moon each to run for a specified term and that Allah knows everything you do. In verses 36:37–40 it is said that Allah "withdraws the day from the night then they are in darkness," that the sun runs for a term by Allah's decree, that Allah "determines the phases of the moon until it returns like an old date stalk," that the sun is "not permitted to reach the moon, nor the night to overtake the day, and each floats in an orbit." In verse 40:61 it is said that it is Allah "who made the night for

Chapter 5 Re-reading Women

you to rest in and the day to give sight." In verses 28:71–73 it is said that if night was "made continuous, no other god would bring you light, and if day was made continuous until the day of resurrection, then no other god would bring you night for rest," and that out of mercy Allah "made the night and the day for you to rest in and to seek his bounty so that you would be grateful." However, let us consider the following problems.

1. In places close to the poles, night can lasts for a long time. People can live in this kind of environment; and

2. Allah could have created human beings without a need for rest in the sense of sleeping at night.

Thus we can see that this kind of argument was for people who do not know about the varieties of the earth's regions and the possibilities of life. I am not saying Allah's level is low, but that it was necessary to adjust to the audience he was talking to, so that we should have no problem replacing those injunctions when we have a different society in which we do not allow slaves, and we should not give women lower status because it was so in the Qur'an.

Let us look at another example. In verse 66:10 it is said, "Allah presents an example of those who disbelieved: the wife of Noah and the wife of Lot. They were under two of our righteous servants but betrayed them, so those prophets did not make them free from the need of Allah at all, and it was said, 'Enter the fire with those who enter.'" People might use this to argue that women are more unreliable, and that women are inherently inferior as the preposition "under" shows.

But as soon as we read the ensuing verses, we can see that one cannot draw the first conclusion. In verses 66:11–12 it is said, "and Allah presents an example of those who believed: the wife of Pharaoh, when she said, 'my lord, build for me near you a house in paradise and save me from Pharaoh and his deeds and save me from those who do wrong.' And Mary, the daughter of 'Imran,[4] who guarded her chastity, so we blew into it through our angel, and she believed in the words of her lord and his scriptures and was of the devoutly obedient." Read together, these verses give examples of pious and impious women, with no implication about their imminent quality to be particularly loyal or treacherous. But people who want to make arguments against women would definitely use 66:10, and it is essential that we read the text carefully to avoid being misled by people with their own agenda.

As for the second conclusion, we should bear in mind the social context which gives rise to this way of speaking. Women did have lower, subordinate status in Noah's and Lot's times. They were less informed because of the lack of social exposure and education. They could only be occupied with what happened at home, and their only source of power and satisfaction would be influence over their husbands and sons, potentially making them frivolous and depressed, giving rise to problematic relationships. But this does not mean that we should keep things this way and think that women are born to be weak and narrow-minded. In developed countries, women have attained an improved status, benefit from equal educational and professional opportunities, and their views can no longer be seen as inferior. The male-dominant hierarchy or social structure in Islamic texts was just incidental, not something that Islam is supposed to defend or uphold. The same changes to women's status can and should happen in Muslim communities.

From such examples we see the importance of reading Islamic texts in context. We need to remember the sort of audience Muhammad was addressing, and not assume that all of his revelations are intended to be eternally suitable for all audiences. It simply does not make sense to see pre-Islamic traders and nomadic Arabs as the zenith of human development and ready for high-level messages which should be followed throughout history.

---

[4] Mary, the daughter of 'Imran, is the Virgin Mary.

Chapter 5 Re-reading Women

Does this mean that Islam is necessarily a backward religion which should be given up? I do not see it that way. Islam has beautiful messages and the Qur'an is a mesmeric work. If we choose appropriate sections of the Islamic texts and jettison inappropriate parts, Islam could become a modern progressive religion in which no groups are oppressed or treated unfairly.

Or we may do the opposite, which is to promote rigid and literal interpretations of the Qur'an and the Hadiths, and create or maintain a patriarchal organisation of society that opposes progress, equality, liberation of women, and any challenge to current power and interests. This is what many extremist groups are doing. We believe that sociologically this could be explained by which groups would benefit. Oil money flows towards conservative religious institutions to maintain the status quo for the male upperclass in power. Poor men failing to move up in urban areas love the worldview in which they are favoured by Allah as long as they follow the simple explicit rules such as prayers and no consumption of alcohol, and then they get to beat women and kill people and go to heaven to enjoy virgins. How do we break this chain?

Education[5] and economic development. Education gives women knowledge, vision, opportunities, and economic independence. Educated women would not take oppression in the name of religion as easily, and they would not be as trapped in families that use them just for sex and raising children.

Islam was not established to perpetuate the suffering of women. If we reason just a little bit we should be able to see that this is not the way to heaven, even if some of the passages in the Qur'an seem to say that. It was for a different time, a different type of social structure, a

---

[5] But not too many university degrees, which gives a false hope of social mobility without the economic development to employ these graduates. It could breed extremism. Read *Engineers of Jihad—The Curious Connection between Violent Extremism and Education* by Diego Gambetta and Steffen Hertog [19] for an illuminating investigation.

different stage of human development. We are past that age.

There is freedom of interpretation in constructing one's faith from an ancient text. You simply cannot have a coherent interpretation without adaptation and extrapolation. Even the objects mentioned in the text are not the ones in use today.

The texts are there, but in this case what we choose to read from them is a reflection of ourselves.

5.1.4 Equal Footing

Living things are frequently said to be created in pairs in the Qur'an.

In verse 4:1 it is said, "O mankind, fear your lord who created you from one soul and created from it its mate and dispersed from both of them many men and women." In verses 6:142–144 people are told to "eat of what Allah has provided for you and do not follow the footsteps of Satan. Indeed, he is to you a clear enemy," and what he has provided are two sheep, two goats, two camels, and two cattle. In verse 7:189 it is said, "it is he who created you from one soul and created from it its mate that he might dwell in security with her." In verse 36:36 it is said, "exalted is he who created all pairs, including what the earth grows and themselves and that which they do not know." In verse 39:6 it is said, "he created you from one soul. Then he made from it its mate, and he produced for you from the grazing livestock eight mates." In verses 51:49–50 it is said, "of all things we created two mates, so that perhaps you will remember. So flee to Allah." In verses 53:45–46 it is said that Allah "creates the two mates, the male and female, from a sperm-drop when it is emitted." In verse 75:39 it is said that Allah "made of it two mates, the male and the female." In verse 78:8 it is said, "we created you in pairs."

It is also emphasised that Allah created both male and female. In verse 49:13 it is said, "O mankind, indeed we have created you from male and female and made you peo-

Chapter 5 Re-reading Women

ples and tribes that you may know one another. Indeed, the most noble of you in the sight of Allah is the most righteous of you. Indeed, Allah is knowing and informed." In verse 92:3 Allah is characterised as "he who created the male and female."

From these passages we can see that the male and the female form a pair and they are both essential parts of humankind. It does not make sense that one is inherently more important and powerful than the other. It was just a stage of social development in which might mattered most, and Islam could only go along with it to a certain extent. But now it is not the case, and it is counter-productive to stick to rules stated in Islamic texts for that particular social context.

In verses 42:49–50 we see similar ideas. It says that Allah "gives to whom he wills females, and he give to whom he wills males, or he makes them [both] males and females, and he makes whom he wills barren." Men and women are both created by Allah. Women are not ordained to occupy an inferior place in the world.

In verse 3:195 it is said, "I shall never allow to be lost the work of [any] worker among you, whether male or female. You are of one another. So those who emigrated or were evicted from their homes or were harmed in my cause or fought or were killed—I will surely remove from them their misdeeds, and I will surely admit them to gardens beneath which rivers flow as a reward from Allah, and Allah has with him the best reward." In verse 4:124 it is said, "and whoever does righteous deeds, whether male or female, while being a believer—those will enter paradise and will not be wronged [even as much as] the speck on a date seed." In verse 16:97 it is said, "whoever does righteousness, whether male or female, while he is a believer—we will surely cause him to live a good life, and we will surely give them their reward according to the best of what they have done." In verse 40:40 it is said, "whoever does an evil deed will not be recompensed except by the like thereof, and whoever does righteousness, whether male or female, while he is a believer—those will enter paradise, being given provision therein without account." From these passages we can see that being male or female does not change one's status with Allah. What matters is what one has done with one's life. Good and evil will be the basis for reward, not one's sex. This should help us correctly read descriptions of heaven from a male perspective. It is because men were dominant among Muhammad's audience that the descriptions emphasised the presence of beautiful women, not because men are the owners of heaven. For more discussion along this line of reasoning, see Section 6.2.

Let us also examine passages in which women are mentioned separately. First, sometimes the female forms of active participle of verbs are added after the male forms, this occurs in 9:71, 9:72, 24:12, 24:31, 33:35, 33:58, 33:73, 47:19, 48:5, 48:25, 57:12, 71:28, and 85:10 for the word مؤمنة *mu'mina*, a female who believes.

In verse 33:35 it is said, "indeed, Muslim men and Muslim women, believing men and believing women, obedient men and obedient women, truthful men and truthful women, patient men and patient women, humble men and humble women, charitable men and charitable women, fasting men and fasting women, men who guard their private parts and women who do so, and men who remember Allah often and women who do so—for them Allah has prepared forgiveness and a great reward." From this passage we can see that men and women are rewarded in the same way for the same moral and pious behaviour.

There are many other similar passages. In verses 9:71–72 it is said, "the believing men and believing women are allies of one another. They enjoin what is right and forbid

Chapter 5 Re-reading Women

what is wrong and perform prayer and give alms and obey Allah and his messenger. Allah will have mercy upon them. Indeed, Allah is strong and wise. Allah has promised the believing men and believing women gardens beneath which rivers flow, abiding in [paradise] eternally, and pleasant dwellings in gardens of perpetual residence, while approval from Allah is greater. That is the great attainment." In verse 57:12 it is said that on judgment day, "you see the believing men and believing women, their light proceeding before them and on their right, 'your good tidings today are [of] gardens beneath which rivers flow, wherein you will abide eternally.' That is the great attainment." In verse 57:18 it is said, "indeed, the men who practice charity and the women who practice charity and [they who] have loaned Allah a good loan—it will be multiplied for them, and they will have a noble reward."

In the same vein, in 85:10 it is said, "indeed, those who have tortured the believing men and believing women and then have not repented will have the punishment of hell, and they will have the punishment of the fire." From this passage we can see that doing bad things to women is just as bad as doing bad things to men. But is this what Muslim communities practise? Or is injustice to women more often condoned than that to men?

Now one may say, these passages only apply to Muslims, but not non-Muslims. But we should remember the volatile situation (Section 4.5.4) and the moral construal of faith (Section 4.1.2). From these qualifications we would be able to derive an inclusive and tolerant interpretation of who is a Muslim and who is not.

In fact, such lists are used for non-Muslims too, for example in 48:4–6 it is said, "to Allah belong the soldiers of the heavens and the earth" "that he may admit the believing men and the believing women to gardens beneath which rivers flow to abide therein eternally and remove from them their misdeeds" "and [that] he may punish the hypocritical men and hypocritical women, and the polytheist men and polytheist women." In verses 9:67–68, 33:73, 48:6, and 57:13 both the male and female forms of the word "hypocrite" are listed. In verses 33:73 and 48:6 both the male and female forms of the word "polytheist" are listed.

Finally, in 4:32 it is said, "and do not wish for that by which Allah has made some of you exceed others. Men are rewarded according to what they have earned, and women are rewarded according to what they have earned, and ask Allah of his bounty. Indeed Allah is ever knowing of all things." From this passage we can see that regardless of whether one is a man or a woman, reward and punishment works the same way. Everyone should abide by the same moral principles. This is the message of Islam that should be promoted, rather than verses with a limited scope of application. I shall talk about this issue in Section 6.2.6.

From the discussions in this section we should be able to see that inequality in Islamic texts between men and women is a result of social limitation, but in terms of moral expectation and cosmology it was clear that men and women were expected to occupy equal roles in society.

5.2 The Rights of Women

Now let us look at concrete issues involving the rights of women.

I showed in Section 5.1.3 that in most cases directions for Muslims are the same for both men and women. But there are indeed rules specifically referring to women, especially in the context of heterosexual relationship. Let us examine them in this section.

5.2.1 Segregation and Tests

In verse 33:58 in the Qur'an it is said, "and those who harm believing men and believing women for [something] other than what they have earned certainly bear the guilt of slander and manifest sin." Similarly, in a Hadith, people ask Muhammad about Muslims and he answers that a good Muslim is "one who avoids harming Muslims with his tongue and hands." [3, 2:9–10] This is a very good guid-

Chapter 5 Re-reading Women

ing principle in thinking about men and women in Islam. Muslims should not harm other Muslims.

But in issues regarding women, the stress very often lies on segregation and covering, which allegedly protect women, rather than on Muslims to act honourably and not do harm. Laws and rules mandating segregation and covering are in place in some Muslim-majority countries.

If one thinks about this, one would find it baffling, because in these Muslim-majority countries, the men are mostly Muslims and are they not required by their faith to control themselves and avoid harming other Muslims, including female Muslims? Why do we not stress more the responsibility of not harming, rather than avoiding any contact between men and women? It is clearly patriarchal psychology rather than what the Qur'an and the Hadiths teach.

In verses 24:30–31 it is said, "tell the believing men to lower their gaze and guard their private parts. That is purer for them. Indeed, Allah is informed of what they do. And tell the believing women to lower their gaze and guard their private parts and not expose their adornment except that which appears thereof and to wrap their headcovers over their chests and not expose their adornment except to their husbands," etc. Here we can see that both men and women are told to be modest.

In verses 23:1–7 it is said, "the believers have succeeded—those who are humble in prayer, and those who avoid ill speech, and those who are giving alms, and those who guard their private parts, except from their wives or their slaves, for indeed, they will not be blamed but whoever seeks beyond that, then those are the transgressors." The verses having to do with men and women are repeated in 70:29–30 where it is said, "and those who guard their private parts, except from their wives or their slaves, for indeed, they will not be blamed, but whoever seeks beyond that, then those are the transgressors." Here we can see that both men and women are responsible for their sexual behaviour. Even though men could have more than one wife, and slaves, this was the particular social institution at that time. Apart from that, men cannot harass every woman they see. Women have no responsibility to lock themselves up. Sadly the situation today is not really better. Polygamy is kept despite a change in social reality, while harassment is not really condemned, and segregation is seen as Islamic.

In verse 33:35 it is said, "indeed, Muslim men and Muslim women, believing men and believing women, obedient men and obedient women, truthful men and truthful women, patient men and patient women, humble men and humble women, charitable men and charitable women, fasting men and fasting women, men who guard their private parts and women who do so, and men who remember Allah often and women who do so—for them Allah has prepared forgiveness and a great reward." Again we see that men are told to guard their private parts. That responsibility should not be imposed upon women. Women should not be hidden and separated from society in order to help men guard their private parts.

The only passages which talk separately about women guarding their private parts are 21:91 and 66:12, which praise Mary, the mother of Jesus. Therefore we can see that women are not the only ones responsible for sexual order in society. But many Muslim communities invoke the danger of promiscuity in order to justify the segregation of women. There is no foundation for this practice in the Qur'an.

One important word that has been used against women in Islam is فتنة *fitna*. In the Qur'an, it can mean trial (2:102), oppression (2:191), discord (9:47–48), treachery

Chapter 5 Re-reading Women

(33:14), etc. But most importantly, in the context of women, temptation. In Abrahamic religions, followers like to ask not to be tempted, because of what they perceive as the inevitable weakness of human beings. And one type of dangerous temptation is women.

So women are to be avoided so that one is not put in the way of temptation?

The link between women and temptation in Islamic discourse becomes a justification for women's segregation. Because men are weak, they should be shielded from temptation, otherwise they will yield to temptation, and that makes them bad in the eyes of God and they will go to hell. So the solution is, men and women are segregated, then men do not face temptation; problem solved. But it does not just mean gender segregation, men and women each getting their designated space. In practice it usually means that women get no public space at all. They are locked at home. So no men outside of the immediate family see them and so the men are protected from their temptation.

But we have to be careful here. In verse 8:28 in the Qur'an, wealth and children are also said to be *fitnas*, in the sense of trials. So why do people not avoid this the same way they prevent men from seeing other women? Actually in this usage everything in life is a *fitna* because how you treat and react to everything in life can be seen as a test and you will be judged for everything you do in life. So does it mean we have to avoid everything in life? Of course this escapist mentality is not what this verse promotes.

In verse 38:23 it is said, "and we certainly tried Solomon and placed on his throne a body, then he returned." Here we can see that even Solomon is tried. There is nothing wrong with trials. They are a part of life. It is not something that we should try to destroy or run away from. Indeed in 29:2–3 it is said that people "who believe will be tested." If you have not been tested, how can you be sure of your faith? How can you know yourself? I discussed the issue of life being a test in Section 4.4.1 when I discussed the concept of fate.

By extension the same should be said about the temptation and trial linked with women. If men can deal only with temptation by locking up women at home, it does not seem reasonable that they will be judged favourably in the context of this trial. It does not seem that they have passed this "test" of treating women honourably.

In verse 9:49 it is said that, among those who asked to be excused from fighting, "is he who says, 'permit me [to remain at home] and do not put me to trial.' Unquestionably, into trial they have fallen. And indeed, hell will encompass the disbelievers." Even though this passage is talking about war, the condemnation of the lack of courage is the same. It is cowardly behaviour of men to force women into segregation in order that they are not tempted and tested, ignoring the rights and needs of women to move freely and realise their goals in life. The escapist and avoiding behaviour by men, or, to put it more accurately, repressive and prohibiting social structure maintained by men in the name of Islam, does not look good in the eyes of Allah. You do not pass a test by not doing it. You fail in this test of adequate interaction between men and women, while other cultures and religions have presented better responses to this social challenge.

However, some people might produce 20:131 in support of segregation. It says that Muslims are told "not to extend their eyes toward that by which Allah has given enjoyment to some of them, for it is in fact the splendour of worldly life by which Allah tests them." And then it is said that the provision of Allah is "better and more enduring." What do we make of this verse? If we read it in the same way as we read 8:28 in which wealth and children are said to be *fitnas*, i.e. tests, to be consistent, then if we are to segregate men and women because of 20:131, then we should also avoid getting rich even if we do it justly, because of 8:28, since both women and wealth are *fitnas*.

In verse 16:90 in the Qur'an it is said that Allah "forbids immorality, bad conduct, and oppression." The word "immorality" would frequently be taken to refer to things

Chapter 5 Re-reading Women

such as extra-marital affairs, and then the preacher would probably alert his male audience about the dangers of women. But it is not imperative that we read it that way. Immorality can refer to any harmful behaviour. It is rather the patriarchal mindset that dictates this reading, and not anything remotely suggestive of this meaning in the surrounding passages. It does not in any way support the segregation and covering up of women.

So we see that this association between temptation and women is used in the service of men seeking to maintain a superior status rather than in the service of a sincerely strict adherence to Islam. It is analogous to earlier attitudes in Christianity regarding women and sin. Many Muslims proudly claim that Islam has a more reasonable outlook on men and women than Christianity, contrasting the warm affection between Muhammad and his wives with the celibacy of Jesus and negative attitudes about sex in Christianity. However, if the association between temptation and women in Islam is not dealt with, the picture of Islamic romantic relations is one that is as misogynist—or more so—than Christian ones.

In verse 24:21 it is said, "O you who have believed, do not follow the footsteps of Satan. And whoever follows the footsteps of Satan—indeed, he enjoins immorality and wrongdoing. And if not for the favour of Allah upon you and his mercy, not one of you would have been pure, ever, but Allah purifies whom he wills, and Allah is hearing and knowing." If purification is according to Allah's will, then social coercion is pointless. Of course then there is no human responsibility to talk about, as I discussed in Section 4.4.1. But in general I think this supports postponement and non-intervention (Section 6.3.1), for these matters should be left to Allah to decide. He will guide and punish whom he wills.

In verses 2:120, 2:145, 5:48–49, 5:77, 6:56, 6:119, 6:150, 13:37, 23:71, 28:50, 30:29, 42:15, 45:18, 47:14–16, and 54:3, every time the word أهواء *ahwā'*, meaning "desires" or "inclinations," is mentioned, it is to warn people against following them. For example, in 54:1–3 it is said, "the hour has approached and the moon is split, and if they see a sign, they turn away and say, 'continuing magic,' and they denied and followed their desires, but there is a settlement for every matter."

Should we conclude from such use of the word "desires" that desire is a bad thing and refraining from its satisfaction constitutes moral behaviour? I argue that this interpretation is not holistic, i.e. taking into account everything we know about Islamic texts, since we know that asceticism is not encouraged in Islam and marriage is a promoted institution. Reflecting on the teachings of Islam on the whole and looking at the context of such verses, we should be able to see that the negative stance towards desires does not refer to everything that we like or specifically to bodily desires, but wanton and unregulated desires. For example in 6:119 it is said, "So eat of that upon which the name of Allah has been mentioned, if you are believers in his signs. And why should you not eat of that upon which the name of Allah has been mentioned, while he has explained in detail to you what he has forbidden you, excepting that to which you are compelled, and indeed many lead [others] astray through their desires without knowledge. Indeed, your lord is most knowing of the transgressors." Here the word "desires" is referring to one's preference or choice.

When we really read the verses with the word أهواء *ahwā'*, we can see that these "desires" or "inclinations" could be material, bodily, or otherwise. It does not refer

Chapter 5 Re-reading Women

to sexual desires alone. Indeed some translation uses the English word "inclination" to avoid undue sexual connotations, for example in [6].

From the discussion above, it should be clear that we cannot take these warnings against following one's desires as evidence that sexual desires or relationships are taboo and dangerous. In fact we need to beware of calls misusing such verses to cleanse the social sphere and to put women into seclusion. Scholars and clerics saying these things please some segment of the population. This mentality comes from male insecurity, using religion as an excuse. Some people experience feelings of shame and guilt in relation to their sexual desires, and feel displeased that other men would have the same thoughts about their loved ones if women move freely in the social sphere, and they read these feelings into the verses. So when scholars and clerics interpret Islamic texts in this way, these people agree and support groups putting these interpretations into action, limiting the freedom of women. It is wishful reading through and through.

An example of this malaise can be found in a fatwa issued by Rashad Hassan Khalil, the former dean of the faculty of Shari'a and Law of Al-Azhar University in Egypt. It states that the marriage of couples who see their spouse completely naked would be annulled. [2] Understandably it caused much controversy. The Hadiths on which this fatwa is based are weak and not from the major compilations. It shows the personal opinion of the one who issues this fatwa rather than what happened in early Islam. This incident shows that some religious scholars see that intimacy between men and women needs to be regulated and limited under the pretext of procreation. Enjoyment of sexual activities is dangerous. This also tends to accompany the view that only the satisfaction of men matters, while the needs of a woman can be ignored.

After examining the issue of segregation, we can see that to reach a conclusion about how to act on the basis of Islamic texts is complicated and takes critical thinking and reasoning. Literalism is dangerous and, contrary to appearance, is not inherently more accurate than non-literal programmes of interpretation.

5.2.2 Fornication

The issue of segregation is connected to the fear of extra-marital sex.

In verses 24:2–3 it is said, "The female fornicator and the male fornicator—lash each one of them with a hundred lashes, and do not be taken by pity for them in the religion of Allah, if you believe in Allah and the last day, and let a group of believers witness their punishment. The male fornicator does not marry except a female fornicator or polytheist, and none marries her except a male fornicator or a polytheist, and that has been made unlawful to the believers."

We need not restrict the instructions given in 24:2–3 to unmarried men and women, even though restrictions regarding their marriage are given. It could be that those are special provisions for pre-marriage female fornicators and both pre- and post-marriage male fornicators since they could still take other wives. But the lashes themselves can apply to everyone.

Verses 24:4–9 give directions about testimony in establishing such accusations. "And those who accuse chaste women and then do not produce four witnesses—lash them with eighty lashes and do not accept from them testimony ever after, and those are the defiantly disobedient, except for those who repent thereafter and reform, for indeed, Allah is forgiving and merciful. And those who accuse their wives and have no witnesses except themselves—then the testament of one of them would be four testimonies [swearing] by Allah that indeed, he is of the truthful. And the fifth is that the curse of Allah be upon him if he were among the liars. But it will prevent punishment on her if she gives four testimonies [swearing] by Allah that indeed, he is of the liars. And the fifth is that the wrath of Allah be upon her if he was of the truthful."

This passage only talks about accusations against

Chapter 5 Re-reading Women

women. Are we to conclude that only married women are to be punished for fornication, when men are not? The reason why a verse has been given about this and only talks about accusations against women is probably that male Muslims asked Muhammad about accusations against women, and women did not ask Muhammad about accusations against men. We should remember that the Qur'an is a compilation of texts Muhammad recited in different times, and frequently in response to what happened or people's questions. Since we already have 24:2–3, explicitly stating the punishment for male fornicators, there is no strong basis to argue that punishment for fornication applies only to women and unmarried men.

And even if that was the basic assumption of Muhammad and his community we need not adopt it now, when society has progressed. We should adopt the improving spirit of Islam rather than particular rules designed for a bygone society.

From this discussion we can see that the text does not guarantee a reading in which women are to be treated more strictly or harshly than men. It is mostly people's preference and bias in reading it which makes it a common belief that Islamic law has to set more boundaries for women than men.

Another issue is the requirement of four witnesses. It would be virtually impossible to have four witnesses for fornication. If people really stick to this requirement, barring false witnesses, it would be very hard to establish fornication. There is an interesting Hadith in which a man told Muhammad he had fornicated, and Muhammad turned away. At the end he gave four testimonies against himself, and Muhammad said, "are you insane?" And ordered him stoned. [3, 63:195]

Thus we can see that unless someone turns against himself it is very hard to establish a case, and people would seldom be punished. It was not a particularly cruel law, given the social context at that time. Life was harsh and women had low status. Concepts of equality and human rights were not developed.

Sadly I think people protecting their "honour" or, more accurately, property do not need four witnesses to convince themselves and inflict harm onto any female family members whom they think are engaged in unlawful sexual intercourse. This is happening today as so-called honour killing, which makes it much more outrageous in the eyes of people who have progressed from Muhammad's days. Islamic texts should not be used for supporting such backward practices. Muslims have to criticise literalism actively and proclaim clearly to the world that Islamic texts are to be interpreted with the social conditions at that time in mind, and no rules or examples are to be followed without careful inspection.

Unfortunately most Muslim communities are not doing this. They only give up rules which seem terrible even to themselves but do not systematically weed outdated views from Islamic teaching.

This will only make enlightened persons leave Islam. But if we reform and modernise Islam carefully, it will survive, and we will be able to preserve its wisdom.

From the examples of the West we can see that these matters are better left to civil resolution and it is not appropriate for criminal or religious law to mandate punishing people for private acts not involving physical harm. It is against liberal principles,[6] and does not contribute to social well-being.

5.2.3 Inheritance and Testimony

In verse 4:5 in the Qur'an, between referring to wives (4:4) and orphans (4:6), one is advised "not to trust one's properties to the incompetent." Selfish men readily interpret it to refer to all wives. Reasonable people interpret it to mean fools of any gender and age, perhaps with an emphasis on women and children. People committed to gender equality find it hard to accept that maybe women are implicitly referred to, but given the historical background that women

---

[6] Please refer to Section 2.3.2 and Section 6.5 for more discussions.

Chapter 5 Re-reading Women

in Arab society at that time were indeed more uneducated and had seen less of the world than men, it need not be a statement asserting an inherent inferiority of women.

Two other issues sparking endless controversy—inheritance (4:11–12 and 4:176) and testimony (2:282)—can be viewed analogously. In both respects it is clearly stated that women receive a lesser share. We can attribute this also to the same historical background, rather than an inherent inferiority of women. If the latter was the case, then such laws would be applicable in any time and age of human society. But one need not subscribe to this view.

In the case of inheritance, it was men's duty to provide sustenance and they had to pay to get married, and in that society it was very difficult for women to work and sustain themselves independently. Therefore the socio-economic structure meant that it made sense for families to bequeath more of their wealth to men than to women. But that is not true in many modern societies.

In the case of testimony, at that time women had low social status, no means of independence, had little opportunity to educate themselves, and most importantly—in a society where there was no central authority—were not as good as men in the ability to fight. She could have been more easily bullied or pressured from speaking the truth. Later on in the same verse (2:282) it is said that the scribe or the witnesses should not be harmed. From this one can see that there was a real danger of threats to the scribe and witnesses. Therefore it was out of practical considerations that a man's testimony was to be counted as more than a woman's. But as we can see from the development of societies, women play prominent and powerful roles in the community when they have the education and opportunities that are necessary. And such provisions are no longer relevant when society is not full of aggression and in a war-like state.

5.2.4 Marriage

When one thinks about Muhammad's audience, the rules about marriage in the Qur'an become understandable. In verse 2:228 it is said that women "have the same rights as men but men have a degree above women." The stipulations given are an improvement on Arab traditions at that time. If the reform had been more radical, it is doubtful if anyone apart from Muhammad's closest associates would have converted to Islam.

Let us also look at 4:34, which states that "men are protectors of women by what Allah has given one over the other and what they spend from their wealth. So righteous women are obedient, guarding in the unseen what Allah orders them to guard. But those [wives] from whom you fear arrogance, advise them, and then forsake them in bed, and then beat them. But if they obey you, seek no means against them. Indeed, Allah is exalted and great." So if a husband fears that his wife disobeys him, he should warn her, stop sharing a bed with her, even beat her. Some commentators say that the Arabic word ضرب *dariba* which is commonly translated as "to beat" could also mean "to explain using an example." So that the passage should mean that after warning your wife and having stopped sharing a bed with her, you should explain the problem to her using an example. I do not find this very convincing as it comes after stop sharing a bed, and the logical sequence should be something stronger and more serious than not sharing a bed.

So what should we do if the word does mean "to beat"?

Muslims do not have to accept it and start beating

Chapter 5 Re-reading Women

their wives when they disobey them. One may ask, how could I reject a verse from the Qur'an? Yes one could. The Qur'an was revealed to a particular audience in a particular time. Do you mean that it is a very confined system? No, any form of communication has to take account of its participants, their limitation in understanding, their social conditions, etc. But we should reach for the message behind, the spirit, the wisdom, not necessarily a letter-for-letter reproduction of the content. So what was an acceptable practice in the past, is no longer acceptable now, even though it is written in the Qur'an. As we shall explain in Section 6.2, if re-interpretation does not work, we may abrogate using our reason.

Salafis object, how could you "change the message" in the Holy Qur'an?

How could we not "change the message" if we are to live in a different age and world? Even extreme conservatives have to use reason to determine if new inventions are lawful, because those inventions did not exist and have not been mentioned in the Qur'an or the Hadiths. So we have to extrapolate about technology anyway. Why not extrapolate in matters between men and women? Has not the situation changed radically? Have not the forms of societies changed radically? Beating one's wives was what Muhammad's audience took for granted but it is not acceptable now and we have better ways to solve marital issues.

Are we not prohibited from reasoning in this realm because it suits male imams' and scholars' interests not to, rather than to adhere to Allah's orders?

In the Qur'an, divorce can be initiated by women. In verse 4:35 it is said, "and if you fear dissension between the two, send an arbitrator from his people and an arbitrator from her people. If they both desire reconciliation, Allah will cause it between them. Indeed, Allah is ever knowing and informed." From this verse we can see that either of them could be the one who wants to separate, and reconciliation is encouraged but it would be ridiculous to deduce from the absence of explicit specifications regarding a woman's request for divorce that this is not allowed. This verse implies that dissension could come from either party and the matter should be fairly arbitrated. Women should be allowed to divorce if they wish, and this is what a reasonable reading of the text would yield. It was conceivably rarer for women to demand it since life was difficult for a divorced woman, therefore the reference was usually to men divorcing women, but it does not imply that it is the only lawful way.

We can find cases of women initiating divorce in the Hadiths. There is a Hadith in which a woman demanded divorce from her husband and this was promptly granted by Muhammad provided that she returned what her husband had given her. [3, 63:197] This should be a case showing clearly that even in Muhammad's age when women were assumed to have lower status, they could obtain a divorce easily if they wanted. In another Hadith, a lady was brought to Muhammad as his bride, and she said, "I seek refuge with Allah from you." And Muhammad left her alone and let her return to her family. [3, 63:181] Even the prophet had to leave a woman as soon as she said this sentence. Now one may say this is before the consummation of the marriage, afterwards it is different. I would say the difference is that it would have been less in a woman's interest to demand divorce after the consummation since people valued virginity and it was difficult for a woman to take care of children if there were any. Muhammad's immediate compliance in this story should be model enough for Muslims to follow. If a Muslim claims that this is a special case not to be imitated by Muslims, I challenge him to provide reasons why he should not do as Muhammad did, with the much more empowered status of women in this age.

Ironically, even though the Islamic texts allow women to initiate divorce, it was not until the 1970s when the film *I want a solution* raised awareness of the lack of such provision in Egyptian law that an amendment is made. Thus we can see that many problematic practices supposedly Islamic do not have any textual basis. It is just that men use Islam for their convenience.

5.2.5 Polygamy

In verse 4:3 of the Qur'an, it is said that if you "fear you cannot treat the orphans justly, then marry two, three, or four women of those who please you. And if you fear that you will not be just, then marry [only] one, or [marry] slaves. That is more suitable that you do not incline" to injustice.

There are many different interpretations regarding this verse, because it is a key verse that is widely discussed and because in a Hadith 'A'isha is recorded to have said that this verse talks about a particular case of a wealthy orphan girl who her guardian wants to marry. Since he cannot pay her a sufficient dowry, the verse is revealed to order him to marry someone else instead. [3, 7:2] But the story, true or not, does not affect our view and interpretation of the Qur'an with respect to polygamy.

First of all, we have to remember the historical background. It was an age in which men died in great numbers in battles and many widows were left behind without any means of making a living. Secondly, it was a very patriarchal society and men had wives and slaves. The discrepancy in number and the social situation made it expedient to allow polygamy.

However, we should ask, do we have the same situation now? Are the number of men as deficient and the situation of single or widowed women as bad as in the Arabian desert in Muhammad's time? Now in most places women can work and support themselves. They lead a better life than women forced by circumstances to marry and produce children like a factory.

We do not keep slavery even though it is permitted in the Qur'an, but why do we permit polygamy? We are applying a double standard for practices that are unjust, unsuitable for present society and detrimental to human happiness. Both should be abolished.

5.2.5.1 Muhammad's Household

People like to use Muhammad's example to argue that polygamy is not a problem. But he lived in a different age and he made political alliances with his marriages. The same cannot be said about most polygamous marriages we see today.

In verses 66:1–5 there is an interesting episode. It says, "O prophet, why do you prohibit [yourself from] what Allah has made lawful for you, seeking the approval of your wives? And Allah is forgiving and merciful. Allah has already ordained for you the dissolution of your oaths, and Allah is your protector, and he is the knowing, the wise. And when the prophet confided a statement to one of his wives, and when she informed [another] of it and Allah showed it to him, he made known part of it and ignored a part, and when he informed her about it, she said, 'who told you this?' [Muhammad] said, 'I was informed by the knowing, the informed.' If you two repent to Allah, [it is best,] for your hearts have deviated. But if you cooperate against him, then indeed Allah is his protector, and Gabriel and the righteous of the believers, and the angels, moreover, are [his] assistants. Perhaps his lord, if he divorced you, would substitute for him wives better than you—submitting, believing, obedient, repentant, worshipping, and traveling, previously married and virgins."

Many scholars agree that the verses have to do with Muhammad sleeping with Mary the Copt in the house of his wife called Hafsa. After Hafsa had found out, he promised Hafsa never to sleep with Mary again in exchange for her keeping silent about it. But then Hafsa told 'A'isha and arguments broke out. Then these verses were revealed to support Muhammad.

For people who see gender equality as a basic principle, these revelations are quite unbelievable. Why would Allah, who is so exalted, intervene in such minor matters? And in support of a man who already has many wives, in sleeping with another woman?

I think the only reasonable way to read it is as some-

Chapter 5 Re-reading Women

thing meant only to solve Muhammad's domestic disputes because he is a man who is useful in the cause of social improvement in seventh-century Arabia. We should not see theses verses as setting an example for married couples in any way.

The social context was different and his role was special in history and religion. We do not condemn Alexander the Great for killing in battle but we would surely do so in other instances of killing. The situation is important in judging whether something is permissible. We cannot just read verses and say that whatever appears in it is permitted or even lauded.

In Arab tradition and in the Qur'an, oaths have to be respected. In verse 5:89 it is said, "Allah will not impose blame upon you for thoughtless oaths, but he will impose blame upon you for oaths that you contracted. So its expiation is the feeding of ten needy people from the average of that which you feed your families or clothing them or the freeing of a slave. But whoever cannot find [the means], then a fast of three days. That is the expiation for oaths when you have sworn. So be mindful of your oaths. Thus does Allah make clear to you his verses that you may be grateful." Compensation has to be given for not keeping an oath, and the price is not small. Freeing a slave is not an insignificant matter. One is also solemnly told to be mindful of his oaths. Therefore the dissolution of Muhammad's oath has to be a special case, and not to be applied in general.

If we use his example to argue for the permissibility of polygamy in general, we can also say that oaths can be dissolved in general. Then verse 5:89 would be meaningless. But reading the verses for what they are, verses 66:1-5 should be much more limited in the scope of application, namely Muhammad's household itself, than verse 5:89, which was intended for all of Muhammad's followers at that time.

5.2.5.2 Pairing

In the Qur'an, there are many verses emphasising the pairwise quality of creation, and for human beings pairing is a more comfortable state than polygamy. Let us look at the numerous examples.

In verse 4:1 it is said, "O mankind, fear your lord who created you from one soul and created from it its mate and dispersed from both of them many men and women." In verses 51:49–50 it is said, "of all things we created two mates, so that perhaps you will remember. So flee to Allah." In verses 53:45–46 it is said that Allah "creates the two mates, the male and female, from a sperm-drop when it is emitted."

In verses 6:142–144 people are told to "eat of what Allah has provided for you and do not follow the footsteps of Satan. Indeed, he is to you a clear enemy," and what Allah has provided are two sheep, two goats, two camels, and two cattle.

From these verses we can see that in Islamic cosmology creation comes in pairs, one male, one female. Therefore it can be argued that Islam is in favour of couples rather than a household with multiple wives, which was a practical measure for Arab society at that stage of development. It is no longer a practical measure in this age. Women do not need to be taken care of. They are highly capable of earning their own bread in modern society. That practical measure is no longer practical now, and arguably hinders social development, especially the improvement of women's position in society.

We should keep in mind that Allah told us to use reason (verse 2:242).

5.2.6 The Veil

Covering your head and your face in the desert is good insulation against the heat of the relentless sun, but in other climates could be extremely uncomfortable and unhealthy. Considering the peculiarity of the place where such a prac-

Chapter 5 Re-reading Women

tice originated, one should not follow this tradition blindly in other places.

Why has this become an issue of so much attention and debate despite its apparent triviality? Because of the public and visible nature of the veil. It is immediately clear whether one wears a veil or not, while it is not immediately clear whether one donates to charity or not.

In the Qur'an relevant instructions appear in several places.

5.2.6.1 Muhammad's Household

In verse 33:53 it is said to Muhammad's followers, "when you ask [his wives] for something, ask them from behind a screen. That is purer for your hearts and their hearts." Some people argue that this sets an example for female segregation in general. Women should not be seen for that would be purer for people's hearts.

However, we need to read the surrounding passages to see if this advice is intended to be extended to others. In verses 33:50–52 it is said, "O prophet, indeed we have made lawful to you your wives to whom you have given their due compensation and your slaves whom Allah has given to you and the daughters of your paternal uncles and the daughters of your paternal aunts and the daughters of your maternal uncles and the daughters of your maternal aunts who emigrated with you and a believing woman if she gives herself to the prophet. If the prophet wishes to marry her, [this is] *only for you, excluding the [other] believers. We certainly know what we have made obligatory upon them concerning their wives and their slaves, [but this is for you] in order that there will be upon you no discomfort, and ever is Allah forgiving and merciful.*[7] You, [O Muhammad], may put aside whom you will of them or take to yourself whom you will, and whoever you desire of those [wives] from whom you had separated—there is no blame upon you [in returning her]. That is more suitable that their eyes be cooled and not grieve and that they

---
[7]Emphasis added by the author of the present book.

should be pleased with what you have given them, all of them, and Allah knows what is in your hearts, and ever is Allah knowing and forbearing. Women are not lawful to you afterwards, and it is not for you to exchange them for [other] wives, even if their beauty were to please you, except your slaves, and ever is Allah an observer over all things."

Then advice is given regarding Muhammad's household in 33:53, "O you who have believed, do not enter the houses of the prophet except when you are permitted for a meal, without awaiting its readiness. But when you are invited, then enter, and when you have eaten, disperse without seeking to remain for conversation. Indeed, that was troubling the prophet, and he is shy of [dismissing] you. But Allah is not shy of the truth. And when you ask [his wives] for something, ask them from behind a screen. That is purer for your hearts and their hearts. And it is not for you to harm the messenger of Allah or to marry his wives after him, ever. Indeed, that would be in the sight of Allah an enormity."

As soon as we read these verses, we see that they show the special status of Muhammad and his household very clearly. We should note the following points.

1. It is stressed that these specifications are only for Muhammad. Other Muslims can at most marry four wives, but Muhammad can marry more.

2. It is said that these provisions are given so that Muhammad does not feel discomfort. This highlights the difficult and special position he was in, and the important work he was doing. It is clear that these provisions do not extend to other Muslims.

3. Widows are not forbidden to remarry in Islam, but Muhammad's wives are. This shows that the commands here are to be applied to his household only.

We should see the set of injunctions here as a special provision due to Muhammad's political and religious sta-

Chapter 5 Re-reading Women

tus. We should not see it as something to be imitated and adopted by others.

There are passages which clearly show that Muhammad's wives are in a special position. In verses 33:28–34 it is said, "O prophet, say to your wives, 'if you desired worldly life and its adornment, then come, I will provide for you and give you a gracious release. But if you desired Allah and his messenger and the home of the hereafter, then indeed, Allah has prepared for the doers of good among you a great reward.' O wives of the prophet, whoever of you should commit a clear immorality—for her the punishment would be doubled two-fold, and ever is that easy for Allah. And whoever of you devoutly obeys Allah and his messenger and does righteousness—we will give her her reward twice, and we have prepared for her a noble provision. O wives of the prophet, *you are not like anyone among women.*[8] If you fear Allah, then do not be soft in speech [to men], lest he in whose heart is disease should covet, but speak with appropriate speech. And abide in your houses and do not display yourselves like the display of the former times of ignorance. And perform prayer and give alms and obey Allah and his messenger. Allah intends only to remove from you the impurity [of sin], O people of the household, and to purify you with purification. And remember what is recited in your houses of the verses of Allah and wisdom. Indeed, Allah is ever subtle and informed." From this passage we can see the special position of Muhammad's wives. Their treatment and reward is different from other people. Therefore we cannot assume that what applies to them also applies to other women.

These special commands show us that advice to

---

[8]Emphasis added by the author of the present book.

Muhammad's wives recommending a screen (حجاب *ḥijāb*) does not apply to other Muslim women. The irony is that this word today is so commonly applied to the headscarf a conservative Muslim woman wears to hide her hair, and is commonly believed to be a practice based on the Qur'an. In the Qur'an it is clearly not the same object.

And even if the screen is required for Muhammad's wives, it is not generalisable to all female Muslims. There is the question of applicability. Muhammad's wives are a special group of women, taking into account the political situation in the last years of Muhammad's life.

We need to establish its necessity by other means if we wish to, since clearly other special arrangements are in the same passage made for Muhammad's wives, for example the injunction that they are not to marry again after Muhammad's death, and that demand is emphatically not applicable to other women. So we cannot simply assume that specifications made for Muhammad's wives can be applied to other women.

As corroboration, we may look at verse 33:6 in the Qur'an in which it is said that Muhammad is "closer to the believers than themselves and his wives are their mothers."

Sura 49 gives some directions having to do with Muhammad and the community of believers.

1. Do not put yourselves before Allah and his messenger.

2. Fear Allah.

3. Do not raise your voices above the voice of the prophet.

4. Do not be loud to him with speech like the loudness of some of you to others, lest your deeds become worthless.

5. Do not call Muhammad from outside his private chambers.

Chapter 5 Re-reading Women

6. Investigate if a disobedient one comes to you with information, lest you harm people with ignorance and become regretful over what you have done.

7. Know that among you is the messenger of Allah. If he were to obey you in many matters, you would be in difficulty, but Allah has endeared to you the faith and has made it pleasing in your hearts and has made hateful to you disbelief, defiance, and disobedience. Those are the guided ones.

8. Make peace if two parties among the believers fight.

9. Fight a faction which oppresses another until it returns to the command of Allah. Make peace between them with justice if that faction returns.

10. Do not ridicule others even if you are better.

11. Do not insult one another.

12. Do not call each other by nicknames.

13. Avoid making assumptions.

14. Do not be a spy, nor backbite each other.

From these directions we can see that the Muslim community was fraught with quarrels, and from 1–5 we can see that Muhammad was probably always summoned to resolve problems, or even "harassed" by Muslims, but he was too nice to push them away. It indirectly gave rise to the use of the screen, setting off areas for his family.

We can see clearly that internal strife was an issue. Muhammad was always busy with the affairs of the community. This is the special historical background to the verses 33:52–53 which mention a screen between the prophet's followers and his wives. It is to preserve a degree of peace and rest for him. It is not a general lesson to humankind.[9]

---

[9] For more historical discussions see Fatima Mernissi's *The Veil and the Male Elite* [31, Ch. 5 and 6].

5.2.6.2 General Instructions

What about instructions for other Muslims?

In verses 24:30–31 it is said, "tell the believing men to lower their gaze and guard their private parts. That is purer for them. Indeed, Allah is informed of what they do. And tell the believing women to lower their gaze and guard their private parts and not expose their adornment except that which appears and to wrap their headcovers over their chests and not expose their adornment except to their husbands, their fathers, their husbands' fathers, their sons, their husbands' sons, their brothers, their brothers' sons, their sisters' sons, their women, their slaves, or those male attendants having no physical desire, or children who are not yet aware of the private aspects of women. And let them not stamp their feet to make known what they conceal of their adornment.[10] And turn to Allah in repentance, all of you, O believers, that you might succeed." From this passage we can see that both men and women are told to be modest. More importantly, women are told to wrap their headcovers over their breast rather than on their hair as required now.

One might argue that since headcovers are mentioned, it is taken for granted that they cover women's heads, and the additional requirement is that women cover their breasts. But I do not think that this argument is convincing. Even though headcovers are mentioned, it does not mean that Allah approves of or requires this type of clothing, it just means that people were wearing it during Muhammad's time. It does not entail that this is required in Islam. The reed pen is also mentioned in 3:44, 31:27, 68:1, and 96:4, does this mean that fountain pens are prohibited in Islam? When we see that something is mentioned in the Qur'an, we cannot automatically reason that it is approved of or praised, it is just what was common at that time. Why do we have no problems with fountain pens, but have such attachment to headcoverings? Does this not show that there is a special fetish and taboo about

---

[10]Such as ankle chains.

Chapter 5 Re-reading Women

sexual issues and changes in this arena? We need to ask ourselves if this is what Allah wants or just our own preconception.

In verses 33:58–59 it is said, "and those who harm believing men and believing women unjustifiably, they will certainly bear the guilt of slander and clear sin. O prophet, tell your wives and your daughters and the women of the believers to bring down their outer garments over themselves. That is more suitable that they will be known [as wives and daughters of the prophet] and not be abused. And ever is Allah forgiving and merciful." Now this seems to establish that in general Muslim women should cover themselves up but if we read the ensuing verse we see that there is a special background for this advice. In verse 33:60 it is said, "if the hypocrites and those in whose hearts is disease and those who spread rumours in Medina do not cease, we will surely incite you against them. Then they will not remain your neighbours therein except for a little while." From this verse we can see that there were problems and quarrels and a war was growing. Bringing down part of the outer garments is a statement in that situation, not a sign of piety. Therefore we can see that this extra covering was for a specific purpose. People were harassing and attacking female believers at that particular juncture, so they are advised to cover themselves and show that they have nothing to be criticised for. But this does not imply that in all periods of time women have to put extra covers upon themselves.

In fact, it is not even clear what exactly is meant by "bring down their outer garments over themselves." Does it bear any similarity to the way hair is meticulously covered with more than one layer of headscarf today among many Muslim women? Is it not an extension rather than an application of what is mentioned here? Does this fit with Islam's emphasis on moderation, as exemplified in a Hadith in which Muhammad showed his distaste for a woman who prays excessively? [3, 2:41]

In verse 24:60 it is said, "and women of post-menstrual age who have no desire for marriage—there is no blame upon them for putting aside their outer garments, not displaying adornment. But to modestly refrain [from that] is better for them, and Allah is hearing and knowing." In reading this we need to be careful. The issue here is different from that above. In the verses above, the topic discussed is that of bringing down one's outer garments (frequently interpreted as covering up one's head), while here the topic is wearing an outer garment or not. What is said here is that an older women does not have to put on an outer garment at all.

From this passage we can see that, even given the social context then, there was room for individual choice to skip the outer garments. We have to remember that law enforcement was not sufficient and it was people's perception that women who cover up are more virtuous, and even in that context a revelation states explicitly that a post-menstrual woman can choose whether to put on outer garments or not.

If we do not subscribe to literalism, then, given the social context now, we should not think that it is pious to cover as much as possible. It would be doing more than is appropriate. In the seventh century, Arabic older women are told to choose for themselves whether to put on outer garments or not. If Muhammad lived in the present age, the Qur'an would be telling us to wear whatever we find appropriate, not instructing us to cover this or that.

We should be able to see that society in which women have freedom and are not required to submit to men is better for everyone. Children are not raised by uneducated and frivolous mothers. Men and women both work for the improvement of society. It is contrary to the reforming spirit of Islam if it insists that women cover up as much as possible and by extension hide away from public view.

5.2.6.3 The Practice Today

When we look at how Muslim women see the issue of the veil, the interesting thing is that, except for extreme conservatives, many Muslim women cover their hair but ignore the injunction that no adornment should be seen. Frequently there is a great deal of adornment on the headscarf itself. Is not that a bit paradoxical?

When we reflect upon it we see that people care about showing their identity more than following Islamic texts. The veil would enable people to identify them as Muslims, while a lack of adornment is hard to notice. Therefore both Muslims and non-Muslims pay more attention to the veil than to the ban of adornment.

This shows us that the veil has more to do with group identity than piety.

5.2.6.4 Metaphysical Meanings of Covering

After discussing the various passages related to women's clothing, let us think about the metaphysical meanings of covering. Reading passages using the cluster of Arabic words having to do with covering and veiling, we see that such words are not used positively. They frequently denote something blocking one from seeing the truth or remembering Allah.

The word حجاب *ḥijāb* is not particularly positive. It frequently refers to a partition blocking people from Allah. In verse 17:45 it is said, "when you recite the Qur'an, we put between you and those who do not believe in the hereafter a concealed partition." In verse 41:5 it is said, "and they say, 'our hearts are within coverings from that to which you invite us, and in our ears is deafness, and between us and you is a partition, so work. Indeed, we are working.' " In verse 42:51 it is said, "and it is not for any human being that Allah should speak to him except by revelation or from behind a partition or that he sends a messenger to reveal, by his permission, what he wills. Indeed, he is high and wise."

In verses 2:7 and 45:23 Allah is said to set a seal on people's hearing and hearts, and it is then said that there is a veil (غشاوة *ghishāwa*) over their vision. It is something that prevents people from seeing the truth.

The word "cover" (غطاء *ghiṭā'*) is not a good thing either. It prevents people from seeing what is important and remembering Allah. In verse 18:101 it is said that the infidels' "eyes were shielded[11] from my remembrance, and they were not able to hear." In verse 50:22 it is said that on judgment day the infidels would be told, "you were certainly heedless of this, and we have removed from you your cover, so your sight today is sharp."

Another similar word is coverings (أكنة *akinna*). In verse 6:25, it is said that among the polytheists there are "people who listen to Muhammad but Allah placed coverings on their hearts and deafness in their ears so that they will not understand." In verses 17:46–47 it is said that coverings have been "placed over their hearts and deafness in their ears, so that they do not understand." And when you just mention Allah in the Qur'an, they "turn their back in aversion." In verse 18:57, it is said that no one is more unjust than one "who has been reminded of the signs of Allah but turns away from them and forgets what his hands have put forth. Indeed, we have placed over their hearts coverings, lest they understand it, and in their ears deafness, and if you call them towards guidance, they will never be guided." In verse 41:5 it is said, "and they say,

---

[11] Literally "in a cover."

Chapter 5 Re-reading Women

'our hearts are within coverings from that to which you invite us, and in our ears is deafness, and between us and you is a partition, so work. Indeed, we are working.' "

Covering is also a sign of fear in Islam. When Muhammad first received Allah's message, he was terrified and covered himself. This is recorded in the beginning of Suras 73 and 74. In verses 73:1–2 it is said to Muhammad, "O you who wraps himself, arise [to pray throughout] the night, except for a little." Similarly in 74:1– it is said to Muhammad, "O you who covers himself, arise and warn, and glorify your lord." This wrapping-up is analogous to what happens to women in conservative Muslim circles. They think that it is safer for women to be covered up, just as Muhammad felt safer when he covered himself and was not seen. But in the long term things just get worse and never improve, for men do not see women in public, and when they see women, it is a rare sight, so they cannot control themselves and they think that those women are not virtuous. This is a vicious circle. Muhammad faced his fear, and received revelations calmly later on. So should Muslim communities. Women should not be hidden in order for men to feel unthreatened.

Finally in 71:5–7 Noah recounts how difficult it is to bring people towards Allah. He says, "my lord, indeed I invited my people night and day. But my invitation increased them not except in flight. And indeed, every time I invited them that you may forgive them, they put their fingers in their ears, covered themselves with their garments, persisted, and were very arrogant." From this passage we can see how people covered their hearing with their garments. Interestingly that is what happens with conservative types of headscarf. One's ears are covered and the ability to listen is weakened. Metaphysically speaking, it prevents people from hearing Allah's call. Allah's veil prevents people from hearing Allah's call—how ironic!

From these examples we can see that covering is not something viewed positively in Islam. It hinders one's relationship with God. One may say clothing is another matter, but it is in fact intimately connected. If women need to cover up everything in order for men not to lose control, then there is no real spiritual liberation for both men and women, for if in society they need all this segregation and excessive clothing in order to maintain order, then if there is any loophole or alternative, people make use of it, giving rise to terrible practices such as the rape and enslavement of young boys in Afghanistan. Until men and women can mix and interact normally, there cannot be general spiritual advancement in society. People would still be obsessed with sex.

Covering prevents one from seeing Allah, and it also prevents people from seeing individuals of the opposite sex as free beings with a mind and a will.

As arguments of course these passages are only tangentially related to the issue of the veil, but in religion insight is very important. As soon as we appreciate and internalise the teachings against metaphysical coverings we would see that covering one's hair and body should never be a key teaching in a religion. It is at most a piece of worldly advice,[12] given the social contest of Muhammad's community.

5.2.6.5 Conclusion

From the above discussion we can see that the case for wearing a scarf on one's head is not strong, and that of covering one's face is even weaker, as one could see from verse 10:27 in the Qur'an. It says that people who do evil will have their face covered with humiliation and pieces of the darkness of the night. So one can see that covering one's face evokes a negative image. It seems unreasonable that this should be required of or seen as good for women, unless Islam is the misogynistic religion that some people claim it to be.

It is each Muslim's choice. If enough people boycott the line of thought that puts women into lower, submissive status, Islam can become the liberal progressive religion which many Muslims aspire for it to be.

---

[12]See Section 7.1.2 for more discussion on this categorisation.

Chapter 6

Reform

In this chapter I shall set out my ideas about the issue of reform in Islam. I shall present an all-round picture of the ideological reform of Islam.

Should Islam be changed? Should we adhere to Islamic texts as much as possible? These are some of the questions which I shall deal with in this chapter.

I shall consider the Salafist approach, then I shall argue for a contrasting approach which I call "abrogation by exaltation."

Afterwards I propose and argue that two things should be done. Adherence to the principle of إرجاء *irjā'*, i.e. postponement, on the part of Muslims, and liberalism, not moral relativism, on the part of everyone.

6.1 Refuting Salafism

The contemporary world is full of new things and new ideas not mentioned in the Qur'an and the Hadiths. How should a Muslim find a lawful way to live in this world?

6.1.1 The Incoherence of Salafism

Maybe by the Salafist approach?

The Arabic word سلف *salaf* means predecessors and ancestors. Thus the word "Salafism" refers to factions of Muslims who advocate that modern Islam is corrupt and Muslims should emulate the predecessors, i.e. Muhammad and his companions as much as possible, and interpret Islamic texts as literally as possible.

Let me demonstrate why the Salafist solution does not work.

First of all, there are very local descriptions in the Qur'an and it shows that there is a specific context to its message.

In verses 16:11–14, it says that Allah "causes to grow the crops, the olives, the date-palms, the grapes and all kinds of fruits," and that he "has subjected the sea for you to eat fresh food from it." In verses 36:34–35 it is said that we "placed gardens of palm trees and grapevines on [earth], and made springs to burst forth in them, that [people] may eat from its fruit." In verses 55:10–13 it is said that Allah "laid out the earth for the creatures. There are fruit and palm tress with sheaths in it, and grain with husks and scented plants, so which of the favours of your lord do you deny?" In verse 22:34–36 it is said that Allah

Chapter 6 Reform

"fashioned, for every community, a rite of sacrifice" and has made the camels and cattle sacrificial animals of Allah, "there is good for you in them." In verse 25:49 it is said that Allah "gives drink to those he created, much livestock and men." In verses 36:71–73 it is said that Allah created livestock, tamed them, and they ride them and eat them, and "there are benefits and drinks in them." In verses 23:19–20 it is said that Allah "brought forth gardens of palm trees and grapevines in which there are many fruits from which you eat," and then it is said that he also "brought forth a tree in Mount Sinai which produces oil and food for those who eat." In verse 27:91 Muhammad is told to say that he is "commanded to worship the lord of this city, the one who made it sacred, and to him all things belong." Even though it says that Allah is the lord of everything, the reference here is very specific. It says that Allah is the lord of Mecca. In verse 6:92 it is said that the Qur'an "is a book we have sent down, blessed and confirming what was before it, so that you may warn the mother of cities and those around it," and in 42:7 it is said that in this way "we have revealed to you an Arabic Qur'an in order for you to warn the mother of cities and those around it and warn of the day of assembly, about which there is no doubt. A group will be in heaven and a group in the fire." Here "the mother of cities" means Mecca. These verses specifically show the geographical location and the people Muhammad was talking to.

Secondly, a messenger is required before a people can be punished. In verse 23:44 while telling stories about Noah and Moses, it is said that we "sent our messengers successively, and every time a messenger came to a nation, they denied him, so we made them follow each other in the path of destruction." The stories of messengers being denied and the subsequent destruction of their people are mentioned in 25:35–40, 26:10–190, 27:45–58, 29:14–40, 37:73–148, 38:12–14, 43:46–66, and 46:21–25, 50:12–14, 51:24–46, 53:50–56, 54:9–42, 69:4–10, 79:15–26, 85:17–20, etc. From these passages we can see that messengers are sent to different nations and their messages were not exactly the same.

For example Lot and Moses did not receive the same revelations. It does not seem appropriate to assume that the messages are universally applicable.

If we are committed to literalism, then only nations near Mount Sinai with exactly such supplies are required to follow Islam. As soon as we read the Qur'an as literalists, we run into a serious problem. For according to this method of interpretation, Salafists should not try to spread Islam in other areas, for those areas do not fit the descriptions of the environment in the Qur'an. If we are not committed to literalism, then adherence to the texts can be relaxed and open to flexible adaptation, and we are not prevented by the texts from spreading Islam. We can see from this logical dilemma that the only consistent way in which one is allowed to proselytise outside the Arabian Peninsula is to adopt a flexible attitude to the instructions given in the Islamic texts.

Let me discuss another theoretical problem of Salafism. One of the concepts in Salafist thought is بدعة *bid'a*. Literally it means innovation. It is derogatory in the context of Salafist doctrinal discussions. It has come to mean new things that have not appeared in the Qur'an or the Hadiths. It also means new interpretations. According to conservative schools of Islam such as Salafis, a good Muslim is supposed to refrain from *bid'a*.

Words from this root are not derogatory in the Qur'an. In verse 57:27 it is said that Jesus was sent and he was given the Gospel, "and we placed in the hearts of those who followed him compassion and mercy and monasticism, which they innovated (ابتدعوا *ibtada'ū*). We did not prescribe it for them except seeking the approval of Allah, but then they did not observe it with true observance, so we gave the ones who believed among them their reward, but many of them are defiantly disobedient." Here we can see that the Christians invented monasticism but Allah does not disapprove. On the contrary, having invented it and yet not adhering to one's monastic oath truly, that is something punishable. In verse 46:9, Muhammad is told to say,

Chapter 6 Reform

"I am not a new one (بِدْع *bid'*) among the messengers, and I do not know what would be done with me or with you. I only follow that which is revealed to me, and I am but a clear bearer of warning." Here Muhammad is trying to say that he follows the tradition of the prophets before him. But there is nothing that is against new things in general. In verse 2:117 it is said that Allah is the "originator of the heavens and the earth, and if he decided a matter, he only says to it, 'Be,' and it is." Similarly, in 6:101 it is said that Allah is the "originator of the heavens and the earth. How could he have a son when he did not have a companion and he created all things?" Here Allah is characterised as the originator and creator of the heavens and the earth, but does it mean that anything original must be explicitly approved by him? I do not think that we can draw this conclusion here. It is reading too much into the text.

As a result of the above survey, we may say that the ban against *bid'a* is itself a *bid'a*, therefore it is self-defeating, so that if it stands, i.e. *bid'a* should be banned, then this practice of *bid'a* itself should be banned. This is like when a Cretan says that all Cretans are liars.

In reply, Salafists might use verses such as 44:2–4 to support their position. In this passage it is said that the Qur'an is revealed in a blessed night "in which every wise affair is made distinct." So things not mentioned in the Qur'an are not wise nor good. So we should stick to old rules and old objects present in the Qur'an.

However, should we interpret this as saying that anything not distinctly discussed in the Qur'an is not wise? This is probably not a reasonable way to read it. It should be read as saying that important things are made clear, but not absolutely *every* wise affair, otherwise Salafists should not use any modern tools. Therefore, just to be coherent and not self-defeating, meaning that one does not do what one objects to, Salafists should read this rhetorically, not as a universal quantifier without limitation. Only in this way can one maintain a coherent position, otherwise not only is it necessary for them to live tribally, but also refuse any modern weapons for example. In that way they would be harmless, and this form of Salafism would have no coherence issue. But any militant Salafist group is bound to be incoherent. They are hypocritical in their adherence to Qur'anic times.

Indeed, if one is absolutely serious about eliminating *bid'a*, then one should not use any modern technology which has not appeared in Muhammad's time. No modern weapons would be allowed, otherwise one would be commiting *bid'a*, since those items of technology are not in the Qur'an or the Hadiths, are without precedent, and therefore are *bid'a*. For example, a pamphlet printed by modern technology is *bid'a*. In the age of Muhammad and his companions, modern printing techniques did not exist. For example, the internet is *bid'a*. It is totally unimaginable in Muhammad's time. How is one to determine whether it is lawful according to Islam or not? It is a great stretch and interpretation of the original message of the Qur'an anyway. But the internet plays a great role in the spread of Salafist Islam. This is an insoluble doctrinal dilemma for Salafists who try to gain influence by modern communication technology or weaponry. But they do not see it, because they do not have a coherent theology.

Now let us, for a little while, follow Salafists and try to avoid *bid'a*. In that case we would need to think about *bid'a* in contrast with إصلاح *iṣlāḥ*. The word *iṣlāḥ* means reform, doing good things, etc. and it is used positively in the Qu'ran. The active participle, one who reforms, does good things, etc. is مصلح *muṣliḥ*. In verse 28:19 when Moses had killed someone, another man said to him, "You only want to be a tyrant in the land but do not want to

Chapter 6 Reform

make amends." So it seems that *iṣlāḥ* is good. But how do we categorise something new as *iṣlāḥ* or *bid'a*? It would be hard to come up with detailed and specific principles. We need to judge by our rational judgment, looking at whether it is something promoting piety and human welfare etc. If you find this way of going through doctrinal discussions reasonable, you would distance yourself from extreme conservatism because clearly some new practices and some new inventions benefit human beings. It is no use following tradition blindly. It is not equivalent to piety. Allah tells us to use our reason (2:242) and the worst living creatures include the ones who do not use it (8:22).

In short, what we see is blind adherence to the Qur'an and the Hadiths in customs such as taking the testimony of women as weighing half that of men, while none of that is done in the field of new technology. Modern utilities, infrastructure, new weapons etc. are also new things that do not appear in the Qur'an and the Hadiths but they are accepted by most Salafists. Why is such *bid'a* allowed? It is because of the convenience it brings. On the other hand, the liberation of women is seen as an inconvenient and unwelcome change to religious authorities, which in Islam consist exclusively of men.

Let me try to give a stronger argument for Salafists. In verse 45:12 it is said that Allah "subjected to you the sea in order that ships can sail upon it by his command and that you may seek his favour; and so that you will be grateful." Now a Salafist would say, "it is wrong to use this and say that the Qur'an is outdated because only old modes of travel like the ship are mentioned, for in the verse following it, namely 45:13, it is said that he has subjected to us everything in the heavens and the earth, so even though modern inventions are not mentioned explicitly, we may make use of them. In contrast, there is no provision for adopting new rules."

Does it mean Salafism with modern weapons is coherent after all? No, I would say, because

1. If we accept using verses saying that Allah has sub-

jected everything to us such as 45:13 to argue that specific references in the Qur'an to objects do not prevent us from using objects not mentioned, then we should also be allowed to use abrogation by exaltation, following the least context-dependent and most exalted verses, as explained in Section 6.2.6.

2. Even if we accept this Salafist argument without accompanying conditions for similar treatment of social rules, for instance, we still have limitation based on nation and period of time (see above and Section 2.2.2) especially when we try to read the Qur'an as literally as possible. Contrary to common perception, literalism can backfire on conservative positions.

In verse 16:70 and again in 22:5 in the Qur'an it is said that some of you are sent back to the most decrepit age, so that you do not know anything, after having had knowledge. Whatever it intends to say, this bleak picture reminds one of Salafism. Going back to the past is not a solution for the dire situation of Islam and Islamic communities.

6.1.2 Rational Disputation

How are new inventions accepted in Islam? By rational disputation no doubt. People reasoned that new machines serve similar functions to existing objects, for example cars serve similar functions as donkeys and camels in the old days. So similar rules should apply to the usage of cars as to the use of donkeys and camels. Therefore the rejection of rational disputation is not rational and is defeated in actual behaviour of self-proclaimed religious authorities and self-regarded pure Muslims.

If one were to use any different things from those used by Muhammad and his companions, be it new technology or different flora and fauna, one reaches the conclusion of its being lawful by means of rational disputation. There-

Chapter 6 Reform

fore every Muslim already accepts rational disputation in deed, even if not in words.

In verses 43:12–13 in the Qur'an it is said that Allah is the one "who created all the species and made for you ships and animals on which you ride, so that you may settle on their backs and then remember the favour of your lord." If we stick to strict literalism this passage is very irrelevant, for the dominant modes of transportation now are not ships and animals.

If we were confined to the exact things mentioned in the Qur'an and the Hadiths, then we should never use modern weapons, because that was not how wars were fought in Muhammad's days. I doubt any Salafist groups would adhere to that principle. Therefore any group with military power would be inconsistent in their beliefs if it does not accept rational disputation.

This method was used in early Islam, and is called اجتهاد *ijtihād*. It refers to the practice of employing independent reasoning in making legal rulings.

In the Qur'an, the phrase أولى الالباب *ūlī al-albāb*, meaning "people of understanding," appears many times, in 2:179, 2:197, 2:269, 3:7, 3:190, 5:100, 12:111, 13:19, 14:52, 38:29, 38:43, 39:9, 39:18, 39:21, 40:54, 65:10, etc. The verb عقل *'aqala*, meaning "to reason," is used about 50 times, from 2:44 to 67:10. The word is mostly used to urge people to use their reason. From such usages we can see that Islam values understanding, and reasoning about doctrines is necessary and beneficial. How else could one really follow a religion? If we do not think about what to adhere to, we would be acting blindly.

On the other hand, conservatives could use Qur'anic verses such as 5:3 which says that Islam has been perfected to argue against innovation, but they cannot avoid innovation themselves. Can they forego modern weapons, modern facilities, electronics, etc.? If they cannot, then they are using double standards, since rules about these things do not exist in the Qur'an or the Hadiths. They have to use analogy and extrapolation to determine how to behave lawfully with regard to these new inventions.

Other passages which perhaps conservatives like to use include, for example, 13:13. It says that Allah "sends thunderbolts and strikes whom he wills, and yet people dispute about him." In verses 22:3–4 it is said of the people "who dispute about Allah without knowledge and follow every rebellious devil, it is decreed that he will misguide them and lead them to the punishment of the flame," and in 22:8–9 it is said of the people "who dispute about Allah without knowledge or guidance or an enlightening book, twisting his neck to mislead from the way of Allah, there is disgrace for him in this world, and we will make him taste the punishment of the conflagration on the day of resurrection." Similarly, in 31:20, it is said that Allah has "subjected to you what is in the heavens and on earth, and has amply bestowed upon you his favours, visible ones and hidden ones, and there are people who dispute about Allah without knowledge or guidance or an enlightening book." In verse 40:4, it is said that no one "disputes the signs of Allah except those who disbelieve, so do not be deceived by their movement in the country." In verse 40:5 it is said that every nation "plotted against their messenger to seize him and they disputed by means of falsehood in order to invalidate the truth with it, so Allah seized them and the penalty was terrible." In verse 40:35 it is said that those "who dispute the signs of Allah without a power that came to them, great is the hatred on the side of Allah and those who believed, thus Allah seals over every heart of an arrogant tyrant." In verse 40:56 it is said that those "who dispute the signs of Allah without evidence that came to them, there is nothing in their breasts but pride." In verse

Chapter 6 Reform

40:69 it is said that those "who dispute the signs of Allah are turned away." In verse 42:35 it is said that for those "who dispute the signs of Allah there is no place of escape." From the above verses we can see that in the Qur'an, the verb جادل *jādala*, meaning "to dispute," is always used in a pejorative way, and it is said that people who dispute about Allah are going to be punished.

A similar example is the word حاجّ *ḥājj*, meaning "to argue." It also always refers to unjustified argument against Allah. It appears in verses 2:76, 2:139, 2:258, 3:20, 3:61, 3:65–66, 3:73, 6:80, and 42:16. In verse 2:139 Muhammad is told to say, "Do you argue with us about Allah while He is our lord and your lord? For us are our deeds, and for you are your deeds, and we are sincere to him."

From these examples it seems that to argue is a bad thing. However, we need to keep in mind that Muhammad was sent to give advice directly, so the revelations should have been much clearer to his audience then than to us now, for the context and references were clear, and the advice was suited to the time. But now if we follow Islam we have much more adaptation to do for ourselves, because the world has changed. So it has become necessary for us to discuss and dispute, while argument about Islam was more problematic and hostile in Muhammad's time.

The case of the verb تمارٰ *tamāra*, to dispute, and its use in verses 42:18, 53:12, 53:55, and 54:36 is analogous to the one above. In verse 42:18 it is said, "those who do not believe in it seek to hasten it, and those who believe are fearful of it and know that it is the truth. Indeed it is unquestionably the truth that those who dispute about the hour have gone far astray." We should understand this negative attitude towards dispute in terms of the situation at that time.

We have to remember, first, the specific context in which the Qur'an is revealed. Muhammad was constantly attacked with words and with weapons for spreading Islam, which threatened the power structure at that time. Disputes would put his followers into disarray and render them helpless in the face of military action, and they could be annihilated. The verse 40:5 saying that every nation "plotted against their messenger to seize him and they disputed by means of falsehood in order to invalidate the truth, so Allah seized them and the penalty was terrible" refers to these issues. It does not apply generally and this is not the situation Muslims are facing in the contemporary world. Muslims need stability and development rather than fighting, because realistically Muslim-majority countries are not competent in military technology. It is irrational to apply an attitude which was expedient in Muhammad's predicament to today, when Islam is spread to people in radically different places and situations. People need to reason and argue about how to best adapt Islamic teachings to their context.

Secondly, we need to consider pragmatics. The Qur'an is a collection of passages which Muhammad received from Gabriel during the establishment of Islam. Islam started as a persecuted movement. It is reasonable that its passages are defensive and not magnanimous, since it was not a powerful institution. Therefore "argue" and "dispute" are always bad words and such actions are seen as undesirable. But this does not apply when Muslims communities need to consider problems of government and co-existence. People need to argue and dispute about their different viewpoints and preferences, so that they can find a mutually satisfactory solution. In view of this, going back to the beginning of Islam, as Islamist movements like to push for, is a misguided enterprise. It does not help Muslim-majority countries to follow the example of Muhammad and his followers. Are we going to live like a tribe in the desert? Does

Chapter 6 Reform

it make our lives holier? No, artificially emulating Muhammad's lifestyle is not piety. God never ordered Muhammad to live like Jesus. People in different communities need different advice and improvement.

A passage which we need to read with similar caution is 4:150–151 in which it is said, "indeed, those who disbelieve in Allah and his messengers and wish to discriminate between Allah and his messengers and say, 'we believe in some and disbelieve in others,' and wish to adopt a way in between, those are the disbelievers, truly. And we have prepared for the disbelievers a humiliating punishment." Context and pragmatics again caused the negative tone in referring to people who choose doctrines. There were rifts and problems in the fledgling community. However, after the more than a thousand years which have passed since Muhammad's time, we are compelled to review Islamic texts and formulate a system of beliefs which are suitable and practical for us.

As a precaution, let me also state that it would be even more unjustified to read the word لغو *lagw*, meaning "vain talk" or "ill speech," as referring to doctrinal disputes, discussion about religious reform, etc., i.e. any dissent in general. It appears, for example, in verses 23:1–3, which say, "the believers have succeeded, those who are humble in their prayer, and those who turn away from vain speech." In verses 28:52–55 it is said that when the believers "hear ill speech, they turn away from it and say, 'For us are our deeds, and for you are your deeds. Peace will be upon you. We seek not the ignorant.' " These verses had specific references, not just any talk. They were talking about people's negative reaction to Muhammad's message. We should not take such passages as advising against religious discussion and expressing different views.

Now let us read verse 40:14 with the above background in mind. In this verse people are told to "call Allah, being sincere to him in religion even if the infidels dislike it." People's dislike would not have mattered if they were not powerful. In most of Muhammad's career his followers endured danger and ostracism. This is the reason why disputes about Allah or among believers were not viewed favourably, because it could mean physical danger for Muslims. However, in the modern world, people can dispute without putting anyone in danger and this is the way whereby people can compare the strength of different ideas. We have to take into account the difference between the context in which such verses were revealed and the context in which we today engage in intellectual debate. In our time, disputation makes possible peaceful compromise, whereas a stifled environment without dialogue makes violent propaganda and mutual hostility more likely to take place.

Other verses which are prone to be used in discouraging disputation are 34:5, in which it is said that those "who strive against our signs to cause failure, there will be a punishment of painful foulness," and 34:38 in which it is said that they will be "brought into a punishment." Conservatives might claim that any dispute about the Qur'an is striving against Allah's signs.

However, do these passages really mean that we should not dispute about Allah? First we need to ask ourselves, regarding what Allah actually wants Muslims to do, are there doubts or disputes? Of course there are. People do not agree, so they need to discuss. Only with rational discussion can people gain a better understanding of different views regarding an issue. Does it mean that they are less pious for disagreeing with what religious scholars say, for example? Of course not. For religious scholars, or anyone else, could be wrong, and they are not divine. On the contrary, it is idolatry to suppose that these people rep-

Chapter 6 Reform

resent Allah and that they are always right in what they say about Allah. Therefore it is not the kind of disputing about or striving against Allah that such verses refer to and are trying to stop.

Again we have to remember the context in which Muhammad conveyed such messages. They were recited to his followers during difficult times in which either Muslims would succeed in getting military control, or they would be persecuted and suffer severely, so it is understandable that the passages required unity and allegiance. But the context is different in our world today. We have developed different political systems and religion can be confined to the private realm. So there is no urgency to stop disagreements. On the contrary, the only way for Islam to make progress and survive is to encourage rational disputation and reach a compromise in religious outlook that would fit modern society. From the above discussion we should see that passages like 13:13 which says that Allah "sends thunderbolts and strikes whom he wills, and yet people dispute about him" should not be used for silencing disagreements, controversies, and challenges to religious authorities.

In verses 52:11–12 it is said, "woe to the deniers" on judgment day "who are playing in vain discourse." Conservatives might read this as an injunction against doctrinal discussion or disputes but we should remember that the context was that Muhammad was struggling with rumours and plots against him, so this verse should not be read broadly to include all types of doubts and disputes, but should be limited to the personal attacks Muhammad was facing.

It becomes even more interesting when we consider verse 31:21, the verse following the one against disputing about Allah above. This verse says that people "follow the way of their fathers rather than Allah, even if it is Satan's way." The passages against disputes about Allah have been ironically used to keep people from changing their forefathers' way, even when it has nothing to do with Islam. Many Muslims mistake what some Arabs do for what is required by Islam. But we need rational judgment and scholarship to review what Islam is, we cannot just follow whatever people tell us is the way of Islam.

In verse 41:52, Muhammad is told to say, "did you see that if it were from Allah and you disbelieved in it, who would be more astray than he who has gone far in opposition?" One could say that this verse condemns doubts and arguments about the Qur'an, and that it tells people to believe without question or discussion. However, as the words "disbelieve" and "far" show, it is talking about people who do not accept Muhammad's message at all, when he was spreading its news. It has nothing to do with the necessary discussions taking place now about how to adapt ancient rules to societies that are vastly different from Muhammad's time. To use such verses to silence discussions is dishonest and doing a disservice to Islam. We should not be stopped when such verses are produced to scare us. We should argue calmly and eloquently that they do not condemn discussions about reform in Muslim communities.

From the discussions above we can see that one should rather remember verse 2:242 which says that Allah "makes clear his verses so that you may use reason." We should use reason to reach reasonable interpretations of Islamic texts, and not accept without close examination traditional, established, or mainstream interpretations. What one regards as traditional, established, or mainstream may be just a fashionable trend for ten years. For all its seeming eternity, religious institutions are man-made structures that are in fact quite transient. We have to scrutinise every point rigorously.

This is very tiring, but this is *jihād* in the way of Allah.

The discussion above connects neatly with our discussion of women's rights in the previous chapter. This field is in dire need of rational disputation and a review of what is historical and what is essential in Islam. When we look at social changes in the modern world, we need to think about the applicability of analogical arguments in determining which rules to keep and which rules to change. So we should keep this section in mind when reading the

Qur'an and the Hadiths.

6.2 Reshaping Abrogation

After discussing the importance of rational disputation, we should also examine the issue of abrogation. It plays a key role in determining the doctrinal position one takes, for it is about whether it is permissible to cancel or replace verses in the Qur'an. By extension, we may also talk about cancelling or replacing rules in Islam in this connection. It may sound radical but it is written in the Qur'an itself.

6.2.1 Origin of Abrogation

The traditional description of abrogation says that verses which were received later cancel verses which were received earlier. The stance regarding the consumption of alcohol is among the examples of abrogation which are commonly talked about. Earlier verses were only against praying when drunk (4:43), whereas later verses were totally against alcohol (5:90).

It is said in verses 2:106 and 16:101 that a verse may be canceled or replaced. In verse 16:101, it is said that when Allah "substitutes a verse in place of another, they say that Muhammad is an inventor." In verses 87:6–7 Muhammad is told, "we will make you recite, and you will not forget, except what Allah should will. Indeed, He knows what is declared and what is hidden." From these verses we can see that the Qur'an has undergone different versions, so to speak. Existing verses were canceled and replaced. And this is just in Muhammad's life time.

We should also remember that the actual compilation of the Qur'an from oral recitation occurred after Muhammad's death. Therefore the Qur'an may not be the perfect final version of Allah's divine instruction as some imams and mullahs would like us to believe. I am not saying that the Qur'an is totally unreliable, just that, as a Muslim, one need not believe that every word of it is totally, correctly, and undoubtedly Allah's message to us.

Is not the Qur'an supposed to be uncreated? How could it be imperfect and improved upon? How can Allah who is all-knowing give a message and decide to change it? These questions should drive any perfectionist Muslims crazy, if they have any sense of logic.

But let us be easy and make ourselves comfortable with it. Allah gives different instructions to different people in different circumstances. There is nothing wrong with that. Different people in different circumstances need to do different things. Therefore Allah gives them different things to do. This makes perfect sense. Only fundamentalists cannot or will not understand that.

It would be great for reform-minded Muslims, if abrogation was allowed.

6.2.2 The Seal of Prophets

Abrogation was indeed allowed during the lifetime of Muhammad. But only during his lifetime, because Muhammad is said to be خاتم النبيين, *the seal of prophets* in verse 33:40 in the Qur'an. A seal indicates that a missive is complete. So it seems that any change to Allah's messages should be impossible after Muhammad's death.

Not so fast! Exactly what does saying that Muhammad is the seal of prophets mean? I argue that it has two reasonable interpretations, namely,

1. Muhammad is an extremely important prophet. His messages confirm previous revelations sent by Allah and negate fabrications made by men.

Chapter 6 Reform

2. Muhammad is the last prophet sent by Allah.

even though mainstream Muslims only accept the latter.

If we look at the context in which the phrase "the seal of prophets" is used, we would probably not read it in the second way. For verse 33:40 says that Muhammad "is not the father of any one of your men but is that messenger of Allah and the seal of prophets." The father part refers to the issue of his adopted son Zayd. It seems totally illogical to read this phrase in a universal sense as putting an end to prophecy when the other half of the sentence is referring to something as particular as the case of an adopted son and marrying his ex-wife. It seems an extreme distortion of the text. It is really surprising how out-of-context this phrase has been used, reflecting how few people have read the Qur'an attentively. Reading it in context decisively points towards the first interpretation of the phrase "the seal of prophets."

Let us ask ourselves seriously, even if the phrase was intended to convey a sense of finality and gravity, should we take the seal to be absolute and forever? Allah can unseal prophecy if he so wills. The world has changed and Islam is not exactly in a good state, maybe Allah would prefer people to live by updated guidance, correcting any miscommunication or misinterpretation that exists.

We should note an interesting coincidence of terms here. In Chinese Mahayana Buddhism there is the concept of the three dharma seals, referring to the three basic doctrines of Mahayana Buddhism, namely impermanence, nonexistence of self, and nirvana. These three seals are the yardsticks against which the authenticity of Buddhist teaching is checked.

It is an interesting idea that can have its parallels in Islam. If we reflect on Muhammad's designation as "the seal of prophets," we see that it makes sense to take it to mean that his central message can act as the yardstick by which the authenticity of teaching in Islam should be checked. It is just an interpretation that has not been suggested.

Even though this interpretation seems unorthodox, in practice we have already seen in various fundamentalist movements that it is disastrous to read this designation of Muhammad as saying that every word of his message needs to be followed in an inflexible way, ignoring the change of circumstances from his time and now. And it does not mean that we cannot propose new teachings in Islam or have new prophets. So it is very reasonable to look at the phrase "the seal of prophets" in a way that is similar to the three dharma seals in Buddhism.

6.2.3 Nation and Prophet

If verse 33:40, which says that Muhammad is the seal of prophets, is worthy of our consideration, then verse 10:47 discussed in Section 4.1.1 above is at least as important, if not more so. In this verse it is said that each nation has its own prophet, and that judgment is between this prophet and his people. Similarly, in verse 13:7, it is said that for "every race there is a guide." In verse 35:24 it is said that there is "no nation but that a bearer of warning has passed inside it." In verse 22:67, it is said that for "every nation Allah has appointed rites which they perform." In verse 14:4, it is said that Allah "did not send any messenger except one who speaks the tongue of his people, so that he make things clear for them." From this verse we can deduce that Muhammad's message is for the Arabic-speaking people he was sent to, and that the instructions are designed for this people. In verses 14:9–10, it is said that Allah sent messengers to the people of Noah, 'Aad, and Thamud, and those after them. Only Allah knows who these other messengers are. So if people follow others, we cannot be really sure that those are not Allah's other messengers.

Most importantly, In verses 13:38–39 in the Qur'an, it is said that messengers have been sent before, and that there is a book for *every period of time*. It is also said that Allah eliminates what he wills and confirms what he wills, and that the *mother of the book* is with him. In verses

Chapter 6 Reform

43:3-4 it is said that Allah "made it an Arabic Qur'an so that you may understand, and indeed it is, in the mother of the book with us, exalted and wise." And then in 31:27 it is said that if "trees were pen and the sea was ink and seven more seas were added to it, the words of Allah would still not be exhausted."

These verses seem to say that the Qur'an was the book for Muhammad's time, just as the Torah and the Gospels were the books for different times. It is a version of the mother of the book for Muhammad and his followers. I discussed this issue in detail in Section 2.2.2.

Reading the specific instructions on inheritance in the Qur'an in 4:1-13 for example, it seems reasonable to suppose that it is a book intended for a particular period of time in the history of the Arabs. In verse 4:11 it is said, "Allah instructs you concerning your children: for the male, like the portion of two females." It was practical in an age where a male was expected to provide for his wife and children. But it is not necessarily the case in other ages. If a prophet was sent from Allah today, the instructions would have be different.

We should reason from the particularity of the instructions in the Qur'an that they were not intended for any age and any form of society, but contained practical advice for Muhammad's audience. This also supports the view that the Qur'an is a message for Arabs in the seventh century. Seen on the grand scale of things, the Qur'an is but a small part of Allah's book. These verses confirm this supposition.

Reading the above passages carefully we should be able to see that they seem to be in conflict with the statement that Muhammad is the seal of prophets if it implies that he is the last prophet. What about people to whom no prophet came before Muhammad? Is there no one to guide them? We have two ways for resolving this issue.

1. The prophets of all other nations have already relayed their messages before Muhammad.

    This could be the case and it would mean that according to *islam*, the prophets of each nation should be looked for before the time of Muhammad.

2. One could interpret the meaning of the phrase "the seal of prophets" as rhetorical only, not saying that there are absolutely no prophets after Muhammad.

This rhetorical turn of phrase is employed because when we try to persuade a not-very-educated people to follow us and fight for us, it does not do to say that our messages are for this situation only, that our messenger is for our nation only, and that our rules are for our nation in this age only. We have to say our messages very strongly and that they are meant for every human being. This is the reason why there is a discrepancy between such strong rhetoric and the occasional allusion to prophets for different nations and the occasional changes to Allah's injunctions. You cannot say that the rules will change after a hundred years, or that the rules are different for different groups. This people whom you are trying to teach will be confused and they will not follow you.

In connection with the second point, let us look at verses 77:49–50 in the Qur'an in which it is said that on judgment day "woe, that day, to the deniers. Then in what statement after the Qur'an will they believe?" If we reflect with reason we should be able to see that it does not mean that everyone who ever lived on earth without following Muhammad's message would be punished. Read with the moral construal of belief,[1] we can see that it is a rhetorical question showing the people's regret for their immoral behaviour in life, on judgment day. It would be unreasonable to read it literally as saying that there is no divine message after Muhammad.

---

[1] Please refer to Section 4.1.2 in which we argued that we can construe Islam as a body of moral guidance.

6.2.4 Allah and King

In verse 6:39 it is said that Allah "wills who is to go astray and who is to go on the straight path." I discussed the problem of will in this verse in Section 4.5.1. However, to try to reach a reasonable interpretation of this verse with respect to the role of Allah, let us look at 20:79, where it is said that Pharaoh "led his people astray and did not guide them." When we compare the wording we can see that Allah and Pharaoh are set up as rivals and that they play similar roles in people's lives.

In Assmann's *From Akhenaten to Moses* [10], there is an interesting comparison between Akhenaten, the monotheist Pharaoh, and Moses but I think that Allah and Pharaohs occupy more parallel roles in Muhammad's community and Pharaonic Egypt respectively. Pharaohs were not simply rulers but were also seen as gods. And Allah claims to be the sole, ultimate, most powerful deity. But he is seen in a similar way as Pharaohs, and his role is to guide nations.

In verses 40:23–54 there is an account of Moses's story, and one again sees a parallel between Pharaoh and Allah. In verse 40:29 a believer in Pharaoh's family says, "O people, sovereign (ملك *mulk*) belongs to you today, dominant in the land, but who would help us from the punishment of Allah if it came to us?" Attention should be paid to the use of the word ملك *mulk*. The word means kingdom, sovereignty, or sometimes possession, but it is used mostly in the Qur'an to talk about the world as Allah's dominion (in 2:107, 2:247, 3:26, 3:189, 4:53, 5:17–18, 5:40, 5:120, 6:73, 7:158, 9:116, 17:111, 24:42, 25:2, 35:13, 38:10, 39:6, 39:44, 42:49, 43:85, 45:27, 48:14, 57:2, 57:5, 64:1, 67:1, 85:9 etc.) while, in contrast, those whom people invoke besides Allah do not possess even a membrane of a date seed, to emphasise the humble nature of human beings. The other times the word ملك *mulk* is used, it either refers to

Solomon's kingdom (2:102), the kingship of طالوت *ṭālūt* (2:247–248), usually identified as Saul in the Christian tradition, the kingship (2:251) and kingdom (38:20) of David, the kingship of Abraham's king (2:258), Abraham's kingdom (4:54), Joseph's sovereignty (12:101), Solomon requesting a kingdom (38:35), the sovereignty of Pharaoh's people (40:29), or the kingdom of Egypt (43:51).

The only times in which the word does not refer to a ruling power in the material world are in 20:12 in which Satan whispered to Adam, "O Adam, shall I direct you to the tree of eternity and possession (ملك *mulk*) that does not deteriorate?" Then in 22:56, 25:26, and 40:16 it is said that sovereignty (ملك *mulk*) on judgment day belongs to Allah, and in 76:20 it is said that if one looks at paradise, one sees pleasure and a great dominion (ملك *mulk*). These are the only exceptions in which the word does not refer to Allah's dominion or human beings ruling power.

Even more explicitly, Allah is called the king (ملك *malik*) in 20:114, 23:116, 59:23, 62:1, and 114:2.

In verses 48:4 and 48:7 it is said, "to Allah belong the soldiers of the heavens and the earth," and in 74:31 it is said "none knows the soldiers of your lord except him." As we know, the possession of soldiers is a trait of leaders and kings.

In verses 58:20-21 it is said, "indeed, the ones who oppose Allah and his messenger, those will be among the most humbled. Allah has written, 'I will surely overcome, I and my messengers.' Indeed, Allah is strong and powerful." This passage shows that the conception of Allah's kingdom is very similar to a worldly kingdom in terms of

Chapter 6 Reform

power structure and command. Then in 58:19 we have a reference to the party of Satan, while in 58:22 we have a reference to the party of Allah. The struggle between good and evil is allegorised into a struggle between the party of Satan and the party of Allah. The word "party" is not as purely political as today but it already meant a group of people with the same aim and goals. Therefore there are many parallels between Allah and a king or a ruler on earth. Such parallels continue to be seen in Sura 59. In verses 59:3-4 it is said that the people of the book deserve punishment "because they opposed Allah and his messenger, and whoever opposes Allah, then indeed, Allah is severe in penalty." What a people oppose is usually a person in command. Allah is seen as a ruler.

When we think about sovereignty we usually think about it in a secular political sense, but originally there is no clear distinction between a human secular ruler and a divine ruler. Allah is a king of the whole world like a human being can be a king of a geographic area. We can reasonably conjecture that this understanding of religion is one of the accepted views of Moses' people and Muhammad's people. Muhammad follows this tradition and therefore Islam gives guidance in all aspects of a Muslim's life, as a king would rule his people.

But this is probably a compromise between the ideal religion and the religion that Muhammad's community would be advanced enough to be able to accept and follow. Therefore we should be careful not to assume that the form of organisation of Muhammad's followers is an ideal model to be replicated in any time, at any place.

As corroboration of the influence of Egyptian society on the concept of Allah, we should note that

1. The word "bracelet" is used five times in the Qur'an, four times describing paradise, and the remaining one is in 43:53, in which it is said that Pharaoh questioned with respect to Moses, "then why have there not been placed upon him bracelets of gold or come with him the angels joined together?" From this we

can see that the sumptuous description of paradise is highly influenced by Egyptian standards.

2. In verse 43:51, the only time in which a river is said to flow under something other than paradise, it is said to flow under Pharaoh. This shows us what ideas the Qur'an is responding and referring to. The Nile River is an enviable asset and the picture of paradise in the Qur'an is probably modelled after the Nile Valley.

If the view as argued for here is reasonable, that the notion of religion in the Qur'an is not the highest form possible but a compromise due to the conception of religion, sovereignty, and obedience at the time, then by extrapolation, we should think that, in our own time, we can have our own books, or we can have a revised version of the previous sacred books, since our conceptions of these things have changed. The revised version should be one which takes account of the political and intellectual changes in the world which happened after those books were revealed. This seems a reasonable reading of the verses discussed above.

This is the way we should consider historical contexts when trying to determine the significance of each section of religious text, in contrast to the way some religious scholars operate. The way they do it is to say that women's rights were improved by Islam—this is the context, and then they say that we should follow literally the rules laid out in the Qur'an—this is the interpretation. This is not what I mean when I say we should consider historical contexts when we interpret Islamic texts.

6.2.5 Islam as a Compromise

In verses 54:17, 54:22, 54:32, and 54:40 it is emphasised that Allah "has certainly made the Qur'an easy for remembrance." In verse 23:62 it is said that Allah "does not charge any soul except within its capacity." When we read the Qur'an and the Hadiths, we have to consider the

Chapter 6 Reform

social environment which Muhammad was in. His message is adapted to the level of his audience and to that environment. We should read Islamic texts with the caveat that it was a compromise between a high ideal and what Muslims at that historical stage would be capable of achieving.

However, various verses in the Qur'an assert that there is no change in Allah's way. In verse 10:64 in the Qur'an it is said that there is "no change in Allah's words," and in verses 17:77, 33:62, 35:43, and 48:23 it is said, "you will not find in the way of Allah any change." If we cannot change anything written in the Qur'an, how should we deal with the difference between seventh-century Arabia, which is the context and background for Muhammad's message, and modern societies? Let us examine these passages one by one.

In verses 10:63–64 it is said, "those who believed and feared Allah, for them are good tidings in worldly life and in the hereafter. There is no change in the words of Allah." Once we read the verse above we can see that it is referring to Allah's promise only. We should not infer that there can be no change in any rule given in Islamic texts.

In verses 17:73–77 in the Qur'an it is said that the blind ones "nearly tempted you away," and that they "were about to drive you away." And then it is said that they "will not remain but for a short while," that it is "our established way for the messengers in the past," and that you will "not find in our way any alteration." In connection with 17:103 below it is probably referring to the story between Moses and Pharaoh, but what do those verses themselves mean? Are we to take from this that Allah's way never changes and that the revelations given through Muhammad hold true literally in all their details always? No, I do not think so. Even though it is said that Allah's way does not change, we can read it in an abstract way, that Allah's way or grand scheme does not change, but concrete rules might change, which has been observed in Allah's evolving covenant with different peoples. There is no conflict between having a second-order, i.e. higher-level way which does not change, and having a different first-order, i.e. lower-level, concrete systems of rules which do change.

In verses 33:60–62 it is said, "If the hypocrites and those in whose hearts is disease and those who spread rumours in Medina do not cease, we will surely let you overpower them, then they will not remain your neighbours in it except for a little, accursed wherever they are found, seized and massacred completely. [This is] the established way of Allah with those who passed on before, and you will not find in the way of Allah any change." From this passage we can see that the "established way of Allah" is only referring to his power of destroying unjust people. It does not refer to each and every rule given in Islamic texts.

Similarly in 35:43–44, it is said that the evil plot devours only its own people, that they are only "waiting for the way of the previous peoples," that you "will not find in the way of Allah any change and you will not find in the way of Allah any alteration," and that if they travelled they would have "observed how the end of those before them was." The absence of change should be read in connection with the end of the previous peoples. Here it is saying that Allah will destroy disobedient nations like he did before, there is no change to that. But how to be obedient is another issue. Since Muhammad is not the final prophet and for each nation there is a prophet, the rules for each people are different and we are not supposed to apply Islamic rules to people other than the tribes which were in contact with him. We cannot use the Qur'an and the Hadiths literally, without deliberation, as a direct measurement of obedience.

Again, in verses 48:22–23, it is said, "if those who disbelieved had fought you, they would have turned their backs, then they would not have found a protector or a helper. [This is] the established way of Allah which has occurred before. And never will you find in the way of Allah any change." Like the examples above, the non-existence of change is referring to the fate of people who disbelieve. However, we need to remember the moral construal of belief (Section 4.1.2) and should not think that we can pre-

Chapter 6 Reform

dict who is going to hell just by looking at who proclaims himself to be a Muslim.

From the discussion above we can see that even in face of the phrase that one does not find in Allah's way any alteration, there can still be reform and change in religious rules and practice. It is only the inflexibility of some human minds which requires that if we have such phrases in the Qur'an then there cannot be change in Islam.

Another example which is slightly less prone to misinterpretation is verse 50:29. Here it is said, "the word will not be changed with me, and I will not be unjust to the servants." Some people would read this and say, "see! we cannot change God's words. Whatever rules he laid down in the seventh century should be followed today." But as soon as we read the surrounding verses we see that 50:29 is saying that Allah's threat of punishment on judgment day does not change, but it does not mean that all of his commands are unalterable. In 50:24–28, the verses immediately before this, it is said that on judgment day Allah will say, "throw into hell every obstinate disbeliever, preventer of good, aggressor, doubter, who made another deity alongside Allah. Then throw him into the severe punishment," and it is said that his companion will say, "our lord, I did not make him transgress, but he was in far-fetched error," and it is said that Allah will say, "do not dispute before me, while I had already presented to you the warning." Only then comes the suggestive passage, "the word will not be changed with me, and I will not be unjust to the servants" in 50:29. We can see that reading the verses together casts a totally different light from reading this verse alone. This example shows how essential it is to pay attention to context in order to avoid people using verses to fool you into doing what they want you to do.

A related piece of text to discuss is the Hadith which says that Muhammad likens himself to the only missing brick of a beautifully built house. [3, 56:734–735] But that is an easy matter if we are willing to adopt a loose interpretation of the phrase "the seal of prophets" in the

Qur'an. The reason is that the Hadiths are, firstly, not as reliable as the Qur'an and, secondly, this simile is also open to interpretation. The house in the simile could be a monotheistic religion suitable for the Arabian Peninsula in the 7th century.

One may say this interpretation seems trivial. On the contrary, is not the interpretation that this house points towards an eternal perfect religion too grandiose? Is this not something that people, because Islam is a popular religion now with hundreds of thousands of followers, carelessly and falsely attribute to its humble beginnings?

In contrast, let us consider another Qur'anic verse. In verse 6:154, it is said that Allah "gave Moses the Book, completing his favour upon the one who did good." If we take the word "completing" literally, then God's favour is already complete with Moses, so all the later prophets are impostors, including Muhammad himself, who conveyed this passage. Of course Muslims do not interpret the word "completing" here literally, and with reason. But the expression "the seal of prophets" is actually analogous. It conveys the gravity of Muhammad's message, not necessarily saying that it is the last one forever and ever.

Let us do a thought experiment, i.e. run a hypothetical situation in our minds. Imagine that we live in a community in which someone is firmly established as a prophet after Muhammad in the Abrahamic fashion.

Now close your eyes, breathe deeply and seriously imagine the situation.

Do you think this community would interpret phrases such as "the seal of prophets" as saying that Muhammad is the last prophet? Or would this community look at the phrase "the seal of prophets" as Muslims read "Allah gave Moses the Book, completing his favour," that is, in a loose sense? I think that the community would.

In fact it seems that, logically speaking, Muslims should accept the Baha'i faith the way they think Jews and Christians should accept Islam. The reason is that Islam acknowledges the revelations of Judaism and Christianity and claims that Muhammad continues this tradition. The

Chapter 6 Reform

Baha'i faith does the same thing. It acknowledges the revelations of Judaism, Christianity, and Islam and claims that the Bab and Baha'ullah continue this tradition. It is really hard to adopt Islam but reject the Baha'i faith.

From the Islamic point of view, Islam (or *islām*) existed before Muhammad and the verses he delivered are not necessarily the only expression of Islam. The Jewish and Christian holy books hold messages from Allah, just that they may have been translated or interpreted wrongly. In verse 4:164 in the Qur'an it is said that prophets "have been sent to you, some we told you about and some we have not told you about." This asserts the existence of previous prophets. What about prophets after Muhammad?

In Sura 26 of the Qur'an a series of stories about the messengers before Muhammad is told. Among them, Shuaib is said to have conveyed some instructions to his people (26:181–184), namely,

1. Give full measure.

2. Do not cause loss.

3. Weigh with an even balance.

4. Do not deprive people of their things.

5. Do not commit evil on earth.

6. Fear the one who created you and the former generations.

Now this list is similar to what other prophets said but is definitely different, for example Moses' ten commandments are different from this list. Are we going to deny any prophets because of their deviation from previous ones? This does not seem reasonable. As long as a person sincerely claims to receive divine revelations and his messages tell people to do good, he is probably a prophet who deserved to be mentioned by Muhammad, if only he lived before Muhammad.

In reading the Qur'an and other Islamic texts, one can see that Allah changes his plans frequently. It does not necessarily mean that he is careless or not prepared, and Muslims should not blind themselves against these records in order to preserve the impression that Allah is perfect. For example, in verse 8:65 it is said that ten patient believers will overcome two hundred, and then in 8:66 it is said that Allah "has lightened the load because there is weakness in you, and now a hundred believers will overcome two hundred."

Maybe Allah is not perfect or prescient enough (prescient means having foreknowledge) but is flexible and reasonable. That should be good enough. It is perhaps a human weakness and selfishness that a so-called perfect God is needed in order for one to believe in him.

And after Muhammad, there have been different people who claimed to be prophets in the tradition of Islam, but all were denounced as impostors by most Muslims. So this issue is definitely not something Muslims are open about. But the present book aims to challenge established views, not just repeat the accepted ones.

We think that Muslims overstate Muhammad's authority when they proselytise because of a narrow conception of Islam, their own desire to dominate, and for the sake of their own ego rather than for love of God and his messenger. Compare the subsection on ego in Section 4.5.1 above.

But I do not need to push this point about the non-final status of Muhammad if you feel this is too much. The fact is, even if no new prophets are accepted, one can and should review the way Islam is taught. Finding the essence of the revelations and living by it is Islam. Reviewing and reforming the messages, the traditions, and the interpretations thereof would be a way towards Allah.

At least we can see that such words as "complete," "perfect," "seal," etc. are only to be interpreted as meaning that it is definite and important *for the time and place in which it is revealed*. As for any passages in the Qur'an and the Hadiths, one has to interpret them with reason and flexibility. These texts come from another time and age and they were never really intended as universal in

Chapter 6 Reform

the *absolute* sense. They were said to be universal in the *rhetorical* sense. I do not say this just because we feel that it is true, but because we can see from the examples given in the present book that interpreting such words literally does not make sense. The messages were intended to help the followers in their particular situation.

I am not saying that later generations cannot believe in a faith established a long time ago, but we have to read the religious texts carefully, because these texts had a context and a situation.

We should adopt the teachings that improve us in this time and age, not the ones which drag us behind, reverting to bad practices which either did exist in the past or are only imagined to have existed in the ideal community of the forefathers.

Following the example of Muhammad, we should abrogate teachings in the Qur'an using our own reason and the core principles we choose from the texts and traditions.

For example, in Section 4.5.1 I talked about the terrible problem of Allah willing people to disbelieve and then punishing them for it. For any thinking and non-egotistic Muslim the view that all non-believers would be punished by Allah should be a problematic doctrine. If we were to abrogate this, Islam would become a much better religion.

Maybe this was just to make sure that people's will was strong enough for battle. It is not true nor important for Islam. Why should we assume that every message of Muhammad is eternal and all-encompassing? It is an idea that causes terrible dogmatism and suffering. We can see that if all of the Qur'an's statements are taken as true universally, then

1. There would be many scientific mistakes which would not be an issue if we see them as simplified stories for an uneducated audience.

2. Islam cannot accommodate modern life because modern inventions are not mentioned in the Qur'an.

So abrogation is necessary.

6.2.6 Abrogation by Exaltation

The principles of the form of extended abrogation that I advocate would be, when there is a conflict between different verses, we should

1. Choose the verse which is less context-dependent.

2. Choose the verse which characterises Allah in a higher way.

3. Choose the verse which exhibits a higher form of wisdom.

Justification of the above principles is not hard. For the first one, as I have argued in Section 3.2.3, Islamic texts were given under particular historical and social circumstances. In order to benefit from the wisdom in these texts, we need to place them in their context and learn the lesson rather than the letter. Therefore, when we see a conflict between different verses, of course we should choose the ones which are less context-dependent, for these are the ones which would be more reasonable for our own situation.

As for the second principle, we can find a great deal of textual evidence. The exalted status of Allah is asserted in verses 2:255, 4:34, 6:100, 7:190, 10:18, 16:1, 16:3, 17:43, 20:114, 22:62, 23:92, 23:116, 27:63, 28:68, 30:40, 31:30, 34:23, 39:67, 40:12, 42:4, 42:51, 72:3, 79:24, 87:1, and 92:20. It is also said in 9:31, 10:18, 16:1, 28:68, 30:40, 39:67, 52:43, and 59:23 that Allah is exalted above what they associate with him, and in 6:100, 21:22, 23:91, 37:159, 37:180, and 43:82 it is said that Allah is exalted above what they describe. In verses 55:26–27 it is said, "everyone on earth will perish, and the face of your lord, owner of majesty and honour, remains."

As for the third principle, we can also find much textual

Chapter 6 Reform

evidence. The word حكيم ḥakīm, meaning "wise," is used about 100 times in the Qur'an for characterising Allah, from 2:32 up to 76:30. It is definitely a very important property of Allah. We should also remember that the Qur'an is said to be made easy for people. In verses 54:17, 54:22, 54:32, and 54:40 it is emphasised that Allah "has certainly made the Qur'an easy for remembrance." In verse 23:62 it is said that Allah "does not charge any soul except within its capacity." Therefore if there are passages with lower and higher levels of wisdom we may conclude that the lower ones are for people not ready for the higher ones.

Let me demonstrate the application of these principles with some examples.

Regarding context dependence, in verse 27:40 it is said that Solomon said, "Whoever is grateful, he is grateful for his soul. Whoever is ungrateful, then Allah is self-sufficient and generous." In verse 31:12 this is again stated as a piece of wisdom given to Luqman. In verse 39:41 it is said that Allah "revealed to you the book for the people in truth, so that whoever is guided it is for his soul, and whoever goes astray goes astray against it, and you are not a manager over them." In verse 42:48 it is said that Allah did not send Muhammad "as a guardian, only notification is upon" him. The point that Muhammad is only responsible for getting the message through is repeated in 3:20, 5:92, 5:99, 13:40, 16:35, 16:82, 24:54, 29:18, 36:17, and 64:12. From these numerous verses we can see that we are each responsible for our own souls and we should take care of them, but not other people' issues. We should let them work out their spiritual path for themselves.

On the other hand, in verses 2:190, 2:193, 2:244, 4:76, 4:84, 8:39, 9:12–14, 9:29, 9:36, and 9:123, people are told to fight in the way of Allah, and fight those who do not believe. But these verses were given during hostilities between Muhammad's followers and people who oppressed them. There was no other way to resolve their conflict except by violent means, given the chaotic state of the Arabian Peninsula at that time. Therefore these verses are very context-dependent, and are not meant to be universal. A verse corroborating this claim is 49:9, in which it is said that if one faction of believers oppresses the other, then fight against the oppressors until they return to the command of Allah. From this verse we can see that fighting was a common way to resolve conflicts because there was no higher judicial authority among different groups of Arabs.

If we use the first group of verses to abrogate violent verses urging one to fight non-believers, then Islam cannot be a violent religion. The problem we see now is that extremists use violent passages to incite fighting and terrorist attacks. If the majority of moderate Muslims make their stance, cancel, and remove such verses in a united way, then it would become much more difficult for extremists to quote the Qur'an and incite violence.

As we said before, the traditional description of abrogation says that later verses cancel earlier verses. But this does not have to be the only case where abrogation happens. It should take place whenever verses are in conflict and the ones that are meant to be applicable in general should abrogate the ones that are only applicable under the circumstances in which they were revealed, for example the wars Muhammad was fighting. The timeline of Muhammad's revelations is frequently controversial, and in view of the long history of compilation and transmission of the revelations, it is more advisable to decide from the content, using one's God-given ability to reason.

It may seem wilful of us to decide which passages to follow, but the problem exists without our wilfulness, for there are conflicts in the text itself. Therefore we are doing only what is necessary when we choose between conflicting verses. And of course we should use our reason to choose, rather than unreliable rules based on the chronology of revelation.

As for characterising Allah in a higher way, let us look at the following verses. In the Qur'an, the word رحيم *raḥīm*, meaning "most merciful," is used 116 times from

Chapter 6 Reform

the very beginning until 73:20 and every time except once it is used for characterising Allah, while the word رحمان *raḥmān*, meaning "most gracious," is used 57 times from 2:163 until 78:38 and every time it is used in order to describe Allah. From these verses we can see that Allah is associated with mercy and graciousness. The word غفور *ghafūr*, meaning "forgiving," is used 91 times from 2:173 to 85:14 and every time it describes Allah. The word عفو *'afū*, meaning "pardoning," is used in 4:43, 4:99, 4:149, 22:60, and 58:2 to describe Allah, and is used to describe Allah only. Allah is also frequently said to be pardoning people, for example in 2:52, 2:187, 3:152, 3:155, 4:153, 5:95, 5:101, 9:66, 42:25, 42:30, and 42:34. In addition to these, we should also pay attention to the characterisation of Allah as affectionate (ودود *wadūd*). In verse 85:14 it is said that Allah is the forgiving, the affectionate, and in 11:90 people are told to "ask forgiveness of your Lord and then repent to him. Indeed, my lord is merciful and affectionate."

From these recurring descriptions we can see that these are extremely important qualities of Allah, so important that they should trump other ones if textual conflict arises. If other descriptions imply that Allah is not merciful, forgiving, pardoning, or loving, they should be discarded in favour of the characterisations above. These qualities are generally applicable in determining what one is supposed to do, while many injunctions were context-sensitive, for example given in war, or dependent on the social realities of the time. Therefore we should give more priority to these characterisations of Allah than to concrete injunctions recorded in Islamic texts.

On the other hand, let us look at verses which are in conflict with the verses characterising Allah as merciful, gracious, etc. as discussed above. For example, in verse 39:54 people are told to "turn to Allah and submit to him before punishment comes to you, then you will not be helped." Similarly, in 39:72 it is said that the keepers of hell will say to the ones who disbelieve, "enter the gates of hell abiding there eternally, and wretched is the residence of the arrogant ones." I propose that such verses use fear to promote good behaviour, because that was most effective for Muhammad's audience. Other violent and fear-inspiring verses should be read in the same way. We do not need to take such verses with as much weight as the ones expounding Allah's mercifulness. In verse 40:3, Allah is characterised as the forgiver of sin, acceptor of repentance, severe in punishment, owner of abundance. We should look at "severe in punishment" as applying to people who commit really serious crimes, not just say that they do not believe. Otherwise it cannot be reconciled with the names "forgiver of sin" and "acceptor of repentance."

One may say, "how can you determine and choose for yourself that mercy and forgiveness are more important than explicit rules given in the Qur'an and the Hadiths?" My answer is that, as I have argued in Chapter 3, we need to read and interpret very carefully. Literal reading does not mean that one is more faithful to the text.

Let us look at another set of contrasting verses. In verses 2:217, 3:22, 5:5, 5:53, 6:88, 7:147, 9:17, 9:69, 11:16, 18:105, 33:19, 39:65, 47:9, 47:28, 47:32, and 49:2, it is said that if people do not believe, what they do would be worthless. On the other hand, in 3:161, 4:40, 4:49, 4:77, 6:160, 10:44, 10:47, 10:54, 16:111, 17:71, 18:49, 21:47, 23:62, 36:54, 36:69, 45:22, and 46:19, it is said that people will not be wronged by Allah, that they are rewarded for what they do. In verses 27:89–90 in the Qur'an it is said that, on judgment day, people are rewarded according to what they have done. In verse 40:17 it is said that on judgment day "every soul will be rewarded with what

Chapter 6 Reform

it earned," that there is "no injustice today, for Allah is quick in account." In verse 95:8 it is said, "is not Allah the most just of judges?" In a Hadith, Allah is recorded to have said that people with just the weight of a barley grain, a wheat grain, or an atom of good would be taken out of hell. [3, 2:42] I argue that the second group of verses and Hadiths should abrogate the first group, i.e. since it is unjust to make non-Muslims' deeds worthless, this claim is null and void. It does not fit with Allah's elevated status and especially his role as dispenser of justice to make people's good deeds worthless just because they do not believe in his existence. Injustice against prophets should be counted as bad acts and this is what was at stake when those verses were revealed but disbelief by itself should not be a serious crime.

For another example, in verse 35:39 it is said that the disbelief of the disbelievers "does not increase them in front of Allah except in hatred." The hatred of Allah is not compatible with his mercy (1:1) and kindness (22:65). Because of his exalted status and being free from need (14:8), it is not reasonable that he should hate. Allah's exalted status is asserted in 2:255, 4:34, 6:100, 7:190, 10:18, 16:1, 16:3, 17:43, 20:114, 22:62, 23:92, 23:116, 27:63, 28:68, 30:40, 31:30, 34:23, 39:67, 40:12, 42:4, 42:51, 72:3, 79:24, 87:1, and 92:20. Therefore the verse about Allah's hate should be abrogated because of its conflict with other more coherent verses.

As for exhibiting a higher form of wisdom, let us look at the following verses. In verses 40:7–8 it is said that those who carry the throne and those around it praise Allah and believe in him and ask forgiveness for those who believed, saying "O our lord, you encompassed everything in mercy and knowledge, so forgive those who repented and followed your way and protect them from the punishment of hell. O our lord, admit them to the gardens of Eden which you promised and whoever was righteous among their fathers, spouses, and offspring. Verily you are strong and wise." The fathers of Muslims may not have known Islam and become Muslims. But they could still be admitted to paradise for their good deeds. Doing good deeds is more important than saying that one believes in Allah. So this passage exhibits a higher form of wisdom than verses which threaten anyone who does not believe with punishment and hate, such as verse 40:10 in which it is said that the ones who do not believe will have called out to them, "the hatred of Allah is greater than your hatred for yourselves when you were invited to faith and you disbelieved."

Another powerful verse with exalted content is 45:20. It says that the Qur'an "is enlightenment for mankind and guidance and mercy for an assured people." Very similar verses are found in 7:203, in which it is said that the Qur'an "is enlightenment from your lord and guidance and mercy for a people which believe" and 28:43, in which it is said that Allah "gave Moses the book" "as enlightenment for the people and guidance and mercy so that they may take heed." The word used in these verse is بصائرٌ *baṣā'ir*, the plural of بصيرة *baṣīra*, meaning "insight." Other verses containing this word are also uplifting. In verse 6:104, it is said, "enlightenment from your lord came to you. So he who sees does so for his soul." In verse 12:108 Muhammad is told to say, "this is my way. I invite [people] to Allah with insight, I and those who follow me."

In verse 78:39 it is said that on judgment day "he who wills may take to his lord a return." This definitely exhibits a higher form of wisdom than passages threatening punishment for disbelief, for example in 2:24 in which it is said, "fear the fire, whose fuel is men and stones, prepared for the disbelievers." In my opinion such punishment is not as it is described in the Qur'an, and it is for misconduct rather than disbelief, as I explicated in Section 4.1.2.

After reading these exalted verses carefully, let us ask ourselves, do we read the Qur'an in a way that is coherent with such verses? If we do not, then we need to adjust our interpretation and choice of verses so that our religious outlook fits with such verses. This is the key meaning of abrogation.

6.2.7 Deviation

After presenting such bold suggestions in view of the dominant *Zeitgeist* in Muslim communities, let me give a preemptive reply to potential attacks.

Maybe conservatives would produce verses such as 41:40 in the Qur'an, in which it is said that those "who deviate from (الحد *alḥada*) our signs do not hide from us. Is he who is cast into hell better or he who comes safe on the day of resurrection? Do what you will, indeed he sees well what you do." And they would say that such verses show that you should adhere to Islamic texts without modification, and that if you do not follow exactly what they say, you will go to hell.

Now we need to read such verses carefully, and not be scared the moment we see it. Yes this verse tells us not to deviate from the signs of Allah, but what are the signs of Allah? The creed or kneeling how many times in a prayer? I suppose we all agree that there are priorities and differences in relative importance in our actions with respect to our faith. Therefore we should also agree that many actions are not tightly tied to faith and that advice found in the Qur'an and the Hadiths is based on the social situation Muhammad and his audience were in. Therefore changing these rules does not threaten one's faith and is not what is referred to in verses such as 41:40. We have to remember the context in which Muhammad received his revelations, and this verse in all probability refers to other groups competing violently with Muhammad and his followers. We should not apply such verses to other situations lightly.

In general, we need to loosen up and not see every change as a sign of the deterioration of Islam. Otherwise this suffocation and lack of freedom will kill every social improvement that potentially could be realised. In fact this resistance to change is a sign of the low self-esteem which Muslim communities collectively feel. Just as a person with hurt feelings becomes sensitive to others' words and actions and sees contempt everywhere, a community with an inferiority complex feels insulted and sees a threat to its faith, culture, or values all around it.

6.2.8 Ending Note

After reading this section one might say, if it is as I argue, then what is religion but what one chooses? My reply is that indeed this is the way it is, for one chooses his own religion anyway. For however conservative one is, he chose the particular school to stick to. So what I am proposing is that we should choose more carefully and in a more reform-minded manner.

One does not need to listen to mullahs and imams who profit from the institutionalisation and petrification of Islam. In verse 9:34 in the Qur'an it is said that the monks and rabbis devour the wealth of people. At the time Qur'anic verses were revealed there were no counterparts in Islam yet, because it had just been established by Muhammad. But now we definitely have people making use of Islam and devouring the wealth of people. They promote teachings, not because they are Islamic, but because

Chapter 6 Reform

they are good for maintaining their power, for example the superiority of Islam and the superiority of men. These are teachings that benefit clerics and hence are promoted.

One should remember that established views are not necessarily correct. They can become established because people in power prefer them.

If trying in this age to do something akin to Muhammad's abrogation of Qur'anic verses seems too radical, one can review interpretations and that should go far enough towards liberalisation and secularisation. Actually why is it so radical? Is it because to try to do what Muhammad did is very presumptuous? Is that not a little bit idolatrous towards Muhammad, who emphasised that he was a humble human being, not a god?

One may argue that if some of the core doctrines are discarded, it is no longer Islam. Islam as defined by the five pillars does not include all these other doctrines. The creed says Muhammad is a messenger of Allah, it does not say that he is the only one or the last one, even though some Muslims seem to assume that he is both. And there are so many other things including the spiritual, cultural aspects, etc. that hold this fluid concept of Islam together.

One can also reflect on the irony that trying to repeat in this context something which Muhammad did seems un-Islamic, but getting rid of modern inventions and societal norms and trying to live like him superficially does not.

If we read the beginning of Sura 26 of the Qur'an with the above discussion in mind, it is as if this is telling us to accept reform,

> If we willed, we could send down to them from the sky a sign so that their necks would bow to it. And yet *no reminder from the most merciful comes to them anew except that they turn away from it*. For they have denied, but news of what they used to ridicule will come to them.[2]

---

[2] Qur'an 26:4–6, my emphasis.

It is people who are against reform. The message conveyed by Muhammad was reformist. It is reading the letter but not the spirit to use that message as being against reform. Liberal reform upsets the status quo, so powerful religious figures do not like it, and socio-economic problems in many Muslim communities cause some Muslims to blame the West or to attribute these problems to non-literalist ways of following Islam, and their proposed solution is to adopt literalist readings of Islamic texts and strict religious rule. But this is not a viable solution. Alleviating the underlying socio-economic problems is important, but so is arguing against literalist trends in Islam. For these arguments act like a vaccine against the radicalisation of Muslims who look for the answer in violent Islamic movements when they suffer from an existential crisis, faced with poverty, impenetrable class divisions, lack of suitable employment, etc.

If individuals could become united in a liberal consensus, and petition for major religious figures in Islam to stand together and openly declare a liberal conception of Islam, it would be the end of Islamism. More on this in Section 6.5.

6.3 Re-examination

In this section I shall review fundamental concepts in Islamic legal and political thought.

6.3.1 Postponement

In Section 6.2, I promoted a wider application of abrogation. In this section, I would like to argue for the connected practice of postponement. Abrogation can be said to be a personal tool of interpretation, while postponement can be said to be the corresponding method on the social level. Abrogation is mainly about finding out how one should live, on the basis of Islamic texts, while postponement is mainly about how to deal with people with different religions or interpretations.

The principle of postponement إرجاء *irjā'* dictates that we should postpone—that is to say—leave judgment to Allah. We can find much textual support for postponement. The classic among the relevant passages would be Sura 109 in which Muhammad is told to say, "O disbelievers, I do not worship what you worship. And you are not worshippers of what I worship. And I am not worshipping what you worship. And you are not worshipping what I worship. For you is your religion, and for me is my religion." Muhammad is not told to wipe them out or anything. Religion is a matter of personal choice. If Allah finds something punishable, he would take care of it. We should only care about our own religious life.

6.3.1.1 Judgment is for Allah

In verses 6:57, 12:40, and 12:67 in the Qur'an it is said that judgment "is only for Allah." In verses 6:62, 28:70, 28:88, and 40:12, it is said that judgment is his. In verses 42:8–10 it is said that if Allah had "willed, he could have made them one nation" and that in "whatever you disagree, its ruling belongs to Allah."

In verse 52:18 Muhammad is told to "be patient for the decision of your lord, for indeed you are in our eyes." In verses 76:23–25 Muhammad is told, "indeed, it is we who have sent down to you the Qur'an progressively. So be patient for the decision of your lord and do not obey from among them any sinner or disbeliever, and mention the name of your lord morning and evening." So what one should do is to wait for Allah's action regarding religion.

It is not necessary for a human being to interfere and force others to live in a way that conforms to his religion. Even if this passage is read as a specific order for Muhammad, we can see that even the prophet is told to leave matters to Allah, so who are we to interfere on his behalf?

To postpone judgment and leave it for Allah would point towards liberal government, so that people have the freedom to adhere to their own religious views.

For more verses supporting this attitude, let us look at 52:31 in which Muhammad is told to say, regarding doubts about him, "wait, for indeed I am, with you, among the waiters." We can wait and see. As long as we try to be as moral and spiritual as possible, we can wait for judgment day to see the details. It is not necessary for human beings to codify religious teaching into bureaucratic rules.

In verse 68:44 Muhammad is told to leave Allah with the matter of whoever denies the Qur'an, and in 68:48 he is told to "be patient for the decision of your lord." If even the prophet is not told to make people behave as Islam requires, how can others be qualified to judge which action is sanctioned by Islam?

6.3.1.2 Reminder Only

The job of Muslims is at most to remind, not to coerce. For even the prophet is not sent to be the guardian of everyone. A Muslim should concentrate on his own piety, not that of others.

In verses 80:5–7 Muhammad is told, "as for him who considers himself without need, to him you give attention, and it is not upon you if he will not be purified." So there is no responsibility for Muslims to convert others or force them to believe, for even the prophet is not burdened with blame if someone does not accept Islam.

In verses 88:21–26 Muhammad is told, "So remind [others], for you are only a reminder. You are not a controller over them. However, he who turns away and disbelieves, then Allah will punish him with the greatest punishment. Indeed, to us is their return. Then indeed, upon us is

Chapter 6 Reform

their account." This passage stresses that Muhammad does not control others and is not responsible for them. People would be returned to Allah and face their account. Muhammad does not need to be concerned about them. Neither do Muslims.

One might say, "but these passages are meant for the prophet, it would be more convincing to look at passages advising Muslims in general."

Let us look at such passages. In verses 6:69–70 Muhammad is told, "those who fear Allah are not held accountable for the disbelievers at all, but a reminder, so that they will fear him. And leave those who take their religion as play and diversion and whom worldly life has deluded, and remind [them] with the Qur'an, lest a soul be given up to destruction for what it earned. It will have no protector and no intercessor other than Allah, and if it should offer every ransom, it would not be taken from it. Those are the ones who are given to destruction for what they have earned. There is a drink of scalding water and a painful punishment for them because they disbelieved." From this passage it is clear that not just Muhammad is told that he is not accountable for disbelievers, but other Muslims too. Similarly, in 83:32 it is said that the believers "had not been sent as guardians over" the disbelievers.

In verses 43:82–83 it is said, "exalted is the lord of the heavens and the earth, lord of the throne, above what they describe. So leave them to converse vainly and play until they meet their day which they are promised." In verses 70:42–44 people are told to leave the disbelievers "to converse vainly and play until they meet their day which they are promised, the day they will emerge from the graves rapidly as if they were hastening toward a goal. Their eyes humbled, humiliation will cover them. That is the day which they have been promised." From these passages we can see that it is not the job of Muslims to force others to believe or punish them for disbelief. That is a matter which should be left for Allah and judgment day.

The commands to leave disbelievers to Allah are seen frequently, in verses 6:91, 6:110, 6:112, 6:137, 7:180, 15:3,

23:54, 43:83, 52:45, 73:11, and 74:8–11. In verse 82:19 it is said that judgment day "is the day when a soul will not have anything for another soul; and the command, that day, is with Allah." This passage means that souls will not be able to help each other and so each soul is only responsible for itself.

In verses 87:7–13 Muhammad is told, "Indeed, he knows what is declared and what is hidden. And we will ease you toward ease. So remind [others], if the reminder should benefit. He who fears will be reminded. But the wretched one will avoid it, [and he] will burn in the great fire, neither dying therein nor living." As Muslims we should believe that whoever deserves punishment will be punished in the afterlife. It is not the job of human beings to interfere. The most we should do is to remind people of the teachings of Islam. It should be people's free choice to decide whether to follow them or not. There should be no compulsion whatsoever.

If Muslims are confident about Islam and the exaltedness of Allah, then we need not worry about whether people receive punishment for disbelieving. The prophet Muhammad is only supposed to give a reminder and Muslims are supposed to leave them alone. Allah will punish them if they should be punished. To supersede Allah and impose punishment shows one's impatience and lack of faith, rather than piety.

Let each person take care of his own religious life. Law should be established for necessary arbitration between human beings only. It is true that the Qur'an gave clear directions about interpersonal affairs, but the times have changed, and they cannot be applied literally anymore. So it does not do to use them for ruling people.

6.3.1.3 Against Postponement

On the other hand, let me discuss verses that opponents of postponement might use. In verse 57:14 it is said that, on judgment day, "the hypocrites will call to the believers, 'were we not with you?' They will say, 'yes, but you afflicted yourselves and awaited and doubted, and wishful thinking deluded you until the command of Allah came, and the deceiver deceived you concerning Allah.' " People against the principle of postponement might say, "look! Allah said that people who wait and doubt are going to be punished on judgment day." But we need to see that "hypocrites" had a specific reference. They were people who undermined Muhammad's campaign and sowed disagreement between his followers, supporting him one day and opposing him on another.

We should not identify people as hypocrites just based on the brief descriptions in the Qur'an. Those do not constitute an exhaustive list of the necessary conditions for being a hypocrite as referred to in the Qur'an. Therefore verses condemning the doubts of hypocrites should not be applied to intellectuals contesting the doctrines and laws of Islam.

6.3.1.4 Conclusion

Because of the above considerations, I contend that my liberal interpretation adheres much more to the original ideas of Islam than the recently popular principle of تكفير *takfīr*, declaring another Muslim as a non-Muslim. Muhammad and his companions never did anything like that. People who joined them were welcomed with open arms and accepted as brothers and sisters. How narrow-minded we have become!

If we emulate the purity and openness of early Islam, we should adopt the principle of postponement. We have no right to declare another person as a non-Muslim. If we adopt the principle of postponement, then there is no inconsistency between Islam and liberalism, because each person is allowed to practise Islam in the way he sees fit. Each person should have the freedom to determine his religious life.

However, people argue that Islam is not just a matter of personal faith, but it pushes for a form of society and governance. In particular, many Muslims call for the adoption of Shari'a rule, meaning that law and government should strictly adhere to what the Qur'an and the Hadiths dictate. Now let us tackle this topic.

6.3.2 Shari'a

In order to discuss this issue, we first have to examine what Shari'a is.

6.3.2.1 Original Sense

In the Qur'an itself, The word شريعة *sharī'a*, meaning "the ordained way," has only appeared once, in verse 45:18. The other words of the root ش - ر - ع which appear in the Qur'an are the verb شرع *shara'a* (42:13 and 42:21), meaning "to ordain," the noun شرعة *shir'a* (5:48), meaning "a law," and the adverb شرّع *shurra'* (7:163), meaning "openly." Altogether there are only a few occurrences.

Let us examine the relevant passages (45:18, 42:13, 42:21, and 5:48) in detail.

In verse 45:18 it is said to Muhammad, "we put you on

an ordained way (شريعة *sharīʿa*) concerning the matter, so follow it and do not follow the desires of those who do not know."

In verse 42:13 it is said to Muhammad that Allah "has ordained (شرع *sharaʿa*) for you of religion what he enjoined upon Noah and that which we revealed to you, and what we enjoined upon Abraham and Moses and Jesus, to establish the religion and not be divided in it. Difficult for polytheists is that to which you invite them. Allah chooses for himself whom he wills and guides to himself whoever turns back."

In verse 42:21 it is asked, "do they have other deities who ordained (شرع *sharaʿa*) for them of the religion to which Allah did not consent? But if not for the decisive word, it would have been judged between them. And indeed, the wrongdoers will have a painful punishment."

In verse 5:48, it is said to Muhammad, "we have revealed to you the book with the truth, confirming what has previously been revealed of the scripture and as a criterion over it. So judge between them using what Allah has revealed and do not follow their desires away from what has come to you of the truth. To each of you we made a law (شرعة *shirʿa*) and a method, and if Allah willed, he would have made you one nation, but [he did not,] in order to test you in what he gave you, so race to the good. To Allah is your place of return all together, then he informs you concerning that over which you used to differ."

From these passages we can see the Qur'anic use of this root as having to do with Allah's order regarding the way we are supposed to behave.

6.3.2.2 Modern Usage

In contrast, let us examine the modern usage of the word شريعة *sharī'a*.

In general it refers to a legal code based on the Qur'an and the Hadiths, executed by judges, courts, prisons, and people carrying out other forms of punishment.

Is it the duty of Muslims to call for or fight for this kind of Shari'a rule?

I argue that it is not. When we look at accounts of Muhammad and his companions, we can see that the community was simple and punishment for crimes was not institutional. The revelations in the Qur'an and the advice and actions of Muhammad were practical in view of the society at the time, but they were not intended to be universal and eternal. I have given plenty of arguments to this effect throughout the present book. Muhammad's message was reformist and we can see evidence that it was a compromise between an ideal religion and one that his audience was ready to accept. Therefore to codify the Qur'an and the Hadiths in a literal and strict way into a legal code is even less in the spirit of Islam than interpreting the Qur'an and the Hadiths as a religious text in a literal and strict way, which is already an unreasonable way to safeguard Islam. Islam cannot survive in this mummified form.

However, Islam and law are indeed seen to be more closely connected than, for example, Christianity and law, and it has raised doubts regarding the possibility of complete acceptance of secular government in Muslim-majority countries. The rise and fall of governments in Muslim-majority countries seem to testify to the incompatibility of secular government and Islam. Let us examine this issue in the following section.

6.3.3 Islam is Law?

Does the core of Islam have to be a system of law?

People argue that the Arabic word دين *dīn* does not mean exactly religion as understood in English, but law.

Chapter 6 Reform

As a corollary, Islam is not a religion in the sense of the English word, which perhaps is mostly understood with reference to a liberal version of Protestantism. Islam is a system of law, while the spiritual side of it is subsidiary or supervenient upon obeying that system of law. In the Qur'an itself the word is frequently used in the sense of judgment in the phrase يوم الدين *yawm al-dīn* "the day of judgment," in verses 1:4, 15:35, 26:82, 37:20, 38:78, 51:12, 56:56, 70:26, 74:46, 82:9, 82:15, 82:17, 82:18, 83:11, 95:7, etc. Once, in 51:6, the word دين *dīn* occurs alone and means judgment. Another word with this root is مدين *madīn*, one who is judged or recompensed. It is used in 37:53 and 56:86.

From the numerous instances in which the word meaning "religion" is also used in the sense of judgment it could be argued that Islam is inseparable from law, that it is a system of crime and punishment.

From this it is also argued that Islam is inherently political and cannot be secularised. A literalist application of Shari'a is essential to Islam. Of course not all Muslims hold this position. But it has a powerful voice in Islam.

However, I do not agree with the view that Islam is essentially a system of law. I shall give my counter-arguments below.

First of all, as I showed in Section 4.2.1, in Islam intention is more important than the act itself or the result of the act. But a system of law is mostly concerned with action, because intention is not observable externally. So a system of law is always secondary. It is just the next best thing to ensure that a society runs smoothly given that observing one's heart and intention directly is impossible for human beings.

Secondly, as I showed in Section 6.2, the change in society justifies a change in Islam. So the system of law could change over time, and it is human stubbornness and force of habit rather than solid theology to think that it is necessary in Islam to stick literally to the rules given in the Qur'an and the Hadiths, otherwise it is not Islam. I argue that these rules do not constitute the essence of Islam. Given enough time, it will be totally acceptable and will not seem strange to any members of the faith that rules for actions are changed to accommodate the changes in the world at large.

Thirdly, even though the word دين *dīn* is frequently used in the sense of judgment, it is mostly limited to the set phrase يوم الدين *yawm al-dīn*. We cannot conclude from this usage that دين *dīn* necessarily means law and punishment and thus Islam is also essentially law and punishment. A counter-example is found in verse 39:14, in which Muhammad is told to say, I worship Allah, sincere to him, my religion. As it talks about sincerity, the word *dīn* here does not seem to denote rules that govern action. It seems to denote spiritual loyalty. There is another verse which is very similar, namely 40:65, in which people are told to "call upon Allah, being sincere to him in religion."

In verse 42:13, it is said that Allah "ordained for you the religion (دين *dīn*) which he enjoined upon Noah" and "what we enjoined upon Abraham and Moses and Jesus, to set up the religion (دين *dīn*) and not be divided in it."

Chapter 6 Reform

Yes, Moses's religion is focused on law, but different systems of law were given to Moses and Muhammad. Therefore we may conclude that Islam does not have to be one unchanging system of law.

One may say, Allah would have given a different system of law if he envisaged that our society would need something different. He was definitely able to see how human societies would develop into what they are now.

However, let us think about this seriously. Let us grant that Allah envisaged what society would be like now. Would it have been practical for him to give a system of law which provides for every epoch and every stage of societies after Muhammad? Allah would certainly be capable of doing it but it would have been too complicated for Muhammad and his followers. Imagine the streams of clauses needed. The legal terms in the Qur'an are already convoluted as it is. It would be difficult even for people in this age with a legal education to deal with a system of law that tries to provide for different stages of society.

The practical way would be, as hinted frequently in the Qur'an, to send different prophets for different nations and times, as we discussed in Section 2.2.2. The Qur'an also said that there are prophets which have not been mentioned in the Qur'an (40:78), and I refuted the claim that Muhammad is the last prophet in Section 6.2.2.

Therefore there could well have been prophets in other nations, and prophets after Muhammad. As submitters[3] we should also submit to these prophets, not just Muhammad and the prophets before. How do we determine who are prophets? By reason. By extension we should also accept reform. The reason is that since we determine which new prophets deserve following by means of reason, we should also be allowed to determine which teachings, ethical rules, and coercive law are acceptable. We have been endowed with our own rational faculty so that we could deal with and adapt to different situations.

On the other hand, as proposed from time to time in

---

[3] Please refer to Section 4.1.1.

the history of Islam, the basis of Shari'a can be one's intellect according to Mu'tazilis, or it can be *maṣlaḥa*, i.e. the greatest good, so that the interpretation bringing the greatest good should be chosen, according to early modern reformists such as Khayr al-Din. [24, p. 92] Muhammad 'Abduh also contend that blind imitation (*taqlīd*) is not commendable. One should distinguish between what is essential in Islam and what is not. Islamic law should be adapted to the times. He promoted the principle of *maṣlaḥa*, i.e. the greatest good, and that of *talfīq*, piecing together the most suitable doctrines of different codes and jurists. [24, p. 150–152] In these cases Shari'a is not seen as a fixed system of law through different times and situations in history.

It has been argued that Shari'a is compatible with liberalism. In his introduction to the book *Liberal Islam: A Source Book* [27, p. 14–18], Kurzman describes three modes of liberal Islam, the *liberal Shari'a*, the *silent Shari'a*, and the *interpreted Shari'a*.

The *liberal Shari'a* mode maintains that Muhammad granted rights to non-Muslims under Muslim rule through the Medina Document. This is a model of constitutional protection of rights. Therefore Shari'a can exist in a form that conforms with liberal ideals. The *silent Shari'a* mode maintains that, on subjects not mentioned in the Islamic texts, there is freedom in ruling. But the problem with this view is that illiberal prescriptions cannot be changed. The *interpreted Shari'a* mode allows freedom in interpretation. Both the *liberal Shari'a* and *interpreted Shari'a* modes allow liberal versions of Islam.

Asad also argued in *Formations of the Secular: Christianity, Islam, Modernity* [9, Ch.7] that Shari'a is not static and changes have always occurred in its application.

From the above arguments we can see that the core of Islam is not *one* explicit system of law. We can, using our reason, change the rules regarding what is approved in Islam and what is not.

6.3.3.1 Reductio ad Absurdum

In logic, there is an argument form called *reductio ad absurdum*. It is an argument form in which the absurd conclusion shows that there are problems in the original premises.

In May 2007, Dr. Izzat Atiya, head of the department of Hadith at Al-Azhar University, issued a fatwa (non-binding religious opinion) advising female workers to breastfeed their male colleagues so that they would have breastfeeding relations and thus be exempted from Islamic laws against the mixing of the sexes and appearing unveiled in front of unrelated males. [26] The fatwa was ridiculed and retracted.

What people do not realise is that in fact it serves as a perfect example of *reductio ad absurdum*, exposing the absurdity of applying Shari'a in modern society literally.

This example shows us that if we follow the practices of Muhammad's age blindly, it would inevitably cause ridicule and outrage in the present age. Therefore it is the responsibility of Muslims to reform and modernise Islam, otherwise it will not survive. We need to remember that the Qur'an and the Hadiths were not intended to serve as strict and timeless guidance for each of our actions. They are records of wisdom and practical actions in the context of seventh-century Arabia. Muslims do not need to follow everything mentioned in these texts.

This controversial incident demonstrates the ridiculous nature of literalist Islam.

6.4 Reaction

After examining the legal and political aspects of Islam, we can see that it is not necessary for Muslims to support Shari'a rule based on literalist readings of the Qur'an and the Hadiths. Therefore postponement is possible and thus liberalism is compatible with Islam.

Indeed in the nineteenth and early twentieth century, much effort was spent in finding ways to modernise Near

Eastern countries and Islam towards systems of liberal government. Kurzman [27] and Hourani [24] provide ample examples of such thinkers.

Perhaps European powers and the U.S. have not been behaving with honour, but it does not mean that personal liberty is something harmful to Muslim communities. On the contrary, as the system of production and trade has changed, it is not beneficial at all to society as a whole to put group pressure on individuals and especially women to follow old ways.

Sadly, the trend now is to give up the difficult project of modernisation, to think that the Islamic world is something "different," on which we should not "impose Western models" of society. This seems to hold both in Muslim communities and in the West.

I do not argue that Muslim communities have to follow the West in every detail, but we have seen the progress possible in East Asia along with relative liberation of women from family control. Therefore we should not think that other societies cannot benefit from liberal ideas.

6.4.1 Regression

Defeat by and reaction to the West make many Muslims desperately search for a stronger identity, and one of the approaches they adhere to is to become conservative, traditionalist, Islamist, or fundamentalist. It is not what Muslims in a confident age would choose.

Ironically, even though such movements advocate a "return to the old ways," the phenomenon itself is modern, inspired by Western political thought.

Muslims without complexes should see that reform should aim at liberalisation, not the opposite. Happiness, piety, knowledge of Allah, none of these are fostered by Shari'a-ization because it is not suitable for this age. We do not have a seventh-century situation of warring states of desert tribes.

It would be a conflicting position to accept technology from the West while condemning their ideas of free speech,

Chapter 6 Reform

gender equality, etc. as بدعة *bid'a*, innovation. If anything, the positive connotation of إصلاح *iṣlāḥ*, reform and doing good things, should outweigh the negative connotation of *bid'a*. The word is used positively in the Qu'ran. In verse 28:19 when Moses had killed someone, another man said to him, "You only want to be a tyrant in the land but not one of the people who amend (المصلحين *muṣliḥīn*)."

A militant Shari'a revolution is nothing good for Muslims, as we see in the actions of Daesh (the Islamic State). Killing people in the name of religion is no longer acceptable when we have solutions in the form of secular government and religious freedom.

It is ironic that the form II participle تكفير *takfīr* of the root ك ـ ف ـ ر *k-f-r* meaning "to deny" and "to disbelieve" is now mostly associated with excommunication. But in the Qur'an it was used to mean to remove people's small sins. In verse 3:195 it is said, "I will not allow the work of any worker among you to be lost, male or female. You are of one another. So those who emigrated or were evicted from their homes or were harmed in my cause or fought or were killed, I will surely remove (كفّر *kaffara*) from them their misdeeds, and I will surely admit them to gardens beneath which rivers flow as a reward from Allah, and Allah has with him the best reward." In verse 4:31 it is said, "if you avoid the major sins which you are forbidden, we will remove (كفّر *kaffara*) from you your misdeeds and admit you to a noble entrance." In verse 5:12 it is said, "if you perform prayer and give alms and believe in my messengers and support them and loan Allah a good loan, I will surely remove from you your misdeeds and admit you to gardens beneath which rivers flow." Here is seen the fickleness of a word's etymological fate, going from removal of sins to excommunicating people, which is perhaps parallel to the transformation of the confident golden-era Islamic world to the contemporary chaos-laden Islamic world.

We need to get rid of this obsession with whether one is a Muslim or not, and we need to get rid of the illusion that religious rule is the solution. Religious rule benefits religious leaders, but they have no incentive to solve deep-seated social problems. I am not saying they do not do charitable or other good acts, but for people to have better lives, we need people with a variety of expertise, in the public sector and the private sector. Religious leaders do not have the necessary knowledge to lead complicated populous countries in the modern world. Reciting the Qur'an might have been enough education for teachers and traders in the past, but there is so much more to learn now, that a person armed only with religious texts would be very ignorant, and if disproportionate emphasis is placed on them, a whole community could not be knowledgeable enough to compete in international trade.

For societies to run smoothly and peacefully, we have to agree on basic rules that rest on rational foundations giving individuals the greatest possible degree of autonomy, so that people can explore and find the best solutions to personal, social, and technological problems.

Some Muslims may argue that everyone, including non-Muslims, should abide by Islamic rules. But this does not work and would only lead to conflict and bloodshed, because in the modern world communities cannot be isolated and people of different faiths and cultures are bound to mingle. If each one wants others to follow his rules, there would be no peace on earth. Therefore we have to accept secular government even though it may not fit perfectly with what is said in the Qur'an and the Hadiths. They were not meant for everyone in all times anyway, as I have argued in Section 2.2.2 and Section 6.2.

We should follow Islam, taking into account changes

in the world that have happened since Muhammad's time. Just as we would use modern technology even though it is not mentioned in the Qur'an and the Hadiths, so we should use secular forms of government even though they are not mentioned in the Qur'an and the Hadiths, because they are suitable for modern globalised society.

The Shari'a system should be viewed similarly.

1. One should remember that it was difficult or impossible to keep prisoners, and that it was impossible to have comprehensive policing in the Arabian Peninsula, therefore severe types of deterrent punishment were recommended. Advice in the Qur'an and the Hadiths was pragmatic, not meant for another age or another set of social conditions.

2. Additionally, the requirement of numerous witnesses for the establishment of crimes was quite progressive at the time Islam was established.

3. As for laws that seem barbaric now, it was the social reality at that time, so that Shari'a was not making it worse.

4. But insisting on its implementation now would be disastrous for human rights and especially women's rights.

So it should be clear that we should have a correct understanding of the historical status of Shari'a law but should not be so naive as to think that it can solve the social problems Muslim communities are facing. These have to be solved by education and economic development.

6.4.2 The New Orientalism

Edward Said [39, p. 40] criticised Western scholars for assuming that Islam is "different" and that the Islamic world does not change. But it seems that Muslims are justifying this assumption by looking for their identity in preserving old practices that are not necessarily part of Islam.

It is self-orientalising to think that Islam should not change and could not change. And the West is engaging in a new form of Orientalism in which the left proposes that Islam should not be criticised and should be left as it is, while the right proposes that since Islam is not improving we should shun and avoid Muslims.

Therefore, unfortunately, the conservative factions of Islam and both the right and the left of the West are on one side, leaving the progressive and secular factions of Islam on the other. Even the progressive and secular factions of Islam are sometimes shackled by political correctness from criticising their co-religionists.

One can smell how bad this is. These are not very promising developments. Neither the left nor the right are contributing to human happiness and peaceful co-existence.

6.4.3 Economic v.s. Civil Liberalisation

And we should be aware that the liberalisation of civil rights does not necessarily imply rightist economic measures. The failure or faults of rightist economic policies should not be attributed to liberalisation of civil rights. In history, losers of economic reform have sometimes done that, and opposed the progress of civil rights.

When reform is resisted, it is crucial to identify where the resistance comes from. Of course some groups lose some control or interests when people have more rights. The people losing do not like it, and they are usually people with power and control in the establishment or government or local governance. We need to push for it wisely and diplomatically, not just give up and say that our people do not deserve a modern society. Or to say that progress or modernity are not genuine or are a result of bias or imperialism or Western domination, and give up the ideas of, or campaigns for, social reform altogether.

6.4.4 Non-liberal Use of Liberalism

In an age where the compatibility of Islam and liberalism is deeply mistrusted and multiculturalism pushed to the subversive extreme of denying progress and the values of liberty and human rights, thus defeating the foundation of the human rights campaign, the present book and the position it expounds is particularly salient.

It is self-defeating to argue for the human right to adopt tyrannical forms of social organisation, such as Salafist or Shari'a groups, within a liberal democratic society. Because if any groups could argue for their own special set of rules without the consent of all its members, then a Flying Spaghetti Monster church could claim an unwilling Salafist as a member, or an Aquarius Club could claim all persons born under the Aquarius sign as its members, appealing to their common destiny, whether they want to join or not. This has nothing to do with human rights.

A woman wants the right to divorce. This is her right. A group wants the "right" not to let its members divorce. This is not a right. Members of the group can choose not to divorce but the group cannot say it is its right not to let its members divorce. It is even more ridiculous for the group to say that people who criticise the group are violating its rights. Liberalism supports the rights of an individual, not the "rights" of a group to limit the rights of an individual.

6.4.4.1 Gender Equality

Gender equality is in a particularly precarious position. People claim that traditional patriarchy is better and that people prefer it. It is all very well if some women would like to hand over power and financial responsibility to men, but the threat of regression is not only about this. It prevents women who want to have higher education, independent lives, financial independence, etc. from doing so, by saying that this is not Islamic. However, from Chapter 5 we have seen that it is not in the essence of Islam to advocate patriarchal society.

6.4.4.2 Freedom of Expression

On the other hand, accusations such as blasphemy, insulting the prophet, etc. have been frequently used in inciting Muslims into demonstrations and violence. Portraying the prophet is seen as idolatry, and criticising Islam has been seen as blasphemy. But we need to remember what Allah said through Solomon and Luqman, that whoever is grateful, he is grateful for his soul, and that whoever is ungrateful, then Allah is self-sufficient and generous. (Qur'an 27:40 and 31:12) Allah does not need Muslims' "protection." It is looking down upon Allah's status and power to think that he does. As the discussion on infidels shows, in subsubsection 4.5.1.1, it is frequently one's ego that is at work.

People in power or who desire power love to use Muslims' eagerness to be pious and their ego to achieve their own agenda. Do not be fooled by exaggerations and distortions of what may only be a harmless exercise of freedom of expression and even well-meaning attempts at dialogue.

Many countries are beginning to give way to this rage; in Western countries in the name of political correctness, multiculturalism, and respect for religions; and in Muslim-majority countries in the name of Islam. Muslims may think there is no harm in limiting freedom of expression in the name of Islam, but non-Muslims will not look at this favourably and at some point may snap and develop very negative views of Islam. It is not good for the image of Islam in the long term, and not good for intellectual engagement among Muslims, because there are so many mines in the field that one dare not speak, for one could be harmed or punished for criticising bad trends in Islam.

6.5 Redressing the New Orientalism

As argued in Section 6.4.2, the assumption that Islam cannot and should not change is a form of internalised Orientalism.

Then the question is, how should we fight it?

First we have to reform the idea that Islam is essentially a system of law. From the evolution of Abrahamic religions one can see that the law changes. They have to change to accommodate different historical circumstances. The essence of Islam is not, for example, in how you brush your teeth.

Judaism has conservative sects which see that abiding by Jewish laws is the most important part of Judaism. But Kabbalist thoughts have influenced many people from different backgrounds, and improve the image of Judaism.

Sufism plays a similar role. Sufi groups could be like gangs and not necessarily progressive, but Sufism definitely produced many interesting ideas and literary works. To examine the mystic traditions conscientiously and preserve and transmit them, is very important. Abu'l-Huda al-Sayyadi [24, p. 107] wrote in this vein but more reformist-mystics are needed. And it would definitely improve Islam and its image in the world. It already presents a better side of Islam to the world.

If we pay attention to the spiritual teachings of Islam more than its laws regulating everyday life, then it would be easier to reconcile modernity and Islam.

6.5.1 Islam and Governance

Shari'a is not compatible with the modern world. Systems of law have much advanced since Muhammad's day. His community was an admirable attempt at a just society, but not in today's world. People have found better ways to govern and delineate the boundaries between individuals since then.

Reform is difficult not because it is against Islam, but because people's interests are at stake. Change in society causes change in people's power and wealth. People in power would definitely not like to lose their power, status, and prestige. Men would not like to lose their higher status and privilege in relation to women. Human beings are the obstacles to reform, not Allah. Of course, unconsidered ideas about religions play a role. Since people frequently follow religious texts that have been written a long time ago, advice or rules suitable for an older society get kept in the name of religion. This is the problem Islam is facing.

However, to follow Allah is to work for a better society, not to follow blindly rules established for another age, another historical situation. We should try to understand the goals of Islamic law, which are to cultivate moderation, wisdom, and virtuous habits. It is an instrument but not the ultimate goal. We can see that the prophet Muhammad gives different recommendations according to the situation.

One might ask, how could you establish that one form of government is better than another one except on the authority of Allah? Yes we could. One form of government is better than another one on the authority of reason, comparing different forms of government and the lives of people living under such systems.

We could see that people lead better and more satisfactory lives with more autonomy and choice. This is not to say that we are against family and community, but these should be voluntary associations. Parental or communal tyranny is no bliss for the people involved.

Therefore we should revisit our ideas of ideal government. We shall argue below that we should adopt liberalism and that it is compatible with Islam.

6.5.2 Liberalism

If everyone is to use their own God-given reason to guide their lives, the logical conclusion is liberalism and J. S. Mill's harm principle, since people should be free to choose and experiment with their life choices.

On this basis religions can co-exist peacefully with each other, providing help and multiple paths for people with different degrees of self-control and autonomy. But for people attaining a high degree of self-control and autonomy, they do not need the jurisdiction of any religion.

Chapter 6 Reform

Therefore the ultimate common arbitrator for everyone in society, regardless of his or her faith, is a system of liberal laws.

Religious organisations can advocate their own additional rules but the system should consist only in the form of oaths, excommunication, and social pressure. And if people see that such organisations are actually getting in the way of cultivating the adherents' wisdom and autonomy, they are free to condemn them openly. They should not be accused of intolerance or of curtailing religious freedom, since the freedom of worship and association is not taken away, only that the organisations or religious personnel are criticised.

As we argue in Section 3.2.1, we should advocate secular rule even from the perspective of a Muslim. This is because Islamic texts dictate radically different lives under different systems of interpretations. Depending on our view of the role of social and temporal context in translating the content of Islamic texts to actual rules, we can say that Islam supports polygamy or that it does not, for example. Therefore it is very dangerous to impose one's view of Islamic law on another, even if that person is also a Muslim. And the natural conclusion to this is that secular rule is preferable to Islamic rule.

As we have seen in Chapter 5, if we take account of the historical context of Muhammad's time, women's rights are compatible with Islam. This is a particular case in the context of liberalism. Since the issue of women's rights in Islam is the one which is most divergent with modern values, if it can be shown in this case that liberalism is compatible with Islam, then in other cases liberalism can also be shown to be compatible with Islam.

6.5.3 Equality

Equality of persons before the law is a foundational principle of democratic societies and a key conclusion reached by Enlightenment thinkers.

"All are born equal" is a normative claim in socio-political treatment, and not a factual claim about people's ability. The truth is that people have unequal abilities.

To take it to mean that people are born equal in ability and only limited by social resources is a dangerous confusion. This is a factual claim that needs to be investigated, but somehow taken to be a moral principle in recent academic discourse in some schools in Sociology and in Cultural Studies.

What is worse is to be politically correct and say that *a priori* people have equal abilities.

But a confusion that is even worse is generated when we say that all cultures and societies are equal. Experience tells me the students go so far as to assert that rape, female genital mutilation, foot-binding, etc. are bad only in societies which condemn them, that we are being limited by our experience and education when we "judge" that they are bad, and that we should not be "judgmental."

If we adopt such unreasonable ideas of equality, we cannot argue for the fight for human rights because however badly a society treats its members, that society is equal to any other society, and we should not intervene to improve it, because improvement is an illusion and an invention of the West.

Western societies have their faults, such as alienation, materialism, nihilism, etc. But they are much better than non-liberal societies. Those faults could be remedied, but not by turning one's back on liberalism or adopting fundamentalism.

6.5.4 Reform with Respect to Women

Christianity, with all its Old Testament baggage, and a view of sex as sinful, has given up much of its misogyny. Why cannot Islam, with its normalisation of sexual relationships, do it? Why should we assume that it cannot, other than out of a wish to keep Muslims from progressing and joining the modern world?

However, without liberating female Muslims it would not be possible for Muslims to progress and join the mod-

ern world.
To achieve this, we have to reform our ideas about Islam.

1. The patriarchal world was a productive mode of social organisation for the stage of technological development in Muhammad's time. That is the reason it existed. But it should not be seen as essential to Islam and kept or returned to because of Islam.

2. One should follow the spirit of Islam, not specific rules which were tailored to the world at that earlier time.

3. Not to move forward is not only harmful to women, but also to men and society as a whole, because women's status affects the workforce, the birthrate, and the education of children.

4. By reforming Islam's ideas about women, one also ensures that Islam will not become obsolete, irrelevant, and extinct.

6.6 Conclusion

In this chapter, we have seen how attempts at reform have failed and how reformist ideas have been buried. We need to unearth these ideas and push for their recognition, otherwise both the Islamists and the regressive left, people who think that it is Islamists' right to subjugate women, will dominate discussions about Islam. To fight against this new form of Orientalism, which rationalises the limitations on personal freedom in Muslim communities, is an intellectual and societal battle of urgency.

Reading the Qur'an

Chapter 7

Reason

In this chapter, I propose that the developmental path of Islam in future should be

1. Secular Islam

2. Philosophical Islam

and I shall give my justification and explanation.

7.1 The Realm of Religion

Everyone would agree that it is a Muslim's duty to learn about and obey Allah. But what does that actually mean? I argue that one needs not only to read Islamic texts but, in view of the importance of interpretation as presented as Section 3.3, to think rationally and choose the best actions.

What should be the realm of religion? I propose that it should be confined to the development of the spiritual aspects of a person. A concrete guide to behavior has then to come from spiritual considerations, how to elevate one's soul. Otherwise it is not religious advice, but social or legal prescription.

As seen in the idea of philosophical religions, the highest goal of religions is the cultivation of reason, not legislature in and of itself. Laws provide guidance, but are for non-philosophers and for training purposes only—not ultimate but instrumental—and not always the best instrument.

One may wonder what is the difference between a religion offering advice for the development of the spiritual aspects of a person, in which development guides actual behaviour, and a religion offering direct advice for actual actions in daily lives and society. The difference is subtle but huge in effect. If a religion offers advice for actual behaviour, people with religious authority can easily abuse their authority; if a religion only offers advice for spiritual development, the influence of people with religious authority on social issues and legal matters would be much less and correspondingly the chance of abuse is also diminished. Being human, they would still try to leverage their authority but followers of a faith would not be conforming so blindly.

We should try to lay out ways to limit and be on our guard against religious authority. This would contribute to a freer society with less coercion and suffering.

The existence of religious laws is to guide imperfect human beings through "degrees of autonomy" [18, p. 198] and finally arrive at rational self-rule.

7.1.1 The Allegory of Satan

In the Qur'an, Allah asked Satan to prostrate in front of Adam, and Satan refused to do so. It was his fall from grace. This story is repeated in verses around 2:34, 7:11, 15:31, 17:61, 18:50, 20:116, 38:75, etc. This is different from the biblical account, in which Satan is said to have fallen because he put himself as high as God (Isaiah 14:14–15) and because of unrighteousness (Ezekiel 28:15).

Interestingly, in al-Hallaj's mystical *Kitab al Tawasin* [5, p. 52], Satan said that he refused to prostrate because of his love of Allah. If he prostrated in front of Adam, then he would have put Adam on the same elevated status as Allah. This would contradict his love for Allah. This is a much higher insight than reading the literal meaning of rule-abiding obedience.

Indeed, if everything is determined by Allah, even Satan's refusal was Allah's choice. [5, p. 53] In verse 38:82, Satan is said to say that he will "mislead them all by the might of Allah, except his servants which are made sincere." Therefore it is by Allah's permission and power that people are misled. As we discussed in Section 4.4.1, this is a difficult problem. However, the good news is we can make sense of this if we take the stance advocated in Section 7.3.2.

The important thing is not to make a decision without reflection. This is the true meaning of the pronouncement that the blind are not equivalent to the seeing, which has been repeated in the Qur'an in 6:50, 13:16, 35:19, 40:58, etc.

7.1.2 Worldly Guidance

One example of worldly guidance is advice regarding slavery. In verse 4:25 it is said, "and whoever among you cannot [find] the means to marry free, believing women, then [he may marry] from your believing slave girls, and Allah is most knowing about your faith. So marry them with the permission of their people and give them their due compensation according to what is acceptable. [They should be] chaste, neither [of] those who commit unlawful intercourse randomly nor those who take lovers. But once they are sheltered in marriage, if they should commit adultery, then for them is half the punishment for free women. This is for him among you who fears sin, but to be patient is better for you, and Allah is forgiving and merciful." Slavery is terrible, but it was a social fact that was hard to change in Muhammad's time. The face that Islamic texts do not condemn it should not be taken as reasons for keeping it. It does not feel comfortable to read this verse even though it takes account of the fact that slave girls did not marry voluntarily and thus the punishment for adultery is less than for free women. Such advice is out-dated in our world.

Similarly, in a Hadith Muhammad is said to have said that a slave who performs what is due to Allah and his masters will receive a double reward. [3, 3:97A] This is outdated in a world without slavery. So we see that worldly guidance frequently becomes out-dated.

Worldly guidance is by nature temporary. It is based on the situation and structure of society at that particular stage in history.

To stick to advice for a different age without flexibility is a stupid practice. Religion does not promote stupidity.

Another example is the ruling about the distribution of inheritance. In Muhammad's time, the rules of Islam arguably raised the rights of women from before. To rule otherwise would encounter too much opposition and no one would stick to it. But now his rules are backward and outdated. We should carry on his spirit of improving society, not dragging it behind.

In verses 16:70 and 22:5 in the Qur'an it is said that some of you are "sent back to the most decrepit age, so that he does not know anything, after having had knowledge." That seems to describe the state of fundamentalist Muslim communities in recent times. It is our duty to fight this trend, as liberal citizens of the world, Muslims or non-Muslims. Do not confuse trying to reform Islam as being hostile to it. One can be hostile to fundamentalist Islam but friendly to reformist Islam. There is no conflict between these two attitudes, and in fact they complement each other.

Be aware though, that the way to achieve it is not to put in place a new programme of detailed laws about behaviour, but to adopt liberal laws and, on the basis of that, discuss how best to conduct oneself, not by legal coercion, as we argued in Chapter 6.

Now let us get back to spiritual guidance.

7.1.3 Spiritual Guidance

In the modern world, the fabric of society has changed, and the best way to guide human beings toward higher degrees of autonomy is not by explicit rules about every aspect of life, but spiritual training and integration of the result of such training into everyday life. Many Buddhist organisations are doing an admirable job in this respect. They focus on spiritual development and charity, not dogmatic disputes.

Let us look at Islam. It has its own body of spiritual wisdom in Islamic philosophy and Sufism, and we should learn and promote that. Sufi groups were not always only spiritual. Intrigues and power struggles also occurred. But we should learn what is worthy to be learnt, and be good guardians of a glorious heritage. Salvage and rebuild what is now in rubble. This is the way to relive the spirit of early Muslims, by imitating their admirable purity and persistence in face of difficulties, not by growing a big beard and putting on a blue burqa.

In verse 49:14 in the Qur'an there is an interesting passage. It says, "The bedouins say, 'we believed.' Say, 'You have not believed, but say, 'we have submitted,' for faith has not yet entered your hearts, and if you obey Allah and his messenger, he will not deprive you of [any reward for] your deeds. Indeed, Allah is forgiving and merciful." Here we can see that the external action of entering Islam and following Islamic rules is not equal to faith. Faith is internal and spiritual.

7.1.3.1 Peace

Here I refer to peace of mind more than peace as in war and peace.

In verse 48:4 it is said that it is Allah "who sent down tranquillity into the hearts of the believers so that they would increase in faith in addition to their faith." Anecdotally many people adopt a religion because of the feeling of peace it brings. Regrettably sometimes a religion adopted for peace of mind turns into a cause of war. Interestingly, this verse is actually given in the context of a military victory.

In popular imagination this tension between peace of

mind and war is particularly relevant in Islam, because the Middle East is riddled with war and conflict. But of course there are many historical, political, and socio-economical factors at work, not just religious ones.

In verses 5:15–16 it is said, "O people of the book, our messenger has come to you making clear to you much of what you used to conceal of the book and overlooking much. A light and a clear book has come to you from Allah by which Allah guides those who pursue his approval by the ways of peace and brings them out from darkness into the light, by his permission, and guides them to a straight path." Here Islam is characterised as "the ways of peace." From this example we can see that people sought peace and tranquility when following Islam.

The name of Islam itself is related to peace, for the root of the word "submission" إسلام *islām* in Arabic shares the same root as "peace" سلام *salām*, which is س - ل - م *s-l-m*. Muslims emphasise this relation between Islam and peace and in the Qur'an we are told to greet other Muslims with "peace be upon you." (6:54) An interesting thing is that the word "peace" is used more than forty times in the Qur'an, much more often than the word "Islam."

In verses 6:126–127 it is said, "this is the path of your lord. We have detailed the signs for a people who remember. The home of peace with their lord is for them, and he will be their protector because of what they did." In this passage Muslims are promised a home of peace with Allah. Unfortunately this phrase is sometimes used to divide Muslims and infidels, and people argue that Muslims belong to the home of peace and infidels belong to the home of war, so that Muslims are justified in fighting them and ruling them because these actions are approved by God. This is an unfortunate reading, for the passage is spiritual rather than political, as would be clearly seen if we continue to read on and reach 6:128 which talks about judgment day.

Another example can be found in verse 10:25, where it is said, "Allah invites to the home of peace and guides whom he wills to a straight path." It is easy to read this as saying that Muslims will get peace and others perhaps not. But as soon as we read on, we see in 10:26–27, "For those who did good is the best and extra, and no dust will cover their faces, and no humiliation. Those are residents of paradise. They are abiding in it eternally. And for those who earned themselves evil doings, the recompense of an evil deed is its like, and humiliation will cover them. They will have no defender from Allah. It is as if their faces are covered with pieces of the night, dark. Those are the companions of the fire. They are abiding in it eternally." From this ensuing passage we can see that, regardless of one's faith, one who does good will receive a good reward, and one who does evil will receive a bad reward. So it is unreasonable to infer from 10:26 that only Muslims can be in a state of physical peace. It is more reasonable to read this as saying that Islam offers peace of mind.

Sura 94 is a very beautiful and soothing example. It says to Muhammad, "did we not expand for you your breast? And we removed from you your burden which had weighed upon your back, and raised high for you your repute. For indeed, with hardship is ease. Indeed, with hardship is ease. So when you have finished [your religious duties], then labour hard, and to your lord direct [your] longing." This passage reflects a spiritual connection between Muhammad and Allah. But it is not something exclusive to a prophet. It is something that can be established between any worshipper and the worshipped. One's breast would be expanded, one's burden removed, ease is found, and there is a place for one's longing. This is peace of mind.

In verses 113:1–5 one is told to say, "I seek refuge in the

lord of daybreak, from the evil of that which he created, and from the evil of darkness when it spreads, and from the evil of the blowers in knots,[1] and from the evil of an envier when he envies." This is another instance of the spiritual solace Islam offers. Sura 114 is similar in this respect.

7.1.3.2 Forgiveness

Forgiveness, if improperly taught, can be condescending. People may think that they have something to forgive and they are magnanimously doing so where actually there is nothing to forgive. Therefore it is important that we establish correct attitudes of interpretation, as I have tried to do in previous chapters, especially the principle of uncertainty (Section 3.2.1), correct attitudes of faith, such as tolerance and ease (Section 4.4.2), a rational mindset (Section 6.1.2), and the practice of abrogation (Section 6.2), before we talk about forgiveness.

In the Qur'an, Allah is frequently described by adjectives like gracious, merciful, pardoning, and forgiving. In the Qur'an, the word رحمان *raḥmān*, meaning "most gracious," is used 57 times from 2:163 until 78:38 and every time it is used it is in order to describe Allah. The word رحيم *raḥīm*, meaning "most merciful," is used 116 times from the very beginning until 73:20 and every time except once it is used for characterising Allah. The word عفو *'afū*, meaning "pardoning," is used in 4:43, 4:99, 4:149, 22:60, 58:2 to describe Allah, and it is only ever used to describe Allah. Allah is also frequently said to be pardoning people, for example in 2:52, 2:187, 3:152, 3:155, 4:153, 5:95, 5:101,

---

[1] "Blowers in knots" refers to people who practice magic.

9:66, 42:25, 42:30, and 42:34. In addition to this, the word غفور *ghafūr*, meaning "forgiving," is used 91 times from 2:173 to 85:14 and every time it describes Allah.

On the basis of the attitudes and mindsets above, we should follow Allah's example and be forgiving. In verse 57:28 it is said, "O you who have believed, fear Allah and believe in his messenger. He gives you a double portion of his mercy, makes for you a light to walk by, and forgives you, and Allah is forgiving and merciful."

People are taught to forgive in the Qur'an. In verse 2:109 it is said, "many of the people of the book wish they could turn you back to disbelief after you have believed, out of envy from themselves after the truth has become clear to them. So pardon and overlook until Allah delivers his command. Indeed, Allah is competent over all things." In verses 4:148–149 it is said, "Allah does not like the public mention of evil except by one who has been wronged, and Allah is ever hearing and knowing. If you show a good thing or conceal it or pardon an offense, indeed, Allah is ever pardoning and competent." In verse 24:22 it is said, "do not let those of virtue and wealth among you swear not to give to their relatives and the needy and the emigrants for the cause of Allah, and let them pardon and overlook. Would you not like Allah to forgive you? And Allah is forgiving and merciful." In verse 42:40 it is said, "the retribution for an evil act is an evil one like it, but whoever pardons and makes reconciliation, his reward is from Allah. Indeed, he does not like wrongdoers." In verse 64:14 it is said, "O you who have believed, indeed, enemies to you are among your wives and your children, so beware of them. But if you pardon and overlook and forgive, then indeed, Allah is forgiving and merciful."

From these verses we can see that forgiveness is a great virtue and we should think about forgiveness before blaming others, especially in the religious realm, where people take offense easily for "disrespect to religion."

We also need to remember that criticism of religion can be good for religion, and with a humble sense of uncertainty we should not think that we know what Allah approves. We should judge with reason alone and give room to personal choice. Over and above that, and only then, would we be able to say that we forgive people's unnecessary sneers and prejudice against Islam.

7.1.3.3 Remembrance

In verse 28:46 in the Qur'an, it is said that Muhammad is "sent to warn a people so that they may remember." The word ذكر *dhikr*, meaning "mentioning," "reminder," or "remembrance," is frequently used in the Qur'an.

It is repeated frequently that the Qur'an is only a reminder. In verse 3:58 it is said to Muhammad, "this is what we recite to you of the signs and wise remembrance." In verse 12:104 it is said to Muhammad that he does not ask people for any payment for the news of the unseen, "it is but a reminder for the worlds." In verses 38:87, 68:52, and 81:27 it is also said that the Qur'an "is but a reminder to the worlds." In verse 21:50 it is said that the Qur'an is "a blessed reminder which we have sent down." In verse 36:69 it is said that this is "but a reminder and a clear Qur'an." In verse 38:1 it is said that the Qur'an contains a reminder. In verse 38:49 it is said, "this is a reminder." In verses 43:43–44 it is said that what is revealed to you is "a reminder for you and your people."

The significance of the remembrance of Allah is also frequently mentioned. In verse 13:28 Muhammad is told to say that Allah "guides to him whoever turns back, those who believed and whose hearts are assured by the remembrance of Allah. Undoubtedly hearts are assured by the remembrance of Allah." In verse 16:44 it is said that Allah

Chapter 7 Reason

"revealed the reminder to you in order that you may make clear to the people that which was sent down to them so that they may think." In verse 20:14 we are told to worship Allah and perform prayer for his remembrance. In verse 20:124 it is said that he who turns away from the remembrance of Allah "will have a depressed life." In verses 24:36–37 it is said that, in mosques, are "men whom neither trade nor sale distracts from the remembrance of Allah and the performance of prayer and alms-giving." In verse 29:45 it is said, "the remembrance of Allah is greater." In verse 39:22 "those hard of heart against the remembrance of Allah" are lamented. In verse 39:23 it is said that the skins and the hearts of those who fear their lord "relax at the remembrance of Allah." In verse 62:9, it is commanded that when we are called to prayer on Friday, we should "proceed to the remembrance of Allah."

The most important example in my opinion is 33:41–42 where it is said, "O you who have believed, remember Allah with much remembrance, and exalt him morning and evening."

In verse 5:91 it is said that Satan wants to "avert you from the remembrance of Allah and prayer." The word صَدّ *ṣadda*, meaning "to avert," is significant. It implies our natural tendency to remember, but some of us have been led away from the path of remembrance. Another word ألهى *alhā* which also means to avert, is used to the same effect in 63:9 in which it is said, "let not your wealth and your children divert you from the remembrance of Allah. And whoever does that, then those are the losers." In a similar vein, in 18:101 it is said that the infidels' "eyes were shielded from" the remembrance of Allah. It is because the eyes were covered that one fails to remember Allah.

Apart from the above examples, the word "remembrance" also appears in verses 7:63, 7:69, 15:6, 15:9, 16:43, 18:28, 20:42, 21:2, 21:7, 21:24, 21:42, 23:71, 23:110, 25:29, 26:5, 36:11, 38:8, 38:32, 41:41, 43:5, 53:29, 54:22, 54:25, 54:32, 54:40, 57:16, 58:19, 72:17, 81:27, etc. I list all these occurrences not for the sake of making the present book longer and heavier, but for the sake of reminding ourselves the significance of remembrance in Islam.

The form II noun تذكرة *tadhkira* with the same meaning appears in verses 20:3, 56:73, 69:12, 69:48, 73:19, 74:49, 74:54, 76:29, and 90:11. In verse 69:12 it is said, "indeed, when the water overflowed, we carried your ancestors in the sailing ship in order that we might make it a reminder for you and attentive ears may grasp it." We should not insist that the stories in Abrahamic religions are accurate but should instead focus on the spiritual content. Here reminder and consciousness are key. The flood is not.

Let us look at other related passages. In verses 51:49–50 it is said, "of all things we created two mates, so that perhaps you will remember. So flee to Allah." This verse is particularly interesting in that it uses the verb to flee فرّ *farr*. It conveys very vividly human beings' need to feel safe and how they would feel peace once they remember Allah.

In verses 57:20–21 it is said, "know that the life of this world is but play and amusement and adornment and boasting to one another and competition in increase of wealth and children, like rain which causes a plant to grow and it pleases the farmers, then it dries and you see it turn yellow, then it becomes chaff. And in the hereafter, there is severe punishment, and forgiveness from Allah, and pleasure. And what is worldly life except the enjoyment of delusion. Race toward forgiveness from your lord and a garden whose width is like the width of the sky and the earth, prepared for those who believed in Allah and his messengers. That is the bounty of Allah which he gives to whom he wills, and Allah is the possessor of great bounty." This is a verse worth reading and reflecting on. It gives a deep description of life on earth, of the fleetingness and lack of permanence of life. But we need not be defeated by nihilism and nothingness. If we remember the true aim of life, seeking God and goodness, then we would be able to live spiritually and meaningfully rather than just for the accumulation of material wealth or power.

We are reminded of this again, this time together with the unexpectedness of death, in verses 63:9–11 in which it is said, "O you who have believed, do not let your wealth and your children divert you from the remembrance of Allah, and whoever does that, then those are the losers. And spend from what we have provided you, before death approaches one of you and he says, 'my lord, if only you would delay me for a term so I could give charity and be among the righteous.' And Allah will not delay a soul when its term has come, and Allah is informed of what you do."

There is a similar passage in verses 59:18–19. It says, "O you who have believed, fear Allah, and let every soul look at what it has presented for tomorrow, and fear Allah. Indeed, Allah is informed of what you do. And do not be like those who forgot Allah, so he made them forget their souls. Those are the defiantly disobedient." If we remember Allah and are constantly aware of the consequence of our actions, then we would be upright and help people in need. Then our lives would be beautiful. That is the true goal of religion, to lead people towards an upright path.

In verse 38:46 it is said we "chose our servants (made them sincere) for a pure quality, remembrance of the home." This is beautiful and makes the important role of remembrance in Islam clear. Just as Plato frequently alludes to the soul and its remembrance, for example in [14, Meno 81d],

> As the whole of nature is akin, and the soul has learned everything, nothing prevents a man, after recalling one thing only—a process men call learning—discovering everything else for himself, if he is brave and does not tire of the search, for searching and learning are, as a whole, recollection.

Islam talks about reminders and remembrance.

We need to remember Allah. Islam is something within us. This is something literalists tend to forget. They emphasise the significance of following explicit rules, not remembering that rules are for particular situations only, but remembrance is universal. We do not need political structures to mandate adherence to Islam. We should adhere to our version of Islam from within ourselves. This emphasis on remembrance gave rise to a variety of Sufi rituals with the name *dhikr*, meaning "remembrance."

We also need to return to Allah. The word أوّاب *awwāb*, meaning "one who often returns," is used very positively in the Qur'an. In verse 17:25 it is said, "your lord is most knowing of what is in yourselves. If you are righteous, then indeed he is ever forgiving to the ones often returning" to him. In verse 38:17 people are told to "be patient over what they say and remember our servant David, the possessor of strength. Indeed, he was one who often returns" to Allah.

Chapter 7 Reason

In verse 38:30 it is said, "to David we gave Solomon, an excellent servant. Indeed, he was one who often returned" to Allah. In verse 38:44 it is said that Allah found Job "patient, an excellent servant. Indeed, he was one who often returns" to Allah.

From these uses of the word أَوَّاب *awwāb* we can see that we need only to return to Allah in the face of vicissitudes, so as to retain our spirituality, and not to turn into worldly and unjust people. This is the higher teaching of Islam, not fear and blind obedience.

Use of the verb *to neglect* highlights, from the negative side, the view of Islam as remembrance. Two verses use the verb to neglect, فرّط *farraṭ*, in talking about one's adherence to religion. Negligence of the hour of resurrection is mentioned in verse 6:31 and negligence with regard to Allah is mentioned in 39:56. In verse 18:28 the word فرط *furuṭ*, meaning "neglect," is used. We are told not to "obey one whose heart [Allah has] made heedless of our remembrance and who follows his desire and whose state was in a state of neglect."

Another word with similar import is heedlessness غفلة *ghafla*. In verses 50:19–22 it is said, "the intoxication of death will bring the truth. That is what you were trying to avoid. And the horn will be blown. That is the day of the threat. And every soul will come, with it a driver and a witness. You were certainly heedless of this, and we have removed from you your cover, so your sight today is sharp." Once the cover is removed, we can see clearly and shall not remain heedless of the spirit. We will remember Allah. It can happen before judgment day, in this life.

The word ساهون *sāhūn* means heedless. In verses 51:8–11 it is said, "you have different views. He who is deluded, is deluded away from [the Qur'an.] The liars are destroyed, who are in a flood, heedless." In verses 107:1–5 it is said, "have you seen the one who denies the judgment? For that is the one who drives away the orphan, and does not encourage the feeding of the poor, so woe to the praying ones who are heedless of their prayer, who show off and withhold assistance." From the use of this word we can see that people who do not act justly as taught by Islam are heedless. Therefore if people become mindful they will act rightly and become close to Allah.

The use of the concept of neglect and heedlessness should be considered in contrast to remembrance. Because Islam is something within us and we can remember it if we want, if we fail to attend to our spirituality, it is due to negligence. Religion conceived this way would not be tied up with detailed rules revealed more than a thousand years ago, because they are not universal nor within us, and we cannot remember these.

In Section 4.2.1 I talked about the importance of intention in Islam. It is said to determine one's reward in the afterlife. There is a higher dimension to that idea. In verse 79:35 in the Qur'an it is said that on judgment day "man will remember that for which he strove." On that day one will review one's life. But if we were able to know and remember our innermost intention while we live, we would truly be able to live fulfilling and meaningful lives.

7.1.3.4 Light

Islam and the Qur'an are frequently said to be light sent down from Allah. Does our practice of Islam fit this noble metaphor?

The image of Allah sending down a light is mentioned many times. For example in verse 4:174 it is said that Allah "sent down to you a clear light." In verse 7:157 it is said that "those who follow the messenger" "followed the light which was sent down with him." In 33:45–46 it is

Chapter 7 Reason

similarly said that Muhammad is sent "as an illuminating lamp" "inviting to Allah." In verse 64:8 we are told to "believe in Allah and his messenger and the light which we have sent down."

The light is said to be a means by which Allah guides. In verse 39:22 it is said that one "whose breast Allah has expanded towards Islam" is guided by a "light from his lord." In verses 42:52–53 Muhammad is told, "you did not know of [this] book or the faith, but we have made it a light by which we guide." In verse 57:28 it is said, "O you who have believed, fear Allah and believe in his messenger. He gives you a double portion of his mercy, makes for you a light to walk by, and forgives you, and Allah is forgiving and merciful."

The image of extracting people from darkness into light appears numerous times in the Qur'an. In verse 2:257 in the Qur'an it is said that Allah extracts those who believe "from darkness into the light." In verses 5:15–16 it is said that "a light and a clear book came to you from Allah, by which he guides those who pursue his pleasure to the ways of peace and extracts them from darkness into the light." In verse 33:43 it is said that Allah is the one who blesses you and his angels ask him to do so "in order that he may extract you from darkness into the light." In verse 57:9 it is said that Allah "sends down upon his servant verses of clear evidence in order that he may extract you from darkness into the light." In verse 65:11 it is said that Allah sent "a messenger who recites to you the clear signs of Allah in order that he may extract those who believe and do righteous deeds from darkness into the light."

An especially expressive passage is 14:1 in which Muhammad is told that the Qur'an is "a book which we have revealed to you that you might extract mankind from darkness into the light by permission of their lord to the path of the strong, the worthy of praise." In verse 24:35 it is said, "Allah is the light of the heavens and the earth. The example of his light is like a niche in which there is a lamp. The lamp is in glass, the glass as if it were a pearly star lit from a blessed olive tree, neither eastern nor western, whose oil nearly glows even if fire did not touch it. Light upon light. Allah guides to his light whom he wills, and Allah presents examples for the people, and Allah is knowing of all things."

The light is also said to be a reward to believers. In my opinion it means that people who truly believe in Islam will not be taken up with the material world, but they will live uprightly and meaningfully. Therefore they will be rewarded accordingly in the afterlife. It should not be taken to mean that Muslims are the only ones who get treated well on judgment day. In verses 57:12–13 it is said that on judgment day "you see the believing men and believing women, their light proceeding before them and on their right. 'Your good tidings today are gardens beneath which rivers flow. You are abiding in them eternally.' That is the great attainment. On the day the hypocritical men and hypocritical women will say to those who believed, 'Wait for us that we may acquire some of your light.' It will be said, 'Go back behind you and seek light.' " In verse 57:19 it is said, "those who have believed in Allah and his messengers, those are the truthful and the witnesses with their lord. For them is their reward and their light. But those who have disbelieved and denied our signs, those are the companions of hellfire." In verse 66:8 it is said, "O you who have believed, repent to Allah with sincere repentance. Perhaps your lord will remove from you your misdeeds and admit you into gardens beneath which rivers flow, on the day when Allah will not disgrace the prophet and those who believed with him. Their light will proceed before them and on their right."

From such passages we can see the centrality of envisaging Islam as a religion of light, rather than of darkness. This is what is said in the text, but are we practising it? Or are we perpetuating darkness by carrying on the vestiges of a bygone society crystalised in the Islamic texts and mistaking that for piety and spirituality?

In Arabic, the word for light نور *nūr* and the word for

fire نار *nār* come from the same root ن - و - ر. If we want people to admire and follow Islam, do we show to the world that Islam is a religion of light or of hellfire?

7.1.3.5 Concluding Remarks

Muslims like to say Islam is a religion of peace. But do we really practise this? If we do, we should always try to promote peace and justice in our thoughts and deeds. The modern world is very different from Muhammad's time and place, and hence the society and the audience he addressed were also extremely different from our own. To live in this totally transformed world, we need to renew and rethink our covenant with Allah, and not accept and adopt without thinking seemingly clear and unchangeable injunctions in the Qur'an and the Hadiths. That is why we need to follow spiritual guidance rather than worldly guidance. The sensible way for religions to develop, survive, and guide human beings towards their fulfilment is to put their emphasis and principles on the the spiritual level, and not on the social-political level.

In considering the merits of every thought and action we should aim at the promotion of peace and spiritual development in oneself and in the community. If we really adhere to this principle, this would put an end to doctrinal clashes and sectarian violence, and all religions would grow and become the best version of themselves. This is the best path for the faithful, whatever one's faith is.

7.2 Philosophical Religion

Philosophical religion was a common concept before the divorce of philosophy and religion after the Enlightenment. Fraenkel has expounded on this concept and its influence on Judaism, Christianity, and Islam admirably in his book *Philosophical Religions from Plato to Spinoza* [18].

7.2.1 Religion and Reason

Fraenkel reminds us that in the Middle Ages, many thinkers were of the opinion that philosophy and reason serve as the higher goal, whereas scriptures constitute a path for lay persons ultimately to transcend religious laws and self-govern using pure reason, i.e. God. He says, "rational insight is revelation" and "for proponents of a philosophical religion one of religion's main aims is to lead all members of the religious community to the highest level of rational autonomy they can attain." [18, p. x] Muslim philosophers holding such views include al-Farabi (ca. 872–951) and Averroes (1126–1198).

In verse 9:19 in the Qur'an, it is said, "the mosques of Allah are only to be maintained by those who believe in Allah and the last day and perform prayer and give alms and do not fear except Allah, for perhaps those will be among the guided ones." From this passage we can see that the goal is to be one of the guided ones. Thus, despite there being so many religious clashes in history, in the Qur'an itself believers and non-believers are really distinguished on the ground that believing is better for the mental state of people at a certain developmental stage. But of course that qualification needs not be said explicitly in the text itself. I argue that more advanced people do not fall under this comparison. I argue that this is the intended meaning of the Qur'an.

Let me produce another piece of evidence for this attitude. Allah is frequently characterised as wise and knowing. These are particularly desirable qualities in Islam. But Muslims do not always remember this. We say that Allah is wise and knowing, but we interpret Islamic texts as if he is a stupid police officer, who does not know anything except bureaucratic rules, applying them mechanically without considering the situation.

The word حكيم $ḥak\bar{\imath}m$, meaning "wise," is used about 100 times in the Qur'an for characterising Allah, from 2:32

Chapter 7 Reason

until 76:30. The word علم *'alīm*, meaning "knowing," is used even more frequently—about 160 times—in characterising Allah. In verse 12:100 it is said, "my lord is subtle in what he wills, indeed, he is the knowing, the wise." In verse 60:10 it is said that Allah judges between you, and Allah is knowing and wise."

The verse 4:92 is a particularly good example. It says that it is never permissible for "a believer to kill a believer except by mistake. And whoever kills a believer by mistake, then the freeing of a believing slave [is required] and a compensation payment [should be] presented to the deceased's family unless they give it up as charity. But if the deceased was from a people at war with you while he was a believer, then the freeing of a believing slave [is required], and if he was from a people with whom you have a treaty, then a compensation payment [should be] presented to his family and the freeing of a believing slave [is required], and whoever does not find [the means to do these], then a fast for two months consecutively, for the acceptance of repentance from Allah, and Allah is knowing and wise." In this long verse we see a list of rules regarding killing. What is required under different circumstances is described. But the world is complicated and exceptional situations obtain. The last clause characterising Allah as knowing and wise should be read as saying that people need to use their own discretion when dealing with different cases, and it should also be read as a hint that, should the world change and different rules become more appropriate, there is no injunction against following them. For these rules were given for Muhammad's audience and it was not necessary nor practical to give rules that would be good for one thousand and four hundred years later. Sticking to rules for a different age does not mean piety. We need to proceed with wisdom and knowledge as the ending of this passage hints, and remember that Allah is wise and knowing when we think about what Islam is.

Words from the root ن - ي - ب *b–y–n* are usually related to the concept of clarity. They are used frequently in the Qur'an. The most frequent words except for the proposition بين *baina* meaning "between," are

1. مبين *mubīn*, meaning "clear," occurring about 120 times;

2. بيّنة *bayyina*, meaning "clear thing," occurring about 70 times; and

3. بيّن *bayyana*, meaning "to make clear," occurring about 40 times.

The verb to make clear is particularly cogent. Allah's message is made clear for people to understand and determine for themselves what is Allah's way. In verse 2:118 it is said, "those who do not know say, 'why does Allah not speak to us or a sign come to us?' Those before them said something like what they say. Their hearts resemble each other. We have already made clear the signs to a people who are certain." The Qur'an is intended to be a clarification of Allah's commands. It shows that Allah's message can be clarified and also modified, as I argued in Section 6.2.2.

In verses 3:102–103 the believers are told to "fear Allah as he should be feared, and do not die except when you are Muslims, and hold fast to the rope of Allah all together and do not become divided, and remember the favour of Allah upon you; when you were enemies, and he joined your hearts together so you became by his favour brothers, and you were on the edge of a pit of fire, and he saved you from it. Allah makes clear to you his signs in this way so that you may be guided." From this passage we can

Chapter 7 Reason

see that we should be guided by the Qur'an in which the signs of Allah are made clear, form a coherent theology for ourselves, and live by it. But what is happening is that people choose what promotes their agenda and use Islam as a tool for accomplishing their desires for power, influence, and status. The misogyny which Muhammad was fighting persists in the name of the religion he was the spokesperson for. This is the irony of ironies, and even Allah has to accept such defeat.

In verse 4:26 it is said, "Allah wants to make clear to you and guide you to the practices of those before you and to accept your repentance, and Allah is knowing and wise." From this passage we can see that the Qur'an is intended as a clarification of what practices are good in the eyes of Allah. But in this age we need much more clarification before we can apply Allah's rules, for the world has changed drastically. What do we do? We need to use our own reasoning, analysing the intention and considerations behind what is said, for we need to live in the spirit of Allah, not in the letter of the Qur'an, because that would be impossible and unreasonable. We cannot live like Muhammad materially and should not. What we can and should do is to emulate his simplicity and spirituality.

From the above discussion we can see that the text being made clear at the time of revelation does not mean that we do not need to think, for centuries of interpretations and traditions have made us forget the original meanings and context in which it was given. We need to keep reminding ourselves of this. And in order to escape from this conglomeration of bias we need to take the text apart and reason step by step so as to reach a reasonable reading.

The frequent use of words having to do with clarity should alert us to its importance in Islam. However, we should ask ourselves, do we honour this in our religious thinking? Do we think carefully before judging if something is obligatory, recommended, neutral, objectionable, or forbidden? I would say that people frequently let their tradition and bias make the decision for them, instead of a critical analysis of Islamic texts and ideas.

Even al-Afghani (circa 1838–1897), an influential thinker who placed great emphasis on Islam as a force in politics, supported human reason and philosophising as the basis of Islamic communities [24, p. 118] because he saw that human reason is in harmony with Islamic prophecy if properly applied [24, p. 125], and prophecy is only necessary for establishing a moral basis, while the rest can be attained through human reasoning, *ijtihād*. [24, p. 127] His view is seen with suspicion by some [24, p. 123] but from thinkers like him we should see that philosophical Islam is not a wilful interpretation of Islam.

If this kind of interpretation, sometimes viewed as esoteric, is adopted by the mainstream of religious people, then religions can be truly peaceful and followers of different religions would have no problem co-existing with each other.

7.2.2 Clarification of Terms

Let us discuss the relevant concepts first.

Faith is one's ultimate conviction, not necessarily supernatural (using today's terms, it could be characterised by not being recognised by scientific theories).

Religion is an organised set of beliefs, usually supernatural. There is usually some institution with authority.

Philosophy is a collection of different sets of beliefs and reasoning, usually not supernatural. There are full-time jobs teaching this in the modern world.

Fraenkel [18] propounds the desirability of an intellectual life for the individual and the social goals that people should aim at as a result. We agree basically with his views but do not share the depth of historical interests he displays, since in relation to our goal we need not concern ourselves too much with the fine points of interpretation and issues such as the origin of the concept of autonomy. [18, p. 29] I would like to convince and "convert" lay people, not academics. An investigation into the historical origin of autonomy does not offer a strong argument for liberalism for an ordinary Muslim.

Therefore I concentrate on the implications of philosophical religion in the context of Islam, liberalism, and social issues.

7.2.3 Jihād

With this rampant talk about and against *jihād*, how should we reclaim the concept of *jihād*?

We need to be honest and admit that, in Muhammad's time, the word *jihād* did frequently mean actual fighting, because in early Islam Muslims had to fight to survive, and the Arabs were constantly fighting before Islam. But we have a different situation now. People still fight for resources and money, but we have advanced, and we have better ways to solve these problems. It is not in our self-interest to promote fighting and violence. We should remember the primary meaning of *jihād* in Islam. The original, more important meaning, is "to fight oneself," "fight with our arrogance, laziness, selfishness, inaction, etc." The goal is to improve oneself, seek knowledge, help others, pursue spirituality, etc.

If this form of *jihād* gets as much attention as the violent form of *jihād*, then the soft power of Islam is in a state with which we can be happy.

7.3 The Rebirth of Religion

7.3.1 The Fall

The fall of religion occurred when reason was seen as antagonistic to religion.

Before the Enlightenment, many theorists (for example, Averroes in [11]) tried to reconcile reason and religion by interpreting religious texts as allegorical rather than literal. A frequently used example is God's being said to be king in the Bible, which theorists tend to interpret allegorically, as saying that God's rank is highest. [18, p. 161]

In the Enlightenment, another solution emerged— giving up religion altogether. [36] Thinkers in the West began to argue that religion in general is inherently irrational, unreasonable, unscientific, and superstitious, Christianity being no exception. Earlier scientists tended to view the scientific enterprise as looking for God's rules in action in nature. The line of thought was that since God is rational, the world created by him is also orderly and rule-governed. The job of scientists was to discover these rules.

However, with the advance of science, many statements in the Bible and by the church have been contradicted. After the promulgation of the theory of evolution, religion and science became enemies and seemingly irreconcilable. So atheism came to be seen as more reasonable than theism. Many religious authorities become more and more radical and irrational, because people who think left religion. And the people who are attracted to religion are attracted through conservatism and populism.

But we see today that the degeneration of religion is not the only possible way to go. We could once more promote reason as central to religion, which supports the advancement of science and education and chooses reform rather than withdrawal from and avoidance of the modern world.

And to bring believers of Abrahamic religions to the liberal side, we should revive the philosophical religious tradition. In this way adherents to a religion could be persuaded to join the liberals, rather than denouncing them as infidels.

7.3.2 Prophets and Priests

In verses 31:23–24 in the Qur'an, it is said that Allah "grants a little enjoyment to infidels, then he forces them to a severe punishment." Why does Allah not do the opposite, punish them a little so that they repent and escape from more serious harm, as verse 32:21 says, that Allah will definitely "make them taste the nearer punishment before the greater punishment so that they may return"? It seems that the verses 31:23–24 constitute an attempt to cover up Allah's inability to punish them in this world. Even if that is the case, it is not a problem. Let the spiritual be with Allah and the mundane be with us. It is not an embarrassment for Allah not to be able to punish people in this world, it is rather another testament to the historical context and the necessity of presenting an image of God that is extremely powerful so that the nomadic Arabs would fear and believe. But it should be something that we have grown out of. We do not need to believe out of fear. We should believe for the sake of our souls.

Weber [41, §C.1.a] made an insightful distinction between prophets and priests as being different professions. Prophets are inspired, while priests seek to stabilise and institutionalise, therefore they have to legislate and rationalise their own *raison d'etre*, otherwise they would have no position or recognition.

In modern eyes the two are associated with religions, while philosophers are seen as another species. But it would be better for the world if we do not follow priests as interpreters of religion, but ideally follow only ourselves, and if that does not work or if we need some guidance or reference, we should rather turn to philosophers and, by extension, intellectuals.

In that way, we avoid the dangers of priests taking power from us in order to benefit themselves. Philosophers are not always to be trusted, but the danger of abuse is much smaller, because it is their profession to question, teach, and write, rather than make people—powerful or powerless—follow their views and attain power in the name of God, or gods.

Prophetic guidance is potentially practical advice for a particular age. But for any other age, reason must be applied in determining whether it is applicable to it, and if it is, to what extent and in what manner. Philosophers perform this deliberation better than priests, because they have no personal stake in it, while priests consciously or unconsciously would like to enlarge their power and jurisdiction.

For example, what do we do with passages such as 2:228 in the Qur'an saying that women "have the same rights as men but men have a degree above them"? That is simple if we allow flexibility in the practice of religion. Consider the age and situation in which the revelation is given. The society in which Muhammad lived was extremely patriarchal. Has it changed? Yes it has. Then should the implementation of such injunctions be changed? Yes it should. The spirit of the law is to attain the best state possible given the age and situation. And now the best form of law in this respect is equal rights for men and women, if we give them the same opportunities for education, work, and political self-determination.

In verses 42:52–53 it is said that Muhammad is "leading to the straight path, the path of Allah, to whom belongs what is in the heavens and what is on earth. Undoubtedly, matters evolve towards Allah." This hints at the idea of letting people explore and ultimately evolve to the highest level of being.

In my opinion, in verse 5:48 in the Qur'an a rare hint is given of the grander scheme of things. In this verse it is said that Allah "gave Jews, Christians, and Muslims each their own laws and programmes so that they will compete in doing good." It seems a bit like evolution, exploring the possibilities and looking at how living beings pursuing different paths fare.

It is a very good explanation for the chaos in religious beliefs and again shows us the fundamental importance of doing good deeds rather then making others accept your religion.

Verse 30:41 says something similar. It says that corruption "appeared in the world by means of what people have earned by their hands in order for Allah to let them taste some of what they did so that they may return." We can see from this verse the idea that what happens in this world is a manifestation of what people desire, so that their ideas are tested and demonstrated in actuality. In this way people can see the consequence of their actions and interactions. In this way we get to learn what happens if our ideas and volitions are actualised. This is a very spiritual view of our lives and the world.

7.3.3 Oneness

In Islam one is supposed to say "in sha' Allah," i.e. if Allah wills, every time one talks about the future. In verses 18:23–24 in the Qur'an it is said, "never say of anything, 'indeed, I will do that tomorrow,' except [adding] 'if Allah wills,' and remember your lord when you forget, and say, 'perhaps my lord will guide me nearer than this to right conduct.' " This is arguably the most influential piece of text in the Qur'an as judged by the frequency its effect is seen in social interactions.

According to this, if Allah wills, then I will do it, whatever it is, and if I do not do it, then Allah does not will it. It is open to debate whether Allah's will is a necessary condition for me to do it, according to classical logic. But Allah's will being the sufficient condition is sufficient to call into question the role of human agency. As long as Allah wills, it does not matter whether the person wants to do it or not.

The only way for this to make sense without eschewing human agency and responsibility, without reducing human beings to fatalistic non-agents, is that everyone is Allah or a part of Allah. Then Allah's will contains one's own will, and it makes sense to talk about each action of every individual as being the will of Allah. Otherwise we are just puppets involuntarily involved in the world.

God is invoked as the source of meaning and ethics. But if everything is Allah's will, it does not make sense to talk about human beings as moral or not because they do not determine this, and Allah is the one who does. As we discussed in detail in Section 4.5.1, the only possible way to reconcile the omnipresent will of Allah and human agency and responsibility is to equate the two, like what the famous Sufi mystic al-Hallaj did in saying "I am the truth." [5, p. 51]

For example, in verses 74:54–57 it is said that the Qur'an "is a reminder, then whoever wills will remember it, and they will not remember except that Allah wills. He is worthy of fear and adequate for forgiveness." In verses

76:29–30 it is said, "indeed, this is a reminder, so he who wills may take a way to his lord. And you do not will except that Allah wills. Indeed, Allah is knowing and wise." In verses 80:11–12 it is said, "Indeed, these verses are a reminder, so whoever wills may remember it." In verses 81:27–29 it is said that the Qur'an is "a reminder to the worlds for whoever wills among you to take a straight path, and you do not will except that Allah, lord of the worlds, wills." These passages do not make sense except if we interpret a person's will as equivalent to the one of Allah, for here it is said that whoever wills will remember, and also they will not remember if Allah does not will. Therefore Allah's will has to be the same as the person's will, otherwise the conditional statements are not true. This is the only way in which Allah's will can determine what happens and yet personal responsibility make sense.

In the Qur'an, the plural pronoun "we" is more frequently used then the singular pronoun "I" when Allah talks about himself. Since the message is given through Gabriel, it is reasonable to suppose that Gabriel was talking together with the totality of angels talking in the name of Allah.

We can see some inkling of this idea in verse 31:28, where it is said that your "creation and your resurrection will not be but as one soul."

In the spiritual world, one and many is not as clearcut as when we have physical bodies to delineate different persons. In this sense, polytheism is compatible with monotheism since polytheism counts the higher beings separately, while monotheism counts the higher beings as a collective.

Extending this idea, the oneness of Allah could also mean that everything is Allah, including us, not just the angels. This is a higher meaning of توحيد *tawḥīd*, which literally means making God one.

Allah knows himself through us. We are Allah. And Allah is us. "I am the truth." Each human being is a part of Allah. The process of all life is the process through which Allah is. It is the way he becomes actual rather than potential. All the ups and downs of our lives are the fulfilment of Allah. Different views on life, different doctrines, and different conceptions of faith are lived out through our diverse lives. That is an advanced level of seeing living physically as a test, discussed in subsubsection 4.4.1.3.

In this advanced version, the test is not for Allah to determine whether one is worthy of reward or not, but for oneself to see how one acts under a set of given conditions in life. In verses 84:16–19 it is said, "I swear by the twilight glow, and by the night and what it envelops, and by the moon when it becomes full, that you will surely experience state after state." People will become spiritually more advanced after living out lives physically, seeing what they did in different situations and the consequences of their actions. They would further reflect on their life lessons and gain from this experience. Perhaps there would be other spiritual states after that but we need not speculate too much. What is important for us to know is that we are social, moral, and spiritual subjects experiencing each of our own situations in life, and benefiting from the experience and the chance to experiment with our behaviour, and our reflection on it afterwards.

In this sense, "there is no god but God" means that we do not need any authority or intermediary to tell us how to live our lives. Each of us is a part of God. We can reach God if we reach within. It should be understood in this way rather than as a condemnation of all practices other than Islamic prayer and pilgrimage. Muhammad used to go to a cave to meditate, [3, 1:1] and, before Muhammad, people worshipped God in a simple way. Both these practices are approved in the Qur'an. In verses 98:4–5 it is said that the people who were given the book "were not commanded except to worship Allah, being sincere to him in religion, inclining to truth, and to perform prayer and to give alms, and that is the correct religion." Islam is much more diversified and non-exclusive in its beginnings than we imagine from Salafi preaching.

Following this picture of life, the judgment is a review and evaluation of these diverse ways of living, not a bizarre demarcation of good and evil that does not rest on appropriate correspondence between agency and moral responsibility, which is what a literal reading of the Qur'an and the Hadiths projects.

7.3.4 Directness

In philosophical Islam, the problem of polytheism would also be solved. I touched on this issue in Section 4.5.5 discussing the status of polytheists. Now let us reflect on this in more detail.

In verse 40:12 in the Qur'an it is said that when Allah "was called by himself, you disbelieved, and if others were associated with him, you believed. So the judgment is with Allah, the high, the great." This seems to be a condemnation of polytheism, but let us read this in combination with 41:6. In this verse Muhammad is told to say, "your good is one god so go straight to him and seek his forgiveness." I would argue that this is a rare case in which we should read the verse literally, that is, the motivation behind Muhammad's push for the abolishment of polytheism is directness. Why make it complicated when we can go by a straight path? This is the true meaning of the frequently repeated phrase الصراط المستقيم *al-ṣirāṭ al-*

mustaqīm, "the straight path"! It occurs nearly 40 times in the Qur'an, from the famous "guide us to the straight path" in the opening chapter (1:6) until 67:22. It does not just mean the moral path, it also means the direct path.

Let me give more examples. In verses 3:51, 19:36, and 43:64 it is said that Jesus says, "indeed Allah is my lord and your lord, so worship him. That is the straight path." From this saying we get a sense of the oneness of the world and however many sects there are, faith can be simple and direct.

In verse 3:101 it is said that who "holds fast to Allah has been guided to a straight path." In verse 6:153 it is said that this is "my path, which is straight, so follow it; and do not follow the ways, for you would diverge from his way. He instructed you this so that you may be righteous." In verse 15:41 Allah said to Satan, "this is a path to me that is straight." In verse 22:54 it is said that Allah is "the guide of those who have believed towards a straight path." In verse 23:73 it is said that Muhammad invites people "to a straight path." In verse 42:52 it is said that Muhammad guides "to a straight path." In verse 43:43 we are told to "adhere to that which is revealed to you. Indeed, you are on a straight path." In verse 43:61 we are told to follow Allah, "this is a straight path." These verses stress that following Allah leads one directly to salvation. It is the simple way.

In verse 6:161, Muhammad is told to say, "indeed, my lord has guided me to a straight path, a correct religion, the way of Abraham, a monotheist. And he was not among the polytheists." In verse 37:118 it is said that "we guided [the prophets] on the straight path." In verse 11:56 it is recorded that Hud said, "my lord is on a straight path." In verses 36:3–4 it is said that Muhammad is "from among the messengers on a straight path." In verses 46:29–30 it is said that the jinn warn their people after hearing the Qur'an, "O our people, indeed we heard a book brought down after Moses confirming what was before it, guiding to the truth and to a straight path." The use of the phrase "the straight path" in relation to previous prophets clearly hints at the directness of monotheism, not its exclusiveness. The verse 22:67 also expresses this sense, "for every religion We made rites which they perform. So let the disbelievers not dispute with you over the matter but invite them to your lord. Indeed, you are upon straight guidance."

In verse 6:126 it is said, "this is the path of your lord, going straight. We have detailed the signs for a people who remember." This should be read reflecting on directness and keeping in mind the comments on remembrance above in subsubsection 7.1.3.3.

It is even granted that the worshiped entities exist. In verses 46:5–6 it is said that on judgment day "when the people are gathered," the ones people invoked besides Allah "will be enemies to them." This verse shows that those entities exist and will be judged on judgment day.

From these verses we should be able to see that the reasons against polytheism should not be Allah's wrath or jealousy, as this is a very primitive view of Allah, but simplicity. When people worship many gods, corruption and superstitious practices may proliferate. When people can worship only one god, and people are urged to abandon superfluous practices, people's religious activities could take a more spiritual form. However, this could also lead to problems as a centralised and exclusive monotheism monopolises power and breeds corruption in another way. But conceptual simplicity in religion has its virtue and appeal. In a way it corresponds to Occam's razor [12] in philosophy of science.

1. If gods explain supernatural phenomena, only one god also explains supernatural phenomena.

2. Polytheists believe that gods explain supernatural phenomena.

3. By using *modus ponens* as a rule of thinking, polytheists should believe that only one god also explains supernatural phenomena.

Chapter 7 Reason

4. By the principle of simplicity, one should prefer a simpler explanation.

∴ Therefore, polytheists should convert to monotheism.

Pushing for simplicity was a sensible thing to do in Muhammad's historical context. It raised people's level of allegiance and religious practice.

If ideas are seen as memes, parallel to genes in the competition of biological evolution as Dawkins suggested in *The Selfish Gene* [16], then we can investigate and try to account for their rise and demise in terms of their interaction with the environment. As a meme, monotheism seems to fare better than other religious memes. From the dominance of monotheistic religions one could argue that they give more strength to their believers, and offer more psychological support. Perhaps it is the fittest to survive in human society.

But things are different now from the age in which Muhammad lived and in which monotheism was probably an improvement on Arabian polytheism. In this age the exclusiveness of monotheistic religions seems to cause more problems than benefit. While offering more psychological support, they also provide more pretext for hatred and aggression.

Furthermore, if everything is Allah, when we worship other gods, we are also worshipping Allah. Aside from the consideration of directness, there is nothing evil or condemnable in worshipping other gods. We should see that the warnings against this were tactical, not universal.

In this age in which many people are ready for the higher meaning of oneness we should not get stuck in monotheistic condemnation of polytheistic rituals. We should push for a form of monotheism without aggression.

I call it summatheism. The Latin root *summa* means summit, the highest point.

7.3.5 Summatheism

Summatheism asserts that the highest being and lower deities exist. This is the factual segment of the school. As for the normative or evaluative segment, in summatheism, people are encouraged to pray to the highest being, but there is no blame on people who feel more connection with a saint, angel, or other deities.

There is no inconsistency between Islam and summatheism. After all, the Qur'an said that there is a prophet for each nation. (10:47) Prophets may transmit different revelations to different people based on their circumstances. Therefore on a meta-level Islam is not against different ways of worship.

Now one may argue by appealing to Islamic texts against polytheism that summatheism and Islam are inconsistent. For example, in verse 61:9 in the Qur'an it is said that it is Allah "who sent his messenger with guidance and the religion of truth to manifest it over all religion, although polytheists dislike it." But that is exactly what summatheism is advocating, the belief of one god over others, which does not have to wipe out or condemn polytheism. Here it only says that Islam should manifest over all religion, not that it needs to replace all other religious schools. Polytheism is only a sin in Islam if other gods are put on the same footing as Allah. But that is not necessarily the case, as I have shown in Section 4.5.5.

Before Islamists tried to purify Islam, a variety of practices were accepted as Islam, and people paid respect to many different figures, with different celebrations and rituals. Sufi groups continue to experience Islam in different ways. All we need to do is to accept such practices in the intellectual realm, instigate no excommunication in the religious realm, and enact no governmental penalty in the administrative realm.

In verses 72:27–28 it is said that Allah "sends before each messenger and behind him observers so that he may know that they have conveyed the messages of their lord, and he has encompassed whatever is with them and has

Chapter 7 Reason

recorded all things in number." This passage is remarkably similar to accounts in Taoism in which heavenly guards are sent to do things for a higher deity. I think we should not take the rejection of associating others with Allah in an extreme way. Polytheism as a spectrum of practice and beliefs is not always incompatible with Islam. As I argued in Section 4.5.5 there are angels in the Islamic account of the spiritual world. They could correspond to gods in other religions. In this passage it is said that observers are sent to run errands for Allah. And we should remember that Gabriel is the one who transmitted the Qur'an to Muhammad, not Allah himself. Therefore different levels of spiritual beings are referred to in the verses and the exact extent to which polytheism is wrong is not clear. I hold the view that Islam tells people not to worship other gods because the polytheists at Muhammad's time were unscrupulous morally, and Islam provided the discipline that the warring Arabs at that time needed.

Now let us re-read the passage quoted above. If Allah is all-knowing, why would he need obervers to follow messengers to make sure that they have conveyed the message? The reference to "Allah," "lord," and "we" is not always precise. Sometimes it may mean a group of higher beings but not the highest. That is the reason why observers would be needed to record and observe messengers. It is reasonable to assume that none of the spiritual beings talking to us would really be the creator of the universe. They, i.e. angels in the Islamic scheme, talk in the name of Allah as a kind of representative but they are not really all-knowing, all-powerful. Therefore

1. We should not read these superlative descriptions, such as "all-knowing," too literally, as they might not be true when it is not clear whether it is the highest being or an angel who is being referred to. Even when they do refer to the highest being there can be many problems, such as free will and responsibility, which I discussed in Section 4.5.1.

2. We should not take the Islamic rejection of polythe-

ism in an absolute sense. Islamic descriptions of the spiritual have similarities with polytheism.

This is the view of summatheism.

Mysticism can also be understood via summatheism. Mystics try to connect with a deity, the highest being, or the universe, etc. with various methods. They can all be easily understood in terms of summatheism. Human beings have a spiritual streak. Different monastic or mystical schools all try to explore and develop this tendency. If we look at different religions from the point of view of summatheism we can see that we are working with the same body-and-soul relationship.

In verses 91:7–10 in the Qur'an, it is said, "by the soul and who proportioned it, and inspired it its wickedness and its righteousness, he has succeeded who purifies it, and he has failed who buries it." The main purpose of life is to purify one's soul, and to realise its purity in actual deeds. If we learn the spiritual lesson here and see the goal of religion as the promotion of this idea, then there would be no religious wars or religious institutions blocking the advance of science.

In verses 70:19–27 there is an illuminating account. It says, "indeed, mankind was created anxious. When evil touches him, he is distressed, and when good touches him, he withholds, except the observers of prayer, those who are constant in their prayer, and those within whose wealth is a known right for the ones asking and the deprived, and those who believe in the day of judgment, and those who are fearful of the punishment of their lord." Here we can see the programme of Allah. Islam teaches mankind how to deal with existential anxiety by the observance of prayer, alms giving, belief in judgment, and fear of God. This is a programme that is effective for many people, but not everyone needs to follow this exact programme. Islam in its sophisticated form need not assert that. It was just easier and more practical to emphasise the necessity of this programme for Muhammad's audience.

In this age, there are more suitable programmes of faith

Chapter 7 Reason

for people seeking spiritual advancement, which may contain creative work, charity, meditation, or other ways of living out our lives.

If followers of different religions reflect on and internalise these views, the world would be such a better place and so would the status of organised religion in the mind of secularists, liberals, intellectuals, and non-followers in general.

Then there would be a rebirth of religion, including Islam. This is my hope and my faith.

Glossary

fatwa فتوى *fatwā* A non-binding religious opinion issued by a qualified legal scholar, usually in response to questions.

Hadith حديث *ḥadīth* An account of what the prophet Muhammad said or did, orally transmitted at first, collected and written down a few generations later. Muslims see Muhammad as a model for good conduct. They look for guidance in the Hadiths for matters about which the Qur'an does not provide clear instructions.

jihad جهاد *jihād* Literally means "effort." It can refer to holy war or one's struggle against weaknesses and temptations.

jinn جنّ *jinn* Said to be made of fire, jinn are beings without a physical body. They are similar to souls but are not associated with human bodies as souls are.

Mu'tazilis المعتزلة *al-mu'tazila* An Islamic school which flourished in the ninth century. It advocates the oneness of God, human freedom, and the creation of the Qur'an.

People of the Book أهل الكتاب *ahl al-kitāb* Monotheists who are not Muslims. In Islam they are not treated as well as Muslims but are preferred to atheists.

Salafi سلفي *salafī* A Muslim who thinks that the correct way to follow Islam is to act like early Muslims as much as possible.

Sura سورة *sūra* Literally a "sign," it also means a chapter in the Qur'an.

Bibliography

[1] Ibn al-'Arabi. *The Ringstones of Wisdom*. Kazi, Chicago, 2004 (written 1229).

[2] Ahmed al Buhairy. Former dean of Shari'a: the couple stripped of their clothes during intercourse invalidates a marriage contract. *Al-Masry al-Youm*, 2006. http://today.almasryalyoum.com/article2.aspx?ArticleID=4256.

[3] Al-Bukhary. *Sahih Al-Bukhari*. Kitab Bhavan, New Delhi, 1984 (completed 846).

[4] Al-Farabi. *Al-Farabi's Philosophy of Plato and Aristotle*. The Free Press, New York, 1962.

[5] Al-Hallaj. *Kitab al Tawasin*. Librairie Paul Geuthner, Paris, 1913 (written early 10th century).

[6] A. B. al-Mehri, editor. *The Qur'an*. Maktabah Booksellers and Publishers, Birmingham, 2010 (compiled mid-9th century).

[7] Rifa'a al Tahtawi. *Manahij al-Albab al-Misria fi Mabahij al-Adab al-'asria*. Dar al-Kitab al-Misri, Cairo, 2012 (first published 1869).

[8] Al-Tirmidhi. *Jami' At-Tirmidhi*. Darussalam, Riyadh, 2007 (compiled 884).

[9] Talal Asad. *Formations of the Secular: Christianity, Islam, Modernity*. Stanford University Press, Stanford, 2003.

[10] Jan Assmann. *From Akhenaten to Moses*. The American University in Cairo Press, Cairo, 2014.

[11] Averroes. *On the Harmony of Religion and Philosophy*. Gibb Memorial Trust, London, 1961 (completed 1179/1180).

[12] Alan Baker. Simplicity. In Edward N. Zalta, editor, *The Stanford Encyclopedia of Philosophy*. Metaphysics Research Lab, Stanford University, fall 2013 edition, 2013.

[13] Leonard Binder. *Islamic Liberalism: a Critique of Development Ideologies*. The University of Chicago Press, Chicago, 1988.

[14] John Cooper. *Plato: Complete Works*. Hackett, Indianapolis, 1997.

[15] Katerina Dalacoura. *Islam, Liberalism and Human Rights*. I. B. Tauris, London, 2007.

[16] Richard Dawkins. *The Selfish Gene*. Oxford University Press, Oxford, second edition, 1989.

[17] Roxanne L. Euben. *Enemy in the Mirror: Islamic Fundamentalism and the Limits of Modern Rationalism: A Work of Comparative Political Theory*. Princeton University Press, Princeton, 1999.

[18] Carlos Fraenkel. *Philosophical Religions from Plato to Spinoza*. Cambridge University Press, New York, 2012.

[19] Diego Gambetta and Steffen Hertog. *Engineers of Jihad: The Curious Connection between Violent Extremism and Education*. Princeton University Press, Princeton, 2016.

[20] Hamid Haidar. *Liberalism and Islam*. Palgrave Macmillan, New York, 2008.

[21] Wael B. Hallaq. *An Introduction to Islamic Law*. Cambridge University Press, Cambridge, 2009.

[22] Nader Hashemi. *Islam, Secularism, and Liberal Democracy*. Oxford University Press, Oxford, 2009.

[23] Aysha Hidayatullah. *Feminist Edges of the Qur'an*. Oxford University Press, Oxford, 2014.

[24] Albert Hourani. *Arabic Thought in the Liberal Age, 1798–1939*. Cambridge University Press, Cambridge, 1983.

[25] Samuel Huntington. *The Clash of Civilizations and the Remaking of World Order*. Simon and Schuster, New York, 1996.

[26] Faraj Isma'il. Fatwa allowing a woman to breastfeed a coworker strictly forbidden to retreat. *Al Arabiya*, 2007. https://www.alarabiya.net/articles/2007/05/16/34518.html.

Chapter 7 BIBLIOGRAPHY

[27] Charles Kurzman, editor. *Liberal Islam: A Source Book*. Oxford University Press, New York, 1998.

[28] Ibn Majah. *Sunan Ibn Majah*. Darussalam, Riyadh, 2007 (compiled 9th century).

[29] Andrew March. *Islam and Liberal Citizenship: The Search for an Overlapping Consensus*. Oxford University Press, New York, 2009.

[30] Joseph Massad. *Islam in Liberalism*. The University of Chicago Press, Chicago, 2015.

[31] Fatima Mernissi. *The Veil and the Male Elite: A Feminist Interpretation of Women's Rights in Islam*. Basic Books, New York, 1991 (first published 1987).

[32] John S. Mill. *On Liberty and Other Essays*. Oxford University Press, Oxford, 1998 (On Liberty first published 1859).

[33] Maajid Nawaz. *Radical: My Journey Out Of Islamist Extremism*. W. H. Allen, London, 2012.

[34] Reynold Nicholson. *The Mystics of Islam*. World Wisdom, Bloomington, 2002 (first published 1914).

[35] The Jewish Publiciation Society of America. *The Holy Scriptures According to the Masoretic Text*. The Jewish Publiciation Society of America, Philadelphia, 1917.

[36] Thomas Paine. *The Age of Reason*. Barrois, Paris, 1794–1807.

[37] Karl Popper. *The Logic of Scientific Discovery*. Routledge and Kegan Paul, London, second edition, 2002 (first published 1959).

[38] John Rawls. *Political Liberalism*. Columbia University Press, New York, 2005 (first published 1993).

[39] Edward Said. *Orientalism*. Pantheon Books, 1978.

[40] Amina Wadud. *Qur'an and Woman*. Oxford University Press, Oxford, 1999.

[41] Max Weber. *The Sociology of Religion*. Beacon Press, Boston, 1993 (first published 1920).

[42] Max Weber. *The Protestant Ethic and the Spirit of Capitalism*. W. W. Norton, New York, 2008 (first published 1904–1905).

[43] Ludwig Wittgenstein. *Tractatus Logico-Philosophicus*. Routledge and Kegan Paul, London, 1922.

Advance comments on Dr Alicia Lie's *Reading the Qur'an*

From Lord Carey of Clifton
This book is an important contribution to the modern debate.

From Ahmed Elbeshlawy, independent scholar, author, and poet
This is a book the Muslim world needs to read—closely. Although it is written in English, it is not written for the consumption of the Judeo-Christian West. Its message is fundamentally directed to Muslims. Some Muslims may think that the West is hypocritical in the way it deals with the Muslim world, but Lie argues that "the hypocrisy of the West does not justify Wahhabism nor discredit social reform in the Islamic world". *Reading the Qur'an* is an exercise in self-critique that is, unfortunately, sorely missing in contemporary Muslim culture. Alicia Lie's work tries to take mainstream Islam—and not just Islamism—outside its closed terminological system and the false scholarism associated with it, which is based on a flimsy hearsay culture that clearly caused a whole religion to go awry and transmogrify into what can be seen as the most divisive and self-defeating religious system in the history of humanity.

Lie's book demonstrates original thought and extensive research. Her stance with regard to religion in general is a courageous critical stance. It is, of course, easier to "either follow a religion blindly, ignoring its critics, or ditch a religion completely and say that it is the opium of the people and has only harmful effects". Islam, in particular, is a paramount focus of this either/or fallacy. Bold in her views about the sorry state of the Muslim world today, Lie asserts that "Islam needs reformation". She does not question the main Muslim tenet that there is no god but Allah and that Muhammad is his messenger. But she assertively writes that "Islam is not perfect". That is precisely what the majority of the Muslim world needs to learn; that one of the fundamental signs of respect towards any belief, ideology, or religion is to subject it to a thorough criticism. In other words, to be able to couple religious belief with critical questioning and bracketing of the 'truthfulness' of the sacred. For the most important lesson in religion, according to Lie, is "the logical gaps between accepting the existence of a deity, and accepting the doctrines of a religion which worships that deity". One's religious belief isn't the 'truth'. And, because one's belief exists in reality along with many other different beliefs, one should be careful and humble when one tries to convey one's 'truth' to others, because others have their own 'truths'.

Beyond the political divide of Sunnis and Shiites as well as the difference between mainstream Muslims and Islamists (including Salafis and violent extremist groups like the Muslim Brotherhood and ISIS), Lie boldly separates followers of Islam into "literalist, moderate, Qur'anist, reformist, and mystic" Muslims. She mostly quotes the Qur'an rather than the Hadiths (sayings of the prophet Muhammad) which have been heavily criticized by a few Qur'anist intellectuals from the late seventies onwards. Her appreciable efforts make her one of the intellectuals who wish to save Islam from its problematic Arabian-peninsula context and make it the universal idea it originally started as and formerly was – giving it liberal as well as feminist dimensions. Religion, to Lie, is nothing "but what one chooses".

Lie writes: "One does not need to become a religious student full-time to take matters into his own hands. One only needs to invest some time in reading and thinking, as Gabriel told Muhammad, 'Read!' " With such ease, just by drawing Muslims' attention to one key word in the Qur'an, Lie pinpoints one of the Muslim world's major ailments: the gaping lack of reading; the inability to get to grips with texts and to replace reciting with real reading in the wider sense of the word. Unfortunately, talking about religion in the Muslim world is still largely the monopoly of the religious 'scholars', known as the Sheikhs or the 'men of religion' as they are ridiculously called sometimes, disregarding the fact that none of the prophet's companions, nor the prophet himself, was a scholar of any sort.

Intellectuals like Lie constitute Islamism's biggest nightmare, which is neither the cultural other per se nor traditional political foes; it is the figure of the thinking Muslim. Islamists look at the thinking Muslim and see in him or her the very demise of a certain corpus of literature that has been accumulated over centuries and which has evidently become not just totally irrelevant to any civil society, but even irrelevant to logic and common sense. Modern-day Islamists are not just simply those who carry out terrorist attacks. They are those people who blindly identify with a certain human, historical, and clearly blood-mongering literature beyond any doubt or criticism. The thinking Muslim is also the antithetical figure of the Muslim world's popular pseudo-critical 'thinkers' who always put forward the mind-boggling argument that Islamism – or Islamic terrorism – is a 'Western' or an 'Orientalist' invention – an argument at once self-deceiving and self-defeating, because it claims that the Muslim world is not even intelligent enough to create the inhuman monster it has constructed out of its own Islamist texts.

Any fair reader of Lie's *Reading the Qur'an* cannot but agree with her that contemporary Muslims do not only need to think of peace with the cultural other—they need to think of their own "peace of mind", which is, to the writer, the very root of the word "Islam" itself.

FROM PROVERSE HONG KONG SELECTED NON-FICTION AND ACADEMIC TITLES

Jean Berlie	The Chinese of Macau a Decade after the Handover.
Gillian Bickley, Ed.	The Complete Court Cases of Magistrate Frederick Stewart.
—	The Development of Education in Hong Kong, 1841–1898.
—	Journeys with a Mission: Travel Journals of The Right Revd George Smith (1815–1871) first Bishop of Victoria (Hong Kong) (1849–1865).
—	A Magistrate's Court in Nineteenth Century Hong Kong, 1st ed. 2005, 2nd ed. 2009.
—	Through American Eyes: The Journals (18 May 1859 – 1 September 1860) Of George Washington (Farley) Heard (1837–1875).
Gillian Bickley	The Golden Needle: The Biography of Frederick Stewart (1836–1889).
Verner Bickley	Steps to Paradise and beyond.
—	Forward to Beijing! a guide to the Summer Olympics.
Rupert Chan	Chocolate's Brown Study in the Bag.
Orville Leverne Clubb	Semper fi! The story of a vietnam era marine.
Richard Collingwood-Selby and Gillian Bickley, Eds	In Time of War (Diary entries and letters by Lt. Cmdr. Henry C.S. Collingwood-Selby, R.N. (1898–1992)).
Jun Fang and Lifang He	The Romance Of A Literatus And His Concubine In Seventeenth-Century China. Annotated translation into English of "Reminiscences Of The Plum-shaded Convent" (Yingmeian Yiyu) by Mao Xiang (1611–1693) with the original Chinese text.
Brian Finch	A Faithful Record Of The *Lisbon Maru* Incident. (Translation from Chinese with additional material.)

Wayne Furlong	Buddha is a Punk Skater.
Peter Gregoire	Mentoring Reversed.
Emily Ho	Memoirs of an Ice-Cream Lady.
Errol Patrick Hugh	A personal journey through sketching: the sketcher's art.
Alan Loynd	All At Sea: A Memoir.
Virginia MacRobert	Gin's Tonic: ocean voyage, inner journey.
James McCarthy	The Diplomat of Kashgar: A Very Special Agent. The Life of Sir George Macartney, 18 January 1867 to 19 May 1945.
Stuart McDouall	All Agog In China.
Gerald Yeung	Wannabe backpackers: the Latin American & Kenyan journey of five spoiled teenagers.

Selected Novels and other Fiction

Andrew Carter	Bright Lights and White Nights.
Philip Chatting	As Leaves Blow.
—	The Snow Bridge and Other Stories.
Feng Chi-shun	Three Wishes in Bardo.
Jennifer Ching	A Painted Moment.
David Diskin	The Village in the Mountains.
Peter Gregoire	Article 109.
—	The Devil You Know.
Lawrence Gray	Adam's Franchise.
—	Cop Show Heaven.
—	Odds and Sods.
Patrricia W. Grey	Death has a Thousand Doors.
Peter Humphreys	Hong Kong Rocks.
Dragos Ilca	HK Hollow.
Gillian Jones	A Misted Mirror.
Caleb Kavon	The Monkey in Me: Confusion, Love and Hope under a Chinese Sky.
—	The Reluctant Terrorist: In Search of The Jizo.
Sophronia Liu	A Shimmering Sea.
Jan Pearson	Black Tortoise Winter.
—	Red Bird Summer.
—	Tiger Autumn.
—	Blue Dragon Spring.
Jason S. Polley	cemetery miss you.
Damon Rose	The Handover Murders.
Hayley Ann Solomon	Under the Shade of the Feijoa Trees and other stories.
Laura Solomon	Hilary and David.
—	An Imitation of Life.
James Tam	Man's Last Song.
Paul Ting	Bao Bao's Odyssey: From Mao's Shanghai to Capitalist Hong Kong.
Olga Walló	Tightrope! A Bohemian Tale (translation from Czech).
George Watt	The Finley Confession
Denis Wong	Revenge from Beyond.

FOR MORE ABOUT PROVERSE AUTHORS, BOOKS, EVENTS AND LITERARY PRIZES

Visit our website: http://www.proversepublishing.com
Visit our distributor's website: www.cup.cuhk.edu.hk
Follow us on Twitter: twitter.com/Proversebooks
"Like" us on www.facebook.com/ProversePress

Request our free E-Newsletter
Send your request to info@proversepublishing.com.

Availability
Available in Hong Kong and world-wide from our Hong Kong-based distributor, the Chinese University of Hong Kong Press, The Chinese University of Hong Kong, Shatin, NT, Hong Kong SAR, China.
See the Proverse page on their website:
https://cup.cuhk.edu.hk/Proversehk

All titles are available from Proverse Hong Kong,
http://www.proversepublishing.com

Most titles can be ordered online from Amazon (various countries).

Stock-holding retailers
Hong Kong (CUHKP, Bookazine)
Canada (Elizabeth Campbell Books),
Andorra (Llibreria La Puça, La Llibreria).

Orders may be made from bookshops
in the UK and elsewhere.

Ebooks
Most of our titles are available also as Ebooks.

www.ingramcontent.com/pod-product-compliance
Lightning Source LLC
Chambersburg PA
CBHW052042220426
43663CB00012B/2405